On This Date in Dayton's History

Remembering the Gem City
One Day at a Time

by Curt Dalton

Also by Curt Dalton

The breweries of Dayton: An illustrated history
Dayton (Postcard History Series)
The Dayton Arcade: Crown jewel of the Gem City
The Dayton Canoe Club: An illustrated history 1913-1996
Dayton inventions: Fact and fiction
Dayton through time
Delicious recipes and food for thought from the NCR Archive
Gem City Jewels I
Gem City Jewels II
Gem City Jewels III
Good for what ails you: Dayton's golden age of patent medicine
Greater Dayton drive-in theatres: An illustrated history
Home sweet home front: Dayton during World War II
How Ohio helped invent the world: From the airplane to the yo-yo
Keeping the secret: The WAVES and NCR Dayton, Ohio 1943-1946
Made do or did without: How Daytonians coped with the Great Depression
Miami Valley's marvelous motor cars
The Mother Home: a history of the Dayton Soldiers' Home in 3-D
Mr. Wulff's eagle-powered balloon
Spilt blood: When murder walked the streets of Dayton
A taste of Frigidaire
The terrible resurrection
Through flood, through fire
When Dayton went to the movies
With malice toward all: The lethal life of Dr. Oliver C. Haugh

All Rights Reserved
Copyright 2017 by Curt Dalton
3236 Wonderview Drive
Dayton, OH 45414
email: cdalton@woh.rr.com

CONTENTS

Introduction	5
January	7
February	39
March	71
April	101
May	131
June	163
July	193
August	225
September	257
October	287
November	319
December	349
Settlement and Progress of Dayton *This is the first history of Dayton to appear in print*	380
Index	389
Photo Credits	414

INTRODUCTION

For nearly a quarter of a century I have accumulated a number of interesting stories on the wonderful history of Dayton. The book in your hands contains 366 I chose from the thousands I found.

Some choices may surprise you. For instance, one of the most significant events that involved Daytonians is the Wright brothers first flight on December 17th. But if you look at the page for that date, you will see a different sort of flight being written about - involving UFOs. The reason is because the Wright flight didn't occur in the Dayton area. But don't worry, the brothers have not been neglected in this book.

Other hard choices had to be made because I stuck to only one subject per day. For instance, on June 27th I had to pick from Dayton's first male child, John Whitten Van Cleve, being born in 1801; or the patent on a calculating toy that used the image of Consul, a cigarette smoking star of stage and screen at the turn of the 20th century - who also happened to be a monkey. If you were hoping for the Van Cleve story, this book may not be the right one for you to enjoy perusing.

And perusing is just exactly how this book should be read. Mini bite-size morsels of the history of the Gem City. There are 366 separate events here, some you may know about, others you might not. And all, I hope, will be a treat.

Speaking of treats... On August 27, 1833 Dayton Lyceum members met to celebrate their first anniversary with a program of music and addresses by local citizens. Of special interest was a speech titled *Settlement and Progress of Dayton*, given by John W. Van Cleve and also printed in the morning edition of the *Dayton Journal*. The account was the first history of Dayton to appear in print. I have included *Settlement and Progress of Dayton* in its entirety. The speech starts on page 380.

It is my hope that this book will both entertain and enlighten you. Enjoy!

January 1

Oliver F. Conklin was the talk of the neighborhood when he began riding what he called his "electric tricycle" up and down the streets of Dayton. An electrician for the Dayton Fan and Motor Company and already the holder of two patents on electric motors, building an electric-powered vehicle came naturally to Conklin.

Conklin's invention was much more than a tricycle. The vehicle was designed to carry the weight of two passengers and their baggage. The machine had a tubular steel frame, wire-bound steel rims, pneumatic tires and a leather upholstered seat. The three-wheels were guided by a single handle bar with one hand, while the other hand manipulated a lever that turned the electric current to the motor on and off. The vehicle could be stopped or reversed almost instantly. The battery could last up to 60 miles on one charge. There were no brakes on the machine, as it was entirely controlled by the current.

By November, 1895 Conklin had been approached by companies with offers to come to their city and manufacture his machines, but he claimed that he wanted to remain in Dayton, as it offered all of the facilities he needed to succeed.

And so it did. The wheels and tubular frame were made by the Davis Sewing Machine company. The Dayton Fan and Motor Company was responsible for the motors and storage batteries, while the S. N. Brown company made the wooden wire-bound rims for the wheels.

The last known public display of Conklin's vehicle was on January 1, 1896, when it was seen by 5,000 people at a New Year's celebration at the downtown Dayton YMCA.

Conklin would go on to obtain over a dozen more patents for electric motors and ignition systems and eventually make a living in Palm Beach as an electrical appliance inventor.

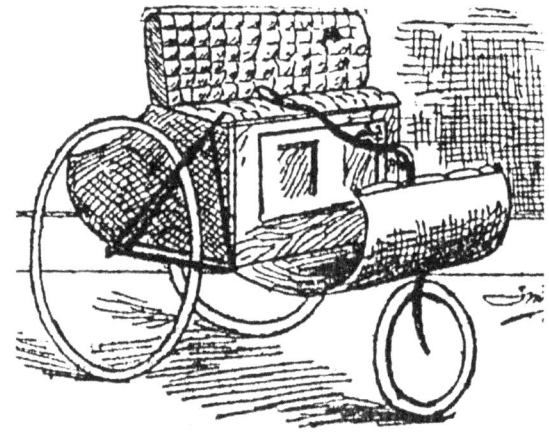

January 2

Before television, ice-skating was the most popular winter sport. The scene below was taken on January 2, 1901 when the ice on the river was twelve inches thick and the temperature fourteen degrees below zero.

During the winter this was a common sight. The most convenient places were Main Street Bridge and the area below the Dayton View Bridge. Another place was the Steele Dam, near where Island Park Dam is now. But the best ice was at the junction of the Miami and Stillwater rivers. After dirt was dredged out of the Miami riverbed to make Robert's Fill, an area of filled-in land where Robert Blvd. was built, a large lake was left near the First Street Bridge. This would quickly freeze and made fine skating. It was filled with skaters almost every afternoon and evening.

In 1941 Charles F. Sullivan reminisced about playing on the river in Dayton when he was a child.

"The boys and young men frequently played polo upon skates, using a tin can for a ball, but it would not be long before it became just a ball of tin. Even then it made enough noise, for players to follow it, even on dark evenings. If you was there to skate, it would be well for you to keep away from that crowd, for if the ball got near you you might be pretty roughly handled by some of them."

Ice skating on the Miami River on January 2, 1901. This picture was shot from the south bank of the Miami River looking east toward the Main Street Bridge.

January 3

On January 3, 1895, *The New York Times* ran a story of how the beer hall at the Soldiers' Home in Dayton was bringing in a profit of $45,000 a year from selling beer. The average amount of beer consumed was well over 5,000 glasses each day. The hall was open every day except Sunday, from 7 am to 5:30 pm. It was a place to relax and greet friends.

"At any time during the day a crowd of several hundred soldiers may be seen in quiet confab, hobnobbing one with the other. The presence of 500 at a time is frequently noted, and during the holiday week a thousand have swarmed the renowned hall. No political or other arguments are allowed, but pleasant and vivacious conversation is ever on tap."

This was not popular with some people. To think that the government was actually furnishing beer to the soldiers smacked of indecency. But the reason behind the move was soon explained. It seemed that many of the soldiers, when given leave to visit the city, would instead stop by the group of saloons that had sprung up not far from the Home; most of which had opened in order to take advantage of the veterans who had some pension money in their pockets. Eventually, things got out of hand. Veterans were found drunk and penniless, and had to be brought home by the matron who went out to look for her lost sheep. In 1876 Henry Mulharon was murdered for the pension money he was carrying while drinking in the city. In 1885 notice was given prohibiting members from walking on the railroad tracks near the Home due to a number of the men killed trying to do so while intoxicated. In an effort to remedy this, the decision was made to open the beer hall to keep the veterans at the Home and out of trouble.

The original hall had proved inadequate, and a new one-story building was built in 1891 with profits from the sale of beer and cigars. A large basement could hold upwards of 2000 barrels of beer, which was less than three months supply for the thirsty vets. Ironically, the old beer hall became the headquarters for the Keely Gold Cure Club, who claimed to be able to cure alcoholism in 95% of its patients.

The sale of alcohol at the Home ended when, in 1906, an appropriations bill passed which stated that any branch maintaining a bar or canteen that sold beer, wine, or liquor after March 4, 1907, would not receive any funding.

January 4

Greencastle Cemetery, located on South Broadway and Miami Chapel Road, is home to a weathered stone slab that marks the final resting place of an unknown woman. On the cracked and faded stone is written, "The Stranger. Died Jan. 4, 1851. Aged 24 yrs." Records indicate that it also once said, "Her kind and gentle spirit gone to a world of light above."

Several stories are associated with the woman buried there. One legend says that the stranger was a daughter of a wealthy Dayton family who died while giving birth to an illegitimate child. The child was supposedly buried with her.

Another story says that she was traveling through Dayton with a tall, handsome gentleman and they decided to stay the night at a local hostelry. That evening the man frantically called for a doctor, but it was too late. The woman died. Inconsolable, the man arranged for the woman's funeral, but he refused to reveal her identity.

Yet another legend says that the woman had been killed by her father after she had told her parents that she was leaving home to go East with a gentleman friend. To keep the tragedy quiet, she was buried without ceremony and without the knowledge of her friends or neighbors.

Supposedly, for years after her death, flowers would mysteriously appear on the grave. Over 100 years later, people would sometimes visit her on Memorial Day and scatter a few flowers in remembrance.

January 5

On the northwest corner of First and St. Clair streets stands Memorial Hall, a monument to Montgomery County war veterans. When it was dedicated on January 5, 1910, thousands gathered to honor the occasion.

At noon a parade formed in front of the Old Guard G.A.R. hall on Jefferson Street. Led by the Sons of Veterans drum corps, the parade marched to the flag staff at Memorial Hall, where a silk flag from the G.A.R. was presented for use to hang outside the building. A fifteen gun salute (one for each township) was given.

Once inside, a number of speeches were given, including a history on how the Memorial Hall came to be. It was also explained how the hall had been designed both for beauty and for functionality. Memorial Hall was planned as a gathering place for veterans; containing assembly rooms for meetings, a reading room, a library and museum, all free of charge. Stained glass skylight windows lit paintings depicting battles that took place during the Civil War.

The dedication ended with a live camp-fire in the auditorium, where a medley of war songs were played, the Dayton Glee Club performed and, of course, many more speeches given. The night ended with the playing of the Star-Spangled Banner.

Memorial Hall as it looked on November 15, 1911. Two bronze statues depicting soldiers from the Spanish American War and World War I were later added on each side of the main entrance in 1923. In 2016, the building is still standing.

January 6

On January 6, 1904, Paul Laurence Dunbar, the renowned African American writer, made a triumphant return to NCR, where he had once worked as a janitor. Dunbar appeared before hundreds of NCR employees, giving several readings and recitations.

Dunbar, whose parents were former slaves, was born on Howard Street in Dayton on June 27, 1872. While at Central High School, he became the president of the literary Philomathean Society and editor of the school paper. Yet when he graduated he found it difficult to find work. His stint at NCR was a short one, as he proved too frail for the job. Later, while working as an elevator operator at the Callahan Building, Dunbar began writing poems. He collected them into a book called *Oak and Ivy*, which he had privately printed in 1893.

By 1895, Dunbar's poems began appearing in national newspapers and magazines, including *The New York Times*. At the time of his death, on February 9, 1906, Dunbar had authored 21 volumes of poetry, four novels, and a number of several short stories, plays, newspaper articles and essays.

Paul Laurence Dunbar recites his poetry to a group of NCR employees in 1904.

January 7

In 1919 the Dayton Museum of Fine Arts was incorporated. The original incorporators included Julia Shaw Carnell, Orville Wright, Valentine Winters and Electra C. Doren. Three years later the name was changed to Dayton Art Institute.

The original art center was situated in a remodeled home at the southeast corner of St. Clair Street and Monument Avenue in 1920. But the group envisioned a museum, a staff of instructors and students. A gift of $2 million by Julia Shaw Carnell allowed this museum to be built on Forest and Riverdale avenues. When Mrs. Carnell presented the new building to the institute on January 7, 1930, she said, "I feel as if I were giving into your hands a child of my own. Be good to it." Until her death in 1944, she covered the annual operating deficit.

Today, the museum continues to collect, preserve and exhibit original works of art. Its collection spans 5,000 years of art history, including important Oceanic art, Asian art, European art, and American fine and decorative art collections. The Dayton Art Institute also hosts concerts, family and youth programs, classes, social events and more.

Modeled after the Villa d'Este, near Rome, and the Villa Farnese at Caprarola in Italy, this Italian Renaissance style building is as beautiful as the artwork that hangs in its many galleries.

January 8

The second election of General Andrew Jackson to the Presidency was celebrated in Dayton on this day in 1833 by a barbecue on land west of the canal basin, now Cooper Park. National salutes were fired during the day. Immediately on the arrival at noon of a canal-boat with from fifty to one hundred citizens of Miamisburg, a hickory tree bearing the American flag was erected. After the erection of the pole a procession was formed, in front of which walked four Revolutionary soldiers bearing liberty caps and two members of the Dayton Hickory Club carrying an appropriate banner, who were followed by another soldier bearing the American flag. After moving through the main streets of the city, the procession passed into the courthouse, where speeches were made and resolutions adopted. From the courthouse they proceeded to the common, where an ox was roasted whole.

  A barbecue was usually an uninviting feast. The outer part of the ox was smoked and scorched, and the remainder uncooked, though the animal was always roasted for many hours. After the feast the almost untouched carcass was hauled off by horses, surrounded by a crowd of boys and dogs, to be disposed of by hogs and hounds.

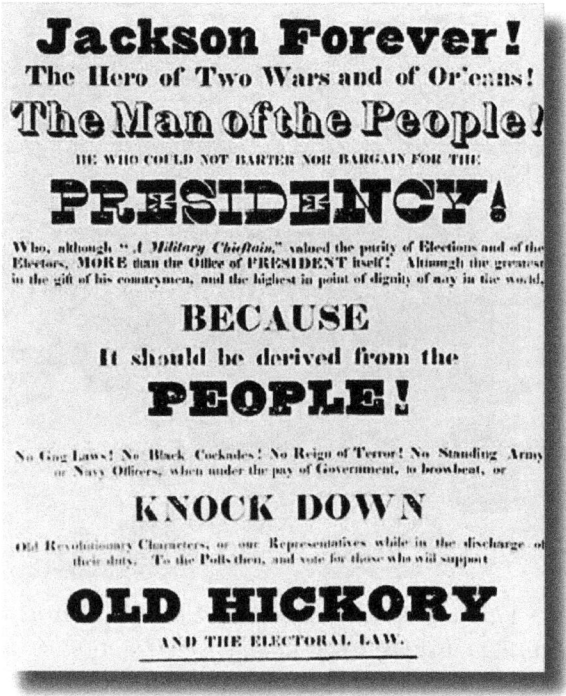

January 9

On this day in 1826, a number of unusual laws were passed in Dayton. Here is but a small sampling.

Be it ordained by the Common Council of the Town of Dayton:

That if any person or persons shall swim or wash themselves (being naked at the time) in the river or mill-race, from the old or corn-mill on the race to the saw-mill on the east of the town or from the old corn-mill down the Miami river within the bounds of the corporation of the town of Dayton, such person or persons so offending, for every such offence, shall be fined in a sum not less than fifty cents, nor more than one dollar.

That if any person or persons shall shoot or fire any gun or guns within the limits of the town lots, at any time, except on the 4th of July, or days of public rejoicing, such person or persons, so offending, shall be fined for every such offence, in a sum not less than twenty-five cents, nor more than three dollars… (F)iring by militia companies on muster days, by command of the officers commanding the same, shall not be considered a violation of this ordinance.

That if any person or persons shall address any wanton or obscene language to or in the presence of another, or shall exhibit any wanton, lewd or obscene gestures or conduct, or shall exhibit himself, or herself, to public view, either naked or in any other way exposed in an indecent manner, he, she, or they, so offending, on conviction thereof, shall be fined in any sum not exceeding ten dollars and costs.

That no privy, shall hereafter be erected within the bounds of the in-lots of this corporation without a vault at the least eight feet deep and sufficiently walled with stone, brick or wood, and any person or persons neglecting to comply with this section, shall forfeit and pay any sum not exceeding ten dollars on conviction thereof…

That it shall be the duty of the supervisor to require of every able bodied male person, who is above the age of twenty-one years and shall have resided three months within the limits of the corporation, being a land holder or house holder, to perform one days labour on the streets and public highways within said corporation annually.

Passed January 9, 1826.
SIMEON BROADWELL, President
ATTEST—WARREN MUNGER, Recorder.

January 10

Historically, Dayton has been known as the home for many patents and inventions. But the city's inventors were not as prolific in the beginning. In fact, over 30 years would pass after the U.S. Patent Office first opened its doors in 1790 before a Daytonian would be granted a patent.

The first patent granted to a Daytonian was to Elijah Converse, on January 10, 1821. His invention was for an improvement in machinery for cutting dyewood. Unfortunately, any text, patent model or patent drawing that existed was lost in a fire that occurred at the U.S. Patent Office in 1836.

But what exactly was Converse's machine supposed to do? It seems that dyewood is exactly what it sounds like: a wood that, when ground up, is capable of yielding a dye. The extracts were sold in both liquid form and for some industries in solid slabs. The products were used for dyeing and tanning in the textile, fur-dressing, wood staining, leather and pigment making industries.

Bark from the black oak tree was capable of yielding a yellow dye, brown dyes came from the bark of apple trees, reds from Brazilwood, Sappanwood and Logwood. In 1500 Spanish ships were exporting large cargoes of logwood from the Yucatan coast. A single ship load of 50 tons of logwood was worth more than an entire year's cargo of other merchandise! Any inventor that produced a machine that could quickly cut dyewoods into pieces suitable for extracting the dyes would end up quite rich.

There is no record of Converse actually producing a working model of his invention. By the end of the 19th century these natural dyes were replaced by synthetic dyes.

It would take 10 more years before another patent was granted to anyone from the Gem City. John Newhall would be given a patent for his washing machine on June 13, 1831.

Eventually, Dayton's inventors began churning out a number of ideas. By 1870, the city ranked fifth in the nation. In 1890, Dayton was granted more patents per capita than any other city in the United States.

January 11

On January 11, 1867, eighteen-year-old Christine Kett was murdered in her home at 641 Oak Street. The girl was found lying on the kitchen floor with her feet hanging down the cellar door and her body covered with blood. The right side of her head had been crushed by a blunt instrument and smears of gun powder were on her face. A revolver belonging to her brother, Frederick, was found by her left side. An axe was found in the cellar.

Police began questioning Frederick, who had found the body He stated that the gun was his, but that he had not used it since New Year's Day.

A short time later, the girl's mother, Christina Kett, arrived at the house. She stated that she had been shopping all afternoon. Frederick was arrested, but later release when it was proven that he had been at work all day. The police then arrested Anthony Goetz, the boyfriend of Christine, but again a perfect alibi was established.

Mrs. Kett was then taken into custody. Neighbors had pointed out that the mother and daughter had frequently quarreled and that the mother possessed a violent temper. But Frederick stated that only he and his sister had known where the gun was located, so they let the mother go.

Finally, a theory was floated that a stranger had come to the home and Christine had gotten the pistol to defend herself. During a struggle the girl was killed. This was thought possible because the house the Kett family lived in had formerly been a brothel, and the family was often annoyed by persons who were looking for that sort of companionship

On March 9, 1884, Mrs. Kett called her son to her bedside. Knowing that she was close to dying, she asked everyone else to leave the two of them alone. She then told her son that she had a confession to make.

On the morning of the murder Christine and another woman left the house together, but the daughter had promised to be home by noon to make lunch. When Christine didn't arrive home until the middle of the afternoon, Mrs. Kett became so enraged that she seized an axe and hit her daughter on the head. Mrs. Kett then took her son's revolver and powder flash, placed her daughter's fingers in the flask, and smeared powder on her face. Then she left the house and did not return until later that evening.

After her confession, Mrs. Kett had her son swear that he would not repeat what she had said. He agreed to do so. His mother died shortly thereafter.

Frederick tried to keep his promise, but after only four days he told his mother's story to the police. Seventeen years after the tragedy occurred, it was finally solved.

January 12

The worst fire that Dayton had seen in years also occurred on one of the coldest days ever recorded in the city. On January 12, 1918, the four-story building at 9-13 St. Marys Street that housed the Dayton Coca-Cola Bottling Company and the Dayton Glove Company was found to be on fire at 5 a.m. Firemen rushed to the scene. In their hurry, several of them were forced to go without socks, while others didn't have the time to grab their boots and were forced to fight the blaze in their shoes.

Normally this would have been only a slight inconvenience, but this was no average day. A blizzard had begun the day before, and snow fell throughout the night. Toward evening the winds rose at an alarming rate. Over the next 12 hours the temperature dropped about 48 degrees, and by the time of the fire it was estimated to be at least 16 below zero.

Due to the extreme cold, at least six firemen were taken to a doctor, suffering from frozen hands and feet. This was especially bad for the men without boots, who had to wade through the freezing snow and water protected only by their shoes.

The fire caused an estimated $25,000 in damage. Dayton Glove Company suffered a total loss, while the heaviest damage to the Coca-Cola company was its stock of syrup and three carloads of bottles. The building was completely gutted, but fortunately the firefighters were able to stop the flames from spreading to adjoining structures in spite of the trouble they had with the freezing water blowing back in their faces.

About 40 people, mostly girls, lost their jobs due to the Dayton Glove Company's loss. The Coca-Cola Company's loss was held to only $5,000 because a majority of the stock had recently been moved to its new quarters on Stratford Avenue.

The Dayton Fire Department was kept busy that day. Burning flues and overheated stoves caused an additional 13 fires that day. Frozen water pipes also demanded a share of their attention.

January 13

On January 13, 1973, thousands flocked downtown for the formal opening of the Dayton Convention and Exhibition Center. The Center was a massive gray concrete building that filled a city block, bounded by Main, Fifth, Jefferson and Sixth streets.

Although the outside of the $6 million, 157,000 square-foot building wasn't exactly beautiful, the functionality of the interior was what really mattered. The first floor of the facility could provide 425 booths, banquets for up to 3,000, and meeting rooms for up to 600. A great hall of 68,352 square feet of column-free space was the major part of the building. Highlighting the spacious main lobby was a mosaic mural made up of 163,296 individual ceramic tiles depicting the first flight of the Wright brothers. The Center was also home to the new Aviation Hall of Fame.

On the second and third floors were meeting rooms divided by sound-proof doors. The third floor also offered a 674-seat auditorium that could be used for a range of activities, from plays to meetings.

Dayton Mayor James H. McGee had high hopes for what the building represented. "I believe the center will be a traffic generator for downtown. It will bring people into the sector and those who come will see what we have to offer. It will generate business and advertise our city."

The Dayton Convention and Exhibition Center as it looked a month before it opened. It was hoped that the "bridge to nowhere", jutting out of the Center and over Fifth Street, would eventually connect to a luxury hotel at some point. Today, the skywalk leads to the Dayton Transportation Center parking garage and the Crowne Plaza Dayton, a four-star hotel with 289 sleeping rooms.

January 14

On May 10, 1897, thirty-nine Shriners assembled in Dayton, Ohio to petition the Imperial Shrine Council for a dispensation to be called Antioch Shrine. On June 14th, 1898 a charter was granted establishing Antioch Shrine Temple. On July 18th, 1898 the first Divan (governing body) was duly elected and installed.

Then, as now, members of the organization devoted much of their time to financing the order's hospitals, where needy disabled children were admitted for rehabilitation.

In 1919, the old Charles Simms' family home on the northeast corner of First and Jefferson streets was purchased.

In 1954, the old home was razed to make room for a new structure. Completed in 1955, the Art Deco/Art Modern building is still in use by the organization. On January 14, 2013, the Antioch Temple was placed on the National Register of Historic Places.

Charles Simms' home. Memorial Hall can be seen on the right.

Antioch Temple today.

January 15

During WWII people were encouraged to work at least 48-hours a week so that factories could produce much needed items for the war effort. Many of the people in the factories were working six days a week and not getting off until 5 p.m. Since most of the downtown stores closed by 5:45 p.m. and were closed on Sundays, this meant that as many as 98,000 workers had little or no time to shop. This led to absenteeism and labor turnover. Companies began offering personal services to help. NCR employees could pay their light, gas and telephone bills at the local Credit Union office. Gas and tire ration requirements were handled by the company. Even auto and drivers' licenses could be obtained.

To help this situation, retailers began staying open on Monday nights until 8:30. This was expanded to also include Wednesday nights in 1943. Dayton was believed to be the first city in the nation to have all of its downtown stores stay open two nights a week.

On January 15, 1943 several Dayton banks began evening hours on Friday nights. This change came into effect as customers began telling banks of how badly evening hours were needed. One man complained about having to carry around $800 because he couldn't get to a bank during the day. Another stated that, although he had three paychecks, he worked during the day and couldn't deposit them, leaving the man without any money to live on. Soon Monday nights were also included. This plan stayed in effect at most of the banks throughout the war.

Workers cash checks at Winters Bank in 1943.

January 16

From 1873 to 1879 the world suffered through a price recession. This period was known as the "Long Depression". In the United States 18,000 businesses failed, defaulting on over a billion dollars of debt, and over a million people became unemployed.

Near the end of 1873, rumors began circulating through the country that Dayton had somehow escaped the fate of the rest of the world. In fact, the city was so well off that people in need could get three meals a day and a place to sleep at night for free. Of course, this was untrue. But during the first week in January, 1874 Dayton "witnessed such an invasion of hoboes and tramps as no American city has possibly experienced at any time in its history," wrote a reporter years later. "When freight trains halted for orders in Dayton, it was the signal for a general unloading of hoboes..."

In order to help the destitute persons and families pouring into the city, the Dayton Women's Christian Association opened a soup kitchen and began serving those in need. On January 16, 1874, a local newspaper reported on how the city was giving tickets away for free food and also allowing people to stay free at the police station.

"Numbers of citizens purchase them," (the tickets could be bought for a nickel), "and when persons come to their house claiming to be hungry, they furnish them soup tickets instead of supplying their wants from their private tables."

Once word got out that Dayton was, indeed, providing free meals, the floodgates opened wide and the police department became overwhelmed trying to cope with the flood of transients steadily pouring into the city.

By now, many Daytonians began to wonder if a serious mistake had been made in establishing the soup kitchen. A committee was formed to try and solve the problem. In the end, the Dayton Women's Christian Association was asked to close the soup kitchen. It required considerable persuasion, but the group finally relented.

The police then began meeting every freight train as it entered Union Station, warning the hobos riding the rails not to even think of getting off in Dayton. It took months to rid the city of those already here. But by early fall Dayton, though still suffering financially, had at least been relieved of her unwanted visitors.

January 17

A few minutes past midnight on January 17, 1880, Policeman Lee Lynam went into Mace Crable's saloon to talk to him. The saloon was located at 109 East Third Street, a few doors east of Jefferson Street. A short time later John Francis came in and made his way to the rear of the room and began talking to George Jackson.

After a few moments Jackson asked Lynam if he wanted a drink or a cigar, to which the policeman said no. Jackson then asked Francis if he wanted something to drink, and the two stepped up to the counter for a beer. After taking a sip, Francis told Jackson about how Officer Lynam had arrested him earlier that day for carrying concealed weapons, but that they hadn't found anything.

Suddenly Francis pulled a gun from his pocket, firing it at Officer Lynam. Lynam threw up his arms, saying, "I'm shot." Francis then tried to shoot again, but the gun didn't go off. Jackson then seized Francis' arm, but Francis pulled away and ran back to the rear room of the saloon.

After a few seconds Lynam pulled his gun and started after Francis. As he reached the swinging doors that divided the two rooms, Lynam staggered, then fell to the floor, blood gushing from his mouth and nose. Hearing the shot, W. S. Hatfield, a private watchman, ran into the saloon. Police officers Pat Hughes and Charles Grauser arrived soon after. Francis handed his revolver to Grauser and gave himself up.

Dr. Henry S. Jewett was called to try and save the injured policeman, but after a few moments Officer Lynam died. He was the first Dayton police officer killed in the line of duty.

After four tries at securing a jury, a change of venue was granted and Francis had his case tried in Butler County. On January 31, 1881, Francis was found guilty of murder and sentenced to twelve years of hard labor at the Ohio Penitentiary in Columbus.

January 18

Known to all as the "Little Mother of the Soldiers", Emma L. Miller first began caring for disabled soldiers after the Civil War at Camp Chase. When the Soldiers' Home in Dayton opened in 1867, Emma Miller was transferred there, along with 450 veterans. For the first 17 years she was the Home's first Matron, then was promoted to Superintendant of the General Depot of the Home, where clothing was made for National Military Home branches across the country. Because of her devotion to the soldiers, a special act of Congress allowed her to wear a little bronze button normally reserved only for veterans of the Civil war.

After Emma Miller died on January 18, 1914, she was laid to rest at the Dayton Soldiers' Home cemetery with full military honors – the first instance in U.S. history of a woman being so honored. On the day of the funeral, Mrs. Miller's casket was placed on a gun carriage drawn by two heavy artillery horses. Her own horse was led in the funeral cortege with an empty saddle; the custom observed with the mount of an officer of the U. S. Army, she having been brevetted a major. After a few words were spoken, a firing squad of eight veterans of the Civil War fired a volley at her grave and a trumpeter played "taps."

Emma Miller's final resting place is on a hilltop grave near the Soldiers' Monument at what is now known as the Dayton National Cemetery, VA Medical Center, Dayton, Ohio.

January 19

In the late 1790s, the United States owned enormous tracts of land to the west and people were encouraged to settle there. Unfortunately, there was no easy way to access the area. When Ohio was admitted to the Union in 1803, Congress knew that it had to act, for now the country had a state that was difficult to reach.

Their answer was to fund a National Road. Besides providing a way for settlers to get to the west, the road was also seen as a way for farmers and traders to move their goods to markets in the east. President Thomas Jefferson signed the bill into law in 1806.

In 1811, the road began in Cumberland, Maryland. By 1818, the road had reached Wheeling, West Virginia. In 1825, Congress required that the National Road had to pass through the state capitals of Ohio, Indiana and Illinois. Springfield, sitting in a direct line between Columbus and Indianapolis, had been reached by 1837. The next section would travel directly westward to Richmond, which meant Dayton would not be part of the route. Arguments were made to move the road four miles southward, so that it would pass through a thriving city instead of a sparsely populated land, but the idea was rejected.

Determined to not lose out on the potential traffic the road would bring through the state, several men decided to form the Dayton & Springfield Turnpike Company, with the idea of building a turnpike from Dayton to the National Road just west of Springfield. The books were opened for subscriptions on January 19, 1838, and contract for construction of the turnpike was made four months later.

In order to persuade travel through Dayton, the turnpike was built in the same style as the National Road, with similar bridges, stone culverts, toll gates, and mile stones. Where the two roads forked together outside Springfield, a sign was erected indicating that the Dayton Springfield Road was actually the National Road, which drove traffic southwest through Enon and Fairfield (now part of Fairborn), to Springfield Street in Dayton.

In order to reach Richmond, Indiana, where the National Road could be picked up again, the Dayton & Western Turnpike Company was formed. This turnpike is now known as West Third Street and, farther out, as Dayton Eaton Pike. Finished in 1840, two toll booths were added to help collect the $131,000 it cost to finish the 35 mile project.

January 20

Although known for inventing the airplane with his brother, Wilbur, Orville Wright also had a lighter side. Nearly twenty years, after being the first man in history to fly in a controlled, powered and sustained heavier-than-air human flight, on December 17, 1903, Orville would file an application at the U.S. Patent office for another type of flying machine.

The toy was made to project a wooden clown into the air, where it would then somersault once, before landing a distance away onto a double trapeze at the other end, on which another clown was attached. The flying clown would catch the upper trapeze with the hooks on its arms and send it spinning around, while both clowns hung on. Orville was granted patent #1,523,989 on January 20, 1925. The flying toy was manufactured by the Miami Wood Specialty Company in Dayton, Ohio under the name "Flips and Flops". Demand for the toy was so great that the company could not make them fast enough. Orville's brother, Lorin, bought into the company, allowing it to buy additional machinery so that the toys could be manufactured more quickly. Lorin would eventually end up as president of the Miami Wood Specialty Company.

Although it didn't prove as successful as Orville and Wilbur's full-size machine, Flips and Flops went on to become a favorite toy of many children.

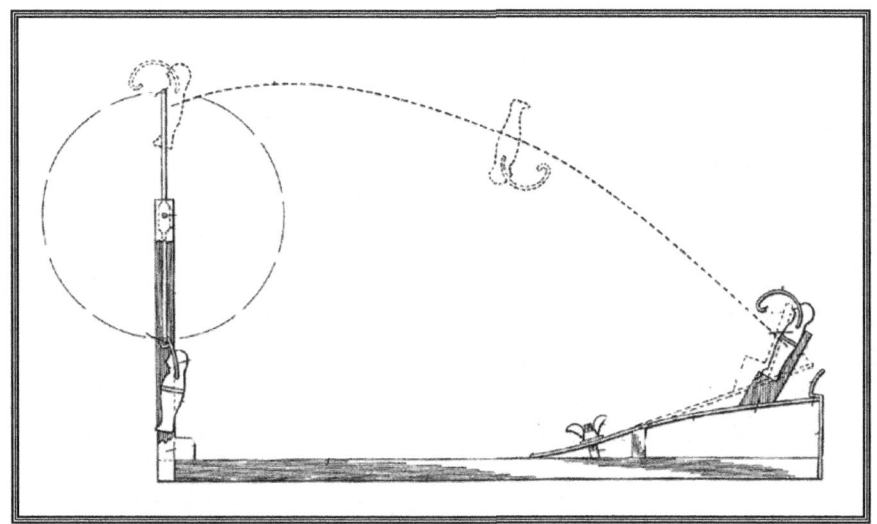

Patent drawing of Orville Wright's toy, showing the catapult and trapeze.

January 21

On January 21, 1914, Dayton's newest motion picture house, the Wayne Theater, was opened by C. Fred Malin, who leased the location from George Richter. Located not far from the Market House that sat on Wayne Avenue, the dark red brick building, with buff pressed brick trimming, was christened "The Theater Beautiful".

No expense was spared on the interior. Designed by Oliver J. Ritzert, the entrance to the auditorium was through a lobby and corridor that were embellished with classic Grecian decorations. Inside the color scheme was green and gold. Side walls were done in silk green color, which complimented the cream colored ceiling. Handsome brass lights softly reflected off a gold fiber motion picture screen. The orchestra pit in front of the stage contained a seven piece Wurlitzer organ that would provide music during the silent films being shown.

Although primarily built to show motion pictures, live acts were also on the bill from time to time. Velvet curtains were used to conceal the performers from view until show time, when they would part to reveal the singers standing against a yellow velvet background. Song novelties included a ragtime soloist, operatic soprano and baritone ballad singer.

By the 1930's Wayne Theater offered a double feature bill, mixing movies with lots of action and adventure with comedy and westerns.

Although the Wayne remained popular up through the 1940's the movie industry was slowly changing. Television, highways and home air-conditioning all played a role in the slow decline of patronage to theaters in the 1950's, and the Wayne was no exception. The theater closed its doors in 1957.

In 1966 Winters National Bank acquired 175 feet of frontage on Wayne Avenue and demolished fourteen buildings, some 80 to 100 years old. This included the old Wayne theater structure. A new branch office was erected to replace the bank's market office at Wayne Avenue and Richard Street which was to be razed to make way for Route 35. The site of the old theater is now a parking area.

January 22

Earl H. Kiser, "The Dayton Dumpling", began racing when he was 16 and later became a two-time world cycling champion. But, bicycling is a young man's sport and Earl announced his retirement at the ripe old age of 23.

In 1901, Earl latched onto another sport involving speed, automobile racing. He soon proved to be good at this as well.

August 12, 1905, was the opening day of a grand circuit meet at he Glenville track in Cleveland, Ohio. A few minutes before the opening race Kiser drove onto the track to warm up his automobile. It was during his second circuit that Kiser somehow lost control of his vehicle and crashed, tearing down over seventy feet of fence. The gasoline tank was destroyed and the car became a mass of flames. Fortunately Kiser had been thrown some ten feet away and so escaped being burned alive. However Earl's left leg was found to be crushed to a pulp, which resulted in it having to be removed.

Afterwards, Earl made an unusual request. A few days later a box, marked "Handle with Care", was delivered to Woodland Cemetery in Dayton. Inside was what was left of Earl Kiser's leg. The leg was buried in a "quiet nook" at the cemetery, to await its owner at some future date. On January 19, 1936 Earl passed away in Miami Beach, Florida. He was reunited with his missing limb three days later when he was buried at Woodland Cemetery on January 22.

Earl Kiser in a Tincher automobile at Harlem Racetrack at Chicago in 1905.

January 23

On January 23, 1916, the *Dayton Daily News* reported on how Stewart, a scraggly fox terrier, braved strange people and unusual events in order to be with his sick owner.

When Michael J. Jennings, proprietor of the Antler Hotel on Sixth Street, had a heart attack, a taxi was called to take him to the St. Elizabeth Hospital. When the taxi arrived, Stewart immediately jumped in to go along. When they reached the hospital, the officials objected, stating that there were rules and regulations to be followed. But Jennings insisted that his friend be allowed to stay, stating that he was rarely without his trusted companion. The fact was, whenever Jennings was called out of town, the 10 year old terrier would refuse to eat or sleep until his master's return.

Rather than have the dog suffer during the days it would take for Jennings to recover, the officials relented. The faithful dog was given quarters in Jennings' room. Stewart refused to leave for any length of time. The nurses, moved by the dog's affection, began bringing him food at the same time Jennings was served his meals.

Fortunately, Jennings recovered, and both he and Stewart were able to return home to the hotel after a few days.

Dayton Daily News applauded St. Elizabeth hospital for the many acts of kindness shown Stewart during the time of Jennings' stay there.

January 24

On this day in 1930, two bandits, one of them armed with a machine gun, held up the South Park Savings bank shortly after it opened for business. The machine gun was used to cover the employees and customers who entered during the robbery. The robbers escaped with about $16,000.

On April 4, five masked men armed with machine guns held up the Xenia Avenue branch of the Union Trust company. Two men remained in an automobile in front of the bank, while the others entered and forced the employees and customers to lie on the floor, threatening to shoot anyone who moved. This time the thieves took over $30,000.

On April 11, seven men held up the Citizens National Bank and Trust Company in Piqua, Ohio. This time an employee sounded a burglar alarm. Ray Alexander, manager, opened fired at the robbers as they made their escape. Over 100 shots were fired, one of the bullets striking Henry Matthews, who owned a nearby delicatessen, killing him. Two others, including Alexander, were seriously wounded.

One of the robbers was later identified as being part of the Union Trust robbery. Fearing that next time it could be someone from Dayton who was killed, the Dayton Clearing House Association donated a modified 1930 Cadillac to the police to be used in responding to bank robberies and other major crimes. It was probably used when John Dillinger was captured in Dayton on September 22, 1933.

Known as the "Bank Flyer", the automobile was equipped with bullet-proof glass and tires, and armor plate shields to protect the radiator and motor. Racks inside held bullet-proof vests, machine guns, high-powered rifles, shotguns and gas grenades.

January 25

When word came that the canal from Cincinnati to Dayton would be completed by 1829, the citizens of Dayton were overjoyed. This was important because farmers could now sell their wheat, corn and tobacco in Cincinnati, where it would bring double the money it did in Dayton.

The first canal boat was scheduled to arrive in Dayton on January 25, 1829. People came from miles around to part of the event. The town had been decorated for the occasion, and Ohio Governor Jeremiah Morrow was to be the town's guest of honor.

About mid-day there was a muffled roar from the neighborhood of the present site of the fairgrounds. A patriotic citizen, anxious to announce the approach of the canal boat *Governor Brown*, had blown up some dynamite as a signal. Instantly the crowd along the banks of canal began cheering.

The *Governor Brown*, with Captain J. D. Archibald of Cincinnati in command, pulled up to the landing at Third Street, where Patterson Blvd. is now. Three other boats would arrive soon after: the *Forrer,* the *General Marion* and the *General Pike*. Each boat was welcomed by the firing of cannon and the enthusiastic cheers.

The three boats were opened to sightseers. A big banquet was held at the National House, where prominent visitors, captains of the three boats, and leading town officials joined in toasts and speeches into the night.

The wood and hay market in 1900. A circus parade passes the Dayton Public Library on the right. The canal (now Patterson Blvd.) can be seen on the left.

January 26

In January, 1841, former Senator Thomas Morris came to Dayton to make an anti-slavery speech at the courthouse under the auspices of the Anti-Slavery Society, which had formed in Dayton in 1839. While he was speaking a disorderly mob began egging him. Doctor Hibbard Jewett tried to help him escape in a carriage, but the mob pulled the driver from the box and caused the horses to run away. When the two men finally reached Dr. Jewett's home, the mob came and plastered it with eggs, then broke in and damaged some of the furniture.

About this same time a light skinned black women came to Dayton and moved to the vicinity of Wayne, Fifth, and Eagle streets, an area of the city where a number of black families lived. This misunderstanding did not set well with a number of people and on the night of January 26, 1841, a mob began an assault at the "Paul Pry", a resort for blacks. Nat McCleary, the leader of the mob, was stabbed and killed.

In retaliation, on the night of February 3, the mob returned and began pulling down and burning a number of houses in the neighborhood. Unfortunately, the temperature that day was below zero. It was believed that some of the owners of the homes, having no shelter from the bitter cold, suffered from exposure and died. Several others sold what goods they had left and moved away.

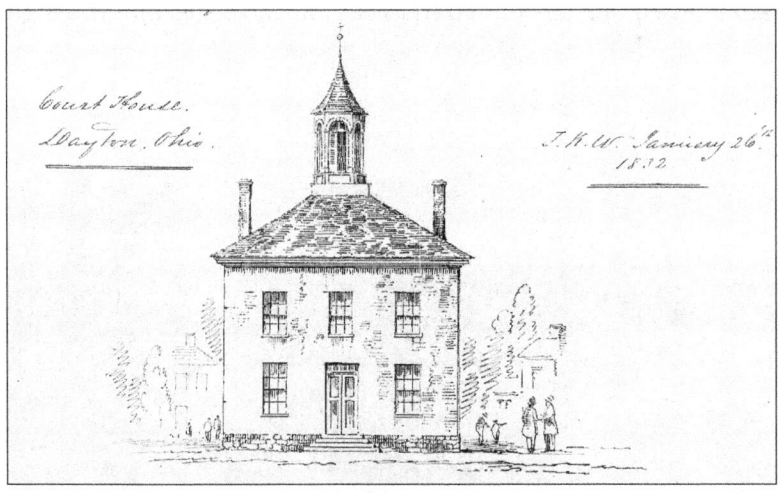

This is a drawing of the brick courthouse where Thomas Morris was egged. It had a courtroom on the first floor and jury rooms on the second. In 1815 a cupola was added. It was razed in 1845 to make room for what is now known as the Old Court House, which was completed in 1850.

January 27

Interest in a railroad connection to Dayton had been going on long before it finally became a reality. Although Dayton had a canal, railroads could carry goods four times as fast as the canal boats. One engine could pull several cars, and each car carried as much as a canal boat.

In 1830, a locomotive and cars were exhibited in the Methodist Church. The city council went so far as to exempt the exhibition from a license fee. A track was run around the interior of the church, and for a small fee parties were carried in the car. For most of the passengers this was their first railroad ride.

In 1847 Dayton men provided money to build a railroad from Dayton to connect with the Mad River and Lake Erie Railroad at Springfield, Ohio. In order to hurry up the work, it was decided to start laying track at Dayton. A work engine, the *Seneca,* was taken apart at Xenia and hauled by wagon to Dayton.

The first railroad to reach Dayton was the Mad River & Lake Erie. A big celebration was held when the first passenger came to Dayton on a train on January 27, 1851.

The first passenger depot at Dayton wasn't much of a facility, just an existing small brick building that had been acquired by the Mad River & Lake Erie Railroad to serve as a place for passengers to get on and off trains and to purchase tickets. The building stood on the north side of Sixth and Jefferson Streets.

January 28

When people began living on the other side of the river from Dayton, two ferries served to connect the settlement with those pioneers. In 1816, a meeting was held at Grimes Tavern to make plans to build a bridge that would span over Mad River, which, unlike the Miami, could not conveniently be crossed by ferry. It was agreed that the bridge would cross over the river at what is now Taylor Street. The contract was given to William Farnum for $1,400. The uncovered bridge had a span of one hundred and sixty feet, and the roadway over the middle of the river was several feet higher above the water than at the abutments. Completed in 1817, the bridge proved to be unstable. Although a new floor was laid and additional braces were put up in 1824, the bridge finally fell into the river in 1828.

A stock company was incorporated in 1817, the purpose being to build a toll bridge across the Miami River at Bridge Street, about where the Dayton View Bridge (also known as the Monument Avenue Bridge) is now located.

Construction on the Bridge Street bridge began in April, 1818. On January 28, 1819, *The Ohio Watchman* newspaper reported that the new bridge was finally open for business.

"The bridge across the Miami at this place is now finished, and presents to the eye a useful and stately structure, highly gratifying to all who feel interested in the improvement of this part of the country, as it is little inferior in strength and beauty to the best of the kind in the State, and renders the Miami no longer an obstruction to the free intercourse with our neighbors on the other side. It is supported by a stone abutment at each end and a strong stone pier in the center. It measures upwards of two hundred and fifty feet in length, and is well roofed and weather boarded."

A toll house stood at the north end of the bridge. The rates for its use were, for a two horse load, 12½ cents, empty wagon 6½ cents, a two wheeled carriage 6½ cents, man & horse 3 cents and a pedestrian 2 cents.

In February, 1832 a flood occurred which washed out the middle pier of the Bridge Street bridge. Although repaired, the bridge would later be completely washed away by a flood in 1852.

January 29

In 1883, Thomas Elder was working as a salesman for Jordan, Marsh & Co., in Boston, one of the largest dry goods houses in the world at the time. That same year he decided to go out on his own and made his way to Dayton. There he met J. Russell Johnston, who had recently moved from Hartford, Connecticut after working 10 years in a dry goods store, and William Hunter, Jr. The three men pooled their resources and opened the Boston Dry Goods Store at 114-116 East Third Street. Two years later the company moved to larger quarters at 24-26 East Third Street. By 1890, Hunter had retired and the business named was changed to Elder& Johnston. In November, 1896, the company expanded once again, moving into the new Reibold Building. By this time Elder & Johnston was thought to have the largest stock of dry goods in the city.

In 1930, Arthur Beerman arrived in Dayton looking for a job that paid enough for him to marry. He first began working for Alder's Home Store, but in the mid-1930s he founded the Beerman Realty Company. In the early 1940s Beerman also began opening several "cotton shops", which first sold house dresses and aprons, and then expanded into children's clothing. In 1945, Beerman incorporated his business and Beerman Stores, Inc. In 1956, he bought Adler's Home Store and opened his first shoe store. This would later become the El-Bee Shoe Outlet chain.

In 1961, Arthur Beerman acquired a controlling interest in Elder & Johnston. On January 29, 1962, Beerman Stores and Elder & Johnston were merged, forming the now familiar Elder-Beerman Stores.

This building, at 16 South Main Street, was the side entrance to the Beerman's Home Store. The store was L shaped, with entrances on both Main and Third streets.

January 30

On October 10, 1947, Orville Wright was hurrying up the stairs at NCR due to being a little late for a lunch appointment with Colonel Edward Deeds. The exertion caused him to have a heart attack. While under an oxygen tent at Miami Valley Hospital, Orville thought of ways that it could be made to work more efficiently.

On January 27, 1948, Orville suffered another heart attack while at his laboratory on 15 North Broadway Street. He would die at Miami Valley Hospital three days later, on January 30, 1948. He was 76 years old.

Orville's funeral took place on February 2, 1948, at First Baptist Church on Monument Avenue. He was buried at Woodland Cemetery. His niece, Ivonette Wright Miller, later described Orville Wright's funeral.

"His services were at the Baptist Church at 2:30 P.M. with Dr. Charles Lyon Seasholes conducting. V.I.P.'s from all parts of the country were there. There was a loud speaker system set up so that the overflow crowd could hear the services from other parts of the church. At the conclusion of the church service we went to our cars. As the funeral procession moved over the Dayton streets, four jet fighter planes from Wright Field flew overhead. Flags were at half staff and the schools were closed at noon. When the services were performed at the cemetery, the planes flew low and dipped their wings..."

Orville Wright's funeral procession makes its way down Main Street in Dayton.

January 31

In 1788, the territory that would later become Ohio and several other states, adopted a blue law that "set apart the first day of the week as a day of rest from common labor and pursuits," and "enjoined that all servile labors, works of charity and necessity excepted, be wholly abstained from on that day."

In 1809, Ohio legislators doubled down on the law, stating that no "sporting, gambling, rioting, quarreling, hunting, horse racing, shooting or common labors" was allowed on Sunday, unless it was necessary work.

In 1959, Ohio legislators decided to eliminate some of the blue laws that were confusing. Stage shows, circuses, parks and fairs would be allowed to entertain on Sundays. Baseball and movies before noon would also become legal for the first time.

However, the bill actually tightened the law which forbid most people from working, and merchants from opening their stores, on Sundays. The only new business activity permitted under the revision was related to transportation, notably gas stations.

After several meetings with local enforcement officers and businesses to hash out what exactly was allowed on the day of rest, Dayton finally began a strict enforcement of the laws on January 31, 1960.

In less than two weeks, nearly a dozen businesses in Dayton were headed for court. But it was Oakwood that actually made the headlines. Malcolm D. McDonald, a private investigator hired by the Assn. for the Remembrance of the Sabbath, filed four affidavits against Dorothy Lane Market for operating on Sunday. In a surprise move, an affidavit charging McDonald of breaking the law was filed by the market's owner, Calvin D. Mayne. Mayne's reasoning was that the investigator had been working when he gathered evidence of the store being open on Sunday.

"Perhaps this will make people realize what they have not seemed to consider - that the blue laws do not only affect retail outlets, but everyone," Mayne was quoted as saying in the newspapers.

Municipal Judge Frederick W. Howell of Oakwood would later rule Ohio's blue laws as unconstitutional and dismiss the affidavits. But two store owners in Dayton weren't so lucky, being found guilty of similar charges by Dayton Municipal Judge Cecil E. Edwards.

By the 1970s, Ohio's Sunday closing laws were being ignored. On June 20, 1973, the Ohio House of Representatives voted to remove Sunday retail sales prohibitions. The law went into effect on November 21, 1973.

February 1

The first public library in Dayton, as well as the first one in the state of Ohio, was formed through an act of the legislature on February 1, 1805. Known as the Social Library Society of Dayton, it charged an annual membership fee of three dollars. The books were kept in Benjamin Van Cleve's cabin, which was also the village post-office, on the south-east corner of First and St. Clair streets. This made sense, as Van Cleve was also the city's first librarian.

The constitution of the Society contained what might considered today to be some rather harsh rules. Borrowers who happened to drip wax from their candle while reading were fined three cents for each drop found on the page, the same was charged for folding down the corner of a page. If a member of the society was caught lending a book to a non-member, they were fined twenty-five percent of what the book was worth. The same fine was levied if the book was carried into a school.

A member was only allowed to borrow one book at a time. If two or more people wanted to borrow the same book, as for instance when a new book was placed in the library, a lottery was held to determine who had first choice, second choice, etc., to borrow the book. This could be very important, for while a book could be switched for another at any time, their return was optional except "on the first Mondays in January, April, July and October, at or before two o'clock in the afternoon." So being fourth on the list could mean the member would have to wait up to a year for their turn to read the book.

The quarterly return of the books was mandatory. Any member not returning their book in time was fined one-eighth the value of the book, plus twelve cents for every week it was detained.

With so many rules in place, members were sure to break one of them from time to time and be fined. Article Eleven made sure that those fines were paid. It read: "Any person fined or assessed and refusing to pay the fine shall be suspended and if not complied with in one year, his or her right shall be forever forfeited."

Upon Van Cleve's death in 1821, the books were moved to the East First Street office of Justice John Folkerth, later Dayton's first Mayor.

For thirty years this library, "two well-filled bookcases", served the small town of Dayton. But, on September 8, 1835 the dreaded words "Library at Auction," appeared in the *Dayton Journal*. This announced the sale of the books and the passing of the Social Library.

February 2

In 1916, Thomas Midgley Jr. began working for the Dayton Engineering Laboratories Company (Delco) in Dayton. His boss, Charles F. Kettering, assigned Midgley to search for the cause of knock in gasoline engines.

It was discovered that the fuel, not the engine, was the cause of the problem. Unfortunately, this knowledge did not bring an answer as to how to solve the problem. It would take another half dozen years and thousands of experiments before Midgley discovered that tetraethyl lead was the answer.

The first test of ethyl gasoline, as it came to be known, was made on December 9, 1921. It was found that, although the knocking ceased, the additive caused lead deposits on the engine valves, which would ruin the engine. Fortunately Midgley found that adding ethylene dibromide solved this.

Ethyl gasoline was first sold to the public on February 2, 1923, at the Refiners Oil Station on South Main Street in Dayton. It proved to be quite popular until environmental laws enacted in the 1970s all but stopped the use of leaded fuel in automobiles.

February 3

If you walk up to the second floor of the Engineers Club of Dayton building you will see a four-cylinder, 180 pound airplane engine in a climate controlled case. This is the third engine built by Charles Taylor for the Wright brothers. Built in 1904, it was never placed in an airplane that flew. Instead, it was used in the brothers' shop as a test-bed for engine experiments and power source for propeller experiments.

The motor was originally loaned to the Henry Ford Museum when the Wright Cycle Shop and Wright home was moved to Greenfield Village in 1937.

On February 3, 1949, the Wright Engine No. 3 was given to the Engineers Club and put on permanent display, which was fitting, as Orville Wright was an early member and past president of the club.

The third airplane engine built by the Wright brothers, was presented to the Engineers Club of Dayton by Milton Wright, their nephew (R). Examining the antique engine with him is John Wright (left), club president. The first engine built by the Wrights is at the Smithsonian, and the second one is in the Wright Flyer III at Carillon Historical Park. Made out of aluminum, the engine was painted black by the Wrights to fool their competition into thinking that it was made of cast iron.

February 4

There are times in emergency situations that a person needs to have his heart manually massaged. The chest compression technique consists of applying force to the chest wall, which pushes air out and allows the elastic recoil of the chest to draw air back in. This technique also helps with the pumping of blood.

Unfortunately, further damage can occur if too much pressure is applied to the chest. The rescuer also needs to try to maintain a constant 60 beats a minute as well.

Daytonians Max Isaacson and Benjamin Smilg invented a cardiac massage and resuscitation device that provided the means to limit the force applied to a person's chest according to age, size and sex. A handle minimized the effort used by the rescuer, so that the massage could be continued for a longer period of time. The resuscitator also provided external mechanical support to the patient's back and ribs, which helped to minimize damage to the ribs and other organs.

The resuscitator was granted patent #3,245,409 on February 4, 1969.

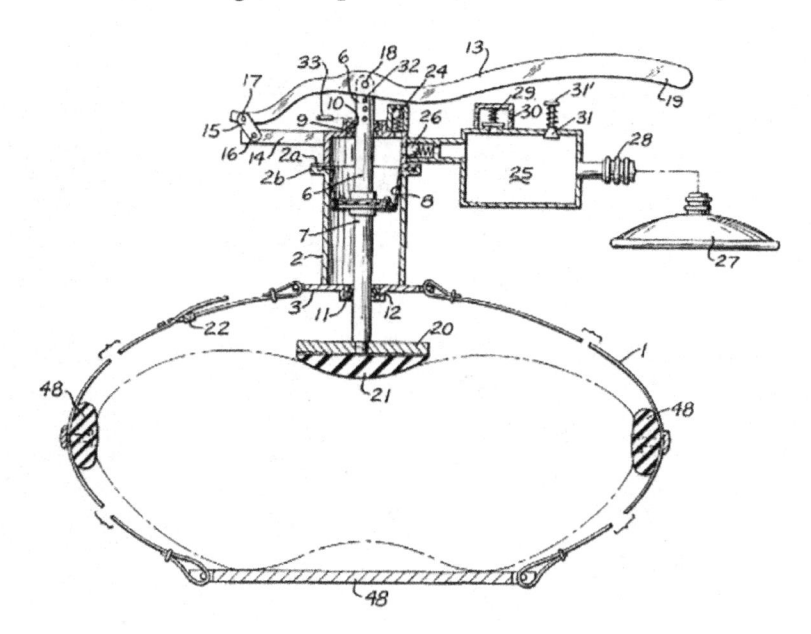

In their patent application Isaacson and Smilg mention that the resuscitator could also be used on animals in an emergency.

February 5

On February 4, 1848 the Dayton Gas Light and Coke Company was incorporated. By the middle of December a gas works was completed and the manufacture of gas for lighting purposes was begun. A mile of gas pipes were laid under the streets of the city. On February 5, 1849, City Hall was handsomely lit by thirteen gas fixtures. A chandelier with eight burners was suspended near the entrance of the hall. Several downtown homes were lit by gas the following day.

To say that Daytonians were impressed is an understatement. One newspaper reported that "the striking beauty of the light, its utility, cleanliness, convenience, all give it claims to consideration which cannot be disregarded, and many who now, perhaps, have no intention of using it will be by force of circumstances and a strong conviction of its utility, persuaded to 'send in their orders.' In a short time orders for more than 600 burners had then been received.

Street lighting came slowly. City council had no authority to levy a tax to pay the expense of both erecting posts and the gas that would be used. They agreed, however, to put up light posts if the property owners on the street would pay for the gas. J. D. Phillips agreed to do so, and had the gas burning at the corner of Main and Second streets. James Perrine also kept a lamp burning at the corner of Jefferson and Second streets.

Unfortunately, the gas, which was manufactured using oil or grease, was expensive to produce. Even when higher prices were put into place, the income scarcely covered expenses, and so the company turned to creating gas from coal. On September 15, 1851, the company switched to coal gas. This proved to create a brighter light at a lower cost.

By 1863 Dayton had 290 lamps lining the streets of the city, and 800 meters in operation. In the 1880s, natural gas was brought to Dayton. But it had a rival… for the city was already starting to turn to the next big idea in illumination – electricity.

On February 13, 1882, electric light was demonstrated for the first time at the *Dayton Journal* newspaper building. Fifty arc lamps were then used to light city streets a year later on February 16, 1883. Dayton was one of the first cities in Ohio to light its streets with electricity.

February 6

On February 6, 1915 a Davis Tri-Car Chemical was delivered to the city of Dayton. Made by the Davis Sewing Machine Company, the vehicle was a new and unusual way to fight fires. The three wheel apparatus looked very much like an automobile from the front, but it was all motorcycle on the back end.

The Tri-Car was built to help fire departments extinguish small blazes. When an alarm would sound at the station, two firemen would jump on the motorcycle and speed to the scene at 45 miles per hour. One of the main advantages was that the vehicle could take narrow streets and short cuts, which usually meant that it got to the fire much more quickly than the larger, heavier fire trucks.

Once there, the firemen could chose to use either the two hand-held extinguishers on board, or unravel 200 feet of hose and spray chemicals from the 35 gallon tank that sat in the front of the motorcycle. Equipped with items such as an ax, a crow bar and a 12 foot extension ladder, the vehicle proved invaluable in controlling fires until larger equipment could arrive.

The Tri-Car Chemical was built along the lines of the company's Dayton motorcycle.

February 7

In 1916, a number of Dayton businessmen decided that their children would be better educated in a private school with more innovative classes than was offered in the public sector. Arthur E. Morgan, the man responsible for designing the five dams after the 1913 flood, was the driving force behind the idea.

On February 7, 1917, Morgan sent a letter to Frank Durward Slutz, Superintendant of Schools at Pueblo, Colorado, hiring him as headmaster. With Slutz in place, the school's supporters selected the name, Moraine Park School, due to the school being located on a moraine.

The first class began on July 1, 1917. Charles F. Kettering offered the use of a large greenhouse located at the corner of Southern Boulevard and Stroop Road. The school included a manual training room, a chemical laboratory, a photograph room, a gymnasium, offices, recitation room, and a lunch room. The Board of Directors included Colonel Edward A. Deeds, Charles F. Kettering and Orville Wright. It was their opinion that students should be encouraged to learn the "kinds of work that will be required of them in the community life in which they will take part after their school days are over."

Progress reports gave points of excellence or weakness on subjects like self expression, acquiring, doing for others, choosing friends, and relaxing. Unfortunately, this did not prepare students for regular college courses and many of them could not get in. The 1926-27 school year proved to be the last one for Moraine Park School.

February 8

On December 23, 1907, the Aeronautical Division of the U. S. Army Signal Corps released Signal Corps Specification No. 486, "Advertisement and Specification for a Heavier-Than-Air Flying Machine." The requirements included that the airplane carry two people having a combined weight of about 350 pounds, travel at least forty miles per hour, be able to stay in the air for at least an hour and carry enough fuel to fly 125 miles. The contract also stated that it was desirable that the flying machine be designed so that it could be quickly and easily assembled in an hour's time and able to be taken apart for transportation in army wagons.

Forty-one applications were received by the Signal Corps. One applicant came from a prisoner in a federal penitentiary whose only payment for building an airplane would be his release from prison. Most of the applications were rejected outright. Of the three that were thought to be able to accompany the feat, the Wright brothers bid to build an airplane for $25,000 was the one that was accepted. The brothers received a telegram telling them of the Signal Corps decision on February 8, 1908.

During the trials in July, 1909, the airplane, piloted by Orville Wright, passed both the speed and endurance tests required of the contract and the Army purchased the Wright's biplane.

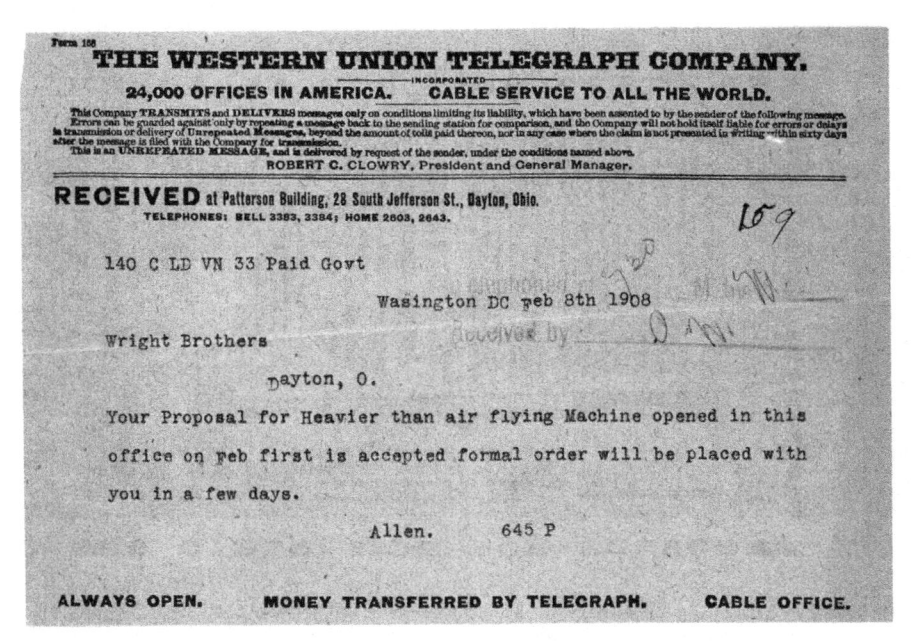

Telegraph the Wright's received stating that their bid had been accepted.

February 9

On January 24, 1848, James Marshall discovered gold on the American River in northern California, while he was working on a sawmill owned by John Sutter. Although Sutter tried to keep it a secret, on March 15 *The Californian* newspaper reported the find. The story was not widely believed. On December 5, 1848 President James K. Polk confirmed the discovery. In his State of the Union address he wrote: "The accounts of abundance of gold are of such an extraordinary character as would scarcely command belief were they not corroborated by the authentic reports of officers in the public service." The gold rush was on.

On February 9, 1849, the Dayton-California Association was formed. A constitution was adopted and by-laws agreed upon. One article of the constitution stated that the members of the company should "cherish each other as brothers and be always ready to help each other in distress.

There were more than fifty in the party when they started from Dayton, but there were some defections along the way. Some of them got cold feet before they were even out of sight of the city and two men jumped off the canal boar at Middletown. Several of the men failed to catch the steamboat in Cincinnati. More left in St. Louis and St. Joseph.

By the time the party had crossed the Rockies there were only twenty-eight members left and the spirit of brotherly love had been smothered. It seems that the men who had been smart enough to bring plenty of provisions for the journey were being pressured by the rest of the outfit to pool everything together and divvy it equally among the members. This did not go over well, and the men with the greater amount of goods split from the company and went on their own.

What was left of the Dayton-California Association finally made it to their destination. The men had excellent luck from the start, panning from $10 to $50 a day; but the cost of living was enough to take their breath away. Some restaurants would charge a dollar for a slice of bread or two if it was buttered. Edward Gould Buffum, author of *Six Months in the Gold Mines* (1850), wrote about eating a breakfast of bread, cheese, butter, sardines and two bottles of beer with a friend and receiving a bill for $43 – which in today's money would come to $1,200.

In the end, most of the men who made the trip came back home to Dayton with little more than they had started with.

February 10

Dayton National Cemetery dates to 1867 when it was established as a final resting place for veterans who died while living at the Central Branch National Home for Disabled Volunteer Soldiers in Dayton, Ohio. Approximately 52.8 acres were originally set aside. The cemetery was in a grove shaded by tall trees near the northwest corner of the grounds, which is now part of the Dayton Veterans Affairs Medical Center campus on West Third Street. The graves were arranged in long regular lines, with a mounted cannon in the center. Large rustic flower vases were placed at intervals.

By 1888, around 3,000 Union veterans were interred in the cemetery. Over 650 African Americans who served in the U.S. Colored Troops (USCT) are buried at the Central Branch, including Joshua Dunbar, father of the famous poet, Paul Laurence Dunbar. The Central Branch cemetery is one of the nation's largest burial sites for black Civil War soldiers.

The last Civil War veteran interred in the cemetery was Theodore C. Witte, who served as a Private in Co. F, 40th Missouri Volunteer Infantry. By 1878 Theodore and his wife, Belle, had moved to Dayton. Over the years he suffered from a number of illnesses, including inflammation of the heart. Witte died at the VA hospital on February 10, 1947, at the age of 99.

Today, the cemetery covers 98 acres, and contains the graves of veterans from every major U.S. military conflict from the Revolutionary War to the Persian Gulf War.

At first the gravestones were made out of wood, as shown here. In 1873, it was decided that a more permanent marker was needed. For soldiers whose names were known a white marble slab was used. The name and rank or affiliation of the soldier was cut into the stone. The part above ground was polished and had a top that was slightly curved. For unknown soldiers, a marble block six inches square and two and a half feet long was used. Only the number used to identify the grave was inscribed into the marble.

February 11

On February 11, 1945 the *Erie Dispatch-Herald* printed an article about Edwin E. Alderman, of Dayton. Before the attack on Pearl Harbor he had been interested in short-wave reception and listened regularly to programs from around the world. When the United States entered the war Alderman continued to listen to Axis broadcasts, and in the Spring of 1942 he began hearing messages concerning American war prisoners, sandwiched between propaganda programs.

Alderman wondered if relatives of the soldiers knew that they were prisoners. He decided to forward on a few of the messages. The response was immediate and so touching he felt obligated to relay all subsequent communications as soon as he received them.

Alderman began spending an average of eleven hours a day without pay in order not to miss any news from overseas. His day started at 1 a.m., tuning into an eight-minute broadcast from Tokyo. Back to bed, then up again at 5 a.m. for a five-minute broadcast. During the day he would send out reports of the men to the next of kin mentioned in the broadcasts. About 5:45 p.m. he donned his earphones and settled in to await the first evening broadcast, a French report from Berlin. At 6:15 p.m. Radio Tokyo came on the air with news and records of prisoners of war. At 7 p.m. Radio Berlin took over with news and prisoner of war reports. These reports also included messages from prisoners of war, most written down and read on the air in English by the enemy.

By 1945, Alderman had relayed to more than 9,000 families the news that their loved ones, many of whom had been reported killed or missing, were alive.

Edwin E. Alderman typing the names of prisoners of war he hears over his short-wave radio.

February 12

On February 12, 1805, the Ohio Legislature passed an act incorporating the town of Dayton. The act provided "that such part of the township of Dayton in the county of Montgomery as is included in the following limits, that is to say, beginning on the bank of the Miami where the sectional line between the second and third sections, fifth township, and seventh range intersects the same; thence east with said line to the middle of Section 33, second township, seventh range; thence north two miles; thence west to the Miami; thence down the same to the place of beginning, shall be and the same is hereby erected into a town corporate, which shall henceforth be known and distinguished by the name of the town of Dayton."

Dayton was governed by a board of seven trustees, a collector, a supervisor, and a marshal, elected by freeholders who had lived in the town for at least six months. The trustees chose one of their number as president and recorder, and also elected a treasurer. The board was called "The Select Council of the Town of Dayton." The president of the Council also acted as mayor.

One of the first acts that almost occurred was the moving of the entire town from its present location. In March, 1805, a combination of the thawing of snow and several days of rain caused the waters of the Miami and Mad rivers to overflow the river banks at the head of Jefferson Street, and just west of Wilkinson Street, covering nearly all of the town plat, bounded by Water (now Monument Avenue), Wilkinson and Perry, Third, and Main streets.

The flooding was worrisome for several reasons. There was a fear that it would become a regular occurrence, which could damage homes and businesses. It also meant that it would be impracticable to plant crops much before June, which greatly shortened the growing season.

Daniel C. Cooper proposed to vacate the original lots of Dayton and lay out a new plat on the hill east of town, pledging that every property owner would be given a lot of the same size they then owned. But a number of people rejected the idea, partly due to not wanting to rebuild their homes again, and so the plan fell through.

February 13

A special dispatch was sent from Dayton to the *Cincinnati Enquirer* so that its readers could also enjoy a peculiar event that had just taken place in the Gem City. On February 13, 1881 the newspaper published the story about the Civil War veteran who had been left toothless by his wife.

When a widow from New London, Ohio read in the newspapers about the Arrears of Pension Act of 1879, which allowed veterans who had fought for the North in the Civil War to reapply for pension and possibly receive back payments, she travelled to the Dayton Soldiers' Home for a new husband. There she met an ex-Union vet by the name of Anderson, who informed her confidentially that he was due $1,800, which would be coming to him as soon as Congress made an appropriation. The woman stated that she had a deep affection for Anderson and insisted he come to her home. Having had enough of living at the Soldiers' Home with a bunch of old men, he agreed. They were soon married and had a short honeymoon, with her paying all of the expenses. She then brought him back to Dayton to await his pension check. She also agreed to have all of his teeth pulled and placed an order for a set of dentures for her husband.

When the newly minted wife returned home a letter was waiting for her, which explained that Anderson was not eligible for the pension and had deceived her. She took the first train back to Dayton and, in the presence of a large number of his friends, gave him a tongue-lashing, telling him that "if you ever dare show your face near my house again I will shoot you".

On her way back home the woman went to the dentist and stopped the order for the fancy $10 dentures she had placed. Anderson was said to be very disconsolate, as he was minus both his wife and his teeth.

The reading room in the Putnam Library at the old Soldiers' Home in Dayton.

February 14

For years it was thought that a road from Dayton to Eaton would be very desirable. The farmers on the west side of the Great Miami River finally agreed to allow a railroad to pass through their lands.

The Dayton & Western Railroad Company was chartered on February 14, 1846. By this time the purpose had changed slightly, with the new plan for the railroad to go from Dayton to the State line between Ohio and Indiana. It is believed the survey was commenced in July, 1848, and the contract let on the April 21, 1849. Track-laying began August 6, 1852.

When it was finished, the Dayton & Western railroad line ran southeast through the heart of the west side of the Gem City, meeting with the Cincinnati, Hamilton & Dayton Railroad just south of Germantown Pike, using the Fifth Street Railroad bridge to reach the other side of the river. This line connected Dayton to Richmond, Indiana. Trains passed over this road to Indianapolis the same year, and the entire road was opened on October 11, 1853.

These two lines gave manufacturers and merchants an expanded market in the Miami Valley to the south and west of Dayton and, in turn, also helped open up the West Side of the city, as residents there could catch the train for a day of shopping in downtown Dayton.

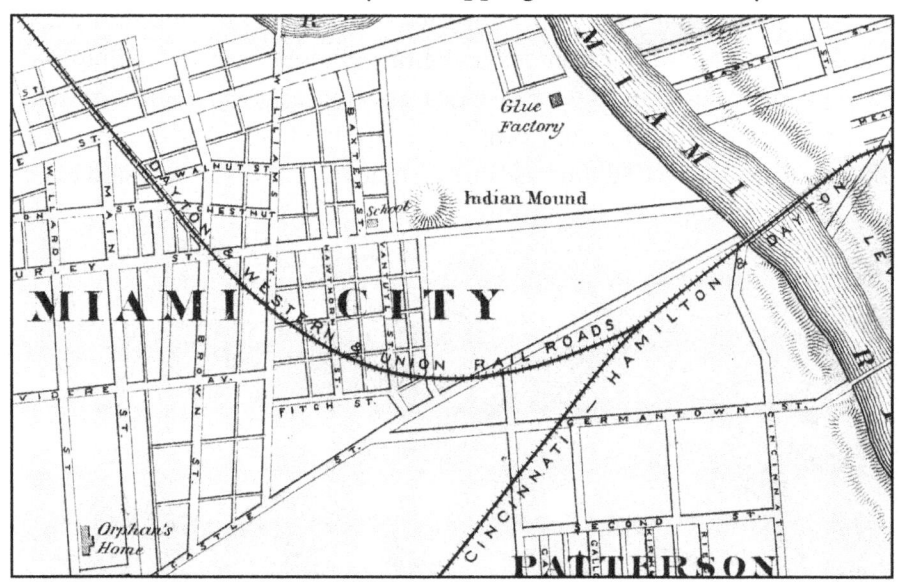

In 1872, part of the west side of Dayton was known as Miami City. Also, Dayton & Western was leasing their tracks to Dayton & Union Railroad, which is why the railroad track says Dayton & Western & Union Railroads on the map.

February 15

Captain Jack Crawford, known as the poet scout of the wild and wooly west, arrived in the Gem City on February 15, 1904. The master storyteller was scheduled to talk to the boys from Steele High School and to entertain the old Civil War soldiers at the Soldiers' Home.

Crawford was a natural story-teller, narrating his life as a seventeen-year-old fighting with the Pennsylvania Volunteers during the Civil War, and his time as a scout for the Black Hills Rangers, a group of men who helped protect the coal miners from angry Sioux tribesmen. His daring ride of 350 miles in six days to carry dispatches to Fort Laramie for the *New York Herald*, telling the news of the victory by Gen. George Crook at the Battle of Slim Buttes during the Great Sioux War of 1876-1877, made him a national celebrity. He also served as an army scout during the Victorio's War of 1880. In between wars, he worked with Buffalo Bill Cody on stage, searched for gold in British Columbia, and published a book, *The Poet Scout: Being a Selection of Incidental and Illustrative Verses and Songs*, in 1879.

With that much material at his disposal, it's no wonder that Crawford was popular on the lecture circuit. He proved to be a hit in Dayton as well. "One of the best entertainments given at Memorial Hall this season was Captain Jack Crawford's lecture last night," reported the *Dayton Daily News*. "He entertained the veterans from his unlimited supply of frontier stories and poems in a way that completely charmed his listeners."

Captain Jack Crawford usually stepped on stage dressed in buckskin pants, homespun shirt, fur-trimmed buckskin coat, and a wide-brimmed sombrero that covered his shoulder-length hair.

February 16

During the Great Depression the Work Projects Administration (WPA) provided jobs and training for young people in a separate division, known as the National Youth Administration. The NYA completed a number of projects in and around the Dayton area, including constructing additional park buildings. The work served as a training school for boys. In 1940, the NYA built various furniture for community centers and assisted in building playground slides and bicycle racks. They also helped reconstruct camps at Eastwood, Elmwood and Mad River parks and build a Sea Scout log cabin at Island Park.

The most permanent work created by the boys of the NYA is the Hills and Dales Lookout Tower. Located on Southern Boulevard, just south of the Patterson monument, the tower overlooks the park. On February 16, 1941 the *Journal-Herald* reported that the tower had finally been completed after a year's worth of work.

The tower was constructed of stone salvaged by the city from condemned buildings. When completed the tower was 56 feet high to the peak of the roof and offered a view of 15 miles around. It was reached by fifty steps from the boulevard and fifty more steps from the entrance to the lookout platform. The walls are more than three feet thick in places. Today, the tower no longer has its roof and is no longer open to the public.

February 17

On February 17, 1808, an act of legislature allowed Daniel C. Cooper to amend the original plot of Dayton, to set aside land east of St. Clair Street, north of Third Street, west of Mill Street (now Patterson Blvd.) and south of Second Street "to be a public walk forever".

In 1836, Daniel's son, David Zeigler Cooper, donated the proceeds from the lease of three lots located on the north side of Second Street, between St. Clair and Mill streets, to the beautification and upkeep of the land. With this fund, the park was enclosed with an iron fence, topsoil added and young saplings of elm and maple were planted. "A fair beginning," he wrote, "for a work which promises to be a credit, as well as an ornament, to the town."

Today, before you enter the downtown branch of the Dayton Metro Library, look at the grounds just north of the building. There, where a monument to President William McKinley stands among the trees, is Cooper Park, named after the man who wanted to leave behind a place for people to gather and relax from the worries of the bustling city.

Cooper Park, with its wide gravelled path, still fairly young trees, iron benches and magnificent water fountain, as it looked from the library in the 1870s.

February 18

During World War II women were asked to turn in their hosiery to help with the war effort. Japan was the sole supplier of silk to the US, and deteriorating trade relations in 1941 cut off the supply. Silk was used for parachutes and for powder bags for naval and artillery guns. Nylon was produced from chemicals vital to the war effort, and was also used for parachutes and tow ropes for gliders.

On February 18, 1943 a drive to gather up old silk and nylon hosiery in the Dayton area began, resulting in the collection of nearly 225,000 pairs of hose in a very short time. In one instance, a woman who had been making rugs from old stockings brought in her partly finished rugs, while another woman donated 118 pairs of stockings she had collected over a period of ten years intending to make rugs. By the first of October 1943, about 46 million pairs of hosiery, or over 2 million pounds, had been collected nationally. This was an amazing feat, due to the fact that no silk or nylon hosiery had been manufactured for quite some time.

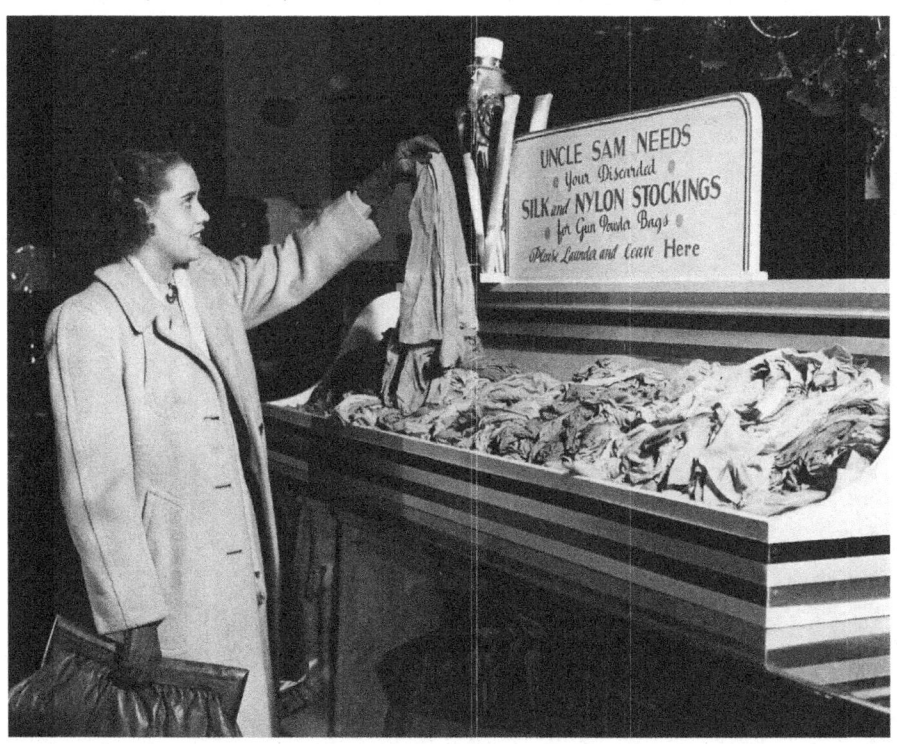

The sign above a bin of collected hosiery reads "Uncle Sam Needs Your Discarded Silk and Nylon Stockings for Gun Powder Bags. Please Launder and leave Here".

February 19

At the turn of the 20th century, Dayton was overrun by hundreds of stray dogs running the streets and barking at all hours of the night. Organizations like the Anti-Noise Society had tried to help pass laws to deal with the curs, but little came of it.

On February 19, 1905, Dayton's health department ordered that all of the dogs in the city limits be quarantined due to several dogs having rabies. A number of dogs had already been bitten by others that were infected, and at least one child had been bitten as well. The quarantine was to last at least nine days and the police were given orders to kill any dogs that were loose. The public agreed with the order, fearing that their children or their own animals might be harmed.

Unfortunately, nothing was put into place to do the job humanely. The police would shoot the dogs as they ran, oftentimes putting the lives of people in danger by stray bullets. Others would club the animals to death. When one man saw this happening and complained, he was arrested and taken to police headquarters, where he was released. The officer then returned and finished the job he had started. Many of the dogs were left where they were slain, which also became a concern. After receiving complaints from a number of people, the police took out three wagons on March 14, and picked up 70 bodies. This did not include the nearly 80 dogs who had been taken to the fertilizing plant earlier in the week.

Calls to city officials, especially to the mayor, began pouring in from frantic dog owners, who feared that their pets might be slaughtered. Others complained of how the dogs were killed in front of children.

On March 26, 1906, the quarantine was finally lifted. The official count of dogs killed was 185, but it was thought that hundreds more had not been reported. During the quarantine, the city council passed a law requiring all dogs to wear a license tag. These were made available on March 28. The tax from the tags went to establish a dog pound, the first in the city. People were warned that any dogs found without tags would be taken to the pound and, if not claimed within three days, the dogs would be euthanized. Edward Clark was hired as the city's first dog catcher. The dog pound officially opened on April 16, 1906, and seven strays were caught by noon. The fine for getting a pet back was 25 cents a day for boarding and the purchase of a dog license.

Today, the period of three days for an unlicensed dog still holds true. Boarding fees are now $15 a day, plus an impound fee of $30.

February 20

On February 20, 1903 E. D. Gibbs, NCR's new advertising manager for Europe, practiced a speech he would be soon be giving in Hamburg, Germany. The crowd consisted of nearly 2,500 fellow NCR employees who had gathered at the Victoria Theater in Dayton to learn about the great strides the company had made overseas and to hear about plans for future activities in Europe.

About the stage, boxes and balcony and gallery railings were flags from a number of nations, a symbol of all the quarters of the globe where NCR had spread. From the dome were suspended streamers of small national emblems, and the background of the stage consisted of huge American flags. The effect of the decorations was very impressive. But they didn't hold a candle to Gibbs' speech.

With a combination of slides and motion pictures, Gibbs conducted an imaginary trip from Europe to the NCR factory in Dayton. The audience was taken on board a steamship at Hamburg, watched it sail from the harbor and saw the motions of the waves as it cut through the Atlantic Ocean to the New York harbor. There, they were transported through the streets of that city to a train, which travelled across the country, arriving at its final destination, the Union Station in Dayton.

After a jaunt around Dayton in an automobile, the trip ended at the NCR factory. The camera then went inside, visiting a number of the various departments, many of which showed the operations of some of the machinery. As can be imagined, the films of particular interest were those which showed the various factory groups, in which most of the audience appeared.

The scenes of Dayton and the factory had been filmed for NCR by the American Mutoscope and Biograph Company, of New York City. This would be the first time that motion pictures had been made in Dayton. The motion picture studio later became a major success, its movie stars including Mary Pickford, Lionel Barrymore, and sisters Lillian Gish (born in Springfield, Ohio) and Dorothy Gish (who was born in Dayton).

Gibbs' speech ended with a flourish, with a number of white doves being released from a basket suspended from the theater's dome. As the birds fluttered to freedom, a shower of confetti fell upon the audience, while from the orchestra pit the NCR band played a brisk military marching tune, bringing the occasion to a close.

February 21

On February 21, 1991, *Dayton Daily News* reported that Curby the Cardinal, a new mascot for the Montgomery County Solid Waste District, had flown into Dayton to teach residents how to reduce, reuse and recycle their trash. It seems that the county's only landfill was due to close and no other site had been developed yet. The hope was that Curby could help lower the amount of trash going to the dump, which in turn could extend the life of the landfill.

Lamar Advertising donated 60 billboards throughout the county, with Curby stating his motto about recycling : "Make it Second Nature." In order to emphasize the importance of the message, all of the billboards were printed on 80 percent recycle paper, manufactured by the Miami Paper Company in West Carrollton. It was the first time in the United States that recycled paper had been used for billboards. Kroger's began featuring a Curby corner display on trash reduction.

As time passed, Curby's popularity grew, and before long he was visiting stores, churches and schools, encouraging and coordinating recycling programs. He even had his own coloring book, which was used for coloring contests, with the winners receiving a certificate honoring them as official Curby Crusaders.

Even though two new waste management sites opened in the late 1990's, the program proved so popular that in 2001, Curby the Cardinal was joined in his crusade by Lucky the Ladybug, the first lady of litter prevention. With the motto, "Take Pride, Ohio!", Lucky asked kids to not litter and to participate in "Litter Bugs Me" cleanup days in their neighborhoods and schools.

Curby the Cardinal and Lucky the Ladybug

February 22

The Fidelity Building, located on the southwest corner of Fifth and Main streets, opened to the public on February 22, 1919. The building was originally 69' x 98' and contained eight floors of offices, most of which were leased by doctors in the dental or medical profession. The Fidelity Building Association, who was responsible for the construction of the building, occupied a corner room on the first floor, along with several other storerooms.

The Fidelity Building Association first began on March 27, 1873 as the Germania Building Association. The organization used customers' deposits and subscriptions to invest in residential mortgage loans of its members to increase home ownership.

The Association held its first meetings in a three-story building at the corner of Eagle and Richard streets. As business grew, the offices moved several times. By 1918, almost 11,000 customers were carrying accounts worth over $6 million. One day's receipts in 1918 equalled about twice as much as the organization handled in one whole year when they first opened their doors.

On May 1, 1918, the Germania Building Association changed its name to the Fidelity Building Association. Some Americans were suspicious of the loyalties of German Americans during World War I. German names of foods, streets, and even places were changed. Fidelity was a much more neutral name than Germania.

The Fidelity Building saw two additions in 1929 and 1930. Today, the 11-story, 120,500 square foot building sits vacant, having closed in 2008 due to damage caused from burst sprinkler pipes.

February 23

On February 23, 1934, a celebrity from Dayton appeared in the comic strip *Strange As It Seems*. Written and drawn by John Hix, the popular feature chronicled unusual facts from around the world - in the vein of *Ripley's Believe It Or Not* - which he also appeared in on October 24, 1931.

The renowned entertainer was Colonel Dudley, a thoroughbred Boston Terrier owned by George C. Kohan. The Colonel understood over 200 commands, including adding numbers, could tell playing cards apart, use a typewriter, play bridge and was said to even be able to read minds sometimes.

Resplendent in his bright red sweater, gem-studded harness and a jaunty derby hat, Colonel Dudley usually had a briar pipe hanging from his jaws - although he also enjoyed a cigar occasionally.

Colonel Dudley held a commission as an officer on the staff of the Kentucky governor. As the official mascot of the Miami Valley Council of the Boys Scouts of America, he made a tour of the United States as the Scouts' ambassador in 1933.

Colonel Dudley appeared on stage and performed on the radio and was a favorite attraction at the Chicago's World's Fair.

STRANGE AS IT SEEMS—By John Hix

COL. DUDLEY -
Wonder radio dog -
SMOKES, PLAYS CARDS,
TALKS AND DOES
ARITHMETIC

February 24

During the Civil War the USS Cumberland, a 50-gun sailing frigate of the United States Navy, was rammed and sunk in an engagement with the Confederate ironclad CSS Virginia at Newport News, Virginia on March 8, 1862. The engagement is considered to be a turning point in the history of world naval affairs as it showed the advantage of steam powered, armored ships over sail powered wooden hulled ships. A miniature man-of-war ship, named after Brigadier General James A. Garfield, was used to take the survivors ashore.

In 1881, *The Garfield* was cut down to a mere twenty-seven feet in length to appear in a parade in 1881 at the inauguration of James A. Garfield as the twentieth President of the United States. The ship was given to the Dayton Soldiers' Home on February 24, 1882, five months after President Garfield died from an assassin's bullet.

On June 14-15, 1882, a Grand Reunion of the Ohio Association of Union Ex-Prisoners of War was held at the Soldiers' Home. On the second day, over 5,000 people watched the launching of *The Garfield* into the Middle Lake at the Home. It became a major attraction to the thousands of tourists who visited the Home each year.

February 25

In 1911 Andrew Carnegie offered the Dayton Public Library $65,000 in funds to build two branches. Sites were secured, plans drawn, contracts let and everything looked towards an early completion of the buildings.

Then came the flood of 1913. The library lost 50,000 books and $25,000 in property and equipment. When the library wrote Carnegie that the building of the two branches would be delayed, he sent a check for $15,000 to be used in the purchase of new books for the branches. The West Carnegie Branch, at 1612 West Fifth Street, became the first branch of the Dayton Public Library when it opened on February 25, 1914. The East Carnegie Branch opened at 22160 East Fifth Street two days later.

After being closed in the 1960's, the West branch remained vacant until it was destroyed by fire in 1979.

The interior and exterior of the West Carnegie Branch, circa 1914.

February 26

On February 20, 1874, Dr. Diocletian Lewis held a meeting at the United Brethren Church in Dayton to talk about starting a war. Dr. Lewis was a prominent temperance leader who believed that saloons were responsible for the majority of human suffering. He felt that his destiny was to go from city to city and rally the local women to come together and wage war against anyone who sold liquor.

Dr. Lewis' speech that night was to the point. He asked the question, were the women strong enough to take on the saloons? If so, then it was time to organize. After a short discussion it was agreed that the time had come to close every saloon in Dayton. That evening a local Woman's Christian Temperance Union group of over 200 women was formed.

On February 26, Dayton became the nation's first city to be subjected to the WCTU's Praying Woman's Crusade. On that day, groups of women visited saloons with the hope of obtaining pledges from them to stop selling liquor. Not wanting the attention, some bar owners promised to close so the women would leave, but then reopened the next day. Others threw water on the sidewalks, trying to make it uncomfortable for the women kneeling in prayer. By mid-March over 150 women had joined in the fight.

After a month's crusading, 226 saloons had closed and 3,000 personal pledges of abstinence were secured. Most of the saloons that closed were located in drug stores and rear-bar groceries. Druggists promised not to sell liquor without a prescription. Groceries lost business from men afraid to be caught drinking.

At the same time, there was a municipal campaign going on and local candidates found themselves pledging "wet" or "dry", the Democrats aligning with the saloons, and the Republicans preaching prohibition or tougher laws.

The day of election, April 6, saw the city full of women banding together to pray at the remaining saloons.

Then came the announcement that every Democrat on the ticket, with the exception of a single constable, had been elected. The next day the police were issued orders to prevent the use and occupancy of the streets and sidewalks of Dayton for public assemblage.

The praying bands dissolved. The war campaign of 1874 came to an end.

February 27

Major Rudolph W. Schroeder served as the Army's chief test pilot at McCook Field. On February 27, 1920, Major Schroeder set a new altitude record by flying upward for an hour and 47 minutes to an altitude of 33,113 feet, an official record that stood for several years.

At this height the temperature was 6 below zero. The plane had an open-cockpit and was unheated. Suffocating from exhaust fumes pouring into the cockpit, the Major lifted his goggles to check his oxygen supply, only to have the film of moisture between his eyelids and his eyeballs freeze. He lost consciousness and with eyes swollen shut plummeted six miles to within 2,000 feet of the ground before recovering his senses and landing the airplane. Major Schroeder's sight never fully recovered from the ordeal.

It was discovered that the sudden change in air pressure during Major Schroeder's fall crushed the gasoline tanks on his plane, which "jolted" him enough to regain consciousness and land the airplane safely.

February 28

When George L. Phillips read in the newspaper about Alexander Graham Bell's success in communicating audibly with a person at a distance, he decided to bring the telephone to his home town of Dayton. A wire could be run from the Western Union Telegraph Office to an "exchange", which would then be run to a customer's place of business.

On the morning of February 28, 1878, workmen completed the wiring between the Western Union and the Beckel House hotel, and before noon the telephones were ready for service. The "exhibition" was to take place in the afternoon and long before the appointed hour the two locations were packed with unbelieving citizens. Then the little bell jingled and people stood in line waiting their turn to listen with childish delight to the voice of somebody two blocks away.

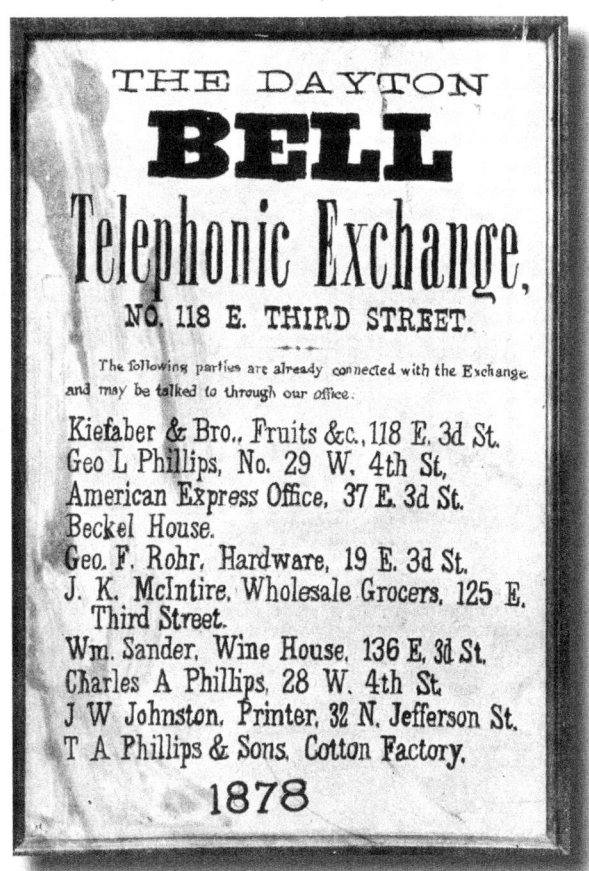

Dayton's first telephone directory. J. W. Johnston printed it in exchange for his first month's use of the telephone.

February 29

It was the end of a 126-year-old tradition when the Central Market House at 22 South Main Street closed its doors on this date in 1956. Since 1829 the site had been used for markets. In 1876, the "new" market house was built.

The three-story building, with its rough wooden floors and lack of modern facilities, had outlived its usefulness, dwindling from 100 stands down to only 20 by 1956. The first four stands were taken out to make room for a garage, then 14 were removed when the municipal court clerk's traffic section used the rear of the market. Supermarkets and lack of parking didn't help the sellers, nor did newer laws in meat inspection and milk pasteurization, which hurt the farmers who butchered their own meat and brought their own milk to sell at the market.

In the end, the city decided to get out of the market business, closing the Wayne Avenue Market as well, on February 25, 1956.

The stone heads of hogs and steers that decorated the entrance to the Market House were turned over to Mrs. Robert Elder and Alfred Swift Frank, heirs of the people who originally granted the land to the city to build the market house.

March 1

On March 1, 1889, seventeen-year-old Orville Wright published the first edition of the *West Side News*, a weekly three column newspaper. Orville was so confident that the newspaper would lead to a life as a publisher that he quit high school so he could devote all of his time on the printing business.

Orville's interest in printing came naturally. His father, Milton Wright, had an office in the United Brethren Printing Establishment at Fourth and Main streets, and Orville would use his time there visiting the pressrooms.

The *West Side News* proved popular enough that in April Orville moved an office at 1210 West Third Street. Orville's brother, Wilbur, soon got involved. The paper expanded from three columns to four, with Wilbur acting as editor and Orville as publisher.

In April 1890, the *West Side News* evolved into *The Evening Item*, which was printed six days a week. *(See July 30)* In addition they printed hundreds of orders for others, including several issues of *The Dayton Tattler* for their friend, Paul Laurence Dunbar. *(See June 16).*

The Wrights maintained their printing business until 1899. They sold it after Ed Sines, who had been doing most of the work on the printing press, had to leave due to a knee injury. The brothers decided to focus on their profitable bicycle business instead.

March 2

On the evening of July 8, 1858, a few Christian gentlemen interested in the "social, intellectual and spiritual welfare" of young men in Dayton, met at the Wesley Chapel on Third Street to discuss the feasibility of organizing a Young Men's Christian Association branch.

A second meeting was held a week later, in which the association was organized, and a constitution accepted. Religious services were held in churches but the organization was abandoned on October 31, 1861 due to some of its members and officers going off to fight in the Civil War.

On March 2, 1870, the Dayton YMCA was official reorganized, with a charter membership enrollment of 247. From 1870 to 1875 the local association met in a rented room over the *Dayton Journal*, just north of the new courthouse. Money was raised and in 1875 the Dunlevy home at 32 East Fourth Street was purchased. A building was erected on its back lot and used as a hall for meetings, lectures and concerts.

By 1886 the building had become too small. Funds were raised to build a new structure on the site of the old one and on February 7, 1887, the YMCA's new four-story brownstone was dedicated. "It is the finest building west of the Alleghenies," YMCA secretary David A. Sinclair boasted at the time. "It will take care of our wants for fifty years to come." By 1908 they had outgrown the building. The structure eventually became the State Theater, which was razed in 1970.

YMCA's next building was erected at the northwest corner of Third and Ludlow, on a site donated by Mary Bell Ecker in her will. At the time it was the second largest YMCA building in the world. Completed in 1908, the structure included Turkish baths, 60 showers, a restaurant, bowling alley and game room. Twenty years later the YMCA had also outgrown this building. The structure is now the Dayton Municipal Building.

When it was announced that the YMCA was going to build a new headquarters at 117 West Monument Avenue, some were against the idea, stating that the location was "out in the country", and too far away to draw members. But plans weren't changed and in 1929 a beautiful building of Northern Italian architecture was completed. In 1992 the building became known as The Landing, a housing and fitness complex. The YMCA remained downstairs, reopening with $160,000 worth of new fitness equipment, whirlpools, sauna and steam rooms, and child-care facilities. The upper floors were converted into 72 apartments.

March 3

On March 3, 1922, Police Officers Charles E. Gross and Walter Newman, who worked for the department as plainclothesmen attached to the auto recovery bureau, were passing the intersection of First and Ludlow streets when they saw a car drive up to the curb and two men leave it.

The officers examined the numbers on the engine and the body and noticed that both had been scratched out. Then they followed the two men to a nearby garage. When the plainclothesmen entered by the back door the two men they were following ran out the front, darting east on First Street. They attempted to allude Gross and Newman by dodging around some parked cars.

The officers drew their revolvers. One of the men, later identified as Albert Pegram, paused a moment and dumped his overcoat into the street. A revolver fell from his pocket. Gross fired at Pegram, the shot going wild. "Pedestrians sought shelter as the lead began to fly on Main Street", the *Dayton Daily News* would later write. Gross fired five shots in all, hitting Pegram in the leg before finally capturing him.

Meanwhile Newman was chasing the other suspect, William Dalton, down Main Street, commandeering a Sifferman Fish Market delivery wagon. Attracted by the shooting, Traffic Officer John Kramer drew his revolver and prevented Dalton from fleeing down East First Street, past the Victory Theater.

Pegram was taken to the hospital in a passing truck. Dalton was taken to police headquarters, where he made a complete confession. The two men had driven into the city the night before, their sedan laden with six cases of whiskey. It seems that their bad luck had actually begun that day, for most or their cargo had been stolen during the night while the automobile was in a local garage. All that was left were 15 quarts of bonded whiskey.

Dalton must have been a very talkative man, as he even confessed to the fact that he and his partner had actually made a trip to Dayton several weeks before, bringing in a large quantity of bonded whiskey to sell.

The two men were to be charged with carrying concealed weapons and with transporting whiskey.

The incident wasn't Officer Gross' first gun battle downtown. About a year before he had shot an automobile thief in a similar fight near the Victory theater.

March 4

As with anything created by man, it all starts with an idea. It began in 1900 when Eugene Barney, Michael Gibbons and others first made plans to build an arcade. In 1900, the Dayton Arcade Company was formed. The area selected was a section of ground that stood midway between Main and Ludlow Streets, running from Third to Fourth streets.

When it was completed the Arcade consisted of four buildings. The front of the Third Street entrance was of Flemish design. Through the center of the building was a 20 foot wide court, with shops on either side. This public passageway, called the Arcade, was protected by a glass roof which shields the first row of offices above.

The Arcade Market gave the complex its distinctive individuality. It had an area of 200 by 198 feet, surmounted by a splendid glass dome that reached upward 70 feet, with a diameter of 90 feet.

During the grand opening of the Arcade on March 4, 1904, over 8,000 visitors marvelled at the 200 stalls, specializing in the sale of items such as vegetables, meat, poultry, eggs, butter, fruits and so on.

Front entrance to the Arcade after completion. Architect Frank Mills Andrews, who designed the Arcade, also designed the Conover building. His studio there on the top floor included an art glass rotunda, which may have helped inspire him as he drew the plans for the Arcade.

March 5

Dayton's citizens were quite upset when the Library Society of Dayton closed its doors in 1835. *(See February 1)* Several social societies like the Dayton Lyceum, the Mechanic's Institute, the Adelphic Society of the Dayton Academy offered books to their members, but the selections were slim and not available to the general public.

In 1847, the Dayton Library Association was incorporated with the purpose of creating a community library. It opened on May 21, 1847 in a second-story room in the Steele Building at 12 North Main Street. But by 1853, the room was getting a bit crowded, and so the books were moved to the second story of the newly built Phillips Building on the southeast corner of Main and Second streets.

That same year the Ohio legislature authorized the establishment of free libraries in the district schools. This was the beginning in Ohio of the present free, tax-supported library system. Instead of scattering the books throughout the school districts, the Board of Education opened the Public School Library in the old United Brethren Building at Main and Fourth streets in 1855. Three years later it was moved to the Central High School. In 1860, the Dayton Library Association donated their collection to the Board of Education. The Public School Library was transferred to the Phillips Building where the Dayton Library Association's collection was located. In 1867, the collection moved once again, this time to the old Jefferson Street Market House.

In 1884, it was decided that the library needed its own building. Cooper Park, on East Third Street, was chosen. The city agreed to allow free use of the land. The Board of Education asked for architects to offer up plans for the new building, with the stipulation that it had to be constructed out of Dayton stone in rock-faced rubble work and it had to be fire-proof.

On March 5, 1885, plans submitted by Peters and Burns were accepted and the castle-like structure opened on January 24, 1888. It would serve the collection and the community well for the next 74 years, until a new building was built adjacent to it, which opened on March 26, 1962.

People never really took a liking to the new building, especially when it was compared to the one before it. But the 1962 structure is now also mostly gone, although some of its bones were incorporated in the building of the latest library, which was completed in 2017.

March 6

In 1909 a battle raged between Frederick A. Cook and Robert E. Peary, both of whom claimed to have reached the North Pole on foot. That was the year Cook announced that he had achieved the goal on April 21, 1908. A week later, Peary stated that he had been the first to reach the North Pole and said that Cook was a fraud.

In January 1911, Peary appeared before the Naval Affairs Subcommittee of the U.S. House of Representatives hoping to receive recognition as the discoverer of the North Pole. Hearing of this, Cook began touring the country, delivering a lecture titled "The Truth About the Pole", giving his version of the controversy.

On March 6, 1911, Cook appeared before about 150 people at the Victoria Theater. The audience was shocked to hear him declare that he had sent a telegram to President William Howard Taft, in which he charged Peary with an attempt to kill a fellow explorer. The *Dayton Daily News* refused to print the telegram, saying that it contained "ugly intimations" which were unsupported and therefore made its publication unjustifiable. However, it did report that the message concluded with "Your hand is about to put the seal of clean approval upon the dirtiest campaign of bribery, conspiracy and black dishonor that the world has ever known."

Unbeknownst to Cook, the House and Senate had already passed a bill, which included placing Peary on the retired list of the corps of civil engineers with the rank of rear admiral "for his Arctic exploration resulting in reaching the North Pole". This included an annual salary of $6,000. President Taft had signed the bill into law on March 4, just two days before Cook's lecture in Dayton.

Cook claimed this photo was taken at or near the North Pole in 1908.

March 7

By the 1830s Americans were spending $8 million each year on imports of silk goods, almost all of it imported from overseas. Congress wanted the money to stay in the United States and so began promoting the raising of silkworms and the planting of the Chinese Mulberry tree. It grew rapidly and sprouted enormous leaves, each being large enough to feed two crops of silkworms per season. It was declared that a family of three could make $300 in six weeks.

On March 7, 1839 the Dayton Silk Company was incorporated with a capital of $100,000. The company advertised that they had on hand 150,000 eggs that they would distribute free to anyone who would sell back to them the cocoons raised from the eggs. Farmers soon began turning their attention to this valuable crop, some actually pulling out other crops to plant them.

However, the farmers and other investors did not realize how much care the silkworms needed to survive, including 24-hour-a-day feeding the last two weeks. Still, money could be made, although it was much more work than the farmers originally thought.

Another fact that the investors didn't know was that mulberry trees are susceptible to cold. The winter of 1839-1840 killed many of the trees. Unfortunately, so many investors across the country had by then been caught up in the silkworm craze that the prices of mulberry trees had risen dramatically. Where at first the one year old trees had sold for $3 to $5 per hundred, the price rose to $500 per hundred. When Dayton farmers went to buy new mulberry trees in the spring of 1840, they found that the price of the trees had become greater than that of the silk that could be obtained from them. The Dayton Silk Company, as well as others who had taken a chance on raising silkworms, went under.

March 8

In 1880, Rev. Augustus Waldo Drury began serving as a professor at Union Biblical Seminary (later renamed Bonebrake Theological Seminary), which was located on First Street and Euclid Avenue on the West Side of Dayton. Drury would remain in that position for fifty-four years.

After writing several books dealing with religious matters, Drury next turned to recording the history of Dayton. When it was released on March 8, 1909, the two-volume set of *History of the city of Dayton and Montgomery County, Ohio* was considered the most complete account of the city ever published. It still serves as one of the best records of the city's earlier times, since some of the sources that Rev. Drury used for research were destroyed in the flood that hit the city in 1913.

The history of the West Side is where the book really shines. Drury's first-hand knowledge from living in the area and studying its past is apparent. From his book we learn a lot about William King. By 1807, King had purchased 1160 acres of land, most of which would later become known as the West Side of Dayton. He would run the first ferry across the Great Miami River and was involved in building a toll bridge across the Miami River in 1817.

By 1900, there were more than thirty churches located in west Dayton, which is why it was known as the "City of Churches". Drury's time spent as supervisor of the Union Biblical Seminary's library gave him the knowledge he needed to write about these institutions, as well as a number of businesses that otherwise might now be forgotten.

Rev. Augustus Waldo Drury would continue to write books and other publications until close to the end of his life, when he began losing his eye sight at the age of eighty-three. He would pass away about six months later, on February 18, 1935.

March 9

Joseph Desch was hired in 1938 to work for NCR in Dayton. He began experimenting on ways to develop an electronic counter. A contract was signed with M.I.T. to develop a 'Rapid Arithmetical Selector'. In 1940, the National Defense Research Committee requested NCR to begin developing electronic defense equipment. The contract grew into the Naval Computing Machine Laboratory, which opened at NCR on March 9, 1942.

Pressure was put on Desch to develop a code-breaking machine. The German military was using a machine called the Enigma, to encode secret messages. British cryptanalysts, using a machine called a Bombe, had been successful in decoding these messages at the beginning of World War II. However, in February of 1942, a fourth rotor was added to the German Naval Enigma, thereby rendering the Bombe all but useless.

The reading of these coded messages was important to the war effort. In 1942, German submarine U-boats sank over 1,600 ships in the Atlantic. Fortunately, the U-boats would communicate with a base on shore to plan their attacks, which enabled the messages to be intercepted. Desch worked with British scientists and was able to develop the first U.S. Bombe.

The U.S. Navy version of the Bombe was a seven foot high, eight foot long and 5,000 pound marvel. Six times faster than its British counterpart, the information was useful in helping the Allies both avoid and destroy U-boats.

March 10

On March 10, 1917, a new resident moved into Hawthorn Hill. It was a sixteen pound St. Bernard puppy that Orville named Scipio. Orville had bought Scipio from Nina Dodd's White Star Kennels in Long Branch, New Jersey for $75.

When Orville went to the train station to pick up the puppy, he took along his nephew, saying that they were going to meet "Mr. Bernard."

The puppy soon became like a member of the family. It is said that the presence of Scipio enriched both Orville and Katharine's lives.

When Orville passed away in 1948, he still had a picture of Scipio as a puppy in his wallet, even though his friend had died in 1924.

March 11

Dorothy Gish was born on March 11, 1898 in Dayton, Ohio. After her father left the family, her mother pursued a career as an actress, and eventually included Dorothy in her act. Dorothy was a natural and made her debut on stage at the age of four as Little Willie in the play, *East Lynne*. Her film career began when her friend Mary Pickford introduced her to director D. W. Griffith in 1912. Thus began a lifetime of acting, with Dorothy appearing in over 100 movies from 1912 and 1963. Dorothy's stage performances included *Young Love, (1928), The Inspector General (1930), By Your Leave (1934), Missouri Legend* (1938) and *Miss Susie Slagle's*, which was televised on NBC in 1955.

Dorothy's last performances were in a 1956 Broadway revival of *Life with Father* and in the film *The Cardinal* (1963). She died in 1968 from bronchial pneumonia at the age of 70 at a clinic in Rapallo, Italy, where she had been a patient for two years. Dorothy Gish was entombed in Saint Bartholomew's Episcopal Church in New York City in the columbarium in the undercroft of the church.

Dorothy (right, with fan) with her older sister, Lillian, who also became a popular movie star. The two sisters appeared in several films together, including Hearts of the World, Orphans of the Storm, *and* Romola. *In 1920 Lillian directed Dorothy in a film called* Remodeling Her Husband; *during which Dorothy fell in love with co-actor James Rennie. The two were married from 1920 to 1935.*

March 12

During World War II Ohio factory workers helped produce $29 billion worth of war supplies. More than 400 Ohio companies would receive recognition for their efforts with the presentation of the Army-Navy "E" award. The "E" award was first begun by the Navy in 1906 to honor excellence in gunnery. When World War II began, the Army and Navy began giving the award to companies whose production facilities achieved "Excellence in Production" ("E") of war equipment.

In 1942, NCR won the award and was given an Army-Navy "E" pennant to proudly fly outside its Dayton factory. The company maintained an outstanding record of performance throughout the war, which earned them a Star Award every six months until their flag carried four stars. At that point, the military increased the interval to one year.

In the April, 1945 issue of the *NCR Factory News*, a letter from Admiral C. C. Bloch, Chairman of the Navy Board for Production Awards was reproduced. Dated March 12, 1945, the letter informed NCR that a fifth star had been granted to the Dayton plant.

"The courageous men on the fighting fronts must have the necessary weapons with which to wage total war," Admiral Bloch stated. "These men appreciate the vital support of the men and women of The National Cash Register Company who have worked with such untiring effort on the production front to supply these needed war materials."

By war's end, only 206 companies in the entire nation had been granted five Star Awards. Frigidaire also earned the honor.

March 13

On the northwest corner of Third and Main sits arguably the most beautiful building in Dayton – the Old Court House. Finished in 1850, today it is considered one of the finest examples of Greek Revival architecture in the United States.

When the contract was first signed, the estimate to build the courthouse was $63,000. However, the final price was in excess of $100,000. It took three long years to finish the project, and all the while the population of Dayton was growing. In fact, by 1857, the county commissioners agreed that a bigger courthouse was needed. A vote was called for a tax levy for the new building. Stung by the high price of the courthouse that was already considered a relic, the citizens of Dayton voted down the levy.

Rather than go through the voters again, on March 13, 1867, the Ohio Legislature passed an act authorizing the commissioners to build another courthouse. Plans were drawn in 1869, but the project bogged down and it took until 1884 before the new county courthouse was finally completed just north of the older courthouse on Main Street.

The 1850 courthouse is on the left, the 1884 courthouse is on the right. By the late 1960's the court functions had moved to yet another location and in 1974 the 1884 courthouse was razed. Some of the stones are now a part of the retaining wall of the 1850's courthouse. The area where the courthouse sat is now a gathering spot known as Courthouse Square.

March 14

On March 14, 1919, a parade and dinner was given in honor of Company G, 372nd Infantry Regiment. The 372nd Infantry was part of the National Guard's all-black 93rd Division during WWI. The regiment's participation in the Meuse-Argonne advance was decisive in ending the war, credited with taking nearly 600 prisoners, and securing large quantities of engineering supplies and artillery ammunition. For its actions the regiment was awarded the Croix de Guerre with Palm.

Company G was the first Dayton war unit to return as a group from military service and the parade gave citizens a chance to turn loose some of their pent-up patriotism. A number of organizations joined the soldiers as they paraded downtown, including the Knights of Tabor, Knights of United Brotherly Friendship, Odd Fellows, Knights of Pythias and Daughters of Jerusalem. Black veterans from the Soldiers' Home who had fought during Civil War slowly marched along, followed closely by the members of Company G, who were last in the parade.

Afterward, a reception was held at the Grace M. E. church at Fourth and Ludlow streets. A number of speeches were served with the food. On behalf of his fellow comrades of Company G, Sergeant Garfield Jones graciously thanked everyone who was responsible for the demonstration. The program was closed by everyone singing the Star Spangled Banner.

Soldiers of the 372nd Infantry Regiment prepare to board a ship in France for their return home to the United States in March 1919.

March 15

On April 4, 1947, the Federal Communications Commission (FCC) granted the Crosley Broadcasting Corporation a construction permit to build a television station in Dayton. This was the first broadcast license issued for the city. Assigned channel 5, the new station's call letters were WLWD, and were part of Crosley's "WLW Television Network", which also included stations in Cincinnati and Columbus. The new station's call letters came from Crosley's Cincinnati radio station, WLW (**W**orld's **L**argest **W**ireless) + **D**ayton.

Excitement must have been high, for WLWD stood a good chance of being Dayton's first television station to go on air, but a number of delays set back the broadcast to March 15, 1949 – twenty days after WHIO-TV began broadcasting. WLWD's office and studio were housed in a former skating rink on South Dixie Drive.

During its very first year, WLWD broadcasted the Dayton Indians baseball games, the first time a Class A team in the country was televised. It was also the first station to show automobile racing, which took place at the Dayton Speedway.

WLWD was switched to channel 2 on the dial on April 27, 1953. Over the next few years the station became known for a number of its great regional programs. Johnny Gilbert hosted a 90-minute daytime variety/talk show that included celebrity guests and a 60-person studio audience. When he left, his time spot was given to *The Phil Donahue Show*, which began on WLWD in 1967. Other regional programs, originating from WLWT in Cincinnati, but also shown on WLWD, included *The 50-50 Club*, hosted by Ruth Lyons (succeeded by Bob Braun after Lyons' 1967 retirement), *The Paul Dixon Show* and the Saturday evening country music program *Midwestern Hayride*.

In June, 1975, WLWD was sold off to Grinnell College in Iowa. The school changed the call letters to WDTN shortly after the sale closed in spring 1976.

Today, several sales, trades and mergers later, WDTN is owned by the Nexstar Media Group.

March 16

When the first settlers arrived in Dayton on April 1st, 1796, they built log cabins, and since the logs were green, it was several years before the cabins became dry enough to become a fire hazard. The first fire of consequence was on June 30, 1820, when Daniel Cooper's mills burned, destroying four thousand bushels of wheat and two thousand pounds of wool.

Soon after, the Dayton City Council passed an ordinance requiring each able bodied man to have two leather buckets at his home, which the city provided. When an alarm was sounded the men were required to run with the buckets and fight the fire. The city also provided ladders, which were hung on the outside wall of the market house on Second Street.

All was well until the night of November 16, 1824, when George Groves' hat store, containing over a hundred fur and a number of wool hats, caught fire. Unfortunately, the fire ladders were not in their place at the market house, which meant that the fire had to be fought strictly on the ground with men throwing water from their leather buckets. Groves' business was completely destroyed, the loss being about $1,000.

An ordinance was passed stating that anyone removing the public ladders from the market house, except in case of fire, would be fined $10. But the city knew this wasn't enough. When H. G. Phillips went on a business trip to Philadelphia in the spring of 1825, he took along $226 from the city and ordered a fire engine to be manufactured.

When the fire engine finally arrived on March 10, 1827, even though it was somewhat crude, it was still the seven day wonder for a time. It held several barrels of water, which had to be filled by forming lines from a cistern to the engine and passing the filled leather buckets along the line. The two pumps were operated to throw the water through the hose on to the fire.

Men were needed to man the newfangled fire engine, and so the first volunteer fire company of Dayton was organized on March 16, 1827. Unfortunately, the engine wasn't taken care of very well, for when a fire occurred on a cold day in 1831, it couldn't be used. It seems that the engine was full of ice, because the firemen had forgotten to empty it after a fire that had occurred several weeks before.

March 17

When someone talks about "patent medicines", we all picture the pitchman from the old movies, pointing with his right hand at a bottle in his left, extolling the virtues of the "brown miracle in a bottle", a tonic that would cure your sore head, aching feet, depressed spirits or even any major diseases you may have.

The phrase "patent medicine" is deceiving in many ways. Rarely were the potions patented and most did not contain any curative ingredients. Then, as now, a patented invention did not need to work, but medicine makers were still leery of sharing their secret formulas, since the patent process would have required them to reveal the ingredients of their dubious products.

However, some patent medicines really were patented. On March 17, 1863, Edward Conway, a dentist from Dayton, was awarded patent 37.901 for an "improved liniment". Called Dr. E. Conway's Linimentum", the good doctor claimed his liniment could be used "For stopping of blood, the cure of rheumatism, cuts and inflammation of every kind." The amber colored liniment was made up of brandy, camphor, cedar bark, ammonia, orrisroot, white-oak bark, whiskey and opium; ingredients sure to stop anyone's blood.

Ads for Dr. Conway's liniment appeared in the Dayton Daily Empire newspaper several times between December 1862 and January 1863. However, it appears that by the time Conway's patent was approved, the liniment was no longer available.

March 18

When the Phillips House opened on the southwest corner of Third and Main streets on October 14, 1852, it was agreed that Dayton finally had a hotel that matched those found in other metropolitan cities. Considered among the leading first-class hotels in Ohio, the four-story high building contained 150 rooms, all heated with steam and lit with incandescent electric lamps. Abraham Lincoln was a guest there while stumping for president in 1854. For decades the Phillips House was the scene of important events and was considered the town's social center. But by 1919, it was getting difficult for it to compete with the more modern hotels that dotted the city at that point.

On March 18, 1919, the *Dayton Daily News* published a story on a proposal to replace the Phillips Hotel with a monument to the Wright brothers, in the form of an 18 story high, 500 room hotel to be called the Wright Hotel. The plan included a roof that could be used for airplane landing, with the upper floor being a garage for airplanes instead of automobiles, as well as headquarters for an airplane club. It was hoped that the hotel would become the hub of airplane business activities.

Perhaps it was the three-million price tag, or maybe the difficulty of landing an airplane on a strip of roof only 200 feet long, which doomed the plan from the very beginning. Instead, in 1922, the land was sold to the Gibbons family, who owned the Gibbons Hotel on Third and Ludlow. They, in turn, tore down the Phillips House in 1926 and then leased the site to the Liggett Drug Co. The Liggett Co. built a two-story that housed their drug store, as well as several other businesses.

The Liggett Company building circa 1927. This building was replaced in 1989 by One Dayton Centre (now Fifth-Third Center).

March 19

A new dry goods store by the name of Prugh, Joyce and Rike opened in Dayton in 1853. In 1908 it was renamed the Rike-Kumler Company, which affectionately was known as Rike's. On March 19, 1912, the company officially opened their new store at the northwest corner of Second and Main streets at a cost of one million dollars. It was considered one of the finest and most modern department stores in the Midwest. The structure included a power plant, laundries, employee club rooms, restaurant, a food market and an alteration department.

Rike's well-planned building offered a vast array of merchandise from around the world. First floor display windows were creatively decorated to show what the store had to offer inside. In 1938, Rike's added a new floor to the existing building, an eight-story addition on the west side, four high-speed elevators, an auditorium and two new restaurants.

In 1960 the building complex expanded into the old Miami Hotel. Later renamed Shilito-Rikes, then Lazarus, the department store closed its doors in 1992. The complex was imploded in 1999 to make room for the Schuster Performing Arts Center.

This picture shows a rare glimpse of Rike's as it was being built. The department store was only four days late from its scheduled opening of March 15, 1912.

March 20

The address of 319 Central Avenue in Dayton, Ohio, was made famous by being where the first electric self-starter for automobiles was invented in Edward Deeds' barn in 1911. But little has been written on the unique company that was formed in a playhouse there by his son, Charles, and Charles' friends the year before.

The company was made up of six children, ranging in age from eight to thirteen years, who agreed to invest two dollars each. Charles Deeds' playhouse was remodeled for the factory. Soon the boys began turning out wooden mission-style waste baskets, stools and paper weights.

Business was quite profitable and so on March 20, 1911 the Juvenile Manufacturing Company was incorporated. Within the first ten months the boys had sold over $150 worth of merchandise. Business had grown to the point that the company issued an 8-page catalog. Besides stools and waste baskets it also offered Indian head plaques, match safes, and card holders, pin holders and ashtrays of solid bronze in various finishes.

Unfortunately, by August, 1912, the operation had closed. The end came when two of the boys, Charles and Evan Whidden, had to move to Canada with their parents. Profits were split six ways and the company shut its doors.

March 21

By Christmas of 1929, the first effects of the Depression was starting to be felt. The Department of Public Welfare and the Council of Social Agencies decided to have a Christmas campaign to give holiday cheer to needy children. Students of the University of Dayton volunteered to hand out dolls and toys. The Colonial Theatre held a children's party, the price of admission being an article of food. The food was passed on to needy families by the Salvation Army.

The year of 1930 saw major changes in the city, the biggest problem being the ability to help give relief to people who required assistance. The burden of relief was placed on local government agencies, including schools, which tried to provide shoes, clothing, medical supplies and other items to school children.

What came as a surprise to many was the fact that, even though the city could barely take care of their own, Dayton went forward with its annexation program, increasing its area by a little over 7 square miles. The suburban districts incorporated were Riverdale and Mt. Auburn, which became part of Dayton on March 21, 1930. On June 1, 1930 the districts of Westwood, Lakeside, Broadway, Belmont, Overlook and East Park were added, and on November 4, 1930 the Wellmeier Plat of 37.3 acres was added. Police and fire protection was immediately provided and the collection of garbage and street maintenance started. In the end about 36,000 more people became legal residents of Dayton.

Complaints poured in, as these annexations placed a burden on the city and its tax payers, since the new regions had to be provided with police and fire protection, garbage collection and street maintenance at a cost of several million dollars. But Dayton officials explained that, along with the debt, the new districts would also generate tax revenue in the amount of around $45 million. Of course this was based on whether the city's new citizens were able to pay their taxes. Due to the economy many could not to do so.

This did not help the city's situation, as this cost the city revenue. Due to state law which made it compulsory for municipalities to live within their income, on September 15, 1930 an ordinance was passed which cut the salaries of all city officers and employees by ten percent. Fortunately additional taxes were collected and the salary deduction was repealed after only two weeks. The city ended the year with only $13,000 left in the bank.

March 22

On March 22, 1904, the *Dayton Daily News* reported that Harry Patterson, a clerk at the Hotel Atlas, was buying life insurance for his bulldog, Colonel. This came as a surprise to the local insurance men. Sure, Colonel could turn the register around for visitors and ring for the bellboy. Yes, he could play dead, shake hands and even put on his own collar - tricks that were pretty impressive for a dog only a year old, but it seemed foolhardy to most that Patterson would insure his furry companion.

Colonel proved his worth, when he was "discovered" in 1906, by an agent of the Keith's vaudeville circuit and given a 32-week contract to perform across the country. Patterson and Colonel packed their bags and headed for the stage.

Colonel wowed audiences with his tricks, which had grown to include kneeling on a seat with his fore paws over the back and his head hung low, as if praying. The bulldog would remain in that position until his master said "Amen". One of the more popular tricks was when Colonel would go to a bar on stage and bark until given a drink, and then relax by smoking a cigar. He would also walk on his hind legs like a soldier and salute the audience in military fashion.

Colonel smoking a cigar and putting on his own collar.

March 23

The trimming of the Patterson Elm on March 23, 1920 marked the passing of a historic living landmark. Legend states that local Native Americans had meetings under the tree's outstretched branches. The elm marked the northern boundary of the farm of Revolutionary War veteran Col. Robert Patterson, who helped found Lexington, Kentucky before moving to Dayton in 1804. A hundred years later the tree would become a quiet place to contemplate for employees of NCR, the company which Col. Patterson's grandson, John H. Patterson, had created.

Unfortunately, the great elm became diseased. Heavy winds often brought limbs crashing down. Most of the limbs were removed, but the main body was kept intact and creeping vines were planted at its base, so that it could continue its centuries of service.

March 24

On March 24, 1922, an experiment in radio broadcasting began, when WFO went on the air from the seventh floor of the Rike-Kumler building on Second and Main streets in downtown Dayton. The AM station had two frequencies at the time. One was used for entertainment purposes, such as music, and the other was for special types of broadcasts, like weather reports and farm information. The station would switch frequencies when it was time to give a weather report.

A room adjoining the radio office was fitted with equipment that included the ability to broadcast concerts given by leading musicians who came to Dayton, as well as prominent men from the Miami Valley, both of which could be heard by radio sets as far as 2,000 miles away.

One example of programming was when Charles F. Kettering gave his first public talk on WFO on March 30, 1922. The Riverdale Methodist church choir also gave a musical program that day. Receiving sets were set up at the Riverdale Methodist church and the Dayton Country Club so that the musical program and Kettering's talk could be heard.

Rike-Kumler was also thought to be the first in the history of radio to broadcast their "store news", which included ads and special bargains. Of course, the store also installed a radio department so that locals could take advantage of the free entertainment. Some of their biggest customers were those living in the rural areas, who listened in for the road reports that covered every road leading to Dayton for a distance of 25 miles, in case there were accidents or congestion, just like today. The advertising service was also well received, due to the fact that potential customers would be informed of Rike-Kumler's special sales several hours in advance of the time they would receive the information in the newspapers.

Farmers were also in the market for the radios Rike-Kumler was selling, for the company also broadcasted market quotations and the weather forecast, which was relayed from Washington.

But the upkeep of the station and the cost of the various programs proved too much, and WFO went off the air on November 23, 1922.

March 25

Three large air masses, one full of moisture from the Gulf of Mexico, another from Canada, and a third traveling across the Great Plains, converged over the Miami Valley in March 1913. There it released nine to eleven inches of rain over land already saturated with melted snow and previous rainfall. Spread over an area as large as the Miami Valley, this became the equivalent of four trillion gallons of water cascading over the land and through Dayton, releasing in five days what would normally flow over the Niagara Falls in a month. The water had no choice but to pour into the Great Miami River, already swollen beyond its banks, which met with Stillwater and Mad rivers and Wolf Creek at Dayton.

On March 25, 1913, after four days of rain, the river finally overflowed the protecting levees. Slowly at first, then with ever increasing speed, the freezing waters of the Great Miami began filling the streets of the city, including the West Side. Soon the brackish, yellow river water was traveling through Dayton at 25 miles an hour, carrying with it everything in its path.

People were trapped in their homes, some having to resort to climbing onto roofs to escape the ever-rising waters. Heat was out of the question, for fear of beginning a fire due to escaping gas. Food was scarce; most of it becoming ruined when the river waters flooded the first floors. Ironically, clean drinking water was even harder to find.

It took three days for the waters to recede… and years for the city to completely recover.

March 26

In the beginning, whenever a new postmaster was appointed, the post office was moved to their homes. In 1861, the office was moved to the Beckel Hotel at Third and Jefferson streets. When the quarters there became too cramped, the post office was moved to the United Presbyterian Church at Fourth and Jefferson streets.

In 1892, Dayton finally obtained its first Federal Building when a post office was built at the southwest corner of Fifth and Main streets. Unfortunately, in less than a decade the city had outgrown the regal stone structure. Although an effort was made in Congress to raise money to expand the post office, it was finally decided that another building was needed. The old post office was sold to help raise money for the estimated $1 million it would cost to erect a new one.

On March 26, 1912, ground was broken at 120 W. Third St.. Postmaster Frederick Withoft delivered a brief speech, stating that he believed the post office would be one of the finest buildings in the country. The contractor, Herbert B. Knox, owner of the Charles McCaul Company, promised to push through the project as quickly as possible.

On January 1, 1915, the new Federal Building was dedicated. The granite structure included a colonnade of 16 monolith columns. Reliefs of eagles, wreaths, and scrolls ordained the entrances while lion heads inspected those who passed by. It would remain in use until 1975.

Slated for demolition in 1975, the building was saved by the local architectural firm of Lorenz and Williams, which used it for the firm's offices. It was renovated again in 1994 and now serves as the home for the U.S. Bankruptcy Court.

March 27

On March 27, 1908, Dayton Mayor Edward E. Burkhart announced that he had begun a crusade against the billboard nuisance in Dayton. This was nothing new, as people had complained about the unsightly structures for years, but nothing much could be done, due to laws allowing signs to stand on private property. But this time the mayor had ammunition. A 30 feet long by 35 feet tall billboard had fallen over the day before and had hit a woman, fracturing her leg and causing internal injuries.

A new law was passed, stating that billboards that were not secure were to be taken down immediately. It also called for any "immoral" ads to be removed. The mayor stated that he had received a number of complaints on a poster for "Sapho", a stage play in which actress Olga Nethersole plays a woman who has love affairs with a number of men. In one scene, she and a man ascend a staircase together, presumably toward a bedroom. Another poster, advertising a burlesque act called "French Maids", could also be seen on some billboards, even though the mayor had revoked the license of the Gayety Theater for showing the "immoral performance".

"The police are to lose no time in scrutinizing the lithographs (posters) all over the city, and must either order the owners to tear them off or have them covered up," stated Mayor Burkhart. Fire Chief Frank D. Ramby also promised to personally investigate the matter at once.

This billboard on West Fifth near Perry Street was typical of the day. And image what the woman on the Sapho poster would look like if she was 10 feet tall.

March 28

In 1824 John and Dolly McAffee were living next door to Hetty Shoup. Unfortunately, John fell in love with Hetty and before long the two began having an affair.

On June 20, 1824 John came home from town with some "medicine" for his wife to drink. She had been ill lately and was prone to having "fits". Sadly, the medicine was in fact opium, a deadly poison. The drug didn't work as quickly as John hoped, and so he strangled her to death. As soon as the act was finished, John panicked. He ran from the house and hid. He was eventually captured and tried for murder. After only five hours of deliberation the jury found McAffee guilty of poisoning his wife. Judge Joseph H. Crane read the sentence out loud in court.

"The Court adjudge and sentence that you, John McAffee, be taken from hence to the prison from whence you came, and that you be taken from thence on the 28th day of March instant, between the hours of ten o'clock in the forenoon and five in the afternoon to the place of execution, and that you be there hanged by the neck and throat, till your body be dead, dead, dead, and may God Almighty have mercy on your soul."

A scaffold was erected where Robert Boulevard and West Third Street would later intersect. Never before had anyone in the city been sentenced to hang, nor had anything ever aroused so much anger in the populace. Being the last week of March, the roads leading into Dayton were over six inches deep in mud, yet thousands trudged through it to see the event. Some came from as far as twenty miles away, an all-night journey at the time.

Although John made no confession on the scaffold, he had supposedly written one in his cell while awaiting his death; in rhyme, no less. The printed confession was sold at the time of the hanging.

Unlike its author, McAffee's confession is alive and well. Known as *The Poisoned Wife* and *Young McAfee on the Gallows,* the poem became a popular ballad that is still sung today. Folklore singer Mike Seeger recorded it in 1964, as did Sandy and Jeanie Darlington in 1966. Ann and Phil Case offer their version, titled *McAfee's Confession*, on their album *Why Should We Be Lonely?* McAffee's tale of death and woe continues to live on in legend.

March 29

On March 29, 1822 a squirrel hunt in Montgomery County began that lasted a day and a half, in which at least one thousand squirrels were killed. These strange migrations of squirrels would occur at irregular intervals. Starting from the Northwest, they would come in countless numbers, and nothing could turn them from their course. Rivers were no impediment to them, and boys would stand on the shore of the Miami and kill them with clubs as they emerged from the water. This was not done out of cruelty, but in self-defense. If left unchecked the squirrels would destroy any cornfield they found in their search for something to eat.

This wasn't the first time, nor the last, that this would happen.

In 1811, Charles Joseph Labrobe wrote in *The Rambler in North America* of a vast squirrel migration that autumn in Ohio.

"A countless multitude of squirrels, obeying some great and universal impulse, which none can know but the Spirit that gave them being, left their reckless and gambolling life, and their ancient places of retreat in the north, and were seen pressing forward by tens of thousands in a deep and sober phalanx to the South …"

Because of the numerous squirrel migrations, John Audubon and John Bachman were convinced that the squirrels on the move were a separate species from the gray squirrels and used the scientific name *Sciurus migratorius*. Bachman once described what a migration was like.

"Mountains, cleared fields, the narrow bays of our lakes, or our broad rivers, present no unconquerable impediments. Onward they come, devouring on their way everything that is suited to their taste, laying waste the corn and wheat-fields of the farmer; and as their numbers are thinned by the gun, the dog, and the club, others fall in and fill up the ranks…"

In August, 1822 a hunt was organized in Columbus to try and control the migration. The farmers in several townships were asked to make arrangements. After three days the official count had reached 19,960 squirrels, but since many of the farmers hadn't bother to make a report, the total was thought to far exceed that number. These hunts continued through the 1850s.

March 30

When the Young Women's Department of the Woman's Christian Association ceased to exist, ten of their members decided to form the Young Women's League in August, 1895. Members were invited to take classes, which included sewing, millinery and gymnastics. A lunchroom was also made available.

Membership grew and by 1898, the society purchased a home at 24 West Fourth Street for $23,500. A nine-day bazaar at the Kuhns Building was held which netted $5,000 - enough for the down payment.

In 1901, James M. Cox, owner of the *Dayton Daily News*, offered to let the league women put out an edition of the newspaper, the proceeds would go towards their mortgage. They readily agreed. And so, on March 30, 1901, the entire editorial staff of the *Dayton Daily News* was composed of women.

The local stories in the issue had a tendency to be geared more toward subjects that league members might want to read, such as charity toward children and higher education for women. But Mabel Withoft didn't hesitate in writing a more gruesome story. "BREAKFAST WAS READY - But the Husband Sent a Bullet to His Brain" told of how William Lacey had committed suicide earlier that morning while his wife was making breakfast. Ill health was thought to be Lacey's motive.

Street sales of the special edition were so heavy that the presses ran several hours overtime to supply the demand. The day's profits netted the league $1,800 toward their building fund.

Left: YWL home, 24 West Fourth Street

One section of the YWL edition of the newspaper was devoted to personal messages of good wishes to the League from the likes of Vice President Theodore Roosevelt, Booker T. Washington, Mark Twain and several others. Twain stated that the League had all the elements of universal brotherhood but one—the sinner. "Yes," he wrote, "what you lack in order to be complete, is an abandoned sinner, an old professional. Would I do?"

March 31

On March 31, 1919, ex-President William Howard Taft delivered a speech at Memorial Hall to an audience of 3,000, in an auditorium designed to hold only 2,500. He spoke of his support in forming the League of Nations, an organization which would provide a forum for resolving international disputes. Taft warned those who opposed the idea that, without international agreement, another war would soon follow, more destructive than the Great War that had ended just the year before. "And, if another war comes," he stated, "it will be a war of world suicide. We must have a League of Nations because we cannot make peace without it."

Although Taft's speech was well received in Dayton, the opposition in Washington, D.C. proved to be too strong. Many members of the Senate believed that the League would commit the United States to an expensive organization that would reduce America's ability to defend its own interests. On January 10, 1920, the League of Nations formed, without the support of the United States. In 1946, the League of Nations was officially dissolved with the establishment of the United Nations.

E. G. Burkham, William Howard Taft, and John H. Patterson together outside of the NCR factory during an earlier visit to Dayton by Taft on November 30, 1918.

April 1

In 1789, John Stites Gano, Major Benjamin Stites and William Goforth made plans for a settlement to be called Venice, which was to be near the mouth of the Tiber River, as they originally named Mad River. On June 13, 1789, the men agreed to purchase the land from John Cleves Symmes. The deed was executed and recorded, and the village of Venice was laid out on paper. The business center of the city was to be located near the present intersection of Herman Avenue and Webster Street. But Indian troubles and some misunderstandings with the landowner and the government led to the abandonment of the project. Fortunately, a treaty was signed with the Indians six years later, and in March, 1796, three parties set out from Cincinnati for the newly named settlement of Dayton.

Although forty-six men had agreed to settle in Dayton, when the time came to start out only nineteen responded, and they set out in three parties, two overland and one by water. William Hamer's party was the first to start, traveling in a two-horse wagon. The group included William and Mary Hamer and thier children, and Jonathan and Edward Mercer. They were delayed and had a long, cold and uncomfortable journey.

On March 21, 1796, the two other parties made their start. The second to travel by land was George Newcom and his wife, Mary, William Newcom, James Morris, John Dorough and family, Daniel Ferrell and family, Solomon Goss and family, John Davis, Abraham Grassmire and William Van Cleve. They were two weeks on the road, which was a rough, narrow, path through the woods and brush, except for a part which led to Fort Hamilton, which, as it was used by the army, was kept in tolerably good condition. They suffered from cold and dampness in camp, as it had rained and was spitting snow.

The third party travelled by water in a pirogue, a long, narrow boat, pointed at each end. This group consisted of Samuel Thompson and his wife, Catherine and family, Benjamin Van Cleve, the widow McClure and her family, and William Gahagan.

The Thompson group made good time, landing at what is now the head of St. Clair Street on April 1, 1796. Mrs. Thompson's daughter, nine year old Mary Van Cleve, is thought to be the first of the settlers to step on Dayton soil.

Today, a bronze plaque proudly marks the spot where the Thompson group disembarked to make a new start in the wilderness.

April 2

The United States was a neutral country when the "Great War" began on July 28, 1914. But after seven boats were sunk by submarines, Congress declared war against Germany on April 6, 1917. On July 20, 1917 ten million American men began registering for the draft.

When William T. Clements heard that war had been declared, he decided not to wait for the draft to begin. On May 26, 1917 he enlisted with the Company D, 6th Regiment of the U.S. Engineers. He first went to Fort Thomas, Kentucky, and then was later assigned to the American Expeditionary Forces and sent off to France, arriving there December 24, 1917.

In early February 1918, Company D was assigned to the British Fifth Army. These engineers were building steel bridges near P'eronne when the Germans attacked and broke through the British line in that area and headed towards Amiens. In desperation every man available was moved to defend that city. These men included Clements. His unit defended the Amiens Defense Line, then moved to defend the woods of Bois des Tallioux, a mile from Warfusee-Abancourt. Unfortunately, the Germans were able to enter Amiens. During the battle for the town Clements was wounded. He died on March 28, 1918, becoming the first man from Dayton to die in the war.

It took nearly three years before Clements' body was recovered. He was finally brought home on April 1, 1921, escorted by a military guard from New York. A funeral was held in his honor the following day at the Woodland Cemetery chapel.

Members of the American Legion attended the service. Members from the Dayton Canoe Club, who fondly remembered their fellow canoeist, were also present, and the flag over the club was put at half-mast. He was buried at Woodland Cemetery on April 2, 1921.

April 3

Even before the United States entered World War I, John H. Patterson, President of NCR, had begun putting together a lecture to teach the causes of the war, how it was effecting Europe and how someday it would also effect America if the country didn't unite in an action that would win the war "over there".

The lecture was finally completed and well deserved it's name, "Wake Up, America". Profusely illustrated with slides and motion pictures, the production also included an entire company of performers, musicians and sound effects men (as this was the age of silent films).

First was shown scenes of devastation in Belgium and France. Then came the unfurling of the American flag and soldiers marching forth to prove that might does not make right and that freedom and liberty would prevail. Audiences were encouraged to take part in singing patriotic songs and shout approval for America entering the war.

On April 3, 1918, the Triangle Club, composed of members of the Knights of Pythias, gathered at the Community Hall at NCR, to listen to "Wake Up, America". The following day, the U.S. Senate voted to declare war on Germany. On April 6, the U.S. House of Representatives endorsed the declaration and America formally entered World War I.

Created by James Montgomery Flagg, this poster was featured in "Wake Up, America" Day in New York City on April 19, 1917. Columbia, who personifies the U. S., is asleep. While she dozes, sinister storm clouds gather in the background. While Patterson's lecture probably did not give Flagg his inspiration for the poster, NCR did add it to future presentations of "Wake Up, America". The lecture was changed to encourage Americans to do everything in their power to win the war.

April 4

From 1907 to 1964, no matter whether you bought it in New York City or San Diego, if it was a United States embossed or printed stamped envelope it came from Dayton.

Mercantile Corporation first won the contract to make the envelopes for the U.S. Government on April 4, 1907. The four-year term was to begin on July 1 that same year. As Mercantile did not actually have facilities when they made the bid, that gave the company less than three months to build and equip a plant that could produce 5 million embossed stamped envelopes a day. They chose First and Front streets to build their printing plant.

Because of the newness of the plant and its organization, Mercantile did not succeed in filling orders as promptly as it had promised, nor in always producing the quality of envelopes the Post Office required. A committee was sent to Dayton at the end of October, 1907 to investigate the ability of the company to fulfill its obligations. Fortunately, it was decided that Mercantile should be given more time to improve. Soon the employees' skills grew and the plant increased its output. Even when it was under water to a depth of eight feet during a flood in 1913, the schedule was disrupted for only 48 hours.

When the Middle West Supply Company of Columbus and Cleveland won the government bid in 1915, Mercantile bought the company. And when International Envelope won the contract in 1928, they acquired Mercantile's facilities and machines and remained in Dayton.

By 1932 the company was turning out 14 million stamped envelopes every day, shipping them to every post office in every state in the U.S. Even in the midst of the Great Depression, the company was employing over 800 men and women. The paper mills of Etna in Dayton, Howard at Urbana and Maxwell at Franklin, were also kept busy manufacturing the paper from which the envelopes were made. A three months' supply of paper was always kept on hand. A reserve supply of 75 million stamped envelopes were also kept at the plant in locked fireproof vaults, a practice started after the two day stoppage during the 1913 flood.

International Envelope lost the contract in 1964 to The United States Envelope Company from West Virginia.

April 5

Raymond Louis Deerwester's love of music and gift for song brought joy to Daytonians for over seventy years. In 1920 Ray began working as a piano teacher and then opened his own studio three years later. But teaching piano was only one of Ray's talents. He also had a knack for writing popular music as well.

In his lifetime Ray would compose over a hundred songs, many of which were used in Dayton schools, as well as television programs. The Paul Dixon Show used several of Ray's comedic compositions during its twenty-year run from 1955 to 1975. One of Dixon's favorite was *(After Taxes) I Still Have You*, a comedic tale of a couple who, while always in the red after the IRS was through with them, at least still had each other.

But Ray had a soft spot in his heart for a piece he titled *The Dayton Song*. The lyrics tell of a beautiful city founded in 1796 "among the hills and dales and where three rivers flow." They speak of how Dayton was famous for being the home of aviation, for its dams, and for having the finest city government, bar none. Copyrighted on April 5, 1955, this would be adopted as Dayton's official song the following year.

The Dayton Song

Dayton, the city beautiful Dayton, we love you. You are so very wonderful in ev'rything you do. We'll try to our very best and pledge allegiance to Dayton, the city beautiful, Dayton, we love you. Seventeen hundred ninety-six, in a valley low, Founded among the hills and dales and where three rivers flow. You're famous for the dams you built and for your bridges too. Dayton, the city beautiful, Dayton, we love you. Dayton, the aviation home, where man learned to fly. You gave birth to many men, whose ideals were so high. Made you the home of industry with workers skilled and true. Dayton, the city beautiful, Dayton, we love you. Dayton, we're proud to call you home, where each family Has ev'ry opportunity based on equality. You have the finest government of any on review. Dayton, the city beautiful Dayton, we love you.

April 6

Following the bombing of Pearl Harbor it was decided that there should be a recreation center for enlisted men. On December 19, 1941, the Soldiers' Service Club opened in the Parish House of Christ Church. Over one hundred soldiers stationed at Wright Field and Patterson Field were guests at a dance that evening which marked the formal opening of the club.

For the first few months the Club's attendance averaged about two hundred men, but as word spread, attendance grew to the point that the Parish House was unable to hold all of the soldiers who wanted to use the club.

On April 6, 1942 the Soldiers' Service Club moved into a portion of the Municipal Building. During the grand opening every patriotic organization in Montgomery County was represented and each soldier there was given an American flag in commemoration of the occasion.

The club offered a lounge, library, washing rooms, showers, kitchen facilities, and a huge game room labeled "Men's Haven", with included comfortable chairs and davenports where soldiers could take a nap. Typewriters were provided for writing letters home. In the music room was a grand piano, drums and a combination radio-phonograph. Voice recordings could be made and mailed to loved ones

The Soldier's Service Club offered skating parties on Mondays. On Tuesday evenings the Motion Picture Operators Union showed a free motion picture. Wednesday night was dance night, with music supplied by a band from either Wright or Patterson Field and once every month a name band was secured.

On Thursday evenings the Soldiers' Service Club Review was held, consisting of both amateur and professional talent, all soldiers. The shows were also broadcast to the public.

Sandwiches and hot liquids were served each day a noon; a light supper was available between the hours of five and seven o'clock, and on Sundays a full course dinner was served in the evening. All of the food was free and only soft drinks needed to be paid for by the men in uniform.

By 1944 over 20,000 soldiers a year were using the club. Many swore that, once the war was over, they would return and make Dayton their home.

April 7

Not very long after the assassination of President William McKinley in 1901, the Commercial Club in Dayton tried to raise funds to erect a monument to him. Not much was raised. As time passed, patriotism for the president was fading and the fate of the monument was uncertain.

On April 7, 1904, it was announced that Augustus Lukeman had agreed to allow the statue of McKinley he had sculpted for the city of Adams, Massachusetts to be reproduced for use in Dayton at a discount of only $6,000, compared to the original, which cost $25,000. The 18 foot tall monument in Adams was quite beautiful, with a bronze statue of the fallen president standing on a base of solid granite.

The *Dayton Daily News* tried to shame its readers to come up with the money. It stated that, while a smaller monument could be built with the money already raised, it was "hoped the citizens of Dayton would not be satisfied with anything but the best... a memorial that would show to the world that Dayton was fully up on public spirit and civic pride."

It would take several more years, but the money was finally raised. It was estimated that over 11,000 people gave toward erecting the statue, much of it from money contributed from school children.

A large crowd, many of them children, attended the unveiling of the monument at Cooper Park on September 17, 1910. It still stands today.

President William McKinley monuments in Dayton (left) and Adams (right).

April 8

Motion pictures were still somewhat in their infancy when Pyramid Film Company was incorporated on this day in 1915. Devoss W. Driscoll, one of the directors, had previously worked as an advertising manager at NCR. It is likely that Driscoll's old job was what gave him the idea to start Pyramid Film, as NCR had been using motion pictures to advertise their company since 1903.

The Pyramid Film Company specialized in commercial and cartoon films that promoted businesses. During World War I, the Green & Green Company, well-known for their baked goods in Dayton, hired Pyramid to film the manufacture of the hard-bread rations given to fighting soldiers in the Army and Navy. On January 7, 1919, over 400 Green & Green employees watched *Hard Tack*, which showed every step of making the "iron ration" as it was known, from the unloading of the flour to the soldering of the tin containers the rations were stored in, to the final shipping of the product to soldiers overseas. A number of Dayton-made tanks were also shown in maneuvers. As they emerged from the tanks, the soldiers were shown cheerfully munching the "hard tack" rations.

By 1921, Pyramid had begun filming various scenes in Dayton, and then renting the motion pictures to local theaters. Advertised as *The Miami Valley Screen Review*, the film would show items of interest that had happened that week in the city. On May 1, 1921 audiences watched as Sao-ke-Sze, Chinese minister to the United States, visited Dayton. Another scene was of a house which travelled from Florida to Dayton on a truck. Also included were *Dayton Daily News* paper boys eating ice cream, the Davis Girls' Bicycle Club posing for the camera, and Betty Hawkins, the only woman automobile salesman in the area.

In 1923, Pyramid produced a film titled *The Spirit of Lincoln*. Made in conjunction with the Lincoln Memorial University of Tennessee, the film depicted the life and struggles of the young men and women who had grown up in the hills of Tennessee, and the work being done by the University to educate them. The film was endorsed by the Daughters of the American Revolution and the Better Films Committee of Atlanta.

In 1928 Pyramid Film merged with Alexander Industries, Inc., of Denver, Colorado, and became known as the Alexander Film Company. It was thought that Pyramid was the oldest advertising service of its kind still in business at the time.

April 9

On this date in 1969, construction started on what would become the largest and tallest building in Dayton - so large, in fact, that it has its own zip code: 45423.

Located at 40 North Main Street, this 30-story Class "A" building was originally called the Winters Bank Building and served as the headquarters for Winters Bank. Eugene Kettering, son of Charles F. Kettering, was responsible for its construction. When Eugene died in 1969, the building came under the supervision of his wife, Virginia. Winters Bank Tower opened in 1972. The name was later changed to Kettering Tower in 1983 when Winters Bank was acquired by Bank One Corporation.

Today, the impressive 496,614 square-foot structure of glass and steel is home to dozens of businesses, including Carmen's Deli, The Dayton Foundation, Dayton Development Coalition, Verizon, Chase Bank, and The Dayton Racquet Club.

April 10

On April 10, 2003, Veterans Affairs Secretary Anthony J. Principi dedicated Building 120 at the Dayton VA Medical Center as headquarters for the American Veterans Heritage Center (AVHC). Constructed in 1880, two side wings were added to the building in 1891, when it became the Patient Library. The building was closed in May 2000 when volunteers could not be found to staff it.

The goal of AVHC was to preserve several of the original buildings at the Dayton VA Medical Center, including the Patient Library, the 1871 Headquarters Building, the 1881 Veterans Clubhouse, and the 1870 Protestant Chapel.

In 2007, the Chapel's roof was replaced and in 2011-2012 the interior was renovated. The Library was stabilized and a museum honoring veterans of all wars was opened. In 2012, AVHC played a key role in the Dayton VA being designated as a National Historic Landmark. That same year the Dayton VA partnered with AVHC and the Ohio State University Extension Master Gardener volunteers to resurrect the grotto and gardens where so many of the old Civil War soldiers would go to relax. The site was dedicated in August 2014.

In 2017, it was announced that the Dayton VA would become the home of the National VA History Center. The national archive will be housed in the Headquarters Building and the Veterans Clubhouse that the AVHC helped make sure weren't lost to history.

The Patient Library as it looked in the 1930's.

April 11

In its April 11, 1900 issue *The Horseless Age* raved about the new Thresher electric automobile, stating that it was "strongly built, and has the appearance of being constructed as an automobile", high praise at a time when most automobiles looked more like someone had stuck a motor on an old horse wagon as an afterthought. The body style was a "brake", where two passengers sat in the front seat and two others would sit in the rear, facing away from the front. The body was provided by Morris Woodhull, of the Dayton Buggy Works.

Woodhull gave a lot of thought to designing the right type of body for use with Thresher's electric motor. The vehicle had a pivoting front axle and special springs which enabled the automobile to make sharp turns at full speed without having the tendency to tilt. The wheels used ball bearings and the tires were 2-inch thick solid rubber. Power for the automobile came from two 1½ horse-powered motors, geared independently, one to each of the rear wheels. The motors pivoted on the rear axle and were flexibly supported on the frame to help relieve jarring from any bumps the vehicle encountered on the road.

Thresher advertised a variety of styles of vehicles, including runabouts, stanhopes, broughams and delivery wagons. But the "brake" body style was probably the only type produced. Manufacturing lasted less than a year.

Besides the usual four passengers, several other people pile on the Thresher automobile as it sits in front of Steele High School, probably to show off its endurance.

April 12

In 1906, while president of the Dayton Malleable Iron Company, Peirce D. Schenck began working on an improved automobile in a barn at his home. His prototype was so successful that Schenck used it to convince others to help him organize the Speedwell Motor Car Company, which was incorporated on April 12, 1907.

The company's first move was to buy four acres of ground and an old factory building on Essex Avenue. The company offered several body styles, all powered using 4-cylinder and 6-cylinder Rutenber engines. This proved to be too expensive and the Rutenber engines were dropped in favor of a 4-cylinder engine that Speedwell could manufacture itself.

By 1912 the factory had begun producing several types of light and heavy duty trucks. Speedwell's prospects to become one of the nation's more successful firms seemed solid.

Enter Cyrus Mead, of the Mead Engine Company. By 1912, rotary valve motors had become quite popular. Mead convinced Speedwell that his rotary valve motor would help sales. The motor had six cylinders and could produce 60 h.p. However, before the rotary motor had a chance to succeed, a flood swept through Dayton on March 25, 1913, leaving the Speedwell factory under several feet of water. Production stopped completely as the company dug through the mud left behind and threw away thousands of dollars of now worthless material and half-completed automobiles.

Speedwell never recovered from the flood. The company had spent a lot of money gearing up for manufacturing the Mead rotary engine, only to see the equipment destroyed. Speedwell automobile dealers closed due to the company's inability to deliver vehicles during most of 1913. To make matters worse, the Mead engine had been rushed through before it was ready, perhaps with the hope that Cyrus Mead could tweak the specs of the engine as problems arose. Regrettably, on January 4, 1914, Mead died in an automobile accident.

By the end of 1914 the company was tens of thousands of dollars in debt. Speedwell stopped all operations in January 1915 and was placed in receivership the following month. Speedwell's glory days had come to a close.

April 13

The determination to help provide a home and education for destitute orphans and other impoverished children began in 1844 when the Dayton Female Association was incorporated for that purpose.

The first children's home, called the Dayton Orphan Asylum, began in a small brick building on Magnolia Street. Unfortunately, donations to help run the home were hard to come by, and in its first two decades only sixty children had been helped.

On March 20, 1866, the Ohio Legislature passed a law authorizing the establishment of children's homes, and under that act the Montgomery County Commissioners decided to take charge of the Dayton Orphan Asylum. In 1867, the trustees approached Benjamin F. Kuhns for the purpose of buying land on the West Side to build a larger, more modern, home for the orphans.

In 1856, Kuhns invented an improved way for agricultural machines to plant seeds. Two years later the firm of Benjamin Kuhns & Co. had formed. Although the factory producing the machinery was located near downtown Dayton, on Third Street near the canal, Kuhns decided to make his home on the west side. By 1860, he had purchased several plots of land and had a home built on the east side of Summit Street, between Fifth Street and Home Avenue.

On April 13, 1867, Kuhns agreed to sell five acres of land on South Summit Street at $1,000 an acre. The Montgomery County Children's Home opened at 528 South Summit Street that same year.

The large three-storied brick building, with cupola and basement, contained 42 rooms that were heated by steam and lit by gasoline. The entire area behind the Home was used for gardening. The Home was partly funded by the state for the support of soldiers' children. The Home was closed when the children were moved to Shawen Acres at 3304 N. Main Street in 1928.

April 14

In 1884, Dayton erected a monument at the intersection of Main and Monument to honor the soldiers who had lost their lives during the Civil War. *(See July 31)* But as the city grew, and automobiles instead of horse and buggies crowded the streets, the monument became an obstacle to traffic. The decision to move the Soldiers' Monument to another site proved to be quite controversial. The Sons of Union Veterans were "bitterly opposed" to the move, said Arthur Stolz, commander of the group. "I don't see why anyone should go to war if the community destroys the memorials to it's heroes", Stolz said, adding that statistics showed there were less accidents at Main and Monument than any other principal intersection in the city.

Once the City Commission voted that the monument had to be moved, the turmoil turned to where to relocate it. Deeds Park seemed to be the first choice, followed by Van Cleve Park and Riverview Park. Riverview Park, located at Riverview Avenue, was finally chosen.

On April 14, 1948, hundreds gathered to watch Pvt. George Washington Fair's removal from his base atop the marble column. Even at this late date, efforts were still being made to try and keep him in place. Levitt Luzern Custer, inventor of both the electric and gas-powered wheelchair, appeared before the City Commission to plead his case.

"They have a rope around his neck right now," said Custer. "I beg of you to let him stand. If you take him down, you might as well take down the Washington Monument, or the Lincoln Memorial, or Constitution Hall," he declared. The commissioners were unmoved.

Pvt. Fair was safely taken down with a 100-foot crane and stored away, while waiting for the rest of the monument to be moved to the new location. The monument was rededicated on September 2, 1948.

In 1991, the monument was moved back to its original location as part of a Main Street revitalization project. However, the original Pvt. Fair was too fragile to take his place on top, so he was recast in bronze and the replica took his place. The 1884 marble version of Pvt. Fair can now be seen under the portico at the entrance of the Dayton VA Medical Center.

April 15

On this day in 1909, a long sought-for dream came true for Moses C. Moore, when Dahomey Park had its grand opening. Located at the junction of Lakeview Avenue and Germantown Road, Dahomey was the first amusement park for blacks that was also owned and operated by blacks. The park was named by Moses' wife, Marion, after a musical. *"In Dahomey"* featured lyrics by Paul Laurence Dunbar and starred her good friends George Walker and Bert Williams.

According to a newspaper ad placed by Moore, the park offered motion pictures, roller skating rinks shooting galleries, dancing auditoriums, soda fountains, a merry-go-round, ice cream parlors, and many other features that supposedly attracted thousands of people a day. By 1910 an enclosed baseball field had been added so that Moore could showcase his new baseball team, the Marcos. The Marcos played as independents, offering to play any semi-professional black baseball teams. One of the incentives Moore used to lure companies, lodges and church groups to the park was to offer 15% of the gross receipts from all of the attractions if they booked the park in advance. Sadly, the park proved unsuccessful, closing at the end of the 1911 season. Moore went back to running a saloon. The Marcos baseball team would carry on under other owners and managers, joining the Negro National League in 1920 and playing into the 1940s.

Dayton Marcos Team in 1920

April 16

It was on this date in 1850 that the shining, new $100,000 courthouse at Third and Main streets opened for business for the first time. Inside, every inch of available space in the courtroom was occupied and the audience spilled out into the hall. The gallery, which encircled the room some 16 feet above the ground floor, was also packed - to the point that some wondered if the floor above could support all the weight.

The crowd hushed when Judge John Beers entered the courtroom accompanied by Robert Brown, one of the three associate justices, and Sheriff David Clark and Prosecuting Attorney Samuel Craighead.

The first judicial act of the court was the swearing in of the 15 men who made up the April term of the Grand Jury. The first civil act was the appointment of a guardian for two minor children. Samuel Murray, father of John, 16, and Jacob, 15, appeared in court and posted bond of $1,400. He was then "chosen" by the two boys in open court to be their guardian.

Constructed of Dayton limestone, the building is considered to be one of the finest examples of Greek Revival style courthouses in the nation.

April 17

When Fort Sumter fell on April 14, 1861, it signaled the beginning of the Civil War. President Abraham Lincoln called for a 75,000 man militia to serve.

At the end of the Mexican War in 1848, several military organizations in Dayton had kept up their interest in military manners – keeping up armories, drilling, marching and taking part in various patriotic parades – so when the call went out, Dayton was ready.

On April 17, the Dayton Light Guard and the Montgomery Guard marched to the railway station and took the train for Columbus, Ohio. At midnight on the same day, the Lafayette Guard also departed.

On their arrival at Columbus, the three groups were assigned to the 1st Regiment Ohio Volunteer Infantry for three months – the Lafayette Guard as Company B, Dayton Light Guard as Company C and the Montgomery Guards as Company D.

The departure of these first troops from Dayton was met with great enthusiasm and excitement. No one dreamed that it was but the prelude to a long and terrible war. By its end, 35,475 Ohio soldiers would lose their lives.

On the evening of May 11, 1861, a crowd gathered at the courthouse on Third and Main to listen to a farewell concert from the Regimental Band. The musicians left two days later to join the 1st Regiment Ohio Volunteer Infantry.

April 18

On February 14, 1863, George Lindemuth, a resident of Germantown, Ohio, came to Dayton to sell his tobacco crop. He had planned to go to the theater later that evening with some acquaintances but had become totally lost on his way there. Instead he managed to find the Coffee House saloon. George stated that he wanted to find his way to the theater. Another customer, John Dobbins, agreed to show him.

About 9 pm John and George stumbled into Jacob Altherr's saloon on South Jefferson Street. By the time they left, the two were quite drunk. This was the last time George would be seen alive.

Around 11 pm that same evening, John went to Thomas Wise's barbershop on Market Street, and got a shave. Wise made a remark about how John's pants were bloody and muddy. John explained that he had been butchering. John then invited the people in the shop to go out with him for some drinks, pulling out a large roll of money.

At 7 am the next day the body of George Lindemuth was found dead on the bank of the river on Monument Avenue, just west of Jefferson Street. George's throat had been cut several times. Soon the search for John Dobbins was on. He was found in Cincinnati and brought back to Dayton to stand trial.

After a hung jury the first time, the second jury found John guilty of first degree murder on November 25th, 1863. The date of execution was set for April 15, 1864.

On the appointed day, when John was taken out of his cell, everyone watched in amazement as he danced while enroute to the scaffold, and attempted a "hoe-down" step while the Sheriff was engaged in preparing the scaffold. Nearby sat a pail of water. Seizing this, John threw the contents on the scaffold and, turning the bucket upside down, proceeded to beat a tattoo upon it with his fingers.

All this merriment was due to the fact that John was drunk as a skunk. He had sold his body for thirty dollars to Dr. Albertus Geiger, who wanted it for dissecting purposes to see what made a murderer tick.

After the execution, Dr. Geiger claimed the body. Before dark that same day, John's body was being dissected in the basement of Huston Hall, a place usually reserved for operas and other forms of entertainment. John was later described by physicians as one of the finest built men they had ever seen. The remains were interred without ceremony in the pauper's field in the City Lot on April 18, 1864.

April 19

When John Crouse, of Dayton, enlisted in Company A of the 11th Ohio Volunteer Infantry on April 19, 1861, he took along a companion - a water spaniel by the name of Curly. Newspaper accounts state that a Mrs. John Shellabarger had too many dogs to take care of and so gave Curly to Crouse, adding that the dog was no good for anything she knew of, so he ought to make a good solider.

Some of the biggest battles the 11th OVI fought in were Second Bull Run, Antietam, Chickamauga, the Siege of Chattanooga, the Atlanta Campaign, the Siege of Atlanta, and Sherman's March to the Sea. Curly joined in all of the battles and was wounded at least twice. In order to assure that Curly would be returned if lost on the battlefield, he wore a steel collar that said "I am Company A's dog. Whose dog are you?"

At the Battle of Chickamauga, Curly stayed on the field with the wounded soldiers. A confederate soldier tried to lure him away by tempting him with some food, but Curly refused to leave his comrades. When a parole was given for the wounded soldiers, Curly went back to the Union side with them. But when he got there, the captain of the 10th Ohio saw him and decided he would like to keep Curly, so he tied the dog to his tent.

Meanwhile, the soldiers from Company A had heard that Curly had come back from the battlefield, and began looking for him. When they found him, the captain of the 10th refused to let Curly go. Fortunately, the colonel of the 10th heard all the arguing, and came to see what was going on. After he learned the story, the colonel ordered that Curly be untied, and Curly rushed back to his companions.

As the regiment came home in 1864, Curly accidently got shoved off a train while it was moving. He was found, but his leg had been broken in the accident. Curly was soon patched up and went to live with one of his old regiment comrades, Oliver P. Baggott.

Curly eventually went to live at the Dayton Soldiers' Home. Here he lived out the last of his 12 years. When he died his friends lovingly buried him in a beautiful spot at the Soldiers' Home.

A drawing of Curly at an encampment.

April 20

Located just off Soldiers' Home-West Carrollton Road, Dayton Speedway's half-mile track was the home to many a race during its operation from 1934 through 1982. Unfortunately, on this date in 1952, four people were killed and at least 50 were injured when a racing car driven by Gordon Reid went out of control on a turn and crashed through the track fence and into a corner of the grandstand.

The race, a 10 mile qualifying heat and the first event of the opening day of the 1952 season, was halted when the accident occurred. The crash came on the fifth lap when Reid's car went out of control in the north turn, tore through a woven-wire fence, struck two barrels of gray paint and smashed into the grandstand. Special Policeman Robert Thatcher tried to help Ruby Ellen Shaffer get out of the path of race car, but both were struck and died. The other victims were Gene Lawson and the driver, Gordon Reid.

Amazingly, few of the 12,000 people at the track were aware of the seriousness of the accident and racing was resumed an hour and a half later.

Reid, father of four children, the youngest 2 weeks old, had been racing hot rods and midgets since the end of WWII. He was to have driven on Memorial Day in the Indianapolis 500 for the first time.

Aerial view of racetrack after the accident occurred on April 20, 1952

April 21

In 1995, Tess Little and Paula Recko had an idea for a unique way to bring the community together through art. The thought was to have people sculpt designs onto 5"x 7" clay tiles, which would then be used to create a sculpture. Their vision became a part of a REACH (Realizing Ethnic Awareness and Cultural Heritage) project to involve minority communities.

In order to include as wide a range of individuals as possible, the tiles were made available at neighborhood churches, community centers, fairs, festivals and schools. In the end, 2800 pieces of art, depicting the history and diverse culture of the Miami Valley, were created. The tiles were assembled by artists and volunteers into a cohesive series of 23 panels, which were then cast in bronze. The panels were installed at Courthouse Square, along the stage area near the Old Court House. The 48' by 3' panoramic bas relief sculpture, known as The Heritage Sculpture, was dedicated on April 21, 1998.

If you look closely at the artwork of buildings, animals, rivers, peace signs, flowers and other interesting representations of life and work, you will see portraits of well-known people from the Miami Valley; including Erma Bombeck, Bing Davis, Paul Laurence Dunbar, Virginia Kettering, John H. Patterson and Orville and Wilbur Wright. The likeness of Tess Little and Paula Recko, without whose vision and determination the sculpture would not exist, can also be found peering back at visitors who come to admire this wonderful work of art.

Right: Section of The Heritage Sculpture

Below: The Heritage Sculpture

April 22

The first few years in Dayton were sparse when it came to entertainment. In fact, it took nearly two decades before any professional shows made their way in the wilderness to the Gem City. A display of "wax works and figures" on February 13, 1815 made up the first show in Dayton history.

On the evening of April 22, 1816, the first theatrical performance was held at the residence of William Huffman, on St. Clair Street. The much admired, elegant comedy play called *Matrimony, or The Prisoners* and the celebrated comic farce called *The Village Lawyer* were presented. Between the play and the farce there were two recitals, *Scolding Life Reclaimed* and *Monsieur Tonson*, a fancy dance and a comic song entitled *Bag of Nails*. The tickets were fifty cents. Gentlemen were asked not to smoke cigars.

Exactly three years later, on April 22, 1819, Reid's Inn charged twenty-five cents for admission to view a live African lion, the first to be seen in the city. Exhibited in the barnyard, patrons were assured that they would be in no danger, as the lion, "the largest in America, and the only one of his sort," was secured in a strong cage. The following April, "Columbus", a large elephant, was placed on exhibit in the carriage house at Reid's.

In 1823, a menagerie, containing an African lion, African leopard, Brazilian cougar, Shetland pony (with rider), Egyptian mongoose and several other animals amused the local citizens. A band, composed of ancient Jewish cymbals and numerous other musical instruments, also accompanied the show.

On July 19, 1825, Reid's Inn was again the place to be, when the first circus came to town. The show had a parade, consisting of several wagons containing wild animals and about twenty horses.

In August, 1827, a traveling museum, consisting of birds, animals, wax figurines, paintings and other objects visited Dayton. One of the main attractions was advertised as "that great natural curiosity, the Indian mummy, which was discovered and taken from the interior of a cave in Warren County, Kentucky, where it was probably secreted in its present state of preservation for one thousand years."

As Dayton grew, halls and opera houses were built to accommodate the ever growing number of repertoire companies that made sure to pass through for a night or three on their way to or from engagements in other cities. By the end of the Civil War, Dayton had become known throughout the country as having the finest theater for any city of its size, the Turner Opera House - now known as the Victoria Theatre.

April 23

On August 24, 1932, fifteen 45-passenger streetcars and three gas buses of the Dayton Street Railway Company were destroyed in a fire that razed the company's maintenance and storage facility on Lorain Avenue. The loss was estimated at $150,000. Although eight 24-passenger streetcars were able to be saved, the fire was a real blow to the company, as it was already struggling due to the Great Depression.

In a bold move, Dayton Street Railway decided to replace their streetcars with "trackless" trolley buses, which would use rubber tires instead of tracks. This meant that instead of using just one overhead wire, two would be needed to power the electric trolleys. The decision was made due to the fact that trolley buses were both cheaper to purchase and to operate than streetcars, which would offset the added expense involved in putting up a second wire. On October 4, 1932, unanimous approval of the city commission was given to the company to put from 12 to 15 trolleys into operation on its Catapla/Linden line at a cost of $250,000.

On April 23, 1933, twelve Brill T-40 model electric trolley buses went into service on Dayton streets, which also marked the inauguration in Ohio of trackless bus service. All fares taken in between 9 a.m. and 5 p.m. that day were turned over to the Baby's Milk Fund, which provided milk to infants in low-income families.

Dayton Street Railway employees and first trackless trolley in the state of Ohio.

April 24

Paul Dresser was one of the most successful songwriters of the 1890's, producing such hits as *On the Banks of the Wabash* (which became Indiana's state song), *My Gal Sal*, and *The Blue and the Gray*. Dresser composed and published over 100 songs, 25 of which hit the Billboard top twenty.

Dresser's had his first hit in 1886 with *The Letter That Never Came*. On April 24, 1898 the *Cincinnati Enquirer* published a story in which he told of what inspired him to write the song. It seems that while Dresser was visiting the Dayton Soldiers' Home he saw a group of old soldiers who had once fought in the Civil War waiting in line to get letters from their friends and families. One sad faced, white haired man stood at the head of the line. The old man walked away empty-handed.

When he enquired as to who the man was, Dresser was told of how the soldier had enlisted at East Liverpool, Ohio, in answer to Lincoln's first call for troops in 1861, leaving behind a wife and baby boy at home. While at the front during the war he looked for a letter from his wife, but never received one during the four years he fought for his country. From the winter of 1865 until 1875 he searched for his wife and child, but never found them. Heartbroken, he came to live at the Soldiers' Home in Dayton. Although deeply depressed, he still never ceased to hope for a letter from his family. His companions at the Home saw to it each day that the man was always first in line for the letter that never came.

Dresser's song is quite sad. Each day the man in the song would ask the postman if there was any mail for him. As always, the letter never came. Here are part of the lyrics to the song.

So one day upon the shore, he was found, but life was o'er
His poor soul, it must have gone out with the tide.
In his hand they found a note with the last words that he wrote:
"Should a letter come, please place it by my side!"

Was it from a gray-haired mother? Or a sister or a brother?
Had he waited all those many years in vain?
From the early morning light, he would watch 'til dark of night
For the letter, but, at last, it never came.

April 25

On April 25, 1919, the twenty-eight prisoners on the second floor of the county jail seemed quite happy in spite of their circumstances, many of them were even singing. It could be understood why Ed Scheidt was joining in, for he had just recently been found innocent in the murder of Mike Brown, a man who had been found slain in West Carrollton, Ohio. Scheidt was still awaiting trial for robbery, but compared to murder, that was nothing. But that still left the rest of them, including Charles Dickerson, who was awaiting trial for first degree murder and Ed Stanley and Jack McLaren, both of whom were being held for grand larceny and shooting with intent to kill. Still, they weren't bothering anyone, so Sheriff William Oldt let the singing continue.

Later that evening the sheriff noticed a noise that sounded like metal against metal. Oldt and several deputies darted into the "bull pen", a narrow corridor that led entirely around the cell block. There they found three men, one of whom was Scheidt, covered with sweat and grime, sawing away at the steel bars of the jail. Their singing had covered up the noise they made while cutting through twenty-one bars of steel to escape the cell block, as well as ten heavy steel fastenings which held a concave set of bars across a window that would have led to their freedom.

Sixteen blades were found. Three blades had been ingenuously fastened into brackets made from broom handles. It was believed that the saws had recently been smuggled into the jail by one of the prisoner's friends. The police estimated that the prisoners had been sawing constantly for at least 27 hours. They had hidden their progress by pasting black tar soap into the crevice made by the saws, finally sawing the rest of the way through the bars that night.

All of the prisoners were placed in solitary confinement. Most claimed that they had been afraid to say anything, having been threatened by the ring leaders of the escape that their eyes would be gouged out if they squealed. Scheidt was pointed out as head of the plot to escape the jail.

When confronted, Scheidt admitted that he had tried to escape, but that he was no snitch and would not tell who had helped him. "A snitch is a coward at heart," Scheidt stated, "and I am no coward."

Although an investigation was held, the accomplice who had provided the saws was never discovered. As for Ed Scheidt, he was later found guilty of robbing a meat market in Miamisburg, and was sentenced to serve on to seventeen years at the Ohio Penitentiary in Columbus.

April 26

In 1939 Trans World Airlines, at the urging the their of major stockholder Howard Hughes, asked Lockheed Corporation to design a 40 passenger transcontinental airliner with a 3,500 mile range. This led to the development of the L-049 Constellation. However, with the onset of World War II, the TWA aircraft entering production was converted to an order for the C-69 Constellation, which was mostly used as a high-speed, long-distance troop transport during the war.

On April 17, 1944, the second production C-69, piloted by Howard Hughes and TWA president Jack Frye, flew from Burbank, California, to Washington, D.C., in 6 hours and 57 minutes, at an average 331 miles per hour, breaking a speed record. On April 26, during the return trip, the aircraft stopped at Wright Field in Dayton to give Orville Wright his last flight, more than 40 years after his historic first flight. Wright sat at the controls of the airplane for a few minutes during the 50 minute flight. "I guess I ran the whole plane for a minute but I let the machine take care of itself," Orville said of the experience. "I always said airplanes would fly themselves if you left them alone." He also commented that the Constellation's wingspan was longer than the distance of his first flight.

Orville Wright climbs up the ladder of a C-69 Lockheed Constellation to take his last flight on April 26, 1944. He even flew the airplane for a few minutes.

April 27

On February 15, 1898, an explosion occurred on the U.S. Battleship Maine in Havana Harbor, Cuba. At that time, Cuba was ruled by Spain and Cuban rebels were engaged in a war for independence. The battleship had been sent to Havana Harbor to protect American interests and present a show of force. When 266 Americans were killed in the explosion, it was believed that the Maine had been sabotaged by Spain. President William McKinley immediately demanded that Spain give Cuba its independence. When they did not, the U.S. declared war on Spain on April 25, 1898.

On April 27, Dayton's Militia and Colonel White's regiment went to the Union Depot to head for Columbus to join in the war. But there was already a Daytonian on the front lines that made history that same day.

Three ships, including the flagship USS New York, were trying to locate hidden defense batteries they knew were guarding the entrance to the Matanzas harbor. Cadet Charles Boone, who had been admitted at the age of seventeen to the Navy Academy four years before, was captain of the New York's midship port gun.

Suddenly, a shot was heard and an eight-inch shell came skipping across the bay toward the New York, missing it by only a hundred yards. Cadet Boone immediately sent a shot in answer. These two shots signaled the beginning of the first battle of the Spanish-American War.

A crowd watches as Dayton regiments go off to fight in the Spanish-American war.

April 28

Dr. Oliver Crook enjoyed the distinction of being the first native-born Montgomery County boy to enter the medical field. Born in Wayne Township on August 14, 1818, he opened an office in Dayton in 1847.

Dr. Crook's troubles began from associating with Dr. Alburtus Geiger, a local doctor who was not a member of the Montgomery County Medical Society. This was not allowed and, after a warning, the second time he was caught consulting Dr. Geiger, Dr. Crook was kicked out on his ear.

In 1861, Dr. Crook began offering a tonic made of pine tree tar. By the end of the Civil War the tonic proved popular enough to be advertised in newspapers outside of Dayton. He also advertised several other remedies, including "Benzoin Elixir", "Citron Balsam", "S-PH-L-S", and "Compound Syrup of Poke Root". By 1871, Dr. Crook had so many remedies that it took an entire column in the newspaper to list them all and what they were capable of curing.

An indefatigable worker, it was believed that he had the largest practice of any Dayton physician of his day. But the unrelenting work was his undoing. Dr. Crook died on April 28, 1873 at the age of 54. Although the local physicians had shunned him, hundreds of mourners came to his funeral. Those who had not been able to gain entrance to the church remained outside to join the long procession to Woodland Cemetery.

Dr. Crook's "Wine of Tar" ads claimed the elixir could cure consumption, coughs, asthma, diphtheria, sore throat, bronchitis, diabetes, diseases of the kidney - and, in case they missed naming your disease - the list ended with the words "and other complaints". "Benzoin Elixir" was used to cure throat and lung diseases. "Citron Balsam" was good for warts, skin ulcers, gangrene and rheumatism. The aptly named "S-PH-L-S" was for syphilis, and "Compound Syrup of Poke Root" was for everything already mentioned above, as well as getting rid of pains in the bones and limbs. Since many of his remedies were 90 percent alcohol, partakers who weren't cure at least felt better afterwards.

April 29

When it was determined that McCook Field was going to be closed by the military, plans were made to convert the airfield into a public airport. However, General Motors, who owned much of the land, decided not to sell the property. Instead, a group of investors chose a 310 acre site near Vandalia, Ohio to build a private airport called the "Dayton Airport", which was dedicated on July 31, 1929.

Unfortunately, the Great Depression began soon after and by 1933 the owners of the airport, Dayton Airport, Inc., fell into receivership. The City of Dayton considered buying the property, but negotiated a contract to lease the airport instead.

During this time there was little improvement to the runways and it became a concern that, since newer transcontinental airplanes would not be able to use the airport, the facilities might have to close. Former Ohio Governor James M. Cox discussed the matter with officials of the Works Progress Administration (WPA), the State Bureau of Aeronautics and the Bureau of Air Commerce. Cox was assured that, if the City of Dayton were to purchase the airport, funding for improvements would be available through the WPA. Cox quickly formed a committee to raise the money needed to purchase the airport. The goal of $65,000 to purchase the airport was reached. On April 29, 1936, the committee handed over title of the airport to the City of Dayton for $1.

WPA workers pour concrete runways at the Dayton Municipal Airport in 1936.

April 30

The Apollo motion picture theater, located at 28 South Main Street, threw open its doors to the public on April 30, 1914. The man responsible for the new theater was Theodore C. Chifos, a street candy merchant who, at the age of twenty-two, became the youngest theater owner in Dayton.

Architect Gustave A. Niehus redesigned the first floor of the Burkhardt building to produce one of the more comfortable silent film theaters at the time. Patrons no longer had to tolerate kitchen chairs that were thrown haphazardly into a room. The 200 seat Apollo had two wide aisles running the full length of the building. The wooden mouldings on the ceiling were done in ivory and gold, the ceiling itself was colored a light tan. The top half of the walls were painted a dark tan, the bottom half a dark brown. Side wall ornaments of blue, green and gold complimented the colors.

In 1923 the theater was purchased by Homer Guy, Benjamin Wheeler and Wendell Pfieffer. While under their management the Apollo began selling popcorn and candy, becoming the first in Dayton to do so.

In 1936 W. A. Keyes leased the movie house and renamed it the Little Playhouse. The Playhouse provided patrons with films of "classic" movies of the past. It operated quite successfully until 1941, possibly closing due to the start of WWII.

"First Run-First Class" movies from Biograph, Vitagraph and Universal, as well as other studios, led to the Apollo being the place to go to watch silent films.

May 1

Dayton's first drive-in theater opened at 2700 Valley Street on this date in 1942. Herbert Ochs, who had already opened several of the eighty-nine or so drive-ins operating in the country at the time, was owner of the theater. Aptly named "The Drive-In Theater", about 700 cars could be accommodated. Uniformed attendants directed patrons to their parking space so that as many cars as possible could be gotten on the lot. Lawn chairs and orange crates set up near the screen could hold about 300 walk-in patrons. Early birds could dance to music on a large terrazzo floor just in front of the screen.

The sound for the movies came from a large central speaker, which was essentially a bullhorn. One patron recalled how the speaker worked a little too well.

"You could hear all right - everyone in town could hear. In Westerns, when there was a lot of shooting, people used to call the police department and say there was a murder going on here."

Movies were changed three times a week and midnight shows were held every Friday, Saturday and Sunday for 'victory workers'. Special emphasis was placed on showing Technicolor films on the 52' x 60' projection screen. Patrons got their money's worth. A typical night consisted of a color cartoon, one or two short subject films, a first-run news reel (usually about the war) and a full length feature movie.

The Drive-In Theater's name was later changed to Drive-In East when Ochs built a new drive-in at 6500 West Third Street and called it the Drive-In West. It again changed names a few years later, being called the Dayton East Drive-In. The theater's final season was in 1982.

May 2

In 1882, the famous playwright Oscar Wilde was making a tour of the United States and Dayton was one of his stops.

On May 2, Wilde took a room at the Beckel Hotel. A reporter for the *Dayton Daily Democrat* paid a visit to the great man, hoping for an interview. The front desk sent the reporter's calling card up to Wilde's room, which was promptly returned, with an invitation to walk in.

When the reporter entered the room Wilde was half reclining on a sofa, a small table with writing material in front of him and a lit cigar nearby. After chatting for awhile, the reporter made the mistake of asking how the playwright liked the hotel room. Unfortunately, it did not live up to Wilde's expectations. He complained that the chair was badly made and that the coffee cup used in the restaurant was so thick and clumsy that "it disgusts me to drink from it."

Wilde was later taken to see the pride of the city, the then new Third Street Presbyterian church. Although he seemed to like the church as a whole, Wilde stated that the stained-glass windows were "not up to the mark", and that the pilasters on each side of the Ludlow Street entrance should have been of granite, not marble. He did, however, seem to enjoy his visit to the Soldiers' Home.

While crossing the river back to downtown Dayton, and learning its name was Miami, he said, "Ah, how lovely are these Indian names!", and agreed that the view presented a beautiful scene, but then spoiled the moment by stating, "You should never let your manufacturers pollute the air with smoke."

Oscar did not seem all that "wild" about his visit to Dayton in 1882.

May 3

In 1901, NCR laid off four molders for alleged incompetency. The union asked that the men be rehired and, when NCR refused to do so, the molders went on strike. A week later the metal polishers joined them.

The factory soon ran out of stock material. And so, on May 3, 1901, John H. Patterson, president of NCR, posted a bulletin closing the factory indefinitely. It also stated that the directors of NCR had been and were still willing to arbitrate with the employees. The sticking point was that, while the company believed in unions, they were not going to give up the right to discharge any person it employed.

As the days turned into weeks, workers and Dayton businesses both began to suffer. At that point NCR employed about 2,300 men and 350 women and had a payroll of $5,000 a day. While the men of the molders' and polishers' unions were getting between $5 and $7 a week from their unions' strike fund, this left nearly 1,500 employees without any pay. Merchants also began hurting from lack of buyers for their products.

Finally, a strike committee was appointed by the unions other than the molders and polishers and they went to Patterson and asked him to reopen the factory. He agreed upon the condition that NCR was to be given absolute freedom to employ non-union labor in any department they wanted. The unions agreed and the factory was reopened on June 19, 1901.

That day, over 500 people applied for jobs, but none were hired, even though none of the molders or polishers showed up for work. At the end of a week, new men were hired to take the place of anyone who had not returned and work resumed at full-staff.

Unfortunately, the Patterson family suffered two great losses close to this time. Captain Robert Patterson, brother to President John H. Patterson and Vice President Frank J. Patterson, suffered a heart attack and died on June 4, a month into the strike. Captain Patterson had been responsible for the Advance Department at NCR, which included helping educate local children through classes in music, woodworking, cooking and gardening.

A month later, on July 4, Frank Patterson also died from a heart attack. He had been suffering from heart problems for nearly two years. It was reported that the stress from dealing with the strike had helped caused the heart attack to occur.

May 4

It all started with a movement toward bringing playgrounds to Dayton. It was believed that supervised play could improve children both mentally and physically. In 1906, the city counsel set aside $100,000 for public parks and playgrounds.

The first site chosen was a lot located at the corner of East Fifth and Eagle streets. At the time it was a vacant lot with a big billboard hiding it from view. The owner, Anna L. Rieman, agreed to sell the land for half of its worth if they would name it after her grandfather, William Bomberger, who originally owned the land.

On May 4, 1907, architectural plans for the new park were published in the *Dayton Daily News*. The original building, swimming pool, pergola and wading pool were designed by William Earl Russ, an architect who had grown up on nearby High Street. Boys and girls had separate playgrounds, the boys having the added feature of being able to be changed into an ice skating rink during the winter. The building was also designed for use in the winter, with a dancing floor and an auditorium that could be changed into a gymnasium.

Dayton's first public playground proved quite popular when it opened on June 30, 1908. It was thought that 2,000 bathing suits would suffice, but people from all over the city began coming, and the numbers grew larger every year. In 1917, an attendance of over 180,000 was recorded.

Much of the original structures above were demolished in 1955. Today, the park offers tennis and basketball courts, a baseball diamond, soccer field and a playground.

May 5

In the late 1970's an unusual man walked the streets of the city, the style of his tattered clothing earning him the nickname "Rags". Not much was known of the tall, grey-bearded wanderer, and he seemed to like it that way. He kept to himself, panhandling only when he needed to, the rest of the time watching crowds of people as if they were a flock of rare birds.

When he died on May 5, 1980 Daytonians found out the rest of his story. Elias Joseph Barauska was born in Waterbury, Connecticut on December 3, 1919, made it to the rank of Corporal before being discharged from the Army in 1946, then tried his hand at carpentry in Florida. Then an idea came to him that he would like to become a Roman Catholic priest. But after four years in a missionary school he met a woman and fell in love. Torn between getting married or becoming a priest ate at him, to the point that Elais suffered a nervous breakdown and was committed to a mental institution. After his release from a second stay, Elias disappeared and eventually made his way to Dayton.

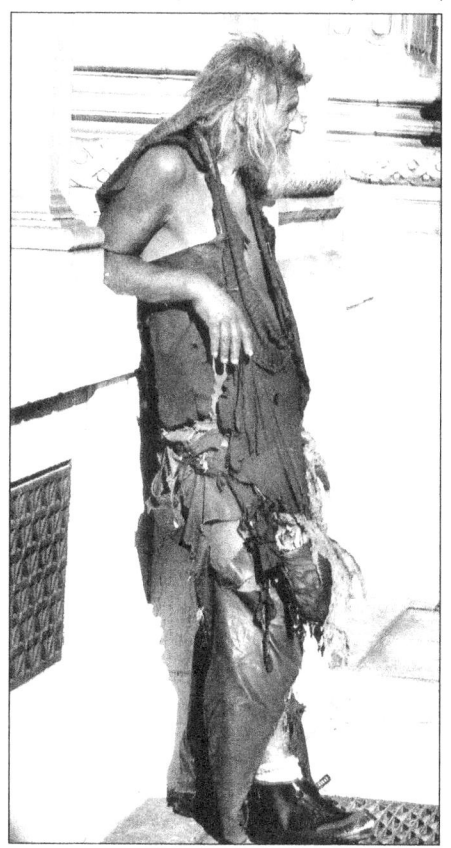

Rags' funeral was well-attended, with over 200 people filing into the Sacred Heart Church for the services. CBS was there to record the event, which was shown on Charles Kuralt's Sunday Morning show. Three priests officiated.

Rags was buried at the National Cemetery located at the Dayton VA Medical Center.

Elias Joseph Barauska, aka Rags, was a fixture downtown for many years.

May 6

On May 2, 1920, Aimee Semple McPherson arrived in Dayton to begin a three week revival meeting at Memorial Hall. By this time she was widely known for her work in faith healing ministries, with thousands testifying to having been cured of diseases and ailments by "Sister Aimee".

McPherson held two meetings a day, one in the morning and another in the afternoon. Though somewhat well attended, the hall was usually less than a third full. A healing meeting on May 6 changed everything.

The first person to ask for McPherson's aid that day was John D. McLardie, who was barely able to walk, even with the help of a cane. After praying, McLardie suddenly threw his cane to the stage and, with tears streaming down his cheeks, walked up and down the stage in front of the crowd.

Encouraged, others surged forward, begging for help. Marjorie Wallace, who had been expected for days to die, arose from the cot on which she had been carried into the hall and walked back to the car that had brought her from Cleveland. Della Hartrum was cured of her gallstones. Seven-year-old Henry Clark, who had been crippled by infantile paralysis, walked in using a crutch and walked out with it under his arm.

And so it went. More than 300 were prayed for that afternoon. This would be the lowest attendance for the rest of McPherson's stay.

As word spread, the crowds grew to the point that thousands of people showed up to each revival meeting, with most having to be turned away. On May 23, the last day of the revival, it was thought that 154,000 people had heard McPherson preach during the 22-day campaign. It was agreed that the number would have been much higher, but the hall was only able to squeeze in about 4,000 believers at a time.

Aimee Semple McPherson proved to be so popular that more than 500 people from Dayton vowed to go to a revival she had planned later that July at Alton, Illinois.

May 7

Although Orville and Wilbur Wright's four flights on December 17, 1903, are well known, it was actually the 1905 Wright Flyer III that was the first airplane capable of sustained, maneuverable flight. On May 7, 2001, a soaring sculpture of the airplane was unveiled on Monument Avenue, between St. Clair and Jefferson streets.

Sitting a little over 10 feet above the ground, the stainless steel and aluminum sculpture was offset with bronze statues of Wilbur lying on his stomach at the controls of the craft and Orville running alongside with his arms outstretched. The 5,000 pound airplane, with its 40-foot wingspan, was set at a five degree tilt, to give the impression that it was ascending. The cantilevered base was made of reinforced steel and weighed an additional 10,000 pounds. Even with all that weight, the airplane, with its basket weave pattern of stainless steel over the wings and rudder, gave it a feeling of lightness, giving the impression that it really could break from its mooring and continue on a path over RiverScape Park across the street and soar above the Great Miami River. This impression was reinforced at the unveiling, when Marion Wright, widow of the brothers' great-nephew Wilkinson Wright, used a remote control unit that made the "canard" front elevator, rear propellers and rudder move, just as the wood and canvas airplane the sculpture represented would have done in actual flight.

May 8

In the mid-nineteenth century people often lamented the fact that, very often, volunteer firemen seemed more intent on fighting each other than fighting fires. Being the fire company to put out a fire was a source of pride, but this sometimes led to bitter encounters when two fire fighting groups ended up at the same fire. When this occurred sometimes the rival companies would cut each others fire hoses, throw stones, and even come to blows while the structure they had come to save would burn to the ground. Dayton was no exception.

On May 8, 1855 a long, red building on Ludlow Street, known as the "Morrison's shop", was discovered to be on fire. Several fire companies responded, including the "Vigilance" and the "Deluge" group of firefighters.

When a well behind the building began running out of water, the Deluge decided to move their fire engine to another well. In turning the engine around, Owen Smith, a member of the Vigilance group, was struck. Thinking that it was on purpose, Smith hit the closest man to him. William C. Richards, of the Deluge group, hit Smith over the head with a fire trumpet he was using to shout orders. Stones and bricks flew like hail as a riot among the groups ensued as the building behind them burned.

At the end of the fight, Richards was found to have a fractured skull and soon died from the injury. He was only twenty-one years old.

An investigation was held, but no one was personally blamed. After a lot of public pressure, the Vigilance company disbanded three days after the incident.

When the *Journal* newspaper was burned by a mob in 1863, the various fire companies refused to show up, afraid that their equipment would be destroyed. After they were assured that the equipment would be replaced the firefighters showed up. But it was too late, the building was lost.

This was enough to move the city council to action. On January 12, 1864, the council passed a resolution that provided Dayton with its first paid firemen. The council also disbanded all volunteer fire companies, which took effect on March 1, 1864.

May 9

One of the more well-known patent medicines made in Dayton was called Tanlac. Touted by the Cooper Medicine Company as a cure-all for almost every illness imaginable, over a million bottles were sold the first year. Part of this was due to an ad campaign of placing testimonies of satisfied customers in the newspaper.

On May 11, 1917, Fred Wick's testimonial appeared in a Tanlac ad in the *Holyke Daily Transcript* newspaper. In it Wick states that he no longer suffered from stomach problems and had in fact gained ten pounds. In the same issue, appeared the notice that "the funeral of Fred Wick was held this morning." Wick's death certificate showed that he had died of stomach cancer on May 9, two days before his testimonial was published!

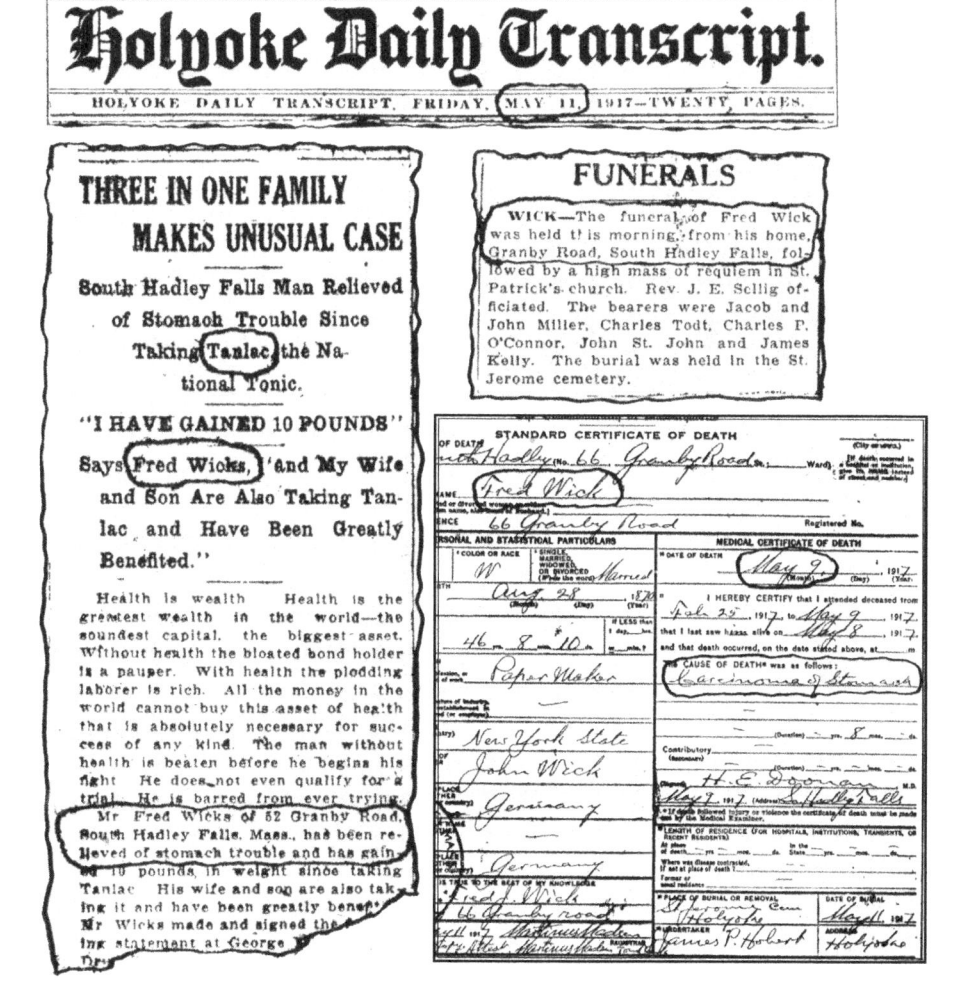

May 10

On April 10, 1910, brothers Louis and Temple Abernathy began a 2,500 mile ride on horseback from Frederick, Oklahoma to New York City, to meet ex-president Theodore Roosevelt. Roosevelt was scheduled to return from a tour of Africa and Europe on June 18, 1910, giving the brothers plenty of time to make the trip.

The amazing thing is that, not only were the boys only six and ten years old, their father allowed Louis and Temple to make the trip alone. Their father, John, had been made a U. S. Marshall of the western district of the Oklahoma Territory by Roosevelt in 1905.

On May 10, 1910, the boys rode into Dayton. Word had reached the city of their coming and an elaborate day was planned. Although the two riders wanted to go on to Springfield so as to stay on schedule, they were enticed to stay with the promise of a free lunch at the Kiefaber cafe, and tickets to the movies. They also visited the Wright airplane factory, where Wilbur Wright showed them around and even allowed them to sit behind the controls of a nearly completed airplane.

The boys spent the night at the Atlas Hotel, and then resumed their trip the following morning.

When Louis and Temple made it to New York City, they were treated like celebrities. They rode their horses in a ticker-tape parade just behind the car carrying Roosevelt.

While in New York, the boys purchased, (or were given for the publicity), a Brush Motor Car, which they drove back to Oklahoma, shipping their horses home by train.

Left to Right: Louis "Bud", John, and Temple "Temp" Abernathy.

May 11

In 1909, Theodore Schirmer had an idea that would change the way business forms were made. He knew that continuous forms could not be fed accurately by means of friction rollers. Schirmer had observed the operation of the chain and sprocket gear that was used when absolute control of movement was required, such as motion picture film through a projector. He thought the same principle could be adapted to business forms.

Schirmer conceived of an autographic register which fed marginally punched forms over pin wheel sprockets on either side of a roller. The idea was unique enough by the U.S. Patent Office that they issued Schirmer patent #940,481 for his "shipping bill register" on November 16, 1909.

Schirmer turned to Dayton businessman John Q. Sherman for help in marketing his invention. Sherman solicited a few investors, and on May 11, 1912, The Standard Register Company was born.

Standard Register was sold to Taylor Corp. in 2015.

Standard Register employees assembling autographic registers, circa 1917.

May 12

At 8:20 p.m., on May 12, 1886, a thunderstorm began, a blinding and continuous fall of water lasting for two hours. When the storm was at its fiercest, a shower of hailstones, some as large as hen eggs, also began to fall. Downtown streets were covered from curb to curb, with some houses and businesses standing in 3 to 5 feet of water.

But it was the upper parts of the West Side where the damage and suffering was the greatest. The rain was especially heavy in the area above Wolf Creek, causing a large amount of loose timber, brush and other materials to float down and lodge against the railroad bridge which today is located near where Blaine and Paul Laurence Dunbar streets meet. The debris created a dam that held the water back to the point that a lake was formed that was ten to twelve feet deep and covered over 100 acres.

The Wolf Creek levee let go at a point near the railroad bridge and when the bridge itself was washed away, the immense lake found an outlet and poured its massive volume of water into the area, converting its streets into canals and overflowing into houses, causing hundreds of families living in one-story homes to stand upon chairs, tables and stools, and those living in two-story houses to seek safety upstairs. The power behind the fast-flowing river swept a number of houses off of their foundations, some floating down to the foot of Broadway and lodging there. Hundreds of families were driven into the darkness to find shelter on higher ground as the water rushed down Blaine Street to Broadway and out Broadway to Second and Third. Soon the area of what is now Dakota, Edison, First, and Second streets was impassable.

As dawn came, the Fansher Bros. soap factory on North Benton Street, near Blaine Street, was also found mostly underwater. The firm produced bars of soap for general laundry purposes, and a laundry chip soap for use by steam laundries at the time. Although the flood was a setback, Fansher Bros. was able to survive for several more decades.

Once again the levees were strengthened. But it was obvious that this was not enough. The following year the course of Wolf Creek was straightened. A new course was dug, starting from the east end of where the railroad bridge crossed, to where it met the Miami River. It is believed that this change is what helped lower the damage to West Side homes and businesses during the severe floods that hit Dayton in 1897 and 1898.

May 13

In 1917, the Dayton-Wright Airplane Company was awarded a contract to produce an American version of the de Havilland DH-4 British bomber. A stripped-down version arrived in Dayton on August 15. The airplane had to be redesigned to take the Liberty engine, machine guns and instruments. The first de Havilland plane was completed and flown on October 29, 1917.

In the spring of 1918, Dayton-Wright contracted with Universal Film Company to make an instructional film showing the complete history of the manufacturing of a DH-4, from the gathering of the lumber to the flying of the airplane, together with the various changes made to it.

Thinking there might be a commercial angle to the film, Universal asked if Orville Wright would mind flying his old Wright Flyer C alongside one of the DH-4's to show the improvements made in just seven short years. Orville agreed to do so and on May 13, 1918, he took to the air from Dayton-Wright South Field, which would also mark his last solo flight as a pilot. *(See April 26 for Orville's last flight as co-pilot).*

The film, marketed as *The Yanks Are Coming,* was scheduled for its first showing on June 23, 1918. However, Universal received a warning not to show the film, as the company had never received a permit to do so, something that was needed for a movie that might contain sensitive war-related material.

In late August, 1918, the ban was lifted on creating motion pictures of airplane operations, so long as it was done under government supervision. Unfortunately, this did not seem to include previously made films. The only known public showing of *The Yanks Are Coming* was on February 20, 1920, when the film was shown by the Pittsburgh Chamber of Commerce to Pennsylvania members of the SAE. It is unknown if copies of the film still exist.

Dayton-Wright built 3,506 of the 4,346 DH-4 aircrafts produced in the United States for the war effort. Although the American DH-4s were in combat for less than four months, they proved their worth. Of the six Medals of Honor awarded to aviators, four were received by pilots and observers flying DH-4s.

After the war, the DH-4 proved to be quite adaptable. When air mail service began in 1918 the durable DH-4 was found to be well suited for the duty of delivering mail. By 1927 a number of DH-4s were modified to be used as forest fire patrol aircraft.

May 14

On May 14, 1959 the Downtown Merchants Retail Association started a shopping event called Downtown Dayton Day. It had picked up the idea from a program using that name in St. Louis. That year over 100 stores participated, including five department stores. It was the first time the downtown stores had gotten together and had a sale on the same day. It was such a success that before the stores closed on the first one, it was decided by the association to have a second in September. In 1960 the group again had two, one in May and one in September. This began a tradition that lasted decades.

Sadly, stores downtown slowly began closing. By 1995, Elder-Beerman was the only department store left. Instead of more than 300 retail outlets in or near downtown, as there were in 1959, by then there were less than 50.

In 2002, the last year of the event, the number of merchants involved had dropped to 15. The stores participating that last year are now, themselves, mostly gone. They were: Cachet G!, Click Camera & Video, Fashion Cents, Gallery Jewelry, Go Home, G. S. Outfitters, Jaffe & Gross Jewelry, Market Wine, Mendelson Liquidation Outlet, Miller Florist, Price Stores, S & V Office & Furniture, Simply Fashions, Tuffy Muffler Shop and Valeria Beauty Center and Day Spa.

ARCADESQUARE — VISIT THESE PARTICIPATING MERCHANTS

American Way	Corn Crib	Cheese Villa	Arcade Seafood Kitchen
Pizza Boy	Rinaldo's	Salad Depot	Strawberry Saloon
Xar's	Hot Dog Builders	Mandarin Kitchen	Jipeto's
Fitzgerald's Cards & Gifts	Goldfinger	Ashley's	Au Coin Artistique
KS Instant Shoe Repair	Moritz Flowers		*(The Tapestry Gallery)*

20% OFF coupon
(Any Single Purchase - 1 Coupon Per Purchase)

Downtown Dayton Day

SEPT. 12

Eighteen merchants in the Arcade took part in the Downtown Dayton Day event in 1985 - three more than participated in the entire city in 2002.

May 15

While in office President Theodore Roosevelt was asked to run for a third term. This was still allowed at that time, but no one had done so before and Roosevelt did not want to be the first. Instead, he groomed William Howard Taft to be his successor in the White House. However, once Taft was elected in 1908, Roosevelt believed that many of the policies he had put into place had been reversed by President Taft. Displeased, Roosevelt ran for president in 1912 to unseat Taft.

On May 15, 1912, Roosevelt arrived by train at the Union Station. He was driven to Lakeside Park, where he spoke to veterans at the Soldiers' Home. Later that evening, he gave a speech before an audience that completely filled Memorial Hall, He made a vigorous appeal to the voters of the city to support his candidacy to the presidency, denouncing his opponent as a hypocrite and unworthy of the support of the people.

At the 1912 Republican National Convention, Taft narrowly defeated Roosevelt for the party's presidential nomination. Undaunted, Roosevelt formed the Progressive, or Bull Moose, Party. In the end, the split resulted in the election of the Democratic contender, Woodrow Wilson, with Roosevelt winning 27.4% of the popular vote compared to Taft's 23.2%, making Roosevelt the only third party presidential nominee to finish with a higher share of the popular vote than a major party's presidential nominee. Wilson, won with 41.8% of the popular vote.

President Theodore Roosevelt in 1912.

May 16

Dayton is well-known for its patents, but few of them are as tasty as Joe Bissett's idea for skewers into a pork loin (or other similar meat) that allowed a person to dine on meat covered with barbecue sauce without silverware or getting the sauce on their fingers. And slitting the meat to tear away in sections also meant that the sauce ended up in their mouth instead of on their face.

Many knew Bissett as the founder of The Grub Steak Restaurant, which opened in 1963 as a small bar and grill at 1410 N. Main Street. It soon turned into a full service restaurant, well-known for its steaks, seafood and, of course, barbecue ribs. His ribs, which he called "Royal Ribs", proved so popular that at one time The Grub Steak was the largest pork tenderloin user in Ohio.

Everyone who came to The Grub Steak loved Bissett's napkin-saving idea, so on May 16, 1969, he applied for a patent. Although it took over two years, Bissett was finally granted Patent #3,635,732 on January 18, 1972.

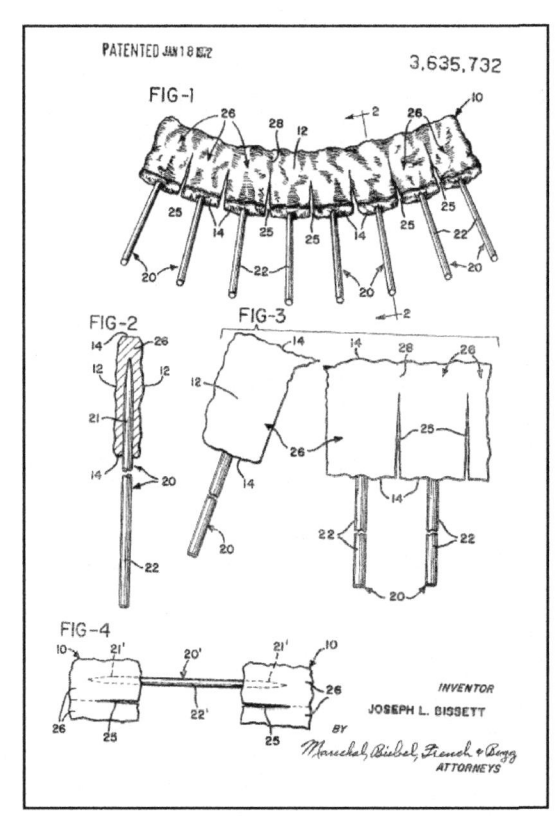

Left: A copy of Joseph L. Bissett's original patent that was filed in 1969. Bissett was also granted Patent #3717473 for a variation of the idea on February 20, 1973.

May 17

After twenty-five years of trial and error, The Siebenthaler Company produced what is considered by many to be the perfect locust tree. Named the Moraine Honeylocust, the tree proved to be so perfect, that it was given Plant Patent #836 in 1949, the first patent for a tree granted in the United States.

The Moraine Locust was unique in several ways. Unlike the Black Locust, the Moraine Locust had no thorns, nor were there any unsightly seed pods that had to be cleaned up in the fall.

With the gradual disappearance of the stately American Elm, due to the ravages of the Dutch Elm disease, the introduction of the Moraine Honeylocust as an alternate choice for use as a shade tree was especially timely. Planted close to a house, the tree would shade the roof and walls in the summer, but allowed the sun to shine through in winter. Attaining a height of 80 to 100 feet, the lower branches of the tree were self-pruning as the top grew wider. This made it desirable for narrow street planting, as sufficient clearance could be maintained for traffic.

Besides the Moraine Honeylocust, Siebenthaler's has also patented the Moraine Ash, the Wright Brothers Maple and the Moraine Sweet Gum Tree.

May 18

In the spring of 1849, cholera made its way to Dayton. The city was familiar with the disease, having lost thirty-three of its citizens to it in 1833. *(See December 26)*

The first fatal case was nineteen-year-old William Munday, on May 18, 1849. He had just come back from Cincinnati by boat a day or two before his death, suffering from a severe case of diarrhea, which continued to worsen until his death. Dr. Michael Garst, who was in charge of the case, advised the authorities to burn the boat and cremate the corpse. Had they followed his advice, the epidemic would probably have been averted or greatly mitigated. But they did not.

Daytonians must have sighed with relief as days passed and no one else died. Then, on June 13, another fatality occurred, marking the beginning of a sixty-one day period of death and disease that lasted until mid-August. Business was almost entirely suspended until September, a Board of Health was appointed. There was no hospital yet and so Mary Hess, who lived on Brown Street near what is now Hess Street, opened her house to the sick. The streets and alleys were white from the quantities of chloride of that were scattered on them in an attempt to disinfect the city.

Drs. David S. Newman and Silas H. Smith were two dedicated physicians who cared for dozens of patients during the crisis. Unfortunately, the two men succumbed to the disease; Dr. Smith dying on July 13, followed three days later by Dr. Newman. Both were buried at Woodland Cemetery. Though thought of as heroes, their deaths served as proof that even doctors didn't always know how to protect and cure themselves from diseases.

Mayor John Howard made a proclamation, stating that July 20 was to be "a day of fasting, humiliation and prayer" and ordered all businesses to close their doors. The churches opened at daybreak and hundreds knelt in the street and prayed.

By mid-summer the disease had run its course, with John A. Throm dying on August 12. In the end, the total deaths from cholera in Dayton that year came to two hundred and twenty-five, or one out of every forty-five people. The loss of life from this devastating event would be more than double the ninety-two deaths reported by the coroner that occurred during the flood that swept through the city in 1913.

May 19

In 1964 brothers Sam, Al and Lou Levin, who were owners of several drive-ins theaters, including the Dixie, Salem, Sherwood and Dayton East, decided to produce their own movie. Sam reasoned that since at the time 'beach' movies and the Beatles were big ticket office draws, a film combining the two ideas was sure to be a hit.

While Lou stayed home to tend the family business, Sam and Al left for Hollywood. There they contracted for a studio and a director. Casting included Martin West and Noreen (Bachelor Father) Corcoran. It also included appearances and songs by Leslie Gore, the Crickets and the Beach Boys. Both Sam and Al starred in the picture. They had cameo appearances as judges of a bathing beauty contest.

On May 19, 1965 the motion picture, entitled *The Girls on the Beach*, premiered at the Dixie and Sherwood Drive-Ins. It was later renamed *Summer of '64*.

Al, Sam and Lou Levin at the premiere of their movie "Girls on the Beach". Dayton Daily Amusement Editor Gee Mitchell reviewed the movie during its premiere.

"It borders on perpetual motion, in fact motion to a rock 'n' roll beat that seldom lets up either, and much of it supplied by a handsome young cast of bikini-clad starlets and muscular young men and cavorting in equally handsome settings. Just watching was exhausting for an elderly codger, but then, these things aren't intended for one who is winded by a two-minute fox trot."

May 20

Though completely blind by the age of 11, that never stood in the way of Eleanor Gertrude Brown. Determined to receive an education, Brown entered the Ohio State School for the Blind in Columbus, and graduated in 1908. Afterward, she began doing piece work for a paper box factory until she had saved enough money to enter Ohio State University in 1909. Although some doubted her ability to be able to keep up in class, she not only did well, but won special commendation in her major subjects, the languages and sociology.

On May 20, 1914, even though she had not yet graduated with a B.A. degree from OSU, Brown was hired to be a teacher in the Dayton Public Schools. She would later receive a master's degree and in 1934 a Doctor of Philosophy degree from Columbia University.

For 40 years Dr. Brown taught German, Latin and world and American history, first at Steele High School, then Wilbur Wright High. Her autobiography, "Corridors of Light," was published in 1958. "Into the Light," a collection of poems later made into a talking book for the blind, was published in 1946.

Dr. Brown passed away on July 21, 1964, at the age of 76. In 1980, she was named "outstanding woman of the year" by the Dayton Federation of Women's Clubs.

Eleanor G. Brown surrounded by her students at Steele High School in 1917.

May 21

Joseph Frank Mikulec, the famous globe trotter, arrived in Dayton on May 21, 1929. It was his third time in Dayton and at least his second time around the world.

Joe, as he liked to be known, had first visited the city in April, 1920, lugging his 31 pound book in which he collected autographs of famous people. During that visit he had added the name of John H. Patterson. He had started from Croatia, his native country, in 1901, his purpose being to circle the world and then write a book on his travels. By his second trip to Dayton on March 2, 1922, Mikulec had covered more than 175,000 miles, toured 26 nations and obtained 50,000 signatures. He claimed the album contained the autographs of every person of note around the world.

Mikulec had an unusual way of making a living during his travels. He neither asked for, nor would take, money offered him. Instead, he would sell postcards of himself, which asked for the person buying it to "Give what you wish". He had originally been offered a deal with an overseas publisher who promised him $50,000 if he gave them an exclusive account of his adventures, but this seemed to have fallen through when World War I began. He did hope to eventually sell both his story and his album of autographs and settle down to a normal life.

Unfortunately, neither wish came true for Mikulec. On May 29, 1933 while visiting Genos, Italy, he died of pulmonary tuberculosis. In the report of his death, on the line of what items Mikulec owned at the time, are the sad words "none other than autograph book". The location of his beloved book has been lost to history.

On May 21, 1929, Mikulec made his final trip to Dayton, in part to add Frederick B. Patterson's signature to that of his father's. The book had by this time gotten so heavy that Mikulec was using a push cart to carry it around, and sometimes had the book shipped from city to city in order to more easily walk the rougher routes.

May 22

During their experiments in 1902, brothers Orville and Wilbur Wright successfully controlled their glider in all three axes of flight: pitch, roll and yaw. In March, 1903 the two brothers applied for a patent on their method of control. The patent's importance was its claim of a new and useful method of controlling a flying machine, powered or not. In fact, it would several months after they first applied for a patent before they brothers were successful in making the first controlled, powered and sustained heavier-than-air human flight on December 17, 1903.

When their application was rejected, they turned to Henry Toulmin, a patent attorney from Springfield, Ohio. By April 1904, the Wrights' patent had been filed not only in the U. S., but also in Britain, France, Belgium, Germany, Austria and other countries. On May 22, 1906, they were finally granted U.S. Patent 821,393 for a "Flying Machine".

Even with this success, the Wrights spent many years in legal battles with aviators and inventors who tried to work their way around the brothers' claims. The suits finally ended with the advent of World War I when aircraft manufacturers established the Manufacturers' Aircraft Association to coordinate wartime aircraft manufacturing in the U.S. All patent litigation ceased automatically.

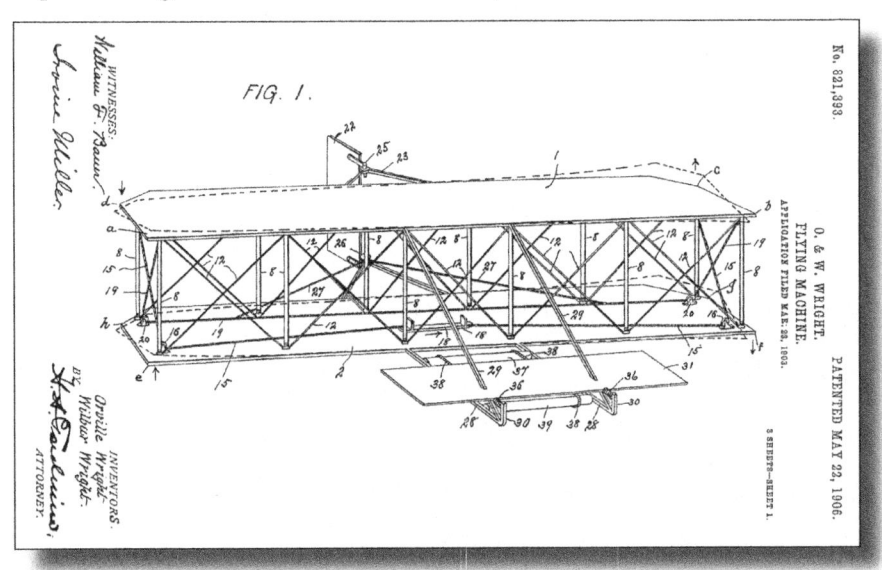

Notice that the patent drawing is of a glider, not a powered airplane. The Wright airplane patent, the basis for their many later patent infringement suits, was for the 1902 glider, not the more famous airplane of 1903.

May 23

The Belmont Auto Theater opened at 2060 County Line Road in Dayton, on August 7, 1947. The Belmont would become the first drive-in in the area to introduce stereo sound, car heaters, 3-D movies and CinemaScope.

In 1954 the Belmont added new sections to its original screen to make a CinemaScope screen 96' wide and 65' high. To celebrate the new screen the owners booked a new 3-D Rita Hayworth movie entitled *Miss Sadie Thompson*, "which, to say the least, should bring out all the young lady's advertised dimensions", noted *Journal-Herald*'s film critic A. S. Kany.

At first Twentieth Century Fox, which controlled the new CinemaScope process, refused to release C-Scope films to any drive-in that did not have a stereo sound system. This was an expensive investment, since it would entail a two box speaker system that allowed a patron to have a speaker for each side of the car. Seeing how well the CinemaScope films were being received in downtown theaters, the Belmont purchased the stereophonic sound equipment.

The first movie to be shown was CinemaScope's *Beneath the 12-Mile Reef* on May 23, 1954. Unfortunately, Twentieth Century Fox soon changed its mind and began allowing drive-ins without stereo systems to show C-Scope movies and Belmont's monopoly of this type of movie came to an end.

In 1983, Miami Valley Research Park bought the land the Belmont sat on as part of a future plan to build a 1250 acre research park. The theater closed in 1997.

May 24

On May 24, 1921 a little five-watts radio station by the call sign WXAX was born. Located in the window of a radio store owned by Stanley M. Krohn, Jr. on the East Third Street side of the Beckel Hotel, WXAX was the first radio station in the Dayton area, the third in Ohio and the thirteenth station in the United States.

In 1922 the call letters were changed to WDBS, which stood for Watch Dayton's Broadcasting Station. In 1926 the owner, Stanley M. Krohn, changed the call letters to match his initials, WSMK. It was here that Benjamin "Scatman" Crothers got his start. When he auditioned for a radio show in 1932 WSMK, the director didn't think his name was catchy enough, so Crothers quickly concocted the handle Scat Man. Later, the nickname was condensed to Scatman by Arthur Godfrey.

In 1939 Charles Sawyer bought the station from Krohn, switching the call sign, at the suggestion of Jack Snow, to WING to honor Dayton's aviation history. *(For more on Snow see July 13)*

In February, 1983, WING was the first radio station in Dayton to go AM Stereo, which improved the sound quality for AM listeners.

Today, WING is a sports-talk station, owned by Main Line Broadcasting.

One of the popular programs the station had over the years was called "The Man On The Street", wherein a radio personality hit the sidewalks and talked to people about various subjects. This picture shows Sidney Ten Eyck surrounded by a crowd, while showing off a carton of Coca-Cola, which was the show's sponsor.

"The "Man On The Street" program was one of the nations' oldest continuous programs with the same sponsor. The last show aired in January, 1980.

"THE MAN ON THE STREET"
Every Week Day — 12:15 P. M., WSMK
Sponsored by
THE DAYTON COCA-COLA BOTTLING CO.

154

May 25

In an effort to help beautify the city, the Greater Dayton Association began placing 368 flower boxes on the Main Street, Dayton View, Third Street and Washington Street bridges on May 25, 1916. Over 20,000 plants were used. Prisoners at the workhouse constructed the boxes out of cypress wood. The organization had been inspired by the work of John H. Patterson, of NCR, who at his private expense, had maintained flower boxes on several bridges south of Dayton.

The project kicked off with the Rotary Club having a parade through downtown, with each member carrying a potted flower or plant. They marched to music provided by the Third Regiment, Ohio National Guard band as they headed toward the Main Street Bridge. A speech was given and then the pots were planted in the several of the 81 flower boxes that ran along both sides of the bridge. In conjunction with this, the Soldiers' Home furnished flowers to adorn the base of the Soldiers' Monument at Main and Monument.

During the two years before this, the Greater Dayton Association had sold trees and shrubs to 676 families for the purpose of decorating their yards. They also had made and sold 1,300 bird houses, provided flowers for McKinley Park and was responsible for over 7,000 feet of window flower boxes in the downtown district.

May 26

On May 26, 1870 the Cincinnati Red Stockings came to town to play an exhibition game against the Daytons, a junior baseball club. Not much was expected from the Dayton team, as the players were all under the age of 18. Plus, the year before, the Red Stockings had posted a 57-0 record, the only perfect season in baseball history. Still, an estimated crowd of about 2,000 showed up at Bimm's Park to watch the battle.

And what a lop-sided battle it was. Playing on a bumpy field that was normally used as an ice skating rink, the Dayton team held their own the first inning, getting four runs against the Red Stockings six. This set the local crowds cheering. But this would be the closest score against the Red Stockings that the Daytons would be the rest of the game.

The Daytons would go on to score another five runs in the fourth inning. Unfortunately, the Red Stockings would score twenty-five runs that same inning. The Daytons team would not score another run the rest of the game.

In the end, the game lasted two hours and forty-five minutes. This was due to the Daytons' unrelenting opponents grim determination to win with as high a score as possible. The local team went down in defeat; the Red Stockings winning by the score of 104-9.

The Red Stockings' winning streak ended at 81 games when Cincinnati fell to the Brooklyn Atlantics, 8-7, in extra innings in Brooklyn on June 14, 1870.

May 27

During World War II, Dayton began using air raid sirens as a signal for citizens to take shelter from enemy bomb attacks. By December 1942 twenty-five "Victory" sirens had been placed throughout the city, the noise of each was touted as being so powerful that "eardrums could be ruptured if one is too close to the siren". But tests indicated that many parts of the city could not hear the sirens.

The Dayton Council for Defense began pushing the city commission to purchase four larger "Victory" sirens to augment the smaller sirens. City commissioners balked at the idea of spending $14,800 for sirens that had proven to be somewhat ineffective. Mayor Frank M. Krebs stated that he was concerned the state would cut further allotments if "the city takes the attitude of not providing badly needed equipment." He believed that the need for proper protection of the city was indicated by the fact that the federal Office of Civilian Defense had supplied Dayton with 5,000 gas masks and helmets along with instructions that the public needed to be on the alert at all times.

Pressure for the city commissioners to buy the sirens began to mount. It was reported that a growing number of emergency corps volunteers were thinking of giving up civilian defense activities if the sirens were not purchased. This helped force the decision to purchase four larger sirens to augment the smaller ones. Three of the new sirens were to have been placed on 50-foot towers in time for the city's first total blackout that was scheduled for May 27, 1943. A combination of bad weather and a shortage of labor delayed the completion of the towers. The sirens were placed on ground-level platforms and used that day anyway.

This did not make residents that lived near the sirens very happy. One resident got so fed up that he fired a shot at the operator of one of the sirens. A second siren suffered a setback when someone cut the gasoline line that fueled it. Two weeks later the power belt of a siren was cut, which effectively stopped the siren from blasting the neighborhood during the next test.

The sirens were finally placed on towers and were tested together on October 9, 1943. The Dayton Council for Defense later reported that the citywide test was "very satisfactory, in fact beyond our expectations".

May 28

Edward "Eddie" Reichenbacher was born on October 8, 1890, in Columbus, Ohio. Due to the anti-German sentiment in the U.S. during World War I, Reichenbacher felt that his Swiss surname sounded too German, so he changed it to "Rickenbacker." He also added the very American sounding middle name of "Vernon." With 26 aerial victories, he was America's most successful fighter ace during the war.

On May 26, 1921, Rickenbacker took off in a de Havilland DH-4 airplane from Redwood City, California. His goal was to reach Washington D.C. in record time, partly to break a transcontinental speed record and also to attend a dinner to be given in his honor by the Metropolitan Club.

After wrecking twice along the way, Rickenbacker finally reached McCook Field at 10 a.m. on May, 28, where he was scheduled to change airplanes. While there he ate lunch and talked to a few of his friends which he had made during his service in the war.

Rickenbacker was given a U.S. D-9 airplane to continue his trip. In spite of having to land again in Hagerstown, Maryland due to a storm, Rickenbacker made it to Bolling Field in Washington, D.C. with forty-five minutes to spare before the banquet would start. He changed into dinner attire and walked into the Metropolitan Club as if nothing had happened along the way. His total flying time was 26 hours, besting the previous record of 33 hours.

First Lt. Edward "Eddie" Rickenbacker with his SPAD S.XIII C.1., France, 1918

May 29

Near the 18th hole of the Community Golf Course at 2917 Berkley Avenue stands a memorial to Montgomery County men and women who died in France and Belgium during WWI.

During the war the Dayton Home Guard had been collecting money to buy uniforms. The signing of the armistice before the uniforms had been bought left the Home Guards with a large sum of money. It was decided that the purchase of a monument would be the most patriotic use for the funds. And so the idea for the Victory Oak Knoll was born.

It was decided to plant a tree for every solider, sailor, marine or Red Cross nurse who had died during the war. This proved to be 180 trees. At the base of each tree was placed a bronze disk engraved with the name, rank and organization of the person for whom the tree represented. A huge boulder was added as well, containing a bronze tablet on which all 180 names were placed.

Dayton Mayor J. M. Switzer accepted the monument on behalf of the city during the dedication on May 29, 1921. The song *The Star Spangled Banner* closed the program.

Today, many of the trees are now gone, but the monument itself still stands, a tribute to those who gave their all in the struggle for world freedom.

The trees are beginning to grow in this photo of the Victory Oak Knoll monument.

May 30

Aurel Vaszin had a dream - to give to Dayton an amusement park and zoological garden that rivaled those in New York, Philadelphia and Cincinnati. In 1927 he took out a long-term lease on a 47-acre tract of land on North Main Street known as Forest Park.

Throughout the winter season skilled workmen were kept busy building amusement rides made by Vaszin's business, the Dayton Fun House and Riding Device Company. Animals were collected for the zoo, with Frederick B. Patterson, of NCR, agreeing to allow animals captured during a recent safari to be housed at the park. Despite a hard winter, workers kept pace in the hope that the Forest Park and Zoological Garden would be ready for the main event – the celebration of Memorial Day on May 30, 1928. Although the park was still not complete, the people who attended that day were not disappointed….

The latest and most popular rides were offered. The most thrilling was a roller coaster named High Diver. The tumble bug ride was a big attraction, as was the aerial swing. A merry-go-round kept the kids entertained, as did the miniature railway. A "kiddie's corner", which had not quite been completed, promised a play center that would include see-saws, slides, ladders, a wading pool and even a large sand box.

The zoo still had a number of permanent homes for the animals that had to be built, but what was being offered that Memorial Day was amazing. Included in the collection was a small herd of English deer and elk, for which a large run had been provided. A red fox could be found, as could a variety of pheasants, ducks, geese, wild turkeys and pigeons and rabbits. The large collection of peafowls proved to be one of the best attractions, although the spider monkey, South American monkeys and a tarantula were also quite popular.

Of chief importance was the group of animals Patterson had given to the park. The collection included a lion by the name of Simba, a leopard, a cheetah and three African monkeys.

Vaszin promised that even more rides and animals would be offered over time. "Our plans are all made, but it must be understood that to be attractive a park must be beautiful, and beautification cannot be hurried," he said. "We are not going to try to do everything at once, but everything we do is going to be done well and for permanence."

Unfortunately, the cost of feeding the animals proved too expensive during the Great Depression and the park was closed in the early 1930s.

May 31

Contributions to help finance World War I were put into a fund known as the "War Chest". One of the best stunts staged to help raise donations occurred on May 31, 1918.

On that day Colonel Edward A. Deeds, one of the founders of Delco, and Howard Rinehart, a pilot for the Dayton-Wright Airplane Company, made a spectacular flight back and forth over the city about six o'clock that evening. The flight was so low that people poured out onto the streets to watch the spectacle - which was exactly what Deeds and Rinehart had hoped for.

It seems that, before starting the flight, five thousand pennies were collected and placed in small envelopes. As the airplane flew over the city, the envelopes were tossed out to the crowds gathered below. Each envelope stated that the finder could keep it as a souvenir "providing you make a substantial contribution to the War Chest."

A wild scramble occurred as people tried to collect the pennies that fluttered down from the sky over the area of Third and Main streets, near a huge old chest that had been erected on the lawn of the Old Court House.

The War Chest campaign in Dayton was a great success, raising over $1 million during the war.

June 1

The War of 1812 was an armed conflict between the United States and the British Empire. The British restricted the American trade and also wanted to set up an Indian state in the Midwest in order to maintain their influence in the region. The Americans were eager to gain their independence from the British Empire once and for all.

At the outbreak of this war, Governor Return Jonathan Meigs called for 1,200 troops and appointed Dayton as the place for assembling them. Three regiments of militia were organized; the first encamped south of Dayton, and the second and third encamped in Cooper Park. General William Hull was made commander, arriving in Dayton on May 25, 1812. Camp was established on Webster St. and became known as Meigs Camp. The final order for 1,600 men to move north to Fort Detroit was given on June 1, 1812.

It was thought that General Hull and his men would be victorious. So it can be imagined the alarm that was raised when on August 22, 1812, news arrived in Dayton of Hull's army surrendering. At first it was thought that Hull had been greatly outnumbered by superior forces, which led to the belief that the British might just be able to win the war. But word later came that Hull had surrendered Fort Detroit to General Isaac Brock without firing a gun, even though he had twice as many men and was well supplied with both provisions and ammunition. Fortunately, the soldiers were released on parole and gradually made their way home.

Gen. Hull was later court-martialed. He was found guilty of cowardice, neglect of duty and unofficer-like conduct and was sentenced to be shot. However, Hull was given a reprieve from President James Madison. Gen. Hull was dishonorably discharged and his name was stricken from the rolls of the army.
General William Hull is the only U.S. general to be sentenced to death by an American court-martial.

June 2

On February 16, 1943 Dayton city commissioners signed a petition from the Dayton and Montgomery County Federation of Churches which called for a voluntary curfew for children. The petition asked for a curfew of 10 p.m. for children up to 12 years of age and of midnight for high school youths for the duration of the war. The petition read in part:

"Inasmuch as juvenile crime and delinquency are on the increase in Dayton, and present-day conditions are causing serious strain on your homes, parents, teachers and children, we do hereby endorse and approve a voluntary curfew of 10 p.m. for children up to 12 years of age, and 12 p.m. for high school youth, unless accompanied by parents or guardian."

Unfortunately, the curfew was not recognized by many of the children or parents. On April 27, 1943 the Montgomery County juvenile court reported that the number of "first time" juveniles brought into the court during January through March, 1943 had increased over 85% from the same period the year before and that 407 delinquency cases had been recorded. At the same time the May issue of Reader's Digest carried an article titled "Trouble on the Street Corner". The article stated that "during the past year...delinquency has doubled in Dayton, Ohio."

The Dayton city council had had enough. Mayor Frank M. Krebs said that police authorities "cannot keep youngsters off the streets nights, unless they have authority covered by ordinance."

On June 2, 1943 a new ordinance passed stating that boys and girls under 15 years of age had to be off the streets and out of public places by 10:30 p.m., unless accompanied by parents or guardians. Dayton law enforcement officers were given responsibility to see that the ordinance was carried out. If the juvenile court found a minor guilty of a violation, the child's parents faced the possibility of a $100 fine, 30 days in the workhouse, or both.

To help counteract the problem, a youth center was opened for high school students at 24 West Fourth Street in October 1943. Financed by the Community War Chest, it offered weekly programs of dances, movies and talent shows, as well as entertainment by two Wright Field swing bands and an all-star high school band that alternated. Along with the YMCA club on West Monument, the club helped give the children a place to go. Both proved popular, with upwards of 200 youths attending the YMCA on some evenings.

June 3

Paul Laurence Dunbar is generally regarded as the first black American to achieve distinction in the literary field. Dunbar became internationally known as a poet, novelist and playwright, having published several books of poetry, fiction and short stories, as well as the lyrics for *In Dahomey: A Negro Musical Comedy*, which was the first full-length musical written and played by blacks to be performed at a major Broadway house.

On June 3, 1904, Dunbar bought a house at 219 North Summit Street (now Paul Laurence Dunbar Street) for $4,100 and moved in with his mother, Matilda. He placed the property in his mother's name. This was probably due to the fact that by this time Dunbar was very sick with tuberculosis and was unsure how much longer he might live.

Even in his weakened state, Dunbar continued to write, including *Howdy, Honey, Howdy* in 1905. This would be the last book published before his death.

Paul Laurence Dunbar died at home in his mother's arms on February 9, 1906. He was 33 years old.

In 1936. the Ohio Legislature dedicated the house as a memorial to Dunbar, the first state memorial in Ohio to honor an African American.

June 4

On this day in 1968, the *Press-Gazette* (Hillsboro, OH) reported an end of an era. Their native son, Joe Rockhold, was retiring after almost 35 years in the entertainment field of radio and television. Rockhold's early days were during the golden years of radio in the 1930s, where he acted in radio shows, including WAJU in Columbus, WXYZ in Detroit, and WSPD in Toledo. Rockhold was willing to do whatever was needed; from playing parts in Lone Ranger and Green Hornet programs, to creating the clomping of horses' hooves and other effects. His greatest success was in Chicago, where he played Doc Green on the Tom Mix show. But today Rockhold is better known in his role of lovable Uncle Orrie.

After taking a break from the business for a few years, Rockhold decided to try his hand at television. WHIO-TV executives were looking for talent and his act as Uncle Orrie, with his Civil War style cap, string tie and wire-rimmed glasses, won them over. His first appearances were on the Kenny Roberts Show, a country singer, who had a children's program. When Roberts left in 1956, Uncle Orrie and Nosey the Clown (Jack Jacobsen) took over. They were later joined by Ferdie Fussbudget (Ken Hardin).

Left: Nosey the Clown & Uncle Orrie

The unscripted show would start with children yelling and music playing, Games would be played, prizes given and a cartoon show. The big deal was to be picked to sing the "BHA means Better Home Appliances" song while Uncle Orrie played guitar, because each child that participated was paid a dollar.

June 5

Although the stock market crashed in October of 1929, it wasn't until nearly ten years later that a food stamp program was created. The first food stamp program was quite simple. When a person received their relief check he or she could use part of it to buy a book of orange stamps, redeemable for food at face value in any store. With every dollar's worth of orange stamps bought the purchaser would get an additional 50 cents worth of blue stamps for free. The blue stamps were also redeemable in any store, but only for foods designated as surplus.

Sponsor of the food stamp plan was the Federal Surplus Commodities Corporation, also known as FSCC. The FSCC tried to help farmers who could not sell their products by buying them and passing them on to the needy through food banks. Unfortunately, complications set in when store owners objected to the competition. People on relief complained that one week they'd get all potatoes, the next week all oranges and the next week nothing.

Once the food stamp program began on May 16, 1939 the surplus food was distributed through regular stores. Rochester, NY was the first to try the program. The next was Dayton, which handed out stamps on June 5, 1939. Before its end in early 1943, over 20 million people across the U.S. had been helped.

On June 6, 1939, Edward Barrett was the first person in Dayton to receive the benefits of the new program, trading in his stamps for an armload of groceries.

June 6

In 1828, at the age of fifteen, John Insco Williams was apprenticed to an uncle, who was a house and carriage painter. Young Williams soon began to think that this kind of art was not suited to his genius, and ran away. He worked at anything he could find to do until he had managed to save up money enough to go to Philadelphia, where he attended an art school. He remained three years, painting all day and studying in perspective and anatomy at night.

While visiting in Louisville, Kentucky, Williams met John Banvard from whom he learned about the painting of panoramas. Williams would soon gain a reputation of a panoramist when in 1849 he painted *The Grand Moving Panorama of the Bible*. His painting represented sacred history from the creation to the fall of Babylon. A booklet explaining the scenes was published. This panorama was exhibited in Dayton at the Jefferson Street Baptist Church for about a week, the last day being June 6, 1849.

When the panorama was destroyed by a fire at Independence Hall, Philadelphia, in March 1851, Williams went to Cincinnati and painted another one on a much larger scale, covering four thousand yards of canvas. He successfully exhibited it across the United States. This panorama was damaged by a flood in Baltimore, which washed off nearly all the paint. Williams came back to Dayton and repainted it, and again exhibited it. It was later destroyed in a fire in 1871.

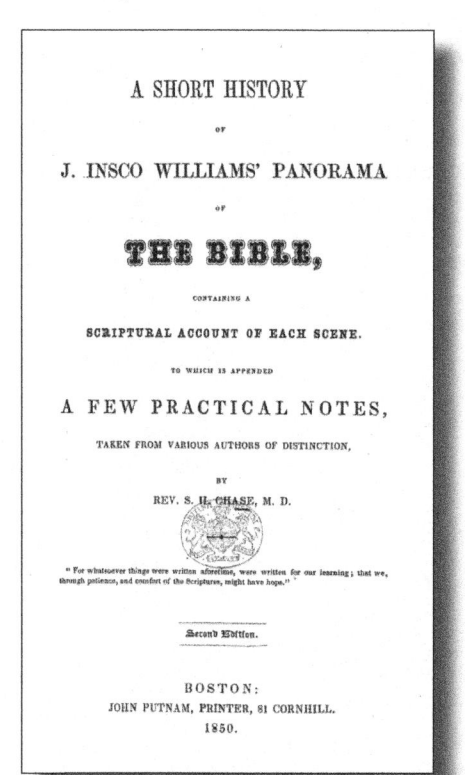

The Civil War inspired a 10,000 square foot panorama entitled *Williams' Great Painting of the American Rebellion* that traveled throughout the East, accompanied by music and lectures. Williams exhibited at the Pennsylvania Academy of the Fine Arts in 1864, and at the Cincinnati Associated Artists in 1866.

Williams died in Dayton in 1869.

June 7

In 1974, President Richard Nixon appointed Gerald Ford as Vice President after Spiro Agnew resigned. When Nixon resigned, Ford became the only President who had never been elected to national office.

On June 7, 1976, President Ford was given a warm welcome by a sea of over 10,000 people who crowded around the Old Court House to listen to him plead his case as to why he should become the GOP nominee instead of his challenger, Ronald Reagan. But not everyone was happy about his visit. One man was arrested for threatening to kill Ford. The Secret Service also received a call that a bomb had been hidden in the Dayton Power and Light building then under construction at Courthouse Square. A search was conducted, but no bomb was found.

President Ford was not the only one to have trouble while in the Gem City. During a speech Reagan gave in the Oregon District the day before Ford's visit, a heckler began shouting about fascism. A scuffle soon developed, in which the protester was punched and kicked until the police were able to pull him from the crowd. Ann Lake, Reagan's press secretary, said the fracas was "the first time anything like this has happened in the campaign."

President Gerald Ford would go on to win the GOP nomination, but lose the bid for president on November 2, 1976, to Democrat Jimmy Carter.

President Gerald Ford at the Old Court House in Dayton on July 24, 1976.

June 8

The body of Bernice Champion was found underneath the Herman Avenue Bridge about 7 a.m. on June 8, 1915, ending nearly four days of searching. Her friend, Etta Hyre had been found in the river just below the Steele Dam two days before.

The two women, along with their friends, Carl Wheelock and Harold Laspe, had been taking part of a canoe carnival celebrating the opening of Island Park on June 5. It was at 9:20 p.m., near the end of the event, when the accident occurred. The four friends were in a canoe together and were part of a procession of 126 boats that took off from Idylwild, just north of the Dayton Canoe Club. The decorated canoes lit up the Stillwater River as they swept past Island Park and circled around near Steele Dam as a 25 piece orchestra filled the air with music. The plan was for the canoes to return to Island Park, where there would be dancing and a display of fireworks.

Unfortunately, somehow in the darkness, Wheelock and Laspe missed the markers on where to turn their canoes. Suddenly their canoe was swept over the dam and into the torrents and whirl pool below.

For hours after the accident it was hoped that the four young people had somehow survived. Police and firemen, along with members of the canoe club and volunteers, searched along both sides of the river for a quarter of a mile. Laspe and Wheelock were finally found clinging to a rocky point of land 75 feet from the dam, which was nearly invisible from the levee at night. Etta Hyre's body was found after a grappling hook snagged a part of her clothing. It was located in deep water just below the dam.

When it was determined that Bernice Champion had most likely drowned, dynamite was brought in and set off in the water below the dam in an effort to try and bring her body to the surface. This did not work, but is thought to have been at least part of the reason that the Steele Dam had weakened to the point that part of the structure collapsed a year or so later. Price Brothers came to Dayton and replaced the dam with a new one in 1917. *(See September 2)*

The same day that Champion was found, Etta Hyre was being buried in Ebenezer, Ohio at Willowview Cemetery. She was twenty-two years old. Bernice would be buried at Davids Cemetery the next day, following a funeral service for her in Murlin Heights, Ohio. She was nineteen years old.

June 9

Hills and Dales Park, located just south of Dayton on South Patterson Boulevard, was originally opened for use by NCR employees in 1907. John H. Patterson enjoyed riding horses and fresh air and believed both were necessary for good health. Hills and Dales reflected this idea, its 294 acres of land offering several miles of horse bridle paths, three baseball diamonds, fully-equipped playgrounds, ten tennis courts, a polo field, a nine-hole golf course, wading pool, club houses for men and women and a dance pavilion.

The city formally accepted Patterson's donation during a celebration on June 9, 1918. Over 10,000 people gathered to watch as a procession of firemen, policemen, Red Cross workers, soldiers from Wright Field and members of several clubs paraded around the grounds.

Due to being injured from falling off his horse, John H. Patterson sent his daughter, Dorothy Patterson Judah, to present the park to the city. It was estimated that the land was worth over $1 million and more than doubled the acreage of land the city had previously for use as parks.

The event was actually a two-day affair, beginning on June 8 and ending the next day with the acceptance of the park from Patterson. Above, several thousand children perform a flag drill while a band plays the National Emblem March.

June 10

During the Great Depression, thousands of Daytonians found a lot of time on their hands, but not a lot of money to spend on entertainment. But they did find ways of having fun that didn't cost much.

In the 1930's Dayton had a Main Library near downtown and twelve branches throughout the rest of the city. As can be expected, these were constantly in use. Yet funding was cut to the point that in 1932 pay for library employees were delayed for four months. Elizabeth Faries wrote about these difficult times in her book *A Century of Service: History of the Dayton Public Library, Dayton, Ohio, 1847-1947.*

"During these years, when staff hours and salaries had to be cut, when branches were closed part time and book funds were reduced drastically, more people than ever turned to the Library for information and relief. Some came to forget their financial troubles in recreational reading, others came to get information on the development of new jobs or to prepare themselves for different positions. Only by a rigid economy and a staff working at top speed, sometimes for several months without pay, was the library able to keep open its doors and make its services available to the throngs of daily visitors."

June 10, 1933 signaled the end of "Book Giving Week". The library had asked patrons to donate books they no longer used. The campaign afforded not only a means of replenishing books, but it also served as a lesson to library patrons of the tremendous pressure of demand for books that could not be bought due to lack of funds.

This shows just a small number of the books collected during "Book Giving Week".

June 11

On August 15, 1898, James M. Cox purchased the *Dayton Evening News*. One week later he renamed it the *Dayton Daily News*. The newspaper proved quite popular. When the newspaper had outgrown its location Cox decided that the new home of the *Dayton Daily News* should be unique. The assignment given to the architect Albert Pretzinger was to design "a building, unlike anything in Dayton, and yet not a freak. A dignified temple to the great profession of journalism, which will mark the development of Dayton and establish the news as a fixed institution of the city."

Land was bought on the northwest corner of Fourth and Ludlow. Pretzinger took Cox's order to heart, basing the new DDN building based on the roman-style temple design of the Knickerbocker Trust building in New York City.

On June 11, 1910, the new home of DDN was thrown open to the public. A 40-piece band played as James M. Cox, Jr., raised a flag over the building. At 11 a.m. President Taft pushed a telegraph key at the White House, sending an electrical current that started the big new color presses at DDN. That day's edition consisted of 210 pages. The 124 tons of paper used was nearly enough to stretch across the entire United States.

When the dedication ended at midnight, over 10,000 people had gone through the new building. Today, it remains one of the most unique structures in the Gem City.

June 12

In January, 1866, a petition came before the Montgomery County Commissioners, asking for the annexation of Miami City to Dayton. By 1866 the name Miami City had come to be generally used for the platted land west of the Great Miami River.

Residents of the West Side were torn on the issue. On the plus side was the fact that annexation would bring with it advantages, such as the construction of a levee that would help prevent the periodical overflow of Wolf Creek, improvement and grading of streets and sidewalks, the introduction of gas lights, steam fire engines for the fire department and a well-manned police force.

On the other hand, all of these amenities did come with a price, higher taxes. Quite a few of the homes on the West Side were individually owned. Most owners had been lured to living on the West Side by the low taxes. A majority of them were mechanics and day laborers. They claimed that, with what little wages they made, it was all they could do to pay the taxes already owed on their property. If they were required to pay additional taxes, it would result in the loss of their homes.

Despite their concerns, on June 12, 1868, the first annexation west of the Miami River occurred, with the new western boundary extending to King Street (later renamed Western Avenue and now James H. McGee Boulevard). Soon renumbering and changing of street names occurred. Walnut and Washington streets west of the Miami River became Fourth Street. Barnett Street, named for Senator Joseph Barnett, was changed to Fitch Street. Senator Barnett was well-known for his part in the Presidential campaign of General William H. Harrison in 1840. Gurley Street, named in honor of Rev. Phineas D. Gurley, was renamed Fifth Street. Rev. Gurley was chaplain of the First Presbyterian Church in Dayton from 1850 to 1854. He later became spiritual advisor to President Abraham Lincoln, and was with Lincoln when the president died

Of course, the greatest historic loss came with the renaming of King Street to Western Avenue in 1895. Today, William King, the man they called "King Dayton", who first settled the land west of the Miami River, and was more or less responsible for creating the legacy of the West Side, has no monument, no street, no river named in his memory.

June 13

It is said that a Harry Myers was caught speeding through Dayton in 1904 in his Winton automobile. Traveling at twelve miles an hour on West Third Street, Myers was issued by Dayton police the world's first paper ticket for speeding in an automobile. While not yet proven, research does indicate that Myers probably was given the ticket.

In its March 12, 1904 issue the *Dayton Daily News* reported that three magnificent Winton touring cars had just been received the day before by the Kiser & Co. auto dealership. The three buyers were James M. Cox, publisher of the *Dayton Daily News*; Edward Reynolds, of Reynolds & Reynolds, and Harry J. Myers, a well-known broker in Dayton.

Myers couldn't wait to drive his luxurious Winton and immediately took it out for a spin. What was it like to drive an automobile that could go up to 40 miles an hour? "As the giant car flies along in the face of the strongest wind the most delightful sensation in the world creeps over the passengers and the blood leaps in wild exhilaration". If he felt that way, it isn't too hard to believe that Myers may have allowed his automobile to creep up to twelve miles an hour… Even Edward Reynolds is described as having his chauffeur drive him "over the Dayton streets with the speed of the swallow…"

In 1952, the Dayton Division of Police began using "black box" radar to catch speeders. On June 13, 1952, Dayton's first radar speeding arrest was made by Patrolmen Harold Murphy and James Hopkins when they stopped a car traveling 45 miles an hour in front of Carillon Historical Park on South Patterson Blvd.

In the 1950s, an unmarked vehicle equipped with a black box radar would set up in a stationary location, such as on Plymouth Avenue to detect speeders rushing by on Grafton Avenue.

June 14

Because he had once worked as a sales clerk, Frederick Kohnle knew how monotonous it was to have to price merchandise. Tags were made on the spot, cut from pasteboard strips, marked by hand with pen and then attached to the merchandise with a string or wire. But many times the tags would fall off or become illegible when handled.

Kohnle designed a machine that would print a tag, make a wire formed pin, force it through the printed paper tag and attach it directly to the merchandise in one operation.

Some of the early machines were placed in downtown Dayton stores, including the Elder & Johnston Company and Traxlers. The machine led the way for Kohnle to establish his own business which would become the Monarch Marking System Company. Still, although retailers liked the table-top machine, it soon became apparent that a better design was needed. Kohnle went back to the drawing board, designing a floor-mounted, foot-treadle version for which he received Patent #762,322 on June 14, 1904.

The foot-treadle ticket machine was an immense improvement over the table-top versions, since it allowed the operator to use both hands in aligning the merchandise for tagging. Today, the Monarch brand is owned by Avery Dennison Corporation.

June 15

The United States entered into World War I after officially declaring war on Germany on April 6, 1917.

Battery D, 134th Field Artillery, 62nd Brigade, 37th Division, more commonly known as "Dayton's Own", was called to service on July 15, 1917. On that day, 193 young men camped at Triangle Park to begin training. Battery D remained there until August 23, when it was ordered to Montgomery, Alabama to continue training at Camp Sheridan. It was here that Pvt. Thomas Hawthorne, a soldier from Dayton, was killed by a stroke of lightning on February 14, 1918. The battery had been out on maneuvers on horses most of the day. When the lightning bolt hit, all 80 horses were thrown to the ground, seriously injuring two other men and killing six horses.

On July 15, 1918, exactly a year after being called for active duty, the soldiers of Battery D arrived at Le Havre, France. From there they went to Camp De Souge, where the soldiers were given extensive training in various army maneuvers. It was on August 24, 1918, that Cpl. John D. Puckett and Pvt. Clarence B. Click, both soldiers from Dayton, were killed when a shell in a field gun exploded prematurely because of a defective fuse. The two men were buried side by side near the camp.

In September, Battery D was ordered to the front. The soldiers took position at Revigny, an important railroad and manufacturing centers along the enemy front. They spent the rest of the war moving to new positions, fighting defensively in the Marbache and Pannes sectors and offensively at Bois-de-Bonseil and Meuse-Argonne. All of the men came through the battles unscathed.

After WWI ended, the battery eventually returned to Camp Sheridan, where they were mustered out on April 16, 1919.

In 1927, it was decided to replace an old bridge on Ridge Avenue, near Triangle Park. On November 11, 1928 the new bridge was dedicated to the soldiers of Battery D. The stone tablet, topped by an eagle, was engraved with the names of all the men from Montgomery County in the battery and a bronze plaque was attached to the bridge. A captured German gun was also placed at the end of the bridge nearest the park.

In 2015, the bridge was once again replaced. The old tablet, along with the German gun, were restored to their former glory and placed near the new bridge.

June 16

Around 1889, a photograph was taken of a number of students that were set to graduate from Central High School in 1890. Paul Laurence Dunbar and Orville Wright were among them. Dunbar was the only black member of the class.

Sometime after the graduation picture was taken, both Paul and Orville decided to quit school. Orville had begun publishing a weekly newspaper, the *West Side News*. He believed that it would lead to a life as a publisher, a field he was quite interested in. *(See March 1)*

By 1889, Paul had already published poems in the *Dayton Herald* and wanted to be a writer. He decided to drop out and publish *The Dayton Tattler*, which was aimed to promote the interests of African Americans. Orville and his brother, Wilbur, agreed to print the newspaper on credit.

"We published it as long as our financial resources permitted of it," Orville later recalled, "which was not for long." Only three issues of the *Tattler* were published.

Unlike Orville, Paul decided to go back and finish his education. He wrote the class song sung at his graduation at the Dayton Opera House on June 16, 1891.

Central High School Class of 1890. Paul Laurence Dunbar (back row, far left) and Orville Wright (back row, fourth from left). Neither men would graduate in 1890.

June 17

When Orville and Wilbur Wright flew for the first time in 1903, even their own home town of Dayton barely appeared to notice. But after the Wrights began receiving acclamations from countries such as England and France, citizens of the Gem City finally took notice and decided to commemorate the brothers triumph over gravity.

The two day celebration began under rainy skies on June 17, 1909. Main Street was decorated with bunting and flags. Columns with the figure of Lady Victory holding in one hand the world and the other a miniature airplane reminded those in attendance why they were there. After a series of speeches by dignitaries at Van Cleve Park, an exhibition parade and drill was held by the Dayton Fire Department, followed by a review of military troops. Next came a reception for Orville and Wilbur at the YMCA building. At dusk, spectators assembled along the Miami River were treated to a fireworks display.

The second day began at the Fairgrounds, where the brothers were presented with a number of National, State and City medals, including Congressional Medals. In the grandstands, children dressed in red, white and blue formed an American flag and sang *The Star Spangled Banner*.

Then came another parade, made up of Federal and State troops, various local civic and fraternal societies and school children, and ended with a large number of floats and automobiles illuminated with lights. The evening ended at Cooper Park, located behind the library on Third Street.

June 18

On June 18, 1910, the *Dayton Daily News* reported on a rival newspaper that had started publishing several months before. Called *The Junior News*, it was a weekly that consisted of four pages, with two columns. The newspaper was printed at 26 Lexington Avenue, home of one of the proprietors, Francis Burba.

But it was no ordinary staff that ran the paper. Francis happened to be 12 years old, and the son of George F. Burba, who was on the editorial staff of the *Dayton Daily News*. The reporter, 7-year-old James M. Cox, Jr., was the son of the owner of the *Dayton Daily News*. The boys had been given an old press and type set that could print one page at a time.

The newspaper proved to be popular in the Dayton View area, having over 400 subscribers. Even at the price of one cent, the boys were able to purchase a small pony and cart to use to deliver their product. The *Junior News* lasted about two years.

On August 9, 1913, brothers Ralph, Ross and Carl Kepler picked up the name and carried on the tradition. It was the first newspaper in Dayton to receive news by wireless, the boys having a ham radio at home through which they gathered information from Washington, D.C.

Unfortunately, America's entrance into World War I would bring a final end to the newspaper.

THE JUNIOR NEWS

PUBLICATION OFFICE, 26 LEXINGTON AVENUE,

VOL. 1   DAYTON, O., MAY, 28 1910.   NO. 17

NEW DEPOT.
For Traction Cars To Be Built.

Dayton is going to have a new union station for traction cars very soon and it is going to be a beauty. We do not know where it will be located but they are going to start to work on it this summer.

BASEBALL.
Dayton Has Been Playing Here.

The Dayton base ball club has been playing at home all the week when it didn't rain. They have been playing good ball but have had bad luck most of the time. As soon as the team gets to batting it will win the pennant.

June 19

The Children's Parade and Pet Show was held in South Park on June 19, 1958. Sponsored by the South Park Business Men's Association, the event began with a parade that started at the corner of Brown and Warren streets, then west on Stewart to Main Street, finishing up at the Montgomery County Fairgrounds, where the contestants assembled on the race track in front of the grandstand. The parade included a number of small hand-made floats, pets of all sizes and well-decorated doll buggies.

A number of contests were held, including "best decorated doll buggy", "boy with the most freckles", "best dressed doll", "boy with the reddest hair" and "best decorated float for boys".

Winners of the various contests were awarded prizes and a good time was had by all.

F. J. Hillgruber, NCR safety director, judged the float of Mrs. Robert Frier, whose husband also happened to work at NCR, as the best decorated float for boys. Hillgruber claimed that no outside influence was used in the judging.

June 20

Just a few miles north of downtown Dayton, where the Stillwater River flows into the Great Miami, was once a park called White City. Named after the White City Amusement Park Company who owned it, the park offered patrons dancing at the dance pavilion, canoe lockers, and amusement rides. Unfortunately, the flood of 1913 washed out the bridge that crossed the Miami River, cutting off access to the park and damaging a number of the buildings.

The city wasn't sure if the park was worth reopening. Then, on July 12, 1913 the Dayton Canoe Club, which was located across the river from the park, held their first regatta. Hundreds showed up to watch the events. Dayton's city officials decided to rebuild White City. After completion, it was agreed that the park needed a new name. When members of the Dayton Canoe Club suggested Island Park, it was enthusiastically received and the rest is history.

The new park opened on June 20, 1914, offering Daytonians a place to go boating, dancing, canoeing and swimming. In 1940, the WPA built a beautiful art deco bandshell, which was named after civic leader Leslie L. Diehl. Today, although most of the amenities of old are gone, the park provides a water-play area and gathering place for picnics and family fun.

As can be seen in this postcard from around 1914, Island Park was a very busy place during the summer. The large building in the background is the Dance Pavilion.

June 21

In 1905, the Dayton Rubber Manufacturing Company began producing garden hose and rubber fruit rings. Three years later the company would enter the tire manufacturing business by introducing the "Airless Tire" for automobiles. Although passengers suffered a bit of a bumpier ride, the invention eliminated the flat tires that had been a problem for automobiles traveling on roads built more for wagons pulled by horses.

Over the next few years, the company would extend its range, offering tires with white sidewalls in 1913, and the first low-pressure tire - the Dayton Thorobred Cord - in 1923. But it was their work in the field of synthetic rubber that really put the company on the map.

On June 21, 1934, the Dayton Rubber Manufacturing Co. announced that it had successfully created the first American tire made out of synthetic rubber. The rubber was made by DuPont using acetylene, which came from coal and limestone, ingredients easily obtained in the U.S., freeing up restrictions of rubber during wartime. However, the Great Depression caused a drop in the need for tires, so the product sat on the back burner.

When World War II began, huge synthetic rubber plants shot up almost overnight, and yet there was still a shortage of tires for public automobiles. Much of this was due to the military requiring tires for heavy-duty, large size truck, bus, artillery, and airplane tires, which required too much material to also allow tires for public use to be made. Instead, they had to rely on tires made of recycled rubber. *(See December 1)*

In 1960, the company's name was changed to DAYCO. The tire division of DAYCO was sold to Firestone Tire and Rubber Company in 1961.

Dayton Rubber Manufacturing Company associates examine the first synthetic rubber tires after an initial road test in 1934. The first road tests were held in secret in Arizona, Maryland and Ohio.

June 22

On June 22, 1927 Charles Lindbergh was flying back to St. Louis for the first time since he had returned from his famous flight across the Atlantic. While on his way, he detoured to Dayton to pay his respects to Orville Wright. Lindbergh landed the Spirit of St. Louis at Wright Field, where Orville and General William Gilmore were waiting.

It was estimated that over 50,000 people lined the streets of Dayton that led to Orville home in Oakwood, in hopes of trying to catch a glimpse of the famous flyer. Lindbergh, however, refused to allow the car to take him through the crowded route. Unfortunately, Lindbergh had promised his financial backers that he would make no public appearances before returning home. Orville understood the flyer's dilemma and the group went straight to Hawthorn Hill.

Determined to see the pilot, thousands of people made their way to Orville's home. Ivonette Wright Miller, Orville's niece, later recalled the commotion that occurred that evening.

"It was not a crowd but a mob, pushing and shoving, trampling the flower beds and bushes, climbing trees, all clamoring for a look at Lindberg... Finally, Orville Wright, more to save his house from ruin than to gratify the crowds, appealed to Lindbergh, and he made a brief appearance on a little balcony of the front portico, tall and boyish, with Orville Wright at his side. The crowd seemed satisfied and dispersed."

Orville Wright, Colonel John Curry and Charles Lindbergh at Wright Field.

June 23

In 1982, Bill Paule and his cat, Muddy Water White, were on a road trip from Dauphin, Pennsylvania to Colorado. While they were in Dayton on June 23, Muddy jumped out of the van. Of course, it was thought that the cat would never be seen again, but in fact the one-year-old black feline was just beginning his own road trip – one that would last three years and cover 450 miles.

On June 24, 1985, Barbara Paule, Bill's stepmother, saw a stray coming toward her home in Dauphin. "It was the most dilapidated cat you ever saw on four legs," said Barbara. "He dragged himself to the front yard like a dying soldier from the Civil War." Barbara fed the cat and, after wolfing down the food, it curled up in her lap.

After feeding him for several days, it dawned on her that the stray might be Muddy. She took him to the veterinarian, who removed 29 ticks that were embedded in the cat. The doctor looked at the now four-year-old cat and came to the same conclusion. His markings were the same, including a "very leatherly bottom lip that we always made fun of when he was little," said Barbara.

Muddy Water White would go on to live almost another four years, passing away on May 28, 1989.

Stories of dogs and cats finding their way home from great distances can be hard to believe, but there are too many documented cases of this happening, even if it takes the pets months or years. Holly, a four-year-old tortoiseshell cat, got lost during a family trip in Daytona Beach, Florida. The cat travelled 200 miles in two months and was found about a mile from its home. A microchip confirmed Holly's identity.

As remarkable as Muddy's story seems to be, there have been stories of cats who have travelled even further. The top winner is Sugar, a cream-colored, part-Persian. Sugar had a hip deformity and also had a fear of cars. When her owners moved 1,500 miles away to Gage, Oklahoma in 1951, they decided to leave the cat with a neighbor in Anderson. However, two weeks later, Sugar went missing. Fourteen months later, Sugar showed up at the family's new home in Gage - a place she had never been. There was no doubt that the cat was really Sugar, for she had an unusual bone deformity in her left hip, one that could easily be felt when the owners petted her.

June 24

In the wee hours of June 19, 1918, the conductors and motormen of the City Railway company, the Oakwood Street Railway company, the Peoples Railway company and the Dayton Street Railway company voted to strike when their demand for an increase in pay was turned down. The strike effectively stopped most of the passenger streetcars that ran in Dayton. The only exceptions were the D. & X., and the Ohio Electric company, which served the lines southeast and south sections of the city.

With transportation all but paralyzed, people could not get to work. This was especially crucial for industrial factories that were working full-speed to fill orders for war materials for the troops fighting overseas. City officials were petitioned to take over operation of the street cars, but the decision was made not to do so.

As the strike headed into its fifth day, Ohio Governor James M. Cox got involved. Cox stressed to the strikers that, while he agreed with their right to negotiate, he had taken an oath to protect lives and property, which he would uphold if he had to.

Whether it was due to the veiled threat, or Cox's promise to go before the National War Labor Board to make sure that the union members got their say, the strike officially came to an end on June 24, 1918.

By the second day of the strike, taxi drivers began gouging the public with excessive fares. Some people even slapped taxi signs on their automobiles to make money. This was soon met by more kind-hearted drivers giving rides to strangers if they were headed in the same direction.

June 25

In order to try and stop people from drinking alcohol, several groups, like the Anti-Saloon League, began spreading the rumor that beer was made of poison. In 1908, The Dayton Breweries Company, the amalgamation of several breweries in the city of Dayton, tried to counter this with a clever campaign.

On May 28, 1908 an ad appeared in several Dayton newspapers that invited readers to supply a name for a new "superior product" that was the best of its kind ever made anywhere in the country, yet it did not supply a description of the item to be named.

The following day, the ad cleared up the mystery, stating that The Dayton Breweries Company would pay $50 each for the first three names accepted for their newest "special brew bottle beer". It went on to describe how the beer was made of the choicest ingredients, like barley and corn, which was mashed and filtered in sanitary machinery, which eliminated any of the product being touched by human hands as the beer was made, aged and bottled. Contestants were given until June 6, to send in a name, along with a letter not to exceed 100 words, telling why they thought their suggested name should be chosen. The ads appeared several times throughout the week.

In order to extend the contest, the ad was changed to a list of names that had been sent in during the contest. Readers were asked to send in the name they thought the judges should chose and the reason why.

On June 25, 1908, the three judges (all of whom were associated with the newspapers who had profited by the ads), posted their final decision. The winner of the contest was Hazel Rauh, with her suggestion of the name "Lily Brew". The new beer was available for purchase a week later.

"The lily itself implies purity," Hazel Rauh wrote in her letter. *"Its name is a slogan of purity, with the purest water obtainable, combined with healthy cereals and hops, brewed by hygienic methods, produces the nourishing Lily Brew".*

June 26

When Paul Laurence Dunbar died on February 9, 1906, he was buried at Woodland Cemetery in a section near Wyoming Street. Within a week steps toward a permanent memorial were being taken. Personal letters were sent out to a number of prominent literary men who had recognized Dunbar's talent early on, asking them to be on an advisory committee, and the Dunbar Memorial Fund was established.

Although it took over three years, the new monument was finally unveiled at Woodland Cemetery on June 26, 1909. A colossal Miami Valley granite boulder with a bronze plaque by Tiffany was unveiled, with the first stanza of Dunbar's "A Death Song" inscribed on the plaque. A willow tree was planted nearby. The new cemetery plot, in Section 101, Lot 3465, was deeded to Paul's mother, Matilda.

The program included an invocation by Rev. G. A. Funkhouseer, a speech by President W. S. Scarborough of Wilberforce College, a prayer by Matilda, several songs by the Philharmonic Society and a benediction by Rev. E. W. B. Curry.

Paul Laurence Dunbar's body was exhumed from his old grave and reburied in its current location the same day as the dedication. When Matilda Dunbar passed away on February 24, 1934, she was laid to rest in the same lot as her beloved son.

It was hoped by the Memorial Fund committee that the dedication of the monument could be held on the poet's birthday, June 27, 1909, but since the date fell on a Sunday that year, it was decided to hold the unveiling on Saturday, June 26 instead.
The plaque is inscribed:

Paul Laurence Dunbar
1872   1906

Lay me down beneaf de willers in de grass,
Whah de branch'll go a-singin' as it pass
An' w'en I's a-layin' low,
I kin hyeah it as it go
Singin', "Sleep, my honey, tek yo' res' at las'."

June 27

On this day in 1916, William Henry Robertson was granted Patent #1,188,490 for a toy. But it was far more than just something for children to play with. When the monkey's feet were set to point at two numbers, its fingers would locate the answer. The deceptively simple device could be used to teach children how to multiply, divide, add and subtract.

Made by the Educational Novelty Company in Dayton, the 6" x 6" tin calculator was named "Consul the Educated Monkey", after a famous performing monkey who was taking the world by storm. The original Consul was a cigarette smoking star of stage and screen at the turn of the 20th century. He would eat with a knife and fork at a table, and ride a bicycle. A 1909 movie, *Consul Crosses the Atlantic*, featured Consul in his first trip to America. Consul would visit NCR the following year.

The patent was actually for the novel idea of using the image of an animal to act as a pointer. It would take another two years before Robertson would receive a patent for the calculating device itself, which he claimed provided "a quick and simple method of finding results on the chart by mechanical means, thereby relieving the eye of having to follow columns and of making mistakes by locating results at the wrong intersections".

June 28

In May, 1869, the General Conference of the United Brethren Church held a meeting in Lebanon, PA. Upon a motion by Rev. Milton Wright, a theology professor at Hartsville University in Indiana, the General Conference directed their newly-appointed board of education to establish a theological school. Rev. Wright served as first chairman of the executive committee of the seminary. The school was to be located in Dayton and at his proposal it was named Union Biblical Seminary.

At the same conference, Rev. Wright was elected to become the editor of the *Religious Telescope*, a paper published by the United Brethren Church that was "devoted to the religious, moral and literary intelligence". Although this was a very important decision, it also meant that Rev. Wright's family would have to move to Dayton, Ohio.

On June 28, 1869, Rev. Milton Wright wrote of his arrival in Dayton.

"Myself and family go, via Richmond, to Dayton, arriving before nine o'clock in the morning. We went to our house, corner of 3rd & Sprague Sts, unpacked and lived."

At the time the Wright family consisted of Milton, his wife Susan, and their sons Reuchlin, Lorin, and Wilbur. In November, 1869, the family moved to Second Street, between what is now Broadway Street and the railroad line. It was here that Susan gave birth to twins, Otis and Ida, on February 24, 1870. Unfortunately, both would die within a month.

When the family moved to their new home at 7 Hawthorn Street in early 1871, Susan was four months pregnant. On August 19, 1871, Orville was born in the upstairs front bedroom. On August 19, 1874, exactly three years later, Milton and Susan Wright welcomed their newly born daughter, Katharine.

In 1878, Bishop Milton Wright moved his family to Cedar Rapids, Iowa, after Milton was elected a Bishop in the United Brethren church and given responsibility for fifteen United Brethren conferences in the "West Mississippi District". They would remain gone from Dayton for eight years.

In June, 1884, the Wright family was finally able to return to Dayton. In 1903, two of the boys, Wilbur and Orville Wright, would achieve the first powered, sustained and controlled airplane flight. The rest, as they say, is history.

June 29

On June 29, 1909 the *Dayton Journal* celebrated its 101st anniversary by printing a newspaper in a hot air balloon. Called the *Hoosier*, the bag was equipped with a hand printing press. It was used to produce a small edition of the *Dayton Journal*, which was edited, type set and printed during the flight. As it soared over the towns copies of the paper were thrown to the ground. The stunt garnished a lot of press for the *Dayton Journal*, but it wasn't completely without risk.

The balloon left Dayton at 10 a.m. The crew consisted of Col. George McCleallan, publisher of the *Dayton Journal*; Dr. P. M. Crume, B. H. Wendler, F. G. Carley, Levitt Luzen Custer, and Howard L. Burba, who was a police reporter for the *Dayton Journal*.

The first edition was dropped over the Dayton Soldiers' Home without incident. The second edition was slated to be dropped in Butler County. When the balloon reached Wood's Station, eight miles east of Hamilton, copies were sent down telling of an exciting experience at Darrtown, four miles from Woods, where a farmer had fired at the balloon with his rifle.

The third edition was dropped over Butlerville, Indiana, just a little distance from where the balloon would finally land. As the balloon started to slowly descend, farmers tried to help by tying a drag rope to a peach tree, but the bag pulled the tree out of the ground instead. As the balloon continued its journey, the line trailed behind, catching on some telephone wires, and knocking out local telephone service.

As far as is known, these three "sky" editions are the only newspapers to have ever been printed in a balloon.

A man shows off the printing press used to print the newspapers during the trip.

June 30

"You're Wright when you smoke the Dayton Flyer Cigar", claims this cigar box label that shows a Wright brothers' airplane flying over Dayton.

The label's design was trademarked by Joseph Friedman on June 30, 1909. He manufactured cigars at 660 East Richard Street in Dayton. The trademark covered the image to be used to sell cigars, cigarettes and cheroots.

Friedman was no doubt inspired by the celebration held for Orville and Wilbur Wright in Dayton on June 17 & 18, 1909. It is unknown if the Wright's were asked for permission to use either their name or the image of their airplane as a means for Friedman to sell his cigars. Since the brothers didn't smoke, drink liquor or even use swear words, it is hard to imagine that this would have met with their approval.

Joseph Friedman registered the name and illustration of "The Dayton Flyer" with the U.S. Patent Office and The United Registration Bureau for the Tobacco Industries on June 30, 1909. He was granted Trademark No. 35408. The art work, shown above, was used as labels on cigar boxes. The cigars sold under the brand name were hand made and used quality tobacco from Havana, Cuba.

July 1

In 1948 Dayton drive-in theaters introduced moviegoers to a new form of entertainment. In addition to the movies being shown, they offered a game called Wahoo. Patrons were handed a Wahoo card at the ticket office, one for each occupant of the car, as they paid their entrance fee. Wahoo cards were similar in appearance to a bingo card.

After the first feature was over, a dial would appear on the movie screen. An arrow would be spun on the dial. The number pointed to would be called off. Patrons finding that number would punch out a perforation below it. To win, the numbers had to be in a straight row across or up and down or diagonally, just like conventional bingo. When someone would win he or she would beep the car horn twice. Prizes and money of various amounts were given, with jackpot payoffs sometimes reaching a thousand dollars or more. To win the jackpot a person had to Wahoo on the first five numbers called. If no one won, the jackpot grew.

On July 1, 1960 Mathias H. Heck, Montgomery County Prosecutor, ordered a crackdown on owners of drive-in theaters who continued to offer Wahoo to their customers. In a letter to the owners Heck wrote "...The sheriff of this county has been informed of our decision that the operation of this scheme of chance is in violation of these (gambling) statues and has been instructed to begin an enforcement program..."

The penalty for violating the law was a fine of not less than $50 nor more than $500, and imprisonment of not less than ten days nor more than six months. The playing of Wahoo at the drive-in came to an end, at least for a little while.

July 2

On July 2, 1932, the Dayton Association of Cooperative Production Units was formed to help Daytonians in need during the Great Depression help themselves. The idea was to place the unemployed into "production units" that would manufacture various goods. Unit members would work a set number of hours each week. In return, the bread, vegetables, or clothing the unit was producing would be distributed according to a member's need. What was left over would be bartered for items the unit did not produce.

The program started in "Tin Town", a black residential neighborhood near McCabe Park, south of Home Avenue and West of Dearborn Avenue. The residents there had suffered immensely from the depression. Almost everyone was on relief, with only one man in the community having a steady job. After a demonstration was held on how people could make clothing and soap and flour, several people were interested in trying the experiment. To help the group, the Community Chest lent the Production Units committee an initial $800 so that sewing machines and other needed equipment could be bought. The first production unit in Dayton was born.

The plan spread rapidly. Within thirty days there were six units in actual operation, varying in size from thirty to eighty families per unit. Most units were involved in more than one particular project. Within a month's time the various groups were making clothing, raising rabbits, gardening, making soap, comforters, brooms, baking bread, making furniture and mending shoes.

At the end of February, 1933, there were more than eight hundred families, or approximately four thousand people, in thirteen production units. In addition to local support, grants totaling over $45,000 were made by the Division of Self-Help Cooperatives of the Federal Emergency Relief Administration (FERA), created by newly-elected president, Franklin D. Roosevelt. The first grant was made in August 1933 and was one of the initials grants.

But it was becoming clear that production units were not the answer to the unemployment problem. One problem was that the families in the units had to have at least some money of their own to pay their rent, water and electricity bills, which meant the majority of them were still on some form of relief. The units were dissolved when it was learned in the fall of 1934 that no further funds would be available from the Federal government to help with the project.

July 3

In 1897, Orville and Wilbur Wright moved their Wright Cycle Co. to 1127 West Third Street. They used the profits from the sales of their bicycles to finance their aviation experiments. It was at this location that the brothers would design and construct their gliders and the first airplane, the Wright Flyer. They closed the shop in 1909 and started The Wright Company, and began manufacturing airplanes.

In 1936, Orville was invited by *Detroit News* aviation editor, James Piersol, to visit Greenfield Village, in Dearborn, Michigan to discuss with Henry Ford the possibility of moving the West Third shop there.

On July 3, 1936, Charles Webbert, sold the two-story structure to Piersol for $13,000, who then donated it to Ford's Edison Institute.

At the time of the sale, a barber shop occupied the space where the Wright's had their bicycle manufacturing plant and repair shop. The second floor, where they had labored over drawings of the Wright Flyer, contained several apartments. Once moved to Greenfield Village, Orville made several drawings of what the original interior looked like so that alterations made after the Wrights had moved out could be eliminated.

The Wright Bicycle Shop, as it is now known, is still a part of the village, as is the Wright home that once stood at 7 Hawthorn Street in Dayton. (*See October 27*)

Charlie Taylor, who was the Wright brothers mechanic, helped with restoring the interior of the building. He was able to find most of the original machine tools that had been used in the shop.

July 4

As a way to celebrate America's 200th Independence Day, David Black was commissioned to create a sculpture with an aviation theme that would serve as the gateway to the south end of Main Street downtown. After some feedback from the public, Black came up with a 150 foot long piece, which he called the Flyover.

The Flyover depicts the first powered flight made by Orville Wright at Kitty Hawk, North Carolina, on December 17, 1903. The steel tubing of the monument is 120 feet long (the length of the first flight) and the gentle curve traces Orville's known path through the sky that day.

The $415,000 memorial to flight stands on a grassy island in the middle of Main Street, between Fourth and Fifth streets.

The dedication of the Flyover took place on July 4, 1996. David Black was joined by Tom Crouch, who was Chairman of the Department of Aeronautics of the National Air and Space Museum at the Smithsonian Institution. Following the dedication, a parade was held, led by grand marshal Gary Sandy, formerly of Kettering, and best known for his role in the television series *WKRP in Cincinnati*. The headline act on the main stage was the Village People, followed by a concert by the Dayton Philharmonic Concert Band. The festivities concluded with a fireworks display on the riverfront.

July 5

The process of microencapsulation involves enclosing a liquid or solid compound into tiny capsules, where it is contained for later release.

Barrett K. Green, an inventor for NCR in Dayton, was the creator of this process. He used his invention to produce the first carbon-free typing paper on the market. Dubbed 'ncr' (no carbon required) paper, the paper contained microcapsules filled with a colorless fluid. Pressure from writing or typing caused the capsules to break open, which created a duplicate copy. This process was granted Patent #2,712,507 on July 5, 1955.

Other improvements and patents on the microencapsulation process quickly followed, as Green partnered with fellow NCR worker Lowell Schleicher. Scratch and sniff advertisements and greeting cards were next. When a person scratched the card, the capsules broke, releasing the enclosed perfume.

Another use is time-released medicine, which consists of a special capsule that slowly releases the medication through its shell, rather than all at once.

Eventually, the process was adapted for use in a number of other products, including detergents, baking mixes and the once popular mood ring.

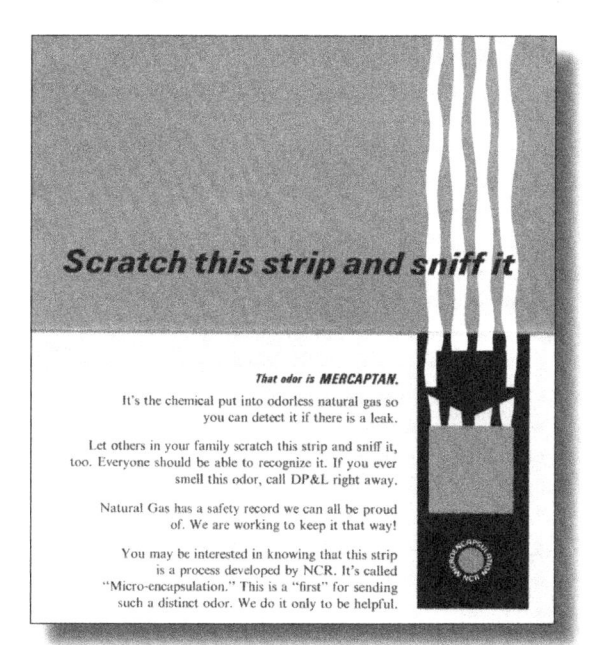

The first use of the scratch-and-sniff process was in cooperation with Dayton Power & Light Company. Cards were sent out that, when scratched, smelled of natural gas. This was used to help educate customers to recognize gas leaks.

July 6

On this day in 1897 a big fight was eagerly watched by a huge crowd in Dayton. It was one for the history books. The fight? It was of the James Corbett-Robert Fitzsimmons boxing match which had been held at Carson City on March 17, 1897.

The fight was a grand success. "I consider that I have witnessed today the greatest fight with gloves that was ever held in this or any other country," claimed Wyatt Earp who had attended the original event.

Although Fitzsimmons had won in the 14th round after delivering a staggering blow to Corbett's chest, some of the spectators had claimed that as Corbett collapsed Fitzsimmons also delivered a blow to his opponent's jaw. If this were so, some of them argued, Fitzsimmons should have lost the fight due to the late foul blow. Fans were eager to watch the film and judge for themselves who the real winner was.

Dayton citizens flocked to the Grand Opera House on July 6, 1897, to watch the fight on film. Unfortunately, only four of the rounds were able to be shown the first night due to the projector breaking down. Col. Billy Thompson, the promoter of the film, apologized and vowed he would remain in Dayton and give a perfect show even if it took all summer. Luckily, it didn't take that long. The show went off perfectly the following night. This would be the first film shown at the Grand - which today is known as the Victoria Theatre.

The Grand Opera House circa 1897

July 7

The month of June, 1911, was one of the hottest on record in Dayton. Still, the temperature was bearable. But that wouldn't last.

When July began, it was as if a blast furnace had been turned on somewhere. In a time without air conditioning, ice was the answer for cooling off. Ninety percent of the families in Dayton began doubling their orders for ice, partly for relief from the heat, and partly for use on the 4th of July. But the ice companies were running out and their horses were exhausted from pulling the wagons through the heat.

The horses weren't the only ones suffering. Factories were told to ease up as the daily temperatures rose in the 90s. After one of their workers collapsed on July 3, Reynolds and Reynolds closed their factory. Others soon succumbed, with a number taken to the hospital. At least two people died from heat stroke.

On July 4, the city folk made a mass exodus to the woods and rivers in an effort to cool off. Unfortunately, a man died from injuries caused by diving into shallow water and a woman drowned in the Miami River.

As the heat rose, the level of the river dropped, causing a shortage of water in the city. By the evening of July 6, many residents were left without water. Police began patrolling the streets to make sure that no one was wasting water by sprinkling their lawns. The owners were warned that any violation would result in their water being turned off.

In desperation, on July 7, the city makes an agreement with the owners of Bimm Dayton Ice and Cold Water Supply to lease their lake for $5,000 a year. Located on Ottawa Street, the 20 acre lake contained water from the hydraulic canal. The lake's gravel bed acted as a natural filter. Within two days it was estimated that between 5 to 10 millions gallons of water had been channeled into the wells of the city. The water crisis was over.

As for the heat, it continued unabated until July 9, when a shower brought the temperature down to a cool 85 degrees. It then rose again until July 11, when a violent storm ripped thought the Miami Valley. Corn stalks were blown over, lightning caused several structures to burn, and some lower lands were flooded. When it reached Dayton, the storm rained down hail the size of marbles. The temperature dropped from 85 to 65 degrees as the wind whipped through the city at 63 miles an hour.

Luckily, the storm signalled the end of the heat wave - at least for that year.

July 8

The first "pumpers" used to put out fires in Dayton were pumped by hand, which meant that the water sometimes did not shoot out with enough power to reach the heart of some of the bigger fires. In 1863, the first pumper that used steam as its power source was bought. It was too heavy to be hauled by man power, and horses were used instead.

About fifty years later, the Dayton Fire Department began testing motorized equipment. It didn't take long to see that, in many instances, by the time the horses would arrive to a fire, other fire fighters using gasoline powered equipment had already put out the flames. It was soon agreed that the entire force be motorized as quickly as the apparatus could be made and delivered.

On July 8, 1917, *Dayton Daily News* reported that the last two fire horses, "Hans Wagner" and "Ty Cobb", were being put out to pasture. Fire Engine House No. 14, on Main Street and Forest Avenue, was the last to modernize their fire-fighting equipment. Horse-drawn fire apparatus was a thing of the past.

Ty Cobb got his name from his sliding ability, while Hans Wagner was given his name when used in the police patrol wagon service because of his speed. Both horses were well-loved and considered among the best ever used in city service.

July 9

During WWII, keeping up morale was important, and that included civilians as well as soldiers. The Memphis Belle was one of the first B-17 United States Army Air Forces heavy bombers to complete 25 combat missions with her crew intact. The aircraft and crew then returned to the United States to sell war bonds. The ten-men crew of the Memphis Belle visited Dayton July 9-10, 1943. The stop-over included a speech at NCR, where the crew drew cheers as they spoke of how the employees were their "team mates" in the war effort.

Major General Lester T. Miller also addressed NCR workers as "Fellow American Soldiers."

"I call you soldiers," he said, "because whether you are in uniform or not, you are doing an important job. You have made possible by your persistent effort, everything that we soldiers in uniform do. You help to make the things that are needed to wage the war against the enemy. And these fine young men are typical of the other parts of the team, the part that uses all of the things you make."

More than 2,500 NCR employees who worked on air craft production jammed the NCR auditorium to see the crew of the Memphis Belle. The crew was joined on stage by the War Production Planning Committee, as well as NCR executives.

July 10

Bott's Studio, at 319 West Third Street, was the place to learn dancing from 1913 to 1949. However, the owner, Fenton T. Bott, was very particular as to what sort of dancing and music should be allowed in public. And one sort especially riled him... Jazz!

On July 10, 1920 Bott declared to a reporter from the *Dayton Daily News* that conditions at the Island Park dance hall was "the worst in the country", largely due to the "shimmy" music being played there. He claimed that the slow, sensuous character of the music encouraged the dancers to make suggestive movements. "If Triangle or Lakeside parks permitted the type of dancing tolerated at Island Park, the authorities would close them," Bott stated.

Some of the "moves" he wanted eliminated included: Tight holding, neck holds, "parking" of cheeks against each other, exceptionally long or short steps and, worst of all, dancing from the waist up.

Bott went on to say that he would soon make an appeal to music publishers, composers, theatrical managers and record companies to improve the "rhythm" of the music they sold. It was also his hope that public opinion would force the city officials to put a stop to any dancers who made "suggestive movements" on the dance floor. The American National Association of Masters of Dancing, of which Bott was serving as president at the time, was printing a manual of dance etiquette that was going to be distributed in all dance halls, studios and academies both the United States and Canada, which he hoped would go a long way toward bringing about dance reform.

Although a week later Mrs. Dewitt, a policewoman, declared that the quality of both the music and the dancing had much improved at Island Park, Bott was not satisfied, since the record companies didn't seem to want to heed his advice about getting rid of, or at least modifying, the type of jazz music they offered. A year later, he was still complaining to anyone who would listen.

"Jazz dancing is a worse evil than the saloon used to be!" he stated in a *Ladies Home Journal* article that appeared in its December, 1921 issue. "It is degrading. It lowers all the moral standards. Those moaning saxophones and the rest of the instruments with their broken, jerky rhythm make a purely sensual appeal. They call out the low and rowdy instinct... and the consequences are almost too obvious to be detailed."

July 11

The Dayton National Cemetery was established in 1867 as a place to inter veterans who died at the Central Branch of the National Military Home for Disabled Volunteer Soldiers, known today as the Dayton VA Medical Center. Records of the Dayton National Cemetery state that the first interment there took place on September 11, 1867 for Cornelius Solly, a veteran of the Civil War. While this is correct, Cornelius is not the first soldier to be buried on the grounds.

In 1800 Henry and Eva Kinsey moved from Virginia to Ohio and took up a section of land of six hundred and forty acres. They left behind their daughter, Hannah, who was married to Jacob Wolf. Hannah's parents wrote that if the couple would be willing to move to Ohio they would give them land.

In 1805, Jacob and Hannah came to the Dayton area, building their log home and barn on land where the Central Branch would later be located.

Jacob Wolf served in the War of 1812 as a Teamster, a Wagon Master and a Quarter Master and was honorably discharged on or about the 30th day of June 1812.

Jacob died on July 11, 1849 and was buried near where the Central Branch would later build a lodge for the person responsible for taking care of deer at the home. Unfortunately, the exact location of Jacob and Hannah's graves have been lost in time, having last been seen in 1940.

A postcard showing the Deer Park and the deer keeper's ivy-covered lodge.

July 12

A depression occurred in 1893 that was the worst in U.S. history up to that time. By the end of that year over 4,000 banks had closed. Over fifty railroads went under and, since this industry was one of the nation's largest, this also caused over fourteen thousand businesses to collapse. Unemployment climbed to 20 percent by 1894, with close to 2.5 million people looking for work.

In an effort to help local families in need of aid, Dayton businessmen came together and held a "Charity Circus". Practically every civic and fraternal organization in Dayton also had a part in the pageant.

The event began with a parade several miles long, with the Columbus and Metropolitan bands, followed by Company I, Third Infantry of the Ohio National Guard. Close behind then were the Knights of St. John and several other bands. Several cages of wild animals, floats, prancing ponies and even dancing girls were part of the parade. It was estimated that over 100,000 people lined the streets to watch.

The parade finished at the fairgrounds, where a big top tent had been set up with two rings and a stage area. The Dayton Turngemeinde showed off their athletic abilities, more music was performed, a troupe of clowns livened the show, as did a mule who performed tricks.

One of the main entertainments was the sideshow tent, which had Hoochy-koochy belly dancers outside the entrance, swaying to Hindu music to entice customers. Inside exhibits included, Professor Gwindle, the human pin cushion, who had innumerable pins protruding through his nose, ears and other parts of his body; Professor Cross, who ate meals made entirely of glass; William Owens, the Zulu king, with rings in his nose and ears; and a strong man who lifted weights with his jaw.

In the end, an accounting showed expenditures of almost $3,000 in staging the event. But ticket boxes were crammed with receipts from the various box offices, and the newspapers announced the next day that the Charity Circus had cleared more than $5,000.

July 13

When L. Frank Baum, the author of *The Wizard of Oz*, died in 1919, twelve-year-old Jack Snow offered to take Baum's place writing the series. Although turned down at first, Snow would eventually write two Oz books: *The Magical Mimics in Oz* (1946) and *The Shaggy Man of Oz* (1949), as well as *Who's Who in Oz* (1954), a guide to the Oz characters.

A longtime radioman, Snow also coined the name of WING radio, in honor of Dayton's aviation history.

After his death on July 13, 1956 Snow's address book of Oz fans was used to create the charter members of a group now known as "The International Wizard of Oz Club", which today has hundreds of members around the world.

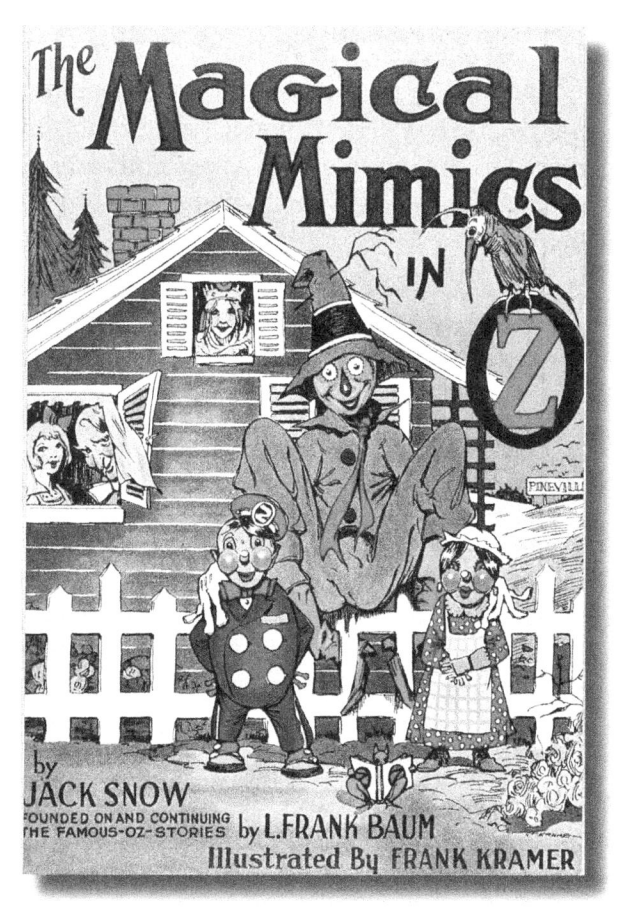

It is rumored that Snow also wrote an unpublished book entitled Over the Rainbow to Oz, but no manuscript has ever been discovered to confirm this.

July 14

St. Henry's cemetery, which opened in 1844, was located opposite the Montgomery County Fairgrounds, bounded by Main, Frank, Ashley, and Rubicon Streets. In the late 1860s, trustees of the cemetery had run out of funds for maintenance and the fence around the cemetery was rotting away. In 1889 plans were made to move the graves from the site to Calvary Cemetery and to sell the former cemetery property. Many of those who had relatives buried in St. Henry's did not want to move their remains.

On March 11, 1891 the trustees filed a petition to allow the sale of the property. The case dragged on for years, resulting in much litigation, one branch of the case going as far as the Supreme Court, where the trustees won it.

Finally, on July 14, 1900, Judge Alvin W. Kumler approved an order for the land to be divided into 36 lots and sold, with those buried there to be moved to Calvary Cemetery. Unfortunately, some of the graves could no longer be identified from their markers. A stone mortuary chapel was erected at Calvary on a lot donated for the four thousand and thirteen unclaimed remains.

St. Henry's Chapel was dedicated on All Souls Day, November 1, 1902.

July 15

Dayton's first daytime air raid drill was held on July 15, 1943. The test, lasting 56 minutes, was deemed to be fairly successful, even though it was reported that five cities in the county-wide defense area never received the signal to take shelter. Nearly 10,000 emergency corps members in the city and county reported to their posts. Approximately 500 women air raid wardens, on duty for the first time, went to their stations.

There was, however, cause for concern, according to Dayton officials. Some local air raid wardens had reported that pedestrians in some sections of the city had continued walking and children had continued playing on streets and yards even after the signal to seek shelter was given.

About a month after the drill, Mrs. Joseph Cates of Dayton found a letter in her mailbox from the Office of Civilian Defense addressed to her 9-year-old daughter, Diane. A similar letter reached the home of Mrs. Richard Thorpe, addressed to her 11-year-old daughter, Phyllis Ann. It seems the two girls were so disappointed with the results of the unsuccessful air raid drill, they had written President Franklin D. Roosevelt, suggesting that American planes "bomb" American cities with false bombs to increase war consciousness.

James M. Landis, the Office of Civilian Defense's director at the time, replied that while their interest in the problem was sincerely appreciated, the method they suggested "...would not be in keeping with one of the guiding principles that has made America a strong and united nation- the principle that our people shall be given facts, uncolored by propaganda or deception, and permitted to decide any issues for themselves on the basis of those facts. Only by adhering to this principle can any nation be certain of full, intelligent, and lasting co-operation on the part of its people. To deceive them in any way, whatever the motive may be, inevitably results in the loss of a priceless national asset - the confidence of the people in the sincerity and integrity of their government."

The mothers, who knew nothing about the letter their daughters had sent, weren't the only ones surprised. The two girls themselves admitted that they had never expected a reply back.

July 16

On July 16, 1902, the City of Dayton awarded a contract to H. E. Talbott & Company for the construction of a reinforced concrete bridge across the Great Miami River at Main Street, replacing the old steel bridge that had stood for nearly a half-century.

It was because of electric streetcars that Dayton chose to build a concrete bridge. When it was found that the city's steel bridges could not support the weight of the cars, an ordinance was passed that required the streetcar companies to pay one-third of the cost of the new bridge.

Talbott agreed to build the bridge for $128,900 and have it completed by December 15, 1902, but a combination of high water, rain and difficulty in finding men to work on the bridge raised the final price to $160,000 and added six months to the project.

On July 22, 1903, the new Main Street Bridge was officially opened to the public. As was normal for the times, a large parade was held and several speeches were given in praise of the magnificent new bridge.

The Main Street Bridge consisted of seven spans, with the length being 588 feet and the width 54 feet. Besides being one of the first concrete bridges built in the United States, the Main Street Bridge was also said to be the longest in the world. This record was soon broken when the Third Street Bridge in Dayton was completed in 1905, it's length being 710 feet and the width 42 feet.

DAYTON, Ohio.   The New Main St. Bridge.

July 17

On July 17, 1866, Benjamin Franklin Ells would be granted Patent 56390A for his unique idea on preserving fruit in a can. But it is the man, not his patent, that was unusual. Ells settled in Dayton about 1835 and began publishing books. The subject matter of his publications included historical, biographical, and devotional books. He also published a number of small pamphlets, known as "penny books", which covered a variety of topics, most of which sold for a penny or two. Some of the material probably wouldn't please today's parents. One such song in "The Juvenile Songster" titled "The Cow" includes the line: "And when she's dead, her flesh is good, For beef is quite nutritious food".

Although his name appeared as either editor or author on many of the title pages, Ells had the tendency to plagiarize a little, taking snippets from other publications and compiling them into a new book, or republishing them in whole without permission of the authors. It was so bad that a biographer on Ells once wrote, "It is difficult to decide whether to list him as an author, an editor, a compiler, an artist with scissors and paste, a publisher or a promoter".

Besides books, Ells also sold patent medicines. These included a miracle drug that had "effected a marvellouse cure of Emeline Yeager", who had consumption. The elixir sold at six bottles for $5, while his books brought 19 to 75 cents. It isn't difficult to see where the business profit was probably coming from.

Perhaps if he had stuck to books and patent medicines Ells might have led a simple, but happy, life. Unfortunately, he decided to go a different route. During the 1850s there was a flurry of dealing in real estate on the West Side, in which Ells engaged in buying and subdividing land. This venture did not work well, as there were not yet enough people wanting to build homes in the area. In 1863 and 1864, there were numerous court sales of Ells' various land holdings and printing equipment.

Still, Ells was left with some money and so turned his attention next to inventing. In 1865, he patented a machine for making bags. The following year he was granted the patent for his fruit can. Neither would bring the inventor a red cent.

Ells would die suddenly during church services on January 11, 1874. The record of his personal property is a sad one. By the time of his death, patent ventures had eaten up what little money Ells had left, leaving only $4.72 to turn over to the heirs.

July 18

In 1876 Nelson Driggs and James Guyon were part of a gang of counterfeiters in Illinois. Driggs was arrested and served eleven years. Guyon escaped, taking with him counterfeit plates and $40,000 in fake cash.

After serving his time, Driggs came to Dayton and began running the United States Hotel, a gambling roadhouse at 3124 Home Avenue. It proved to be quite popular with the men from Soldiers' Home, with a trolley car depositing the ex-soldiers directly from the Home's grounds.

In March 1889, having heard that some of the counterfeit money was circulating and that Driggs was the middle man for the sale of the money, John S. Bell, Chief of the Secret Service, came to Dayton to try and catch Guyon. Pretending to be an attorney, Bell began visiting the hotel and soon became friends with Driggs. He eventually broached the subject of counterfeit money to Driggs, who offered to get $40,000 for him.

While Driggs was going to collect the money in Cincinnati, Bell called in Detective Denello to assist him. When Driggs returned he only had $10,000 on him, saying that Guyon would come later that night with the rest of the money. Guyon did show up and Driggs gave Bell an additional $21,000. Driggs was then placed under arrest and guarded in his room.

The next morning, July 18, 1889, the decision was made to try and capture Guyon as well, who was thought to still be hiding out in the nearby woods waiting for his part of the payment for the counterfeit money. Bell, who had called in five more secret service officers, had three of the men search through a nearby wooded lot. Although Guyon was indeed hiding in the woods, the men passed by without seeing him. He hadn't gone far when he was spotted.

The agents began firing at Guyon, who hid behind a tree and returned fire. It was later estimated that at least 40 shots flew through the air during the ensuing gun battle. Detective Denello caught a bullet, which went through his right ear and glanced over his scalp.

Guyon quickly retreated and got away, although one of the agents claimed to have wounded him. Driggs was acquitted of charges and led an uneventful life from then on. He died December 18, 1895 at his home in Dayton. The fate of Guyon is unknown, although a report in the May 4, 1895 issue of *The Illustrated American* magazine laments the fact that he had "cost the Treasury thousands of dollars, yet he is a free-man today", due mostly for the Secret Service's desire to make sure they would get the plates as well as the counterfeiter during an arrest.

July 19

In 1946, Wallace Monschke was making ends meet by working at Wright Field during the day and a root beer stand in Springfield, Ohio at night. After talking it over with his wife, Virginia, the couple decided to open their own food stand. They borrowed everything they could, and on his vacation from the Field in May 1946, Wallace and two carpenters built the first Parkmoor restaurant at 2801 Linden Avenue.

On July 19, 1946 Virginia picked up Wallace at Wright Field and the two of them rushed to the restaurant for opening day. Everything had been prepared beforehand. The ice cream had been made using a second-hand freezer. Barbecue sandwiches and hot dogs were at the ready, as was popcorn that had been made in an antique corn popper they had bought second hand. Because of the sugar rationing they were only serving orange and root beer drinks.

Business was slow, the restaurant bringing in only $42.00 that first night. An early cold spell in October forced the Monschke's to close, due to there not being any heat in the restaurant, except from the two-burner hot plate they used for cooking.

Fortunately, business improved. Soon customers were flocking to Parkmoor for a taste of its "Dixie Golden Fried Chicken."

The first Parkmoor as it looked in 1946. Between 1946 and 1961, Parkmoor would open sixteen restaurants in the Dayton area. However, the popularity of the restaurant waned during the 1970s, the last Parkmoor closing in the 1980s.

July 20

The Masonic lodge, and the first fraternal organization in Dayton, was St. John's Lodge No. 13, the charter of which was granted by the state Grand Lodge at Chillicothe, OH on January 10, 1812. The lodge members met at a number of places over the years, until a Lutheran church located on Main Street, between Fourth and Fifth streets, was bought by the Masonic Temple Association on January 9, 1905 for $126,000.

The church was only a stopgap for a membership that was growing by leaps and bounds. In 1925, a building site for a new temple was chosen. The site was a four-acre tract located at Riverview Avenue and Belmont Park. The land was presented to the Masonic fraternity by the Ancient and Accepted Order of Scottish Rite of Dayton, one of the 14 Masonic bodies who were going to occupy the new structure.

The temple was a massive undertaking. The $2,250,000 construction contract was awarded to H. R. Blagg Co., who was already busy building the new Masonic Temple in Springfield, Ohio. On July 20, 1925, Henry Coleman, President of the Masonic Temple Association, operated the steam derrick which lifted the first shovel of ground from the site. Attorney Charles D. Heald gave a speech in which he urged respect for the principles of harmony and tolerance as set forth by the Masonic order.

The Masonic Temple took 450 workmen two years and nine months to construct, the temple opening on April 1, 1928.

Now called the Dayton Masonic Center, the building's construction includes Bedford stone and hard limestone and marble from Vermont, Alabama and Tennessee. It is estimated that it would cost $30 million to rebuild today.

July 21

Daytonians were supposedly so overjoyed with the beautiful Union Station that they danced during its dedication on July 21, 1900. The new depot, located at Sixth and Ludlow streets, included a clock tower, a portico along Ludlow Street, five station tracks and three station platforms.

The decorations of the station were lavish, with flags flying, Chinese lanterns and colorful lights sparkling, and the massive columns wrapped in blue and white. Entertainment included a variety of band concerts, dancing, refreshments and, of course, speeches by a number of railroad men singing the praises of the new station. E. M. Thresher's recollection of how the first Cincinnati, Hamilton, and Dayton Railway Company locomotive came to Dayton in 1851 was especially well received.

All agreed at the end of the day that Union Station was the best evidence that Dayton was a cultured and sophisticated metropolis.

As time passed, Union Station began to deteriorate while passenger trains steadily declined. Most of the building and its clock tower was demolished during a renovation in 1964. In 1971 Amtrak took over the route and passenger trains were no longer serviced after 1979. The depot was vacated in 1986 and what little remained was demolished in 1989.

July 22

In 1775, Colonel Robert Patterson built what may have been the first log cabin in Lexington, Kentucky. His grandson, John H. Patterson, of NCR fame, bought the cabin in 1901 and moved it to Dayton.

The pieces lay at the corner of Far Hills and Oakwood Avenue for three years. Once the foundation stones were accidently used in building a roadway and had to be taken out again. It was finally decided to erect it on a tiny triangle piece of land at the intersection of Main and Brown streets. When rebuilt, only hand tools were used and much of the timber used to replace some of the rotted logs came from the land where the cabin had originally stood.

On July 22, 1905, John H. Patterson invited a number of guests to what he called a "garden party" at Far Hills. The guest list included all of NCR's employees and their families, as well as others who had welcomed Patterson when he returned to Dayton from a world tour three weeks before. In the end, over 10,000 people were treated to live concerts and a dinner. Robert Patterson's little log cabin was also opened to the public for the first time that day.

Robert Patterson's log cabin still stands today. It may be found on the campus of Transylvania University in downtown Lexington, where it was moved to in 1939.

July 23

By 1932, with the end of the Great Depression nowhere in sight and the city and charities running low on money to help the poor, a number of proposals were made to try and help people become more self reliant.

One idea was that an "exchange store" should be opened; working under the principle of exchanging goods or labor among people, without any money being involved. Instead, this barter system would use certificates that could only be used in the store. For instance, a farmer could bring in vegetables and other produce and would be given certificates, instead of money. He could then use the certificates to buy clothing or other items in the store. This idea appealed to several Dayton businessmen, including Charles F. Kettering and Adam Schantz III, and so on July 23, 1932 the Dayton Mutual Exchange was born.

Activities included exchanges with local farmers, manufacturers and merchants for their surplus goods and produce in return for certificates. In time, some of the local manufacturers began giving the certificates they received to their employee's as part of their wages. The employees would then in turn redeem them for goods at the exchange. Even some dentists, doctors and lawyers began accepting the certificates.

Unfortunately it ended when the National Recovery Administration (NRA) was formed to create codes of fair practices and set prices. One of the codes prohibited paying wages with scrip certificates. This soon led to the closing of the Exchange.

Amount 25 Cents   N⁰ 39

GOODS CERTIFICATE

This will be accepted at the value above stated in exchange for our goods as listed. It will not be redeemed in money.

DAYTON MUTUAL EXCHANGE
(*Signed*) *Walter S. Carr, Treas.*

per..
Authorized Agent

July 24

Roger Payne, Cambridge University graduate and the "world's most educated hobo", arrived in Dayton on July 24, 1920 while on a tramp across the country. The "hobo philosopher", as Payne called himself, explained how he decided to chuck it all away in 1915, after suffering a breakdown from overworking as a building contractor. He began jumping trains, riding in boxcars and sleeping under porches in a sleeping bag. He carried simple cooking gear and got used to living on less than 50 cents a day.

Payne supported himself by selling pamphlets and lecturing on how the majority of mankind was spending too much time struggling for food and shelter. A socialist, Payne advocated that, if people worked together and were not competitive, then the time spent working could be cut considerably.

During the last years of his life, Payne peddled *The Bowery News* in Manhattan whenever he ran low on money. The publication ran poetry, stories, cartoons, photos, and news from the hobo community.

Despite his lifestyle, Payne was still healthy at the age of 81, when he was struck by a taxi. He remained unconscious for several days before dying on February 23, 1955. His body lay unclaimed for a time, but was eventually buried at Cedar Grove Cemetery in Flushing, New York.

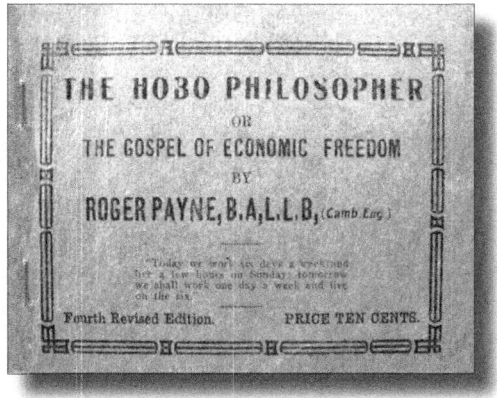

Left: Roger Payne with his walking gear
Above: One of Payne's earlier editions of his pamphlet, with his philosophy on the cover: "Today we work six days a week and live a few hours on Sunday; tomorrow we shall work one day a week and live on the six."

July 25

Billed as "The Greatest Show on Earth", the Ringling Bros. and Barnum & Bailey Combined Shows performed in Dayton for the first time on this date in 1919. The new name was given to the circus extravaganza when Barnum & Bailey's Greatest Show on Earth merged with the Ringling Bros. World's Greatest Shows earlier that year.

Among the many offerings at the circus was an act that comprised of "a quarter of a million pounds of elephants", with some forming a pyramid while others stood on their back legs in a line along the entire length of the hippodrome track. Another popular act number consisted of fifty pigeons, twelve white collies, six fox terriers, two Angora cats and a milk-white stallion by the name of Sir Gallihad. The group would end their act with Sir Gallihad pulling a chariot along a track, with the doves perched at regular intervals along his back and harness, the collies riding in the chariot and the terriers risking life and paws running in and out between the wheel spokes and between Gallihad's legs.

The circus clowns that performed that day included two Dayton boys, Walter and Paul Jung. Their parents had an acrobatic act in vaudeville, and the boys performed with them at a young age. Paul Jung would later appear on boxes and ads for Kellogg's Sugar Smacks in the 1950s.

Crowds gather to see the various side shows presented by Ringling Bros. and Barnum & Bailey in Dayton on June 6, 1940. Attractions included the Leopard People, thin man "Shadow" Rogers, and tattooed lady Betty Broadbent.

July 26

On July 26, 1894 the Montgomery County Fairgrounds was inundated with people, all eager to see the greatest show on earth – the Barnum & Bailey Circus. One of the reasons for the excitement was Chiko, a giant chimpanzee from Portugal who stood five feet three inches tall and weighed 142 pounds. Captured in Africa at the age of about a year and a half, he had originally been kept at the Zoological Gardens in Lisbon. He was brought to America in 1893 when he was about nine years old. Before long Chiko became such a star attraction for the circus that Mr. Bailey had once been offered $10,000 for him. Bailey turned the offer down, stating that the chimpanzee was worth over $50,000 in gate receipts to the circus.

Unfortunately, at the end of the last performance that night, Chiko died. The cause was thought to be dysentery, induced by the hot days and cool nights. The circus owners called on O. P. Boyer, a well-known funeral director in Dayton, with a strange request. They wanted Chiko's body embalmed. Boyer agreed to the unusual task. After the body was prepared, it was shipped to the Museum of Natural History in New York, where it was later mounted and placed on display.

This Barnum & Bailey poster also shows Johanna, a female chimpanzee, who had been bought by the circus in 1893 to be a companion to Chiko.

July 27

On July 27, 1911 ground was broken for a new building at NCR. Located at 1350 South Main Street, the NCR Hall of Industrial Education was built to hold conventions of the company's salesmen and sales agents. Each work afternoon, employees were entertained by educational motion pictures, or programs including musical numbers and interesting lectures. An addition was put on the building in 1913, which included the distinctive 30-foot columns in front. A third addition in 1922 expanded the seating capacity from 1,200 to 2,274. The structure was renamed the NCR Schoolhouse in 1932 and then the NCR Auditorium in 1938.

In the 1920's NCR began holding 'children's meetings'. Thousands of children spent many a Saturday morning there watching movies. Another tradition was the party held the Saturday morning before Christmas. Children would be given a bag of hardtack candy and a silver dollar.

By the 1970's, usage of the Auditorium had declined. NCR attempted to find someone to take over the building, even offering to donate it to various community organizations. However, the building was located next to the NCR power house and all of the utilities, including steam and electricity, came from there. Without the power house, which was torn down by NCR, the building would have to be rewired and the plumbing changed. It was estimated that the renovation would cost a minimum of $2 million, a price no one was willing to pay, even if the building was given to them for free. The NCR Schoolhouse was razed in 1980.

July 28

On July 6, 1838, an organized camp of more than 500 members of The Church of Jesus Christ of Latter-day Saints (Mormons) began making their way from Kirtland, Ohio to Far West, Missouri, a distance of 870 miles. The migrants were fleeing from religious persecution and seeking new homes and religious freedom. Known as Kirtland Camp, the train of 59 covered wagons and 189 head of livestock stretched a distance of nine miles.

On July 28, the group had spent nearly all of their money already, yet still had over 600 miles to reach their final destination. They decided to set up a semi-permanent encampment in a beautiful grove owned by W. Huffman, along the Mad River, near what is now Huffman MetroPark.

While there, several of the men took jobs building a segment of a turnpike between Dayton and Springfield. Others worked at various jobs in the Dayton area, building dykes and levees. The turnpike project lasted nearly the entire month of August and paid them one thousand two hundred dollars.

The Mormons resumed their trek on August 29, 1838. Unfortunately, a number of the members were sick during the encampment, including five children who died and were buried along the river.

On October 4, 1838, Kirtland Camp reached its final destination of Far West, Missouri.

On July 27, 2013 hundreds of people, including twenty-five descendants of members of the Kirtland Camp, attended the unveiling of the Mormon Migration, Kirtland Camp marker placed at Huffman Five Rivers Metropark by the Ohio Historical Society. The marker commemorates the 175th anniversary of the Kirtland Camp's encampment along the Mad River and their contributions to the city of Dayton, Ohio.

July 29

After WWII Daytonians began putting up plaques and monuments to honor the men and women who had made the ultimate sacrifice during the war. The Gold Star Mothers Memorial was unveiled at 1:30 p.m. on July 29, 1951. Located at Riverside Park on Sunrise Avenue the seven foot tall pink granite monument was dedicated to the men and women of Montgomery County who had lost their lives in World War I and II.

During the dedication four wreaths were placed on the monument to depict the four branches of service. Over nine hundred people attended the dedication of the monument.

Members of the Tony Stein Post 619 of the American Legion were put in charge of erecting a war memorial honoring North Dayton service men who had fought in all wars up to that time. Known as the North Dayton Patriots Memorial, the $10,000 monument is located at the intersection of Keowee and Valley Street.

The monument has a circular base 30 feet in diameter, with three granite pylons, each rising 19½ feet. In the center of the monument stands a globe and an eagle, both of which were sculptured in Vermont.

The 661st Air Force Band participated in the Gold Star Mothers Memorial ceremony. To be a member of the Gold Star Mothers you had to have a son or daughter who had died while serving in the armed forces. A flagpole honoring the local dead of the Korean War was placed nearby in 1957.

July 30

For thirteen months the Wright brothers printed a community newspaper called the *West Side News. (See March 1)* In April 1890, the *West Side News* evolved into *The Evening Item*, which was printed six days a week. Unfortunately, it wasn't well received. In the last issue, printed on July 30, 1890, the brothers explained their decision to quit publication.

> Our Parting Word.
>
> With this issue the Item closes its brief but illustrious career. The reason can be stated in a few words: More money can be made with less work in other kinds of printing, etc. During the time the Item has been issued we have found that a daily paper can be published on the West Side, but the profit for the first year or two will be small.
>
> If a man had capital and was willing to work for very little money the first year, a daily could be established which would pay a reasonable profit. As for us, we have only a small capital and do not care to wait a year before we begin to receive reasonable profits. We think we can make reasonable profits in other lines of printing without waiting a year or two. If the people of Miami City as a whole had manifested a genuine interest in the paper we would have continued, but too many were content with promising to subscribe for the paper after awhile. We could not afford to wait on them.
>
> The greatest difficulty we had to contend with is the fact that the people of the West Side will not believe that "any thing good can come out of Nazareth." They seem to have a way when something new is started up over here of standing back and saying they do not believe it can succeed, instead of once doing something to support it.

The decision to stop publishing *The Evening Item* must have been made at the spur of the moment, for the last issue still had a section stating that subscription rates were "Four Weeks for 25 cents", as well as a sentence under LOCAL NEWS that read: "Subscribe for the Item, four weeks 25 cents", while at the same time stating that anyone who had paid for a subscription to the newspaper in advance would be refunded their money. This sloppiness was probably due to them not wanting to reset type for the issue, which was all ready to be printed. Instead, they probably just changed the type in the first column and the top of the second one to tell their readers that the newspaper was closing down.

July 31

After the Civil War, Dayton citizens decided to erect a monument for the soldiers who had lost their lives in the war. The original accepted design was of a figure representing the Goddess of Liberty. Ex-Civil war soldiers protested vehemently, however, requesting that the goddess be substituted by a Union private soldier. George Washington Fair, a 6 foot tall, 200 pound bricklayer and an ex-Union soldier, served as the model.

The three-day dedication celebration began on July 29, 1884 with a reunion of ex-war prisoners. Over 100,000 people were on the streets the next day to view the Grand Army parade. A mock naval battle was also held on the Great Miami River near the Main Street bridge, between forts on the north side and a fleet on the water.

After yet another parade on July 31, the crowd gathered at Main and Monument for the unveiling. But when Ohio Governor George H. Hoadley pulled on the rope that would release the covering around the statue, it broke. A ladder was obtained, but it was twenty feet short of reaching the broken end of the rope. Fortunately, Clarence E. Ward, who worked as a steeple jack, came along and made his way to the top of the monument. He pulled the canvas off and there was a loud hurrah that could have been heard all over the city.

George Washington Fair's ordeal while getting his picture taken for use by the sculpturer for the statue was described by Dayton Journal reporter John Tomlinson.

"It was a steaming hot day when Mr. Fair, wearing a heavy soldier's overcoat, and accoutered with musket belt, scabbard and cartridge box, posed before the camera for four separate pictures: front, back and two side views.

"The picture gallery was like a furnace room on that sweltering day, and the ordeal undergone by the soldier thus clad in heavy clothing as if for mountain picket duty in mid-winter was almost as trying as facing death on the battlefield."

August 1

In the beginning all letters received by the Post Office had to be sorted by hand and then cancelled. By the early 1960s the Post Office began looking for a better way to reduce this extremely time-consuming process. But if a machine were to be used, it would somehow have to first find the stamp on a letter before it could cancel it.

The Post Office began experimenting with stamps that were coated with phosphorescent material that glowed under ultraviolet light. Airmail stamps glowed a red-orange, while commemorative issues were coated with material that glowed green. This enabled the sorter to automatically sort airmail from regular first-class mail. The first sorter/canceler was installed at Dayton, Ohio. Limited quantities of the 8¢ Jet Airliner over Capitol airmail stamp were first used on August 1, 1963. The tagged air mail stamps were faced and cancelled with almost 100 percent accuracy at the rate of 30,000 pieces per hour.

Some Christmas stamps issued in 1963, 1964 and 1965 were tagged, as were 5¢ commemorative stamps, including the Marine Corps, Great River Road, Savings Bonds and Women's Clubs. At first the machines were only 86 percent effective, as there were problems with the photo electric cells sensing the stamps on mail in brown envelopes. They were also sometimes fooled by foreign stamps, trading stamps and similar contrasting spots. Slowly improvements were made and the stamps were declared a success in 1965.

The carmine 8-cent Jet over Capitol air mail sheet stamp was selected for use in the first field test of luminescent tagged stamps. A calcium-silicate luminescent ink, which glows an orange-red color under short-wavelength ultraviolet light, was overprinted on the air mail stamp.

August 2

On June 2, 1909 the Courier Car Company was incorporated. The new company was, in essence, a subsidiary of the Dayton Motor Car Company, manufacturers of the highly successful Stoddard-Dayton line of automobiles. Stoddard-Dayton models were quite pricey and out of the reach of the common man and it was felt that a cheaper automobile would help build sales.

On August 2, 1909, the Courier Car Company opened operations at their plant on the southwest corner of Wayne Avenue and State Street (now Fourth Street), with the first Couriers rolling into the showrooms in January 1910. At first two body styles were offered: a five-passenger touring car and a two passenger roadster. Both models came with a 4-cylinder, 25 h.p., water cooled engine with a selective type transmission, double brakes system and magneto ignition. The company would later add a commercial wagon, which had the appearance of an open body pleasure car, but it also came equipped with a removable rear seat. Extension side boards could then be slipped into place, creating a wagon that could hold up to 750 pounds of cargo. Also offered was the Courier 2 1/2 ton truck.

In 1910, along with its parent company, the Courier Car Company became a part of the United States Motor Company. The autos were renamed the Courier Clermont. Unfortunately, United States Motor soon failed and production of the Courier stopped in 1912.

This Courier Model 10-A-1 was made with a gasoline tank instead of a rumble seat.

August 3

In 1939 traffic surveys were being made of how many vehicles passed through intersections located in the congested sections of Dayton. The information gathered was used to determine the locations and timing of traffic lights. A check of available parking facilities was also done.

A problem of parking spaces in the business district of the city was soon noticed. There was not sufficient space to accommodate the large number of automobiles This resulted in many people being unable to find a parking space and resorting to double parking, which caused congestion in traffic flow. An ordinance was passed limiting the parking time in the congested district, but the Police Department lacked the necessary man power to properly enforce the law.

In the fall of 1939, four parking meters were installed on the west side of Main Street, between First and Second Streets, as an experiment. These meters provided for five minutes of free parking, twelve minutes for one cent and sixty minutes for five cents. The results were so favorable that on August 3, 1940, sixteen meters were installed on Ludlow Street, from Third Street to Fourth Street. Both business owners and the public approved of the meters, as it made for a better shopping experience.

Today, there are 1,300 parking meters in the 40 block district of downtown Dayton.

Draftsmen work on traffic surveys at the Dayton City Planning Board office.

August 4

On August 4, 1902, *Dayton Daily News* reported that, after being in the saloon trade for decades, James "Jake" Ritty, inventor of the cash register, had retired from the business. This included the selling of his beloved Pony House Restaurant and Saloon at 125 South Jefferson Street.

When Ritty began the saloon he had no idea what to name it. One day his friend, Samuel Heinman, a horse buyer, called on Ritty with his young son. When the boy rode his horse into the pub, then and there Ritty decided to call his new business the Pony House. Originally the home of the "English and French School for Young Ladies", Ritty completely redesigned the interior, which included an ornate bar of Honduras mahogany, carved by workers from the Barney and Smith Car Works. The Pony House became a favorite stop for prize fighters, including early champs like John L. Sullivan, James J. Jeffries and James J. Corbett.

It was due to trouble at one of his earlier saloons that led Ritty to invent the cash register. In 1877, Ritty had opened the Empire Saloon at 10 South Main Street. Unfortunately, although a lot of liquor was being sold, profits were low. Ritty began suspecting his bartenders were stealing from him. With the help of his brother, John, James invented a way to keep tabs on sales - a cash register. The two were granted a patent on November 4, 1879.

Ritty was able to sell a few cash registers, but he decided that the sales weren't worth the effort, so when he was offered $1,000 for the rights to the invention, Ritty accepted. This led to him purchasing the Pony House.

The ornate bar that once graced the Pony House is now at Jay's Seafood Restaurant at 225 East Sixth Street in the Oregon District.

August 5

At the turn of the 20th century Barney and Smith Car Works was one of the oldest and most established factories in Dayton, and was one of the most important manufacturers of railroad cars in the country. It was known the world over for its passenger cars, the insides of which were ornately decorated with expensive wood paneling.

However, by 1905 business had slowed, so the company decided to also begin building electric street railway and interurban cars made of steel. This created a need for a large number unskilled workers, something that was in short supply. But Barney and Smith believed they had a solution - hire a foreign-labor contractor by the name of Jacob Moskowitz who had helped Malleable Iron Works with the same problem a few years before.

On August 5, 1905, Jacob formed the Dayton Realty Company for the purpose of establishing what would become known as the Kossuth Colony. This would be where the Hungarian immigrants he would hire to work for Barney and Smith would live. Twelve acres of land were purchased, the boundaries being Baltimore Street, Mack Avenue and Notre Dame Avenue above Leo Street. About 40 houses, a central club house and general store were built, all of which was surrounded by a twelve foot high wooden fence. The fence had only one entrance which was guarded by a watchman. Residents were required to make all their purchases in stores within the colony, using brass tokens they were given as payment for their work at Barney and Smith. If a resident was caught bringing in any item from outside that could also be obtained from a store in the colony, they were immediately fired from the Car Works and evicted from their home.

During the 1913 flood, boards from the fence were used to build rescue boats and never replaced. The Barney and Smith Car Works never fully recovered from the flood damage and the homes were sold in the early 1920s.

The Kossuth Colony was listed on the National Register of Historic Places in 1979.

August 6

The Korean War is sometimes called "The Forgotten War." Fought between World War II and Vietnam, Korea sometimes gets overlooked. But not in Dayton. On September 9, 1995, the Ohio Korean War Veterans Memorial in Riverbend Park, on Riverside Drive, was dedicated. In front of a 13-foot-high granite statue were granite memorials with the names of Ohioans who gave their lives during the war. The names of all 8,182 people missing in action from across the United States were engraved on granite slabs and bricks at the memorial.

On August 6, 2003, a special ceremony was held at the memorial, with the U. S. Postal Service honoring Korean War veterans with a new postage stamp. The year 2003 marked the 50th anniversary of the armistice that ended the hostilities. The stamp depicted the Korean War Veterans Memorial in Washington, D.C. The memorial there features nineteen stainless-steel statues of servicemen from the army, the marines, the navy, and the air force. Shown marching in a wedge formation as if on patrol, the statues represent an ethnic cross section of the United States. Portfolios depicting the stamp were presented as gifts to the 30 Korean War veterans attending the ceremony.

A second new stamp, honoring veterans who had been awarded the Purple Heart, was also unveiled. More than 20 Purple Heart recipients living in the area attended the ceremony.

The Purple Heart is awarded in the name of the President of the United States to members of the U.S. military who have been wounded or killed in action. According to the Military Order of the Purple Heart, the medal is "the oldest military decoration in the world in present use and the first award made available to a common soldier."

The photograph on the Korean War Veterans Memorial stamp shows the memorial just before dawn and shrouded in heavy snow that fell during a storm in January 1996.

August 7

During the presidential race in 1920, the Republicans nominated Senator Warren G. Harding, while the Democrats chose Ohio Gov. James M. Cox.

Gov. Cox had started his newspaper empire by purchasing the *Dayton Evening News*, renaming it the *Dayton Daily News*, so it was only fitting that he would return to Dayton to accept the nomination of his party. To help his campaign, Cox had chosen Franklin D. Roosevelt as his running mate, who had come along for the occasion.

When Cox arrived he was told that there would be a parade in his honor. But instead of watching from the sidelines, both he and Roosevelt led the parade, marching from the Soldiers' Monument on Main Street to the Fairgrounds. Once there, Cox watched as the parade made its way around the race track. Despite the heat, over 60,000 people joined in the celebration, carrying banners that said "Our Friend in Ohio Will Be Our Friend in the Nation". Delegates came from as far away as Wisconsin to show their support. The parade itself consisted of over 20,000 people and took over an hour and a half to pass by the spectators lining the streets.

The next day the *Dayton Daily News* reported that Gov. Cox's speech that day "absorbed all by its force and directness".

Gov. Cox would lose to Harding that November. Harding's victory (60.3% to 34.1%) remains the largest popular-vote percentage margin in presidential elections.

James M. Cox and Franklin D. Roosevelt near Main and Sixth streets as they make their way to the Fairgrounds in Dayton on August 7, 1920.

August 8

In May, 1887, the White Line Railroad Company was formed. The name is a little misleading, for the company was actually a line for street cars. What made the White Line unique was that they were the first in Dayton, and one of the first in the United States, to power their street cars with electricity instead of with horses.

The White Line extended from the north end of Main Street, southward and westward to Roseyard Avenue and later to the Soldiers' Home, now known as the VA Medical Center, on Third Street and Gettysburg Avenue.

At first people were afraid the electric street cars might be dangerous. It was thought that passengers might be shocked and that their pocket watches would be ruined by being magnetized by the electricity. To help still this fear, free rides were offered on August 8, 1888, the line's first day of business. So many people wanted to try the newfangled ride that several fist fights occurred as they struggled to get a seat on the electric street car.

But that did not alleviate the distrust of the public for the new cars. In fact, when it was heard that the Davis Sewing Machine plant would come to Dayton the following year the White Line petitioned the city to lay tracks along Richard Street to the factory. At about the same time the Fifth Street Railway Company made a similar petition to lay tracks to the Davis plant. The city had to decide between a company that used horse power or electric power.

Unfortunately, a number of electrical accidents had happened recently in which people had been shocked to death. Although none of these involved a street car, the council decided to award the franchise to the Davis plant to the Fifth Street Railway Company.

As time passed, with no one electrocuted and their pocket watches still humming along, the attitude on electric street cars changed. So much so that the entire system of the City Railway Company was electrified in 1894 due to popular demand for a faster, cleaner way of traveling the streets of Dayton.

August 9

On July 3, 1896, William Dalton was appointed to the Dayton Police Department, having moved from Miamisburg where he had served as the city's marshal. Officer Dalton's job was to patrol the streets, using a horse to cover his beat. After three years of service, in which he was involved in a number of criminal arrests, it was the pursuit of a lowly panhandler that led to Officer Dalton's death.

On August 9, 1899, Officer Dalton spied a man begging for money near the corner of Germantown and Baxter (now called Fitch) streets. The man began running away in an attempt to escape, but the officer had the advantage of being on a horse and took off in pursuit.

While riding at almost breakneck speed into the street, Officer Dalton was met at the intersection by two horse and buggies and a wagon also being pulled by horses. Discovering it was too late to stop, he tried to guide his horse through an opening, but the animal caught his forefeet in the back wheels of one of the buggies. Its speed was so great that the buggy was wrecked and the horse somersaulted onto its back. Officer Dalton was hurled to the paved street and knocked unconscious. The police ambulance was called and the injured patrolman was rushed to St. Elizabeth hospital. Here it was discovered that he had sustained a fractured skull and a number of other injuries. His wife and 15-year-old daughter were by his side when he died from his injuries 15 hours later, at 7 a.m. on August 10.

During the day of the funeral, thousands watched the procession of policemen in full dress uniforms escort the hearse from Officer Dalton's home to Sacred Heart Church. Officer William Dalton was buried at Calvary Cemetery with full police honors on August 12, 1899.

August 10

While working at Wright-Patterson Air Force Base, Daytonian Peter N. Van Schaik developed an astronaut maneuvering device. The unit contained a life support system, which allowed astronauts to venture outside their space capsule, as well as enabling them to attach themselves to the surface of the vehicle without having to used fittings.

The first astronaut to "spacewalk" was Edward White II, who exited from the Gemini 4 space capsule on June 3, 1965. White used a hand-held propulsion gun, which shot jets of nitrogen, to maneuver in space. Van Schaik claimed the idea came to him from reading the Buck Rogers comic strip. He received patent #3,199,626 for the attachment portion of the maneuvering device on August 10, 1965.

The propulsion gun can be seen in Astronaut Ed White's right hand while he takes the first US spacewalk on June 3, 1965. He was outside Gemini 4 for 21 minutes, and became the first man to control himself in space with a maneuvering unit.

August 11

On August 11, 1905, the Dayton Soldiers' Home posted a story of how one of their residents was almost swindled out of money by someone he thought was his son. William Lloyd, who was formerly a corporal during the Civil War, was trying to locate the whereabouts of his son, Willie, who had disappeared from Niles, Ohio about nine years before. The various methods he used included placing advertisements in a number of newspapers. To his surprise, Lloyd's ad in the *Salvation Army War Cry* was answered with a letter from a man signing his name as Frank Myers, who claimed that he could get in touch with Willie. Lloyd answered the letter and shortly afterward received another letter on letterhead from a San Francisco hotel, signed Willie Lloyd, claiming that he was the old soldier's missing son. Willie wrote that if his father would telegram the money needed for transportation, he would return and never leave again. Lloyd sent a telegram to the owner of the hotel, stating that if Willie would telegraph the maiden name of his mother, the money would be sent at once. Lloyd got an answer back from the hotel that Willie had left the day before.

Soon after, Lloyd received another telegram from Willie, this time from Ogden, Utah,. He once again asked that money for traveling back to Ohio be sent. The anxious father answered "Send your mother's maiden name and transportation will be telegraphed." That was the last time Lloyd ever heard from Willie.

One of Lloyd's daughters, wanting to learn more about the man who claimed to be her brother, wrote to California. She received an answer from the chaplain of the ship on which Willie claimed he had been assigned to while in the U.S. Navy. The letter stated that the person who had represented himself as her brother was a fraud by the name of Henderson. It seems that Henderson had forged and passed an $18 check. When he was found out, the man ran off and hadn't returned. As far as the Navy was concerned, Henderson was a deserter.

Needless to say, Lloyd was unhappy that the man was not his son, but was relieved for not having fallen into the trap of sending money.

August 12

Before 1914, Dayton had a federal plan of government, with a mayor, auditor, treasurer, solicitor and 15 councilmen, one elected from each of the 12 wards and three from the city at large. It worked well, but not well enough. Many people believed that the city government had turned into a politically driven machine that hampered Dayton's progress. The city seemed to be in debt, yet there were "no city-owned parks, no welfare department and no civil service worthy of the name". It was hoped that a city manager-commission government would give Dayton a more progressive and business-like operation.

In 1912, a committee composed of several successful business men and civic leaders, including John H. Patterson, Colonel Edward A. Deeds and Frederick H. Rike, met to consider a way to change how the city was governed. At the conclusion of their study they decided in favor of the commission-manager form of government. This was a system of local government that combined political leadership of elected officials in the form of a commission, with the managerial experience of an appointed local government manager. The commission would be responsible for the legislative function of the municipality such as establishing policy and passing local ordinances and resolutions. It would also appoint a manager to oversee the administrative operations, implement its policies, and advise it.

Although opposed by some people as an autocratic form of government, the movement was given an assist when in 1913 flood waters poured into Dayton. People saw men like Patterson and Deeds assume duties that the city administration could not cope with during the days following the flood and the charter was adopted by a vote of 13,318 for to 6010 against.

On August 12, 1913, Dayton became the first sizeable city in the United States to adopt a commission-manager charter; which became effective on January 1, 1914.

Today, the Dayton City Commission is comprised of the Mayor and four City Commissioners. Each City Commission member is elected at-large on a non-partisan basis for four-year, over-lapping terms.

August 13

On August 13, 1897 the *Dayton Daily News* reported that a "distinguished woman of remarkable business qualifications… is in the city in the person of Mrs. Juana Achey Neil, wife of the late Dr. Neil of this city." The article went on to explain how she had been away for a time, but had returned to discuss the proposition of opening a "horseless vehicle" factory in Dayton.

Several of Dayton's most influential men attended a meeting held by Mrs. Neil, including John W. Stoddard, of Stoddard Manufacturing Company. Stoddard stated that he had recently come from Chicago where he had taken a ride in one of Mrs. Neil's electric carriages. He was very impressed with the way the vehicle had handled and with how fast it could go, the auto reaching speeds of up to ten miles an hour. While photographs were being passed around, Mrs. Neil explained that a total of $730,000 would need to be raised in order to buy all rights to the automobile and to have working capital for the newly formed company. The men must have had some interest in the idea, for they formed a committee to meet with Mrs. Neil in Chicago later that week.

On October 14 of that same year, Mrs. Neil returned to Dayton, bringing along with her representatives of The Chicago Electrical Vehicle Company and two electric automobiles. The town went crazy, with thousands of people lining up to watch the noiseless vehicles careen up and down Main Street. But, even with this turnout, there were no backers to be had for the project.

Stoddard never lost his ambition to get involved in the automotive industry. In 1904, Dayton Motor Car Company succeeded the Stoddard Manufacturing Company, making its first Stoddard-Dayton model that year. By 1907, the Dayton Motor Car was producing over 2,000 automobiles a year and soon became the second largest employer in Dayton, second only to Barney and Smith Car Works, who made railroad cars.

Dayton Motor Car merged with United States Motor in 1910. In 1911, no less than 26 separate and distinct body styles of "pleasure" cars were listed, with a choice of four different engine sizes.

Perhaps the expense of producing such a wide variety of products left too little profit for the company. Whatever the reason, the United States Motor was placed into receivership in 1912. Assets of the company were bought by Maxwell Motor in 1913. This would prove to be the last year the Stoddard-Dayton models were available.

August 14

The Soldiers' Home Panorama Company was organized in Dayton on August 14, 1886 for the purpose of building the Battle of Gettysburg cyclorama. The cyclorama was a 360 degree circular oil-on-canvas painting depicting Pickett's Charge, a climactic event of the Battle of Gettysburg and the defining moment of the Civil War when Confederates attacked the Union on July 3, 1863.

The exhibit, estimated at approximately 42 feet high by 365 feet long, was hung in a specially built 16-sided wooden rotunda and opened for public viewing near the Dayton Soldiers' Home (now the VA Medical Center) on July 4, 1887. Viewers stood on a central platform, placing them in the center of the battle. The illusion was completed with a three-dimensional earthen foreground littered with real cannons, stone walls, broken trees and fences jutting from the painting.

The painting was exhibited for four decades, but eventually could not compete with the popularity of motion pictures. In 1927, the Battle of Gettysburg cyclorama shut its doors. The building was razed and the canvases placed in storage for possible future use. Unfortunately, a year later they were destroyed when the warehouse where they were being housed caught fire.

The Battle of Gettysburg cyclorama. Today, all that is left of the memory of the cyclorama is the name of the street where it was located, Gettysburg Avenue.

August 15

During the War of 1812, a temporary military hospital was open in Dayton. At the outbreak of cholera in 1849, the house of Mary Hess on Brown Street was improvised as a hospital. But the city needed a permanent place to help those in need of medical care.

St. Francis Sisters of the Poor began seeking a site for the opening of a hospital. A family by the name of Zwiesler graciously offered to give the sisters a two-story brick building at 116 Franklin Street, opposite Emmanuel church. The old residence was remodeled and 12 beds were made available for those in need.

On August 15, 1878, St. Elizabeth Hospital, Dayton's first public hospital, was dedicated. The first year alone 183 patients received care. The number continued to grow over the years, to the point that a larger location was needed. In 1882, a 200 bed hospital was built on Hopeland Street.

In July 1996, St. Elizabeth became the Franciscan Medical Center-Dayton campus. Ironically, four years later the city's oldest hospital would close, due in part to Dayton having more medical facilities in the area than were needed.

Before being converted into a hospital, the old building at 116 Franklin Street had boarders, as well as a saloon run by the building's owner, John Zwiesler.

August 16

In 1875, an old jail at the corner of South Main and West Sixth streets was converted into the City Workouse. It was used to hold people charged with misdemeanors sentenced to due time by the municipal courts.

During the wee hours of Saturday, August 16, 1919, seven prisoners used the cover of darkness to escape from the Workhouse. The men had to file through a three-quarter inch iron bar, jump 10 feet from the cell window to the ground and then scale a 10 foot wall. Their escape was discovered when the men failed to answer during roll call at 5 a.m. Some of the men were regarded as dangerous and were wanted by authorities in other cities, so a posse of armed deputies immediately started combing the city. However, it was believed that the prisoners may have hopped a freight train that had passed nearby on Sixth Street early that morning.

Among the prisoners who escaped were Albert Gaudy and Preston Maddox, both charged with carrying concealed weapons; Glover Harris, charged with assault and battery; and Dan Callahan and William Brimhall, both arrested on burglary charges. The others were Robert Hampton, charged with adultery, and James Woodruff, for discharging a fire arm within the city limits.

As the days passed, it looked as if all of the prisoners would remain free, but on September 27, 1919, word was sent from Cincinnati that Dan Callahan had been caught trying to rob a store in that city. As for the rest of the escapees, no record of their capture has been found.

City Workhouse

August 17

As late as 1883, the Dayton Police Department had no official way to transport its prisoners. Whenever transportation was necessary, a market wagon or a horse and buggy owned by a private citizen was pressed into service. John L. Miller, Dayton's mayor, decided that had to stop.

On August 17, 1883, the patrol wagon system was adopted. Before the wagon could be bought a place was needed to store it. A building on Brown Street, just south of Fifth Street, was remodeled. John L. Baker, who ran a carriage shop, was then contracted to build the wagon. The vehicle was placed in commission on December 12, 1883. John Hauser, the wagon's first driver, later recalled what it was like in the early days of its arrival.

"We spent the first two or three days shining up the new wagon and keeping the dust off it – and praying for some fellow to make an arrest away out on the edge of town, so we could show off the wagon."

Hauser didn't have to wait long. Buffalo Bill was in town giving an exhibit at the old Music Hall, now known as the Victoria Theater. A drunken man in the audience made a bit of a ruckus and was arrested.

"The call came for the wagon," Hauser remembered, "and my hopes were realized. I hauled the drunk up to the Sixth Street station house – the first trip ever made over the streets of Dayton by a patrol wagon."

August 18

For decades people have wondered how Dayton received the nickname of "Gem City". No one knows for sure, but of all the different theories, the most accepted one is an article that appeared in the *Cincinnati Daily Chronicle* newspaper on August 18, 1845.

The reference was made by a reporter known only as "T", who wrote:

"The most indifferent observer will not fail to notice Dayton. The wide streets, kept in excellent order, the noble blocks of stores, filled with choice and, of course, cheap goods, and more than all, the exceeding beauty and neatness of the dwellings, you at once mark with a 'white stone.' It may fairly be said, without infringing on the rights of others that Dayton is the gem of all our interior towns. It possesses wealth, refinement, enterprise, and a beautiful country, beautifully developed."

Does that settle it? Not really. Dayton would continue to be called "Rochester of the West" or "Valley City," the latter term appearing more frequently. A quarter of a century would pass before the word "gem" would be associated again with the city.

Published in 1871, the book *Buckeye Blossoms*, by author Mrs. M. E. Porter, has a chapter devoted to describing the various cities in Ohio.

"Dayton. 'Gem of the West'. Never was title more fittingly bestowed. The observing visitor will be impressed, particularly, with five things, adding direct worth and beauty to this 'gem city.'"

In the 1879 *Proceedings Montgomery County Horticultural Society*, members are asked to "contribute your parts towards making this 'Gem City' more of a gem than ever by removing your fences."

In the October, 1879 edition of *Our Dumb Animals*, the magazine mentions a story that had recently appeared in the *Dayton Journal* newspaper.

"W. P. Levis, proprietor of the Gem City paper-mills, has a miniature zoological garden at his mills on East Water Street..."

This is the first mention of any business in the city using the term "Gem City" in their name.

During 1882-1883, Major William D. Bickham, editor of the *Dayton Journal*, began a campaign to have Dayton called the Gem City. In 1887, a new board of trade was organized and began to use the nickname with regularity.

August 19

It was during the Great Depression when Myron E. Scott came across three boys racing homemade, engineless cars down a hill. A photographer for the *Dayton Daily News*, Scott had the idea of holding a race and taking photographs of it for the newspaper. He told the boys to come back the next week to participate in a race that would offer a trophy for the winner.

When nineteen boys showed up with their racers, Scott knew that he had to expand the idea. The *Dayton Daily News* agreed and on August 19, 1933 an astounding 362 racers showed up. It was estimated there were 40,000 watchers lining the street. David Wyse won the division for boys under ten and Randall Custer won in the division for older boys. A film of the race was shown in theaters across the country. Scott began receiving calls from other newspapers who wanted help in organizing their own races so that they could send their local champions to compete in Dayton in 1934.

The following year, races were sponsored by Chevrolet and leading newspapers in 34 cities. On August 19, 1934 the winners gathered in Dayton to race in the "All-American Soap Box Derby". The national championship was won by Robert Turner, age 11, of Muncie, Indiana.

In 1935, the race was moved to Akron, and that's where it's still held today. Myron Scott lived long enough to see his idea become a national tradition.

August 20

On a trip to Germany John H. Patterson, founder of NCR, and Col. Edward A. Deeds, saw fireless steam locomotives in use at a factory. Patterson was fascinated by the fact that they did not use coal, but were instead "charged" or filled with water and steam, on which they could run on for up to 4 hours.

The large tank in which the steam was stored was essentially a huge "thermos bottle" for the storage of super-heated water. The insulated tank would be filled about half full with cold water. A pipe would be used to pump steam into the tank. In about four hours the water would heat up to 366 degrees F., hot enough to create steam to run the locomotive.

On his return Patterson had three locomotives built; the *Rubicon* in 1909, the *South Park* in 1910 and the *Dayton* in 1913. These became the first fireless locomotives in use at a manufacturing plant in the U.S.

In 1962 the locomotives were replaced with a deisel-electric locomotive. The Rubicon was taken to Carillon Park and placed on permanent exhibit in a new building which was erected to house the locomotive. A ribbon cutting ceremony was held on August 20, 1962 to celebrate the opening of the exhibit.

The Rubicon fireless steam locomotive was used to gather the large amount of debris left in the streets by the flood that poured through Dayton in March, 1913.

August 21

On February 27, 1913, a law was passed by the State of Ohio stating that when fruits and vegetables were sold, they had to be sold by avoirdupois weight (avoirdupois is a system of measuring weight based on the fact that sixteen ounces are in a pound), or by individual count. The only legal way to sell produce by measure - by the bushel, for example - was if both the buyer and the seller had a written agreement. Sellers who did not follow the law were subject to fines up to $100 and three months in jail. This did not set well with the sellers who felt the law was unfair. Even with the penalties, many did not follow the new rules.

On August 21, 1913, warrants were served on sixteen owners of market stands by Inspector W. C. Gear, on behalf of the Ohio Agricultural Commission, and City Sealer Charles A. Schultz, whose job was to regulate sales or purchases done by weight or measure and also test and certify scales and means of measures used in Dayton. The sellers were summoned to appear in court in September.

Gear made it clear that he was determined to make sure the law was followed. "(Scultz) may appoint as many men and women as he desires to purchase market products in order to detect the violators of the law", Gear stated. "If the people who do not want the law enforced they must appeal to legislature to repeal it."

And so they did. A test case involving a grocer from Columbus, Ohio, who was arrested, fined $10 and thrown in jail, made its way through the courts. When the Franklin County Common Please Court declared the law unconstitutional, the case was sent to the Ohio Court of Appeals and then the Ohio Supreme Court. The Ohio Supreme Court upheld the Franklin County Court's decision, stating that the law was unconstitutional because it restricted the right of everyone to decide on how they wanted to buy, as well as placing an unreasonable and burdensome obligation on the seller. The Supreme Court also ruled that the arrest of sellers was not a proper use of the police force, since the selling of produce by measure had no relation to public safety nor preventing fraud.

When asked about his views on the law being declared unconstitutional, Schultz stated that he had always been skeptical about its validity, but he felt that it was his duty to enforce it. "It is my duty to protect the consumer against the dishonest dealer," he stated, "and I intend to do so whether the weight law is constitutional or not."

August 22

The XNBL-1 "Barling Bomber" was built for the U.S. Army Air Service in 1923. General William "Billy" Mitchell asked Walter H. Barling to design a bomber capable of carrying enough bombs to sink a battleship. Mitchell's goal was to demonstrate the effectiveness of air power by sinking a battleship from the air, and needed a large, strategic bomber in order to accomplish this feat. The sixty-five foot long, 27,000 pound aircraft had three wings and a 10-wheel landing gear. Components for the airplane were assembled at Wright Field, since McCook Field was deemed to be too small for the plane to take off and land safely.

The first flight was on August 22, 1923. Although the Bomber had the capacity to carry over 5,000 pounds of bombs, it only had a range of 170 miles before it needed refueling. On a test flight from Dayton to Washington, D.C. the Bomber wasn't able to clear the Appalachian Mountains and had to return to Dayton. Part of the problem was that the Engineering Division had been forced to use Liberty engines, which were underpowered for the job, because of an abundant supply of the engines. To power the Barling Bomber, four Liberty engines were mounted between the lower and middle wings, and an additional two in a pusher position. The complex structure of three wings and their struts and bracing wires created so much interference drag that the six engines could barely compensate. The experiment was a failure.

General "Hap" Arnold later stated "if we look at it without bias, certainly [the Barling] had influence on the development of B-17s... and B-29s."

August 23

Built in 1942, the Deeds Carillon was funded by Edith Walton Deeds as a tribute to both her husband, Col. Edward A. Deeds, and her family. The idea was inspired by chimes she heard in a belfry while visiting Bruges, Belgium.

The tower originally had thirty-two bells, visible from all directions, unlike the usual carillon design where the bells are hidden. Of these, twenty-three were electrically-rung, each inscribed with the name of a living family member. The other bells were silent and carried the names of deceased family members.

On August 23, 1942 hundreds gathered for the official dedication of the Deeds Carillon. The first program was played by Mrs. Deeds, which lasted about a half-hour. Plans were made for programs to be played on Wednesdays and Sundays, which consisted of favorite songs personally selected by Mrs. Deeds.

Deeds Carillon, showing the original bells. Now a fifty-seven bell carillon, it has been modernized to play up to 10,000 tunes remotely or a carillonneur can operate the bells via a mechanical keyboard.

August 24

At the Dayton Soldiers' Home stood a marble pillar, once a part of the United States Bank in Philadelphia, PA. Beautiful as it was, the pillar needed a finishing touch. It was decided that a statue of a volunteer soldier should be placed on top that would overlook the cemetery.

In order to raise the money needed to buy the statue an announcement was made that a unique celebration that could not be missed was going to be held at the Home.

Trains from as far away as Indiana and Kentucky were filled to standing room only capacity as they pulled into Dayton on August 24, 1876. Hundreds of carriages, buggies and wagons also arrived, all bound for the same place, the Soldiers' Home on West Third Street.

Part of the activities involved a balloon, aptly named the *Bridal Chariot*. The balloon was placed on the lawn in front of the Home Headquarters building. Father David Winters was joined in the basket by Ferdinand Stahl and Nellie Russ. Twenty sand bags were removed and the balloon rose one hundred feet into the air.

The people below strained to hear every word as the couple was joined in marriage. After the ceremony was completed the balloon was lowered so that Father Winters could jump out. Then, with the Soldiers' Home band playing, the newly wedded couple sailed off, along with the balloon's owner. The crowd watched as the couple floated away on their honeymoon.

Although this marble pillar from the United States Bank in Philadelphia was beautiful in its own right, there was still something missing. While it did get a soldier on top, other statues were also added. See September 12th for the rest of the story.

August 25

The Classic Theater's grand opening took place on August 25, 1927 at 817 West Fifth Street. Built by Carl Anderson and Goodrich Giles, two men from Piqua, the Classic is thought to be the first theater in the United States to be built, operated and managed by blacks. Movies were shown downstairs, while live entertainment, such as Duke Ellington, Ella Fitzgerald and Count Basie, took place upstairs in the ballroom.

Anderson and Giles built the Classic because blacks were discouraged from attending the downtown theaters. Some theaters, like the Colonial, Keith and Mecca, would allow blacks to sit in balconies separated from the rest of the patrons. It wasn't until 1941 that the Dayton NAACP convinced downtown theater owners to begin admitting blacks.

Classic's first-floor theater had seats for 500, and though first-run movies were shown, the organ recital that proceeded the showing of each film was a popular attraction.

Television helped kill off patronage to the theater, as did the building of I-75, which cut off the area from downtown. The Classic closed its doors for the final time in 1959. The theater was razed in 1991.

In 1945, patrons lined up in front of the Classic Theater to watch Louis Jordan, known as the "King of the Bobby Sox Brigade", in his new movie, Caldonia.

August 26

The Mecca was the newest and largest motion picture theater in Dayton when it opened at 1217 West Third Street on August 26, 1914. The front of the building was 40 feet wide and 167 feet long. The architectural design was reminiscent of the Renaissance period, with two large castle like towers on each side of the entrance. Each tower sported an electrical marquee with the word MECCA spelled out in large letters. The auditorium and interior of the building were decorated in white and green, with ivory white ceilings, tan colored walls and Spanish leather wainscot. The stage area was fully equipped to look as if a play were about to be put on. Movies were shown on the screen in a black velvet shadow box, which was specially constructed from over 150 feet of a special velvet.

The front row of seats sat back twenty-three feet from the screen so that patrons in the front row could see the entire projected picture in comfort. Music was provided by a specially constructed hand-played Seeburg Orchestra piano. In the main lobby a large, brightly lit sphere pendant hung from the ceiling to guide the patrons to their seats, helped along the way by thirty small ornamental lamps and several shaded side wall brackets.

By the late 1930's, until it closed in 1953, the theater showed mostly second run movies. Still, the promise to show good movies was mostly kept over the years, even if the films were a bit old by the time they reached Mecca's silver-screen.

August 27

In 1832, the Dayton Lyceum Association was formed. A literary group consisting only of men, its objective was, "the diffusion of knowledge and the promotion of sociability." Meetings were held every week "for lectures, essays and discussions of all subjects except theology and the politics of the day." The latter rule seems to have been included to help keep disagreements centered more on scientific ideas than emotional ones.

On August 27, 1833 Dayton Lyceum members met to celebrate their first anniversary with a special program of music and addresses by local citizens. Of special interest was a speech titled *Settlement and Progress of Dayton*, given by John W. Van Cleve and also printed in the morning edition of the *Dayton Journal.* The account was the first history of Dayton to appear in print. That John had the honor of giving the address was fitting, as he was the son of Benjamin Van Cleve, who was one of the first settlers in Dayton on April 1, 1796. Tradition also says that John was the first male child born in Dayton, his birthdate being June 27, 1801.

The speech included how the original contract was signed by Arthur St. Clair, James Wilkinson, Jonathan Dayton and Israel Ludlow had made with John Cleves Symmes for land extending from the Great Miami to the Little Miami rivers. It told of floods that hit Dayton in 1805 and 1814, the city's rapid growth during the War of 1812, the coming of the canal and the first newspaper printed.

John also spoke of how the lots on the east side of Main Street, near Third Street, were considered to be so far out that it was thought the city would never extend that far and so they were designated as a graveyard. This proved to be too close and so another area, a square bounded by Fifth, Wilkinson, Sixth and Ludlow streets, was chosen to be used in 1805.

John W. Van Cleve would go on to help shape the history of Dayton with deeds as well as words. He would become mayor of the city and, when the second cemetery's land proved to become too valuable, he took the initiative to help create Woodland Cemetery.

For those of you interested in reading *Settlement and Progress of Dayton*, it has been included in its entirety in the back of this book. *(See page 380)*

August 28

The very first wedding in Dayton took place on August 28, 1800, when Benjamin Van Cleve and Mary Whitten were married. But Mary was not the one Benjamin first had his heart set on having as his wife.

Although he was able to raise a good crop of corn in 1796, before he could harvest it he came down with a severe case of ague (an acute fever) and was unable to work again until the following spring. He spent twenty dollars for a cow and it died. He gave eighty dollars for a yoke of oxen and one of them was shot. In the end he was forty dollars in debt. Benjamin wrote of his woes in his diary.

> "When I came to Dayton it was my intention to settle myself permanently & for this purpose I had paid my address to Sarah Lawson Kemper... She was a worthy girl, but my circumstances were now so changed, & my prospects of supporting a family so gloomy that I was compelled to abandon my favorite anticipations of happiness."

That isn't to say that Benjamin and Mary weren't happy. He later wrote in his diary about his wife.

> "She was young lively industrious & ingenuous. My property was a horse creature & a few farming utensils & her father gave her a few household or kitchen utensils so that we could make shift to cook our provision, a bed, a cow & heifer, a ewe & two lambs, a sow & pigs & a saddle & spinning wheel. I had corn & vegetables growing. So that if we were not rich, we had sufficient for our immediate wants & we were content & happy."

Mary gave birth to five children between 1801 and 1809. Their son, John W. Van Cleve, would serve three terms as Mayor of Dayton between 1830 and 1832.

Mary died on December 28, 1810. Benjamin married Mary Tamplin on March 10, 1812. They would remain married until Benjamin's death on November 29, 1821.

August 29

In 1996, The New Neon Movies became the main focus of a number of magazines both here in the United States and around the world. In order to explain how that came to be, we have to travel back to 1952.

Cinerama was a 35 mm process intended to lure people away from their televisions and back into the theaters. Cinerama required a three-camera assembly; the center camera shot the front view, and two side cameras shot the peripheral perspectives.

In the theaters, the three film strips would be projected side by side from three different projectors, producing an image 48' wide and 18' high, onto a screen bent 146 degrees to match the curve of the human eye. Sounds from the movie would be blasted over eight stereo speakers, giving the audience the feeling of being in the middle of the action.

The first film produced was *This is Cinerama* in 1952. Created to show off the Cinerama process, the motion picture includes scenes of the roller coaster from Rockaways' Playland, the temple dance from the La Scala opera company's production of Aida; a performance by the Vienna Boys' Choir; a bullfight in Spain; and scenes from Cypress Gardens amusement park featuring a water skiing show. After the debut of *This is Cinerama*, came the travelogues *Cinerama Holiday* (1955), *Seven Wonders of the World* (1956), *Search for Paradise* (1957), and *South Sea Adventure* (1958). Only two features were shot in three-camera Cinerama: *The Wonderful World of the Brothers Grimm* (1962) and *How the West Was Won* (1962). The movie, *It's a Mad, Mad, Mad, Mad World*, was also scheduled to be filmed in three-camera, but instead it was shot using the single-lens 65mm UltraPanavision format. Although softer focus and less "you are there" peripheral vision, that process proved to be much cheaper, and less expensive to film and show.

In order to accommodate the three projectors and other Cinerama equipment, 88 of the theater's 300 seats had to be removed. But the experiment proved to be a success. On August 29, 1996 film buffs from across the world lined up outside The New Neon Movies for the showing of *This is Cinerama*, the first time it had been shown in America in over 32 years. The film, *How the West Was Won*, also proved to be very popular. Over the years, the theater attracted such luminaries as Hollywood director Quentin Tarantino and film critic and historian Leonard Maltin.

Originally scheduled to run until May, 1997, various Cinerama films continued to be shown at the theater until February 2000.

August 30

In 1795, John Cleves Symmes, a land speculator from New Jersey, sold Arthur St. Clair, General James Wilkinson, Israel Ludlow and New Jersey Congressman Jonathan Dayton, land that became known as the "Dayton Purchase." When the village was laid out, it was agreed that it should be named after Congressman Dayton.

Unfortunately, Symmes later failed to meet his financial obligations to the federal government. When the U.S. Government offered to sell the property to Ludlow, St. Clair, Wilkinson, and Dayton, they declined. In 1800, the government offered to sell the land to the residents, but at $2.00 an acre, most of them could not afford to do so, as they had already given most of the money they had saved to purchase the land from Symmes. Fortunately, one of the men was Daniel C. Cooper. He paid the government their asking price, buying over 3,000 acres of land, including the town site. The town was replatted and clear titles given to the few settlers that were left. *(See September 9)*

In 1802 Cooper married Sophia Greene Burnett. He brought the first African American to Dayton, a woman who worked as a servant in his home. Soon after her arrival, she had a son, whom she named Harry Cooper. Harry was the first African American to be born in Dayton.

On August 30, 1805, when Harry was two and a half years old, he was indentured to Daniel Cooper until his twenty-first birthday. The indenture stated that "Harry shall faithfully obey the said Cooper's lawful commands, his secrets keep (and) shall behave himself in a becoming manner unto the said Cooper, his heirs or assignees." In exchange, Daniel Cooper was obligated to make sure that Harry was taught everything about the farming and milling business.

It is unclear just how much farming and milling Harry was actually taught, because most of his life he worked in a sawmill that Daniel owned. Unfortunately, Harry broke his leg while working. It proved bad enough that the leg had to be amputated. Harry was fitted with an artificial leg, and Daniel Cooper awarded him a pension of a dollar a day for the rest of his life.

Supposedly, even with the wooden leg, Harry was able to work almost as well as before the accident. But it proved to be a hindrance, for he drowned after falling in the sawmill race, near where it crossed Third Street.

August 31

On August 31, 1969, Channel 22 held its first telethon for the Muscular Dystrophy Association. Bernard A. Wullkotte, who wrote for the *Dayton Daily News* under the byline 'B.W.," played the host when the national telethon would cut to Channel 22 during its 21½ hour program. The Jerry Lewis MDA Labor Day Telethon started on the Sunday evening preceding Labor Day and then continued until late Monday afternoon.

Over the years various well-known Daytonians, including Johnny Walker and Don Brown, would host the program. Local viewers were well entertained during the segments, with guests like Steve Kirk, Bob Kwesell and Lou Emm.

But times changed. Jerry Lewis' final show as host was in 2010. In 2013, MDA discontinued the format of being syndicated to individual stations, airing on ABC for only two hours. The last event was held in 2014.

The picture above shows the studio at Channel 22 in the 1970s. Johnny Walker was the host when a male stripper named Jeremiah was performing. Comedian Dom DeLuise, who was in Dayton to help entertain the audience, became so enthused by the performance that he ran over and danced with Jeremiah.

September 1

By far the most ambitious project in Dayton during the Great Depression was the elimination of railroad crossing at street level in the city. With Dayton located mostly on flat land and served by four railroads, it was inconvenient having to wait for trains that ran through many of the city's main streets. The plan was to elevate the railroad tracks, thus allowing cars to pass under the trains as they roared through Dayton.

In 1926, Dayton's citizens approved an $8 mil bond issue for the project. The rest of the $23 million was provided by the railroad companies who entered the city. Work for laying track began on March 5, 1930. Although by this time the city was having financial problems, the money from the bond issue had been set aside, which enabled the work to continue. B & O Passenger Train #59 was the last train that passed over the street level tracks on September 1, 1931. The old rails were taken up the next day.

Traffic backs up for the final time at the busy intersection of Main and Sixth streets as the last train chugs through downtown Dayton at street level.

September 2

In his autobiography, *Build For Tomorrow*, Harry Price writes of his building the Island Park Dam in 1917. But first the old Steele Dam had to be removed due to being weakened when dynamite had been used in 1915 to bring up the body of a girl who had drowned. *(See June 9)*

Harry Price confided to city manager Henry Waite that massive charges of dynamite would be needed to break the dam into more manageable pieces, and admitted that the blasts would "break a hell of a lot of windows and your phone will be ringing like crazy." Wanting the job finished, Waite agreed, but asked that Price wait until Saturday, when he'd be unreachable and the Chief of Police would be out of town.

The following Saturday "water geysers and chunks of concrete went shooting 300 feet into the air" and about 175 windows were shattered by the blasts. Fortunately, no one was hurt and Monday morning the city had a crew of glaziers out repairing the damage.

Harry Price finished the Island Park Dam in August, 1917 and it was officially opened on September 2, 1917. Thousands of people turned out to see the water go over the top of the new dam.

Harry Price wrote about the grand opening in his book.

"I bet Henry Waite a good 50-cent cigar that the first trickle would go over at a certain hour; Henry picked another time, close to mine. It was almost a draw, so we each paid off on the spot and each enjoyed smoking the other's cigar."

The newly finished Island Park Dam from the west bank, taken on September 17, 1917.

September 3

When the Ohio legislature approved the money to build a canal into Dayton there was a lot of controversy as to where it should be located in the city. One suggestion was that the channel should be made no wider than 40 feet across, which would allow it to run down the center of Main Street, which would still allow a wagon road 34 feet on each side if the sidewalks were narrowed to only 12 feet across. This plan "would make Main the handsomest street in Ohio."

The reason this plan had at least some approval was because it meant that it would be located within the city limits, allowing easy access to load and unload merchandise from the canal boats. It was decided to build along the far eastern section of Dayton, where Patterson Blvd. is today. Excavation at the basin between Second and Third streets began on September 3, 1827. A cannon salute was fired in celebration of the event.

The first canal boat built in Dayton was launched near Fifth Street on Saturday, August 16, 1828, at 2 p.m. The citizens of Dayton were invited to join in the festivities, with that ever present cannon being fired off to announce the launch. The boat was called the Alpha and was built for McMaken & Hilton by Solomon Eversull. The Alpha was pronounced by many superior to any boat on the line of the Miami Canal. As water had not yet been placed into the canal, a temporary dam was built across the canal at the bluffs, and water was turned in from the sawmill tail-race at Fifth Street. Although it was found that there were some leakages in the new canal's embankment, the excitement didn't dampen, as trial trips were made from the dam to Fifth Street and back. The Dayton Guards, a military company of boys organized a few weeks before, made the first trip on the Alpha.

In early December, 1828, "a party of ladies and gentlemen" made a trip to Holes Creek and a week later the Alpha took a group to Miamisburg, which was the end of the line of the canal at the time.

But it wouldn't be for much longer. The canal was very close to being finished. *(See January 25)*

September 4

St. Mary's School for Boys began offering classes in 1850. The school was incorporated in 1878, becoming known as St. Mary's Institute. The name was changed to St. Mary's College in 1912.

Within a few years, however, the college was held back in its efforts to grow due to its cramped facilities. With no room to expand, applications for enrollment had to be rejected. A plan was put in place for expansion, part of which involved changing the name of the institution yet again. On September 4, 1920, it was announced that, from that day forward, St. Mary's College would be known as the University of Dayton.

Rev. Joseph Tetzlaft, president of the college, pointed out that the name of the college was changed in honor of the city and that by drawing a large number of students from outside the area to Dayton, the college had been a benefit to the area in both a commercial and civic way.

The plan included the erection of a number of buildings, including an alumni hall, college building, modern gymnasium and a science hall. Fully equipped law and commerce schools were also to be added.

Located at 300 College Park, the University of Dayton now offers more than 80 undergraduate and 50 graduate programs in arts and sciences, business administration, education and health sciences, engineering and law.

Views of St. Mary's College before it became the University of Dayton in 1920.

September 5

After it was deemed that the Ohio Lunatic Asylum in Columbus was incapable of handling the estimated two thousand patients that were considered insane in the state in 1852, the Ohio Legislature passed an act for the building of two additional "Lunatic Asylums". Dayton was chosen as one of the sites. On September 5, 1855, the Southern Ohio Lunatic Asylum opened on 50 acres on the hill at the intersection of Wayne and Wilmington avenues. The building was based on the first uniform plan of hospital construction, developed by Dr. Thomas Kirkbride of Philadelphia, an expert on asylum architecture. The original building contained six wards, three on either side of the administration building, with a capacity of 164. In 1861, the capacity of the Hospital was increased to 600 by the addition of six wards on each side. In 1891, it was again enlarged by the addition of congregate dining rooms.

Over the years, the facility changed its name several times. In 1875, it became the Western Ohio Hospital for the Insane; in 1877, the Dayton Hospital for the Insane; in 1878, the Dayton Asylum for the Insane; and in 1894, the Dayton State Hospital. In 1970 it was renamed the Dayton Mental Health Center.

A fire in 1983 destroyed much of the main building, including the dome. After major renovations, the building reopened in 1986 as 10 Wilmington Place, a private apartment complex for senior citizens.

The Dayton State Hospital in all its glory, with the magnificent dome still in place.

September 6

The Midget Theater, at 1019 West Third Street, was run by Sherman W. and Benjamin F. Potterf. Built at a cost of $33,000, the 300 seat theater was named in honor of Sherman, who was a "midget" and in the show game, before taking over the managership of the theater. "Home of the quality photo plays", the theater took advantage of Sherman's 42-inch height by advertising that there was "Nothing small about the Midget - Only the manager". Just as many people went to the Midget's grand opening on September 6, 1913, in the hopes of getting a glimpse of Sherman, as there were ones to watch the movie being offered.

The theater was quite successful. Patrons of the two story building sat in comfortable opera chairs. The stage area where the screen stood had beautiful green velvet drapes and drop curtain. The curtain that hid the screen was in itself unique. On it was a painting of the original Third Street bridge which had been razed around the turn of the century. It was surrounded by advertisements from other West Side businesses.

Business really boomed when the brothers began showing Renfax Musical Talking Motion Pictures in 1915. The Renfax pictures were synchronized with a record disc that could be played so that the movie actors could be heard to "talk".

The Midget closed its doors in 1928, probably due to competition from two new neighborhood theaters, the Classic and the Palace. The building that housed the Midget still stands, one of the few remnants left of the days of the nickelodeon theaters.

After the theater closed, Sherman and his wife, Sadie, operated a miniature railroad concession at Celoron Park, New York

September 7

Birds hitting flying aircraft have been a problem from almost the very beginning of flight. According to the Federal Aviation Administration (FAA), more than 255 people have been killed and over 243 aircrafts destroyed since the 1980s due to wildlife strikes. Incidents rose from 1,851 in 1990 to 11,313 in 2013. In all, there were over 142,000 recorded strikes in this time period.

The first recorded incident of a bird strike on an aircraft occurred on September 7, 1905. The Wright brothers were taking turns flying the Wright Flyer III at Huffman Prairie that day, having rebuilt it during the summer to try and solve the pitch instability that had hampered Flyers I and II. Their mechanic, Charles E. (Charlie) Taylor, was also there, helping time the flights and keeping notes in a notebook.

Although it is widely reported that Orville Wright was the pilot during the flight, it was actually his brother, Wilbur. It was during the third test of the day. Wilbur flew 4,751 meters in 4 minutes 45 seconds. After the flight Taylor inscribed the following in the notebook:

"Four complete circles. Twice passed over fence into Beard's cornfield. Chased flock of birds on two rounds & killed one which fell on top of the upper surface and and after a time fell off when swinging a sharp curve."

As can be seen in the entry, it seems that all three men kept track separately as to the time each flight lasted.

263

September 8

On September 8, 1942, an intense publicity campaign was begun to acquaint Dayton residents with the importance of collecting tin cans for the war effort. "Many an unsuspecting Dayton housewife helps Hitler every day," claimed the *Journal Herald*. "One look at the city dump shows why. For there, resting in peace, are thousands of rusty cans from which the vital tin can never be reclaimed for the war effort."

It was pointed out that there were some pretty important reasons why the plea to salvage tin cans should be heeded. Two tin cans contained enough tin for a syrette, which was used for administrating sedatives on the battlefield to help prevent shock. They also were used on airplane instrument panels, aircraft bearings and for solder used in electrical equipment on a plane. And since tin was the only metal that wasn't harmed by salt water, it was used to ship food overseas.

On October 19, 1942 the War Production Board stated that it was mandatory to collect discarded tin cans in any city with a population of 25,000 or more. The order called for the segregation of tin cans from ordinary trash, something that Dayton had already been doing for more than a month. The day after the order, Judge Robert Martin, chairman of the Dayton-Montgomery County Salvage committee, announced that Dayton had already collected over 52,000 pounds of tin towards the war effort since the campaign had begun.

Nearly every day the local newspapers ran a story on the large amount of tin cans being collected at the various schools. Soon it became a challenge to collect the largest amount of tin cans. It wasn't unheard of for a school to collect 4 to 5 thousand pounds of tin cans a month. Brown School was highlighted in January 1943, for bringing in over 10,000 pounds of tin, with Fairview Elementary coming in a close second with 9200 pounds.

The first concentrated effort to collect tin yielded approximately 172,000 pounds, or about six railroad carloads, of tin. As the war raged on tin continued to be collected, usually at the rate of close to 100,000 pounds a month.

September 9

The original plat of Dayton was made by Israel Ludlow on November 4, 1795. All lots were ninety-nine feet wide by one hundred and ninety-eight feet deep. The streets are not named in the plat. The plat was certified to by Ludlow on April 27, 1802 and recorded in Cincinnati the next day.

Unfortunately, John Cleves Symmes, the original owner of the land, failed to meet his financial obligations to the federal government. Daniel C. Cooper then stepped forward and bought the town site. *(See August 30)*

On September 5, 1803 Cooper made a new plat, which was entered on September 9, 1805. Names were added to the principal streets, most of which are still in use. Jefferson St. was named for President Thomas Jefferson; Ludlow St., for Israel Ludlow, who platted Dayton; General James Wilkinson, who fought with Mad Anthony Wayne; and St. Clair for Arthur St. Clair, governor of the Northwest Territory. Cherry St. later became Perry St., named for Commodore Oliver H. Perry. Water Street later became Monument Avenue in 1884 when a monument honoring the Civil War veterans was erected at the intersection at Main Street. Mill St. is now Patterson Blvd.

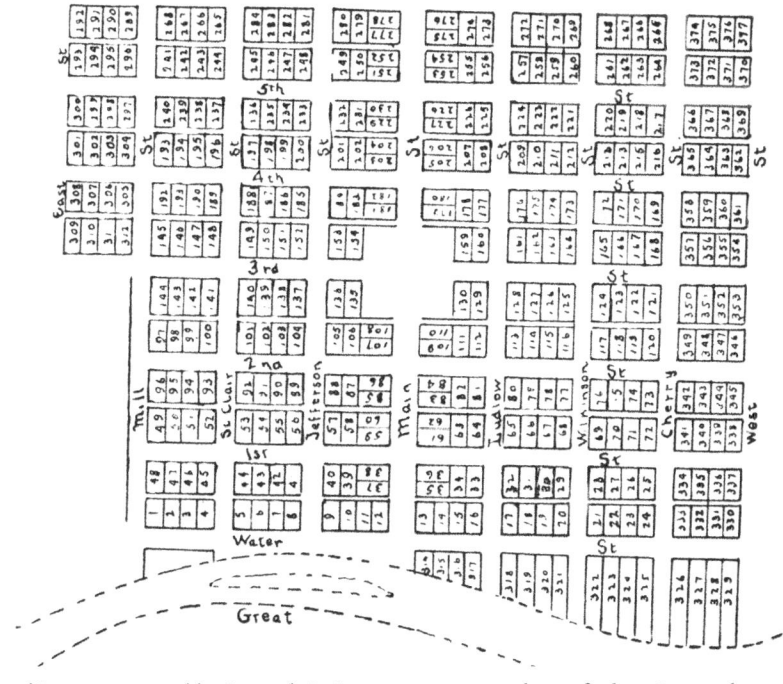

Plat of Dayton created by Daniel C. Cooper in 1803 and certified on September 9, 1805.

September 10

Around 1 a.m. on the morning of September 10, 1833, a fire broke out in an uninhabited house on Ludlow Street. An alarm was given and naturally a number of people came to help. Charles R. Greene was one of the fire wardens, whose job was to form lines of people who would pass buckets of water along to fill up a small pump engine that would then throw the water onto the fire.

Matthew Thompson showed up as well, but instead of helping, he stood on the sidelines, mocking the others. Seeing this, Greene ordered him to get in the line. Thompson refused, using some colorful language while doing so. When he refused a second time, Greene used a board he had in his hand to knock Thompson's hat off, and upon Thompson's use of even fouler language, Greene struck him on the head.

That morning Thompson, who was quite drunk, began hunting for Greene, saying that he was going to kill him. He then went to a judge for a warrant for Greene for assault and battery. The judge refused to issue a warrant until the fees for doing so were paid.

When he returned with the money, but before the warrant was issued, Greene showed up, having been told what was happening. He stated that, under the same circumstances, he would act the same way, and told Thompson that if he kept up he would "knock your heels over your head".

When Greene turned to walk away, Thompson brought up a three foot club he had in his hand and, seizing the end of it with his left hand, struck Greene in the head. Greene died four hours later.

When taken to court, Thompson's defense was that the blow to his head was of sufficient violence to derange his mind, which meant that he was technically insane when he struck Greene. The jury did not agree and returned a verdict of guilty of murder in the second degree.

The judge had harsh words for the prisoner during sentencing.

"You have sunk deeper and deeper, from vice to crime, until you have taken the life of your fellow man, and plunged your family and friends into ruin and disgrace, and are brought to end your own days in prison. Cut off forever from society, or the hope of restoration, you will live a spared monument of clemency of your country's laws; but you will live without civil rights, as one dead - your wife a widow, and your children fatherless."

The judge then sentenced him to life imprisonment.

September 11

Levi and Matilda Stanley were known as the King and Queen of the Gypsies, Levi carrying on the title after his father, Owen, died in 1860. They owned land in Harrison Township and Dayton became their summer home.

Matilda was much loved by her people and it was a great sadness to many when she died in Vicksburg, Mississippi on February 15, 1878. The body was sent to Dayton and placed in a vault at Woodland Cemetery until September 11, 1878 so that word of her death could spread, and give those who wanted to come to her funeral time enough to do so. And come they did.

On that day the immediate family, along with several hundred gypsies from other sections of the country, assembled along the banks of Mad River in the neighborhood of the present Keowee Street bridge. Here the funeral cortege formed, carriages having been provided by McGowan and Lake, a pioneer Dayton livery firm. In the files of a newspaper of that date we read:

"The funeral services were very simple. The casket had but to be removed from the vault to the grave. While the procession did not form until 1:30 p. m., before noon people began to go toward the cemetery from all parts of the city. The street cars on Wayne and Brown sts. could not commence to accommodate all of those who sought to ride. It seemed that the entire city had turned out, and that everyone in the rural districts who had a vehicle was in town. Probably 1000 vehicles, of every description, were grouped about the entrance to the cemetery and far out along every street and alley approaching it. People covered the hill and strolled about the grounds until the cemetery was black with them.

"The body was laid away in the large stone pit that had been constructed at the direction of the head of the Stanley family. It measures 10 feet long, eight feet wide, and is 10 feet in depth. The father, sons and some of the women mourners climbed down into the pit after the casket had been placed in it to take their last farewell of their dead. They threw themselves upon the coffin, kissing the hard wood, and it was with difficulty that they were persuaded to ascend from the vault so the service could be concluded."

However, when Levi Stanley died in 1908, his funeral was attended by only thirty family members. Times had changed, with many of the gypsies having settled down to more permanent homes.

September 12

After over a year of raising funds, a statue of a volunteer soldier was finally placed on top of a pillar that had been donated to the Dayton Soldiers' Home as a monument to Union Civil War veterans. *(See August 24)*

On September 12, 1877 President Rutherford B. Hayes came to Dayton to celebrate the 10th anniversary of the Home and to unveil the Soldiers Monument. Unfortunately, when the president tried pulling the canvas off the statue, the cord broke. Judge Hugh L. Bond, of the United States Circuit Court, of Baltimore, remarked: "Mr. President, that is the first failure of the Administration." President Hayes was not amused and the remark was met with a stoney silence.

The President remained standing until a long ladder was procured and the unveiling was completed amid cheers from the estimated 25,000 onlookers who had come for the ceremony.

Still not everyone was satisfied. While the ten-foot tall soldier atop the column was certainly quite impressive, something seemed to be missing. It was decided that all branches of the service should be honored as well. Four figures were soon added along the base. Carved of white marble, they represented the Infantry, the Artillery, the Navy and the Cavalry.

The beautiful Soldiers' Monument still stands today, overlooking the Dayton National Cemetery at the VA Medical Center on Third Street.

September 13

On the evening of September 13, 1913, satisfied crowds left the Majestic Theater after the final showing in Dayton of *Harry K. Thaw's Fight for Freedom*. People had flocked to see the short documentary - maybe because it came very close to not being shown at all.

The controversial film deals with Thaw's escape from prison while awaiting trial for the murder of Stanford White, a famous architect known especially for the Washington Square Arch in New York City.

Thaw, a Pittsburgh millionaire known for being mentally unstable, chased after Evelyn Nesbit, a chorus girl, begging her to be his wife. She resisted, knowing she would have to tell Thaw that she had been with another man, something she knew would make Thaw jealous. Finally she told of how, when she was 16 years old, White had drugged her and then sexually assaulted her while she was unconscious. But Nesbit was careful not to mention that she had continued to rendezvous with White consensually for years.

Although Harry Thaw and Evelyn Nesbit married on April 4, 1905, he could not cope with the fact that, in his opinion, Stanford had sullied his wife's reputation. On June 25, 1906 Thaw purchased tickets for himself and his wife for a new show, *Mam'zelle Champagne*, which was playing on the rooftop theatre of Madison Square Garden.

During the show, White appeared, taking his place at the table that was customarily reserved for him. During the finale, Thaw drew a pistol, and fired three shots at Stanford White, killing him. He then stood over White's body, shouting "I did it because he ruined my wife! He had it coming to him. He took advantage of the girl and then abandoned her!"

Thaw was tried twice for the murder of Stanford White. During the first trial it was ordered that the jury members be sequestered, the first time in the U.S. that this was ordered. The trial ended in a deadlock.

At the second trial, Thaw was found not guilty by reason of insanity, and sentenced to Matteawan State Hospital for the Criminally Insane for life. In 1913, Thaw walked out of the asylum, headed to Sherbrooke, Quebec, but was soon recaptured. On July 16, 1915, a jury found Thaw no longer insane, and set him free.

After protests were made against showing the film on Thaw due to it dealing with murder, Majestic's manager agreed to have Father Galinger of Corpus Christi Church and Father Schenghof of Holy Trinity decide the fate of the movie. In the end, they approved and the film was shown.

September 14

In 1909 Charles Pinkney Jr. was playing for the Dayton Veterans, a Central Division minor league baseball team.

On September 14, 1909 a double header was held at Fairview Park, with the Dayton Veterans battling the Grand Rapids Stags.
Pinkney started off the first game with a home run. The Stags didn't stand a chance, losing 10-0.

In the last inning of the second game the Stags were leading 5-3. Clouds had begun to darken the sky. As the light grew dim, the Grand Rapids pitcher was having a hard time throwing a pitch over the plate. It was one man on, with one out, when Pinkney came to bat.

The pitcher threw three balls Charley's way. The fourth looked to be a ball which would entitle the batter to his base. It was a fast ball which approached the home plate like a shot from a rifle. Probably due to not being able to see the ball clearly in the darkening light, Charles did not begin to duck until too late. The baseball struck Pinkney behind the left ear, fracturing his skull. The young man never regained consciousness, dying shortly after noon the following day.

Charles Pinkney Jr. was buried at Lakewood Cemetery, located in Cleveland, Ohio. Lakewood also serves as the last resting place for Cleveland Indian Ray Chapman, the only Major League player to have been killed by a pitched ball.

September 15

When the Dayton Public Library began planning a new building to be located in Cooper Park in 1888, the second floor was set aside for the purpose of eventually including a natural history museum. In 1893, legislation was passed by the state giving the Dayton Board authority to use money from the library funds to finish and furnish the second floor of the Library Building for a museum.

Almost immediately a number of people came forward to donate both money and objects to the project. Cases were made to closely match those used by the Smithsonian Institution. Examples of local fauna, flora, fossils, minerals and archaeological relics were gathers, together with photographs and documents pertaining to the history of Dayton. The museum was formally opened to the public on September 15, 1893.

The museum proved to be quite popular, especially after the library bought a number of ethnological and natural history exhibits that had been on display at the Columbian Exposition, which had closed in October 1893. The museum hours were extended to include Sunday afternoons so that men who were working six days a week could be given the opportunity to enjoy the museum with their families.

The Dayton Public Museum as it looked in 1922 after it was transferred to new quarters in the Steely Building on the corner of Ludlow and Second streets. Many of the items are now housed at the Boonshoft Museum of Discovery.

September 16

On September 16, 1837, a committee met at the courthouse to see about organizing a zoological museum. The idea was suggested by William Jennison, who was an accomplished naturalist, having spent years doing such work in Germany before moving to Dayton and opening a plant nursery at his home on what is now Linden Avenue near Huffman Avenue.

Jennison was also an expert in the field of taxidermy, having a number of birds he had prepared himself, which were arranged in handsome glass cases. He also had hundreds of insects classified and arranged in scientific order. He offered to place his entire collection in a public museum, and to devote part of his time to the work of increasing the collection.

This offer was no small matter. Jennison was well connected with a number of societies of naturalists overseas, which meant he would be able to procure from abroad almost any specimens desired, merely by asking for them and paying the cost of transportation. Their eagerness to help was also due to Jennison's willingness to send them items that were desirable. Many times he could be seen, net in hand, collecting butterflies for his cabinet and natural history specimens to exchange with his friends across the Atlantic.

A room was rented at the head of the canal basin between Second and Third Street and the collection put in place. Unfortunately, it was soon determined that the location was unsuitable for a museum and the project was abandoned. It would take another fifty-six years before Dayton would finally get a permanent natural history museum. *(See September 15).*

This watercolor painting by Thomas K. Wharton shows the head of the canal basin in Dayton in 1831. It proved to be a poor spot to open a zoological museum.

September 17

On September 17, 1859, Abraham Lincoln came by train to Dayton to speak. Attorney Lewis B. Gunckel later recalled meeting Lincoln that day.

"I was on the reception committee. When we called at his room in the Phillips House and knocked at the door there was a hearty western response. 'Come in.' Opening the door we were surprised to find him in his shirt sleeves and his wife brushing his hair. She afterwards put on his collar and cravat, he talking to use meanwhile without any apology for his undignified appearance."

The committee walked with Lincoln to Third and Main Streets, where he chose to stand on the pavement while the audience stood on the Court House steps. He was welcomed by Robert C. Schenck, an old friend who had served with Lincoln in Congress. It was during his introduction to the crowd that Schenck became the first person to publicly mention that Lincoln was running for president of the United States.

The newspapers differed in their reporting of the event. The *Journal* (Republican) stated that there were five thousand people to listen to him. The *Empire* (Democrat) said editorially: "Instead of tens of thousands of persons being assembled in our city to hear Mr. Lincoln and the streets deluged with people as one of our morning contemporaries prophesied would be the case, a meager crowd of barely two hundred was all that could be drummed up. And they were half Democrats, who came out of curiosity. Mr. Lincoln is a seductive reasoner but his speech was a network of fallacies and false assumptions."

A short time later the future president caught a train to Cincinnati.

Democrat D. L. Medlar was not inspired. In his diary Medlar wrote: "He (Lincoln) spoke in front of the Court House from 2 to half past 3 o'clock, to an audience varying from three to five hundred people. He has a thin, weak voice, and is by no means an eloquent or forcible speaker."

The portrait shows Lincoln in 1859. He had not yet grown his trademark beard.

September 18

The first regularly published newspaper in Dayton was *The Dayton Repertory*. Published by William McClure and George Smith, the first issue was printed on September 18, 1808. It contained four pages of two columns each, was eight by twelve and one-half inches in size, and printed with old-fashioned type on a second-hand press. It was principally filled with foreign news up to several months old, but some local news items were also added.

After five issues, *The Repertory* was suspended till 1809, when Henry Disbrow and William McClure revived it as a twelve-by-twenty-inch sheet. It was published on Second Street, between Main and Jefferson streets, its last issue coming out on December 4, 1809.

There is a legend of a newspaper before The Repertory. Supposedly, in July 1806, Noah Crane, from Lebanon, Ohio, printed a few issues. He became ill, returned to Lebanon, and abandoned his project. No proof of this newspaper has been found.

September 19

September 19, 1910 marked the beginning of a six-day celebration known as the Dayton Industrial Exposition and Fall Festival. The focus was to showcase "The City of a Thousand Factories", and to display what Dayton had to offer the world. Over 200 manufacturers set up exhibits to show the estimated 100,000 people that they hoped would come to the festival.

Each day offered something different. The first day included a parade, with a number of floats built by various factories to show off their wares. Other events included "Carnival Day", Secret Societies Day" and Sister Cities' Day". Street pageants were held, as were band concerts, balloon races and a wide variety of vaudeville-type acts.

On September 22, Dayton celebrated "Aviation Day", which included airplane flights around Simm's Station and balloon races competing for the Dayton Cup, with the big finish being Orville Wright flying over the city at 5 p.m.

Long before Orville's flight was to take place, crowds gathered along the banks of the Mad and Miami Rivers, with 50,000 people stretched out in a line over a mile long. This was the first attempt at flying over the city and, in fact, the first flight of either of the Wright brothers within the corporation limits. They had previously refused to fly over the city, claiming that it was too dangerous and could cause serious damage to buildings and people should something go wrong and there was a crash.

As Orville took off from Simm's Station, *Dayton Journal* photographer K. M. Kammer snapped off a shot with his camera, then climbed into a Republic automobile driven by Fred Devoe in a race to beat Orville back to the city so that he could take another photograph of the airplane as it circled downtown. The *Hamilton Journal* stated that Orville "looked down on the 60 horsepower Republic going as fast as it could and kept about even with it until it was necessary to go ahead; then he let the wings of his air bird flap a little faster and he went by the Republic like a shot."

Orville's approach to the city was heralded by a number of factory whistles and clanging of street car bells. He circled the city at an altitude of about 3,500 feet and then swung over his home on Hawthorn Street in West Dayton, before returning to Simm's Station. The entire trip of 22 miles took less than 25 minutes.

The event was considered a great success, with the Dayton Chamber of Commerce expecting to clear at least $5,000, which would be used to further boost the city in the future.

September 20

When the first fairs were held in Ohio transportation was hard to come by. People who attended mostly came from the area in which it was being held. To increase interest and attendance, the Ohio Board of Agriculture decided to hold the State Fair in a number of different cities. In 1853, Dayton was selected as the site for the 4th Annual State Fair.

Although Dayton had been holding local fairs since 1839, no permanent buildings had been erected. A site was chosen south of the city, where the Montgomery County Fairgrounds was later located until 2017. Large tents were erected for the various exhibits, ranging from cattle and farm implements to flowers, fruits and machinery.

On September 20, 1853, the gates to the grounds swung open. Even though admittance was a dollar people seemed to have gotten their money's worth. Although earlier fairs had focused on agriculture, in 1853 it was decided to add some entertainment as well. Stage performances were held at the Rogers Theater, while the nearby Welch's Hippodrome, with its clowns, horse and riders, raked in the dimes. The mural of an erupting Mount Vesuvius was a favorite, as was the tent offering up "The Only Living Ourang-Outang in Captivity."

The fair must have been a success, for it was held in Dayton four more times; in 1860, 1861, 1866, and 1867.

The State Fair would find a permanent home in Columbus in 1874. This decision did not set well in Dayton and the city vowed revenge. *(See September 29)*

A contemporary drawing of the State Fair held in Dayton at the fairgrounds in 1853. Although sparse by today's standards, the fair proved to be quite popular.

September 21

Gebhart's Opera House opened to public acclaim at 22 East Fifth Street on March 12, 1877. In 1889 it was renamed the Park Theater. On September 21, 1896, exhibitor Harry Clark brought with him a Vitascope projector and several movie reels. Unsure as to whether the movies would be enough to attract an audience to the theater, Clark played it safe by hiring the American Vaudeville Company to provide live entertainment between reels. These short films would be the first motion pictures to be shown in Dayton.

Although many of the films shown that day had titles, they were not advertised. In fact, if it weren't for a *Dayton Journal* reporter's review of the show, no record would remain of what played on that momentous night. As it is, only vague descriptions were given. But from these few clues an educated guess can be made as to the names of some of the films shown. Among them are: 1) *The Milk White Flag*, showing scenes from Charlie Hoyt's musical comedy. 2) *Bucking Bronco*, where a bucking horse from Buffalo Bill's Wild West show was filmed in a corral at the rear of Thomas Edison's studio. 3) *The May Irwin Kiss*, where actors May Irwin and John C. Rice reenacted the climax of the musical comedy *The Widow Jones*, when the widow and Billie Bikes kiss. This became one of the most popular Edison films of the year, as well as the most controversial, as many people believed showing a kiss between two unmarried people was too risqué. 4) *Watermelon Contest*, which showed the participants hurriedly eating watermelons. When this picture played in Maine, one theater manager claimed that patrons considered it "nasty and vulgar because of the spitting and slobbering" that occurred in the film. He wrote the Vitascope Company and asked that it be replaced with a different picture.

Other reels viewed that evening included views of Niagara Falls and Atlantic City, scenes of President McKinley at his home in Canton, Ohio, a speeding train, the movements and drill of a battery of artillery, ocean waves and a whirlpool. Together, with the vaudeville acts, it made for an unforgettable evening.

In 1907, the theater was renamed the Lyric, then the Mayfair Theater in 1934. The Mayfair closed its doors in 1968 and the building was demolished in 1969. Today, the Convention Center is located on the site.

September 22

The Colonial Theater, at 141 South Ludlow Street, was the first Dayton theater to regularly feature 'talkies', which were often referred to, and rightly so, as the 'squawkies'. On September 22, 1928, the theater presented Dayton's first all-talking, full-length picture, *Lights of New York*. Although neither the plot nor the acting was of high quality, this did not deter the people from attending.

"The first actual talking picture ever exhibited - a picture without subtitles, where in all the characters speak their parts, opened yesterday for a week at the Colonial theater," reported the *Journal Herald*. "And to say that the novelty intrigued the fancy of the audience is to speak with undue restraint of Warner Brothers epoch-making departure *Lights of New York*. There was an odd pleasure in hearing the screen favorites, like the pleasure of becoming better acquainted with neighbors we have only nodded to."

The sound was not on the film itself, but on phonograph discs, which were played in sync with the talking of the actors. Audiences loved "talkies" so much that by the end of 1929, Hollywood was producing sound films exclusively.

September 23

In the 1870s, many slaughterhouse owners operated their own yards, which were scattered across the city. Since both buyers and sellers of livestock needed a central place to transact business, the idea of a union stockyard was conceived. A number of butchers and livestock dealers decided to get together and incorporated themselves into a joint stock company, to be known as the Southern Ohio Stock Yards Company. Their thought was to build the stockyard on the West Side. Among the incorporators were Adam Schantz, a butcher; William Burkhardt, whose company manufactured various meat products, including sugar-cured hams and breakfast bacon; Charles and Nicholas Jacobs, who dealt in fresh, salt and smoked meats; Frank Kimmerle, whose sausage factory and pork packing plant was located on Germantown Street, almost directly across the railroad tracks from where the stockyard would be located; and Jacob Stickle, owner of the City Brewery. Why was Stickle involved? It was because a decision was made to also include both a hotel and a saloon on the property of the stockyard, and Stickle would provide the beer.

Another unusual person on the list was Colonel Edwin F. Brown. Colonel Brown was appointed Governor of the Dayton Soldiers' Home. Having easy access to livestock was very important, as the amount of food to feed the men at the Home was enormous. The potpie served on Wednesdays required twenty-one sheep, seven barrels of potatoes, a hundred pounds of flour, and six dozen eggs. Over three thousand eggs and thirty hams could easily be consumed for breakfast. It is understandable why the colonel would want to be involved in a stockyard so close to the Home.

On September 23, 1875, the Southern Ohio Stock Yards Company officially opened on South Mound Street, just north of the Dayton and Western Railroad line, and about a half-block north of Germantown Street. The eight-acre complex included a number of covered and uncovered pens for cattle, hogs, sheep and calves, with the hotel and saloon being completed soon after. The stockyard would be responsible for bringing a number of jobs to the West Side.

On October 24, 1900, the Southern Ohio Stock Yards was dealt a blow when the Union Stock Yards Company opened in the 1000 block of Springfield Street. By the spring of 1901, the Southern Ohio Stock Yards had closed its doors.

September 24

In 1899 Vincent G. Apple began the Dayton Electrical Manufacturing Company in Dayton. The company's line included the manufacturing of Apple Gas, Gasoline and Petroleum Engine Igniters, Dynamos, Motors and Dayton Incandescent Lamps and Storage Batteries.

One of Dayton's most well-known machinists, Charles E. Taylor, worked for Apple, until he was hired away by Orville and Wilbur Wright to work on an engine for their airplane. But when the Wright brothers needed help with their airplane's electrical system they turned to Taylor's old employer for a solution, an Apple magneto.

In 1902 Vincent invented what some believe to be the first electric self-starter for automobiles. In 1907 Apple pioneered the use of tungsten bulbs in auto lamps for the first time. This lead to Vincent organizing the Apple Electric Co, which began selling its products under the trade name "Aplco" in 1908. In 1914 he developed a method of bar winding starting motor armatures, a method that was used for decades, as well as the first starting system for Ford automobile, using a silent chain drive.

When Vincent Apple died on September 24, 19 1932, he still had 149 patents under his control, 42 patents were pending, 38 patents were prepared to be filed, and 264 inventions in process which applications for patents were to be filed. In time, over 350 patents would eventually be approved. This makes him Dayton's greatest inventor, with over 200 patents more than Charles F. Kettering.

Vincent Groby Apple

September 25

In 1799, Daniel C. Cooper began to raise hogs on his farm, the first seen in this part of the county. The hogs were described as "long-legged, slab-sided, ugly and savage". The hogs proved to be quite popular, for they needed little care, fattening on the great quantity of acorns and beech nuts found in the woods. Others also began raising hogs. They were marked by their owner with a particular notch on an ear, and then turned loose to feed and fatten. Then in the fall, when butchering time came, the settlers would hunt them up in the forest and shoot them with a rifle. This had to be done, for over time the hogs would become very wild. They had also learned as a matter of defense to travel in droves. When threatened, the hogs would form a circle around their young pigs, and when a wolf approached too near, the hogs would tear him to pieces with their tusks. Unfortunately, this also meant that some of the hogs grew quite dangerous.

On September 25, 1806 the city council passed an ordinance barring hogs from running loose in the streets. If found, an offending animal would be taken into custody, slaughtered and sold. History indicates that enough hogs turned up their snouts at the law to provide a fat municipal income. The ordinance seemed to be enforced only once in awhile - probably more forcefully as money was needed by the city, since Daytonians were inclined to vote down any proposed taxes.

This picture of Main Street in Dayton, taken sometime in the 1850s, shows that even a half-century later the problem of loose hogs had still not been solved.

September 26

In the early 1900's, the Dayton Spice Mills Company had a good reputation for their spices, baking powder and coffee. Established in 1885, the specialties of the house were their brand name Jersey Coffee, Jersey Spices and Jersey Baking Soda. The company's products were carried in stores throughout the tri-state region.

In order to broaden their market, Dayton Spice Mills came up with a new product, which they called Dutch Java Blend, a fancy roasted coffee. Little did they know that about the same time the U.S. Department of Agriculture had passed the Food and Drugs Act of June 30, 1906.

On September 26, 1908, Dayton Spice Mills shipped 270 cases of roasted coffee to Frank S. Fishback, whose business was in Indianapolis, Indiana. Each case was labeled "100 pounds of Dutch Java Blend", for a total of 27,000 pounds of coffee. As luck would have it, the Bureau of Chemistry of the Department of Agriculture chose to take samples of the coffee and have them analyzed. It was found that the coffee contained little or no Dutch Java coffee, but was instead chiefly composed of an inferior grade of coffee. This proved that the label appearing on the cases describing the coffee was false, misleading and deceptive, and in violation of the Food and Drugs Act. The facts were reported to the United States attorney for the district of Indiana, who seized the shipment. Fortunately for the company, they were able to file a bond that released the coffee back to them on the condition that the product be sold by legal means.

After the verdict, the Dayton Spice Mills Company had another problem. Although they had been advertising their new product as Dutch Java Blend coffee, the ruling no longer allowed them to sell it under that name. The difficulty was to popularize the new name, Old Reliable Coffee, and at the same time to hold all of the buyers of the old brand without making use of the printed word "Dutch". The advertising card on the left shows how ingeniously they accomplished this. A boy in wooden shoes approaches a woman wearing a Dutch bonnet. In his basket is a box of Old Reliable Coffee. The atmosphere of the card would unmistakably suggest this as the old brand of coffee that so many customers loved. The ads must have worked, for Old Reliable Coffee became the company's best selling product.

September 27

After several days of rumors, on September 27, 1919, it was officially announced that General Motors had acquired the Domestic Engineering Company, Dayton-Wright Airplane Company, and the Dayton Metal Products Company.

The Domestic Engineering Company was responsible for the Delco Light System, which consisted of a small combustion engine operated by gas, gasoline or kerosene, directly connected to a generator which provided electricity. A storage battery stored the electricity. This provided power to people living in rural areas not yet electrified. The company also sold various electrical appliances, all of which could be operated by the electricity produced by the Delco-Light systems.

Dayton-Wright Airplane Company was formed in 1917, when the United States declared war on Germany. The company was awarded war contracts to produce an American version of the de Havilland DH-4 British bomber. The DH-4 was the only American-built aircraft to serve with the U.S. Army Air Service in World War I. It would continue to build airplanes for several years after the war ended in 1918.

The Dayton Metal Products Company was known for its highly efficient research division, much of it due to the scientific and engineering ability of Charles F. Kettering. This would soon become the research division of General Motors. At the time of the sale, the company had been experimenting with air-cooled engines and improvements in fuel. This would lead to the discovery of ethyl gasoline in 1921.

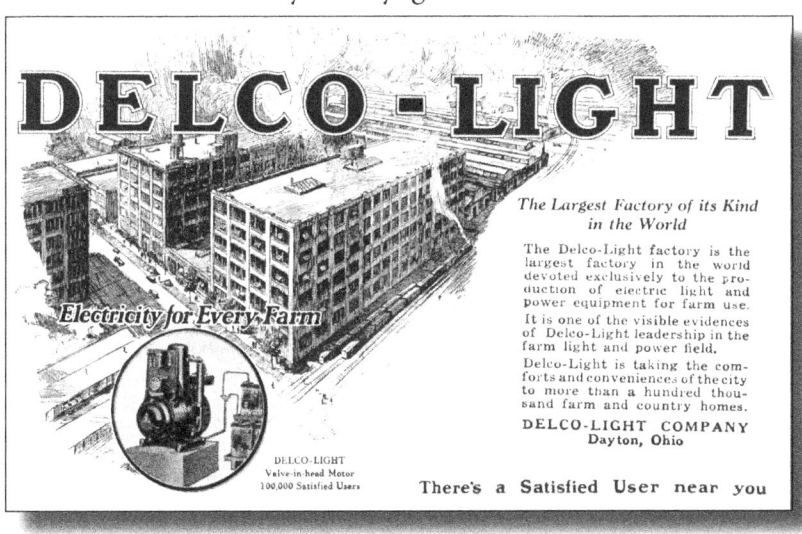

DELCO-LIGHT

Electricity for Every Farm

The Largest Factory of its Kind in the World

The Delco-Light factory is the largest factory in the world devoted exclusively to the production of electric light and power equipment for farm use. It is one of the visible evidences of Delco-Light leadership in the farm light and power field. Delco-Light is taking the comforts and conveniences of the city to more than a hundred thousand farm and country homes.

DELCO-LIGHT COMPANY
Dayton, Ohio

DELCO-LIGHT
Valve-in-head Motor
100,000 Satisfied Users

There's a Satisfied User near you

September 28

On September 28, 1916, the Harley-Davidson Motor Company, well known for their motorcycles, announced that they were was adding a full line of adult and children's bicycles to their products.

The Davis Sewing Machine Company in Dayton made the components and shipped them to Milwaukee to the Harley-Davidson plant for assembly. Bicycles came in one color, military drab, with detailing in black, gold, and white. Bicycles were built to look like a Harley motorcycle in an attempt to make young boys want the real thing when they grew up. Beginning in 1917, they were mainly sold through Harley dealerships. However, sales were slow and production ended in 1921.

1917 Harley-Davidson bicycle

September 29

When the first fairs were held in Ohio transportation was hard to come by. People who attended mostly came from the area in which it was being held. To increase interest and attendance, the Ohio Board of Agriculture decided to hold the State Fair in different cities, including Columbus, Cleveland, Cincinnati, Mansfield, Sandusky, Springfield, Toledo, and Zanesville. Dayton held the honor in 1853, 1860, 1861, 1866 and 1867.

Finally, the Board decided that the Ohio state capital should be the permanent site for the state fair, and it moved to Columbus in 1874. This did not set well in Dayton. A delegation went to Columbus and pled their case for having the fair placed permanently in Dayton instead. When they were turned down, the city decided to get revenge by holding a fair of their own.

On September 29, 1874, the Southern Ohio Fair opened its doors on Main Street, where the Fairgrounds is still today. The response was overwhelming. Large crowds inspected the various exhibits, including livestock, floral arrangements, a Siberian fur robe worth several thousand dollars, and even a set of chinaware made in China!

By the third day, when the famous racehorse, Goldsmith Maid, was scheduled to run, it was estimated that over 43,000 people went through the gates that day alone. The day before, all of the railroads into the city had been at full capacity, some even being forced to use box cars and coal cars in order to accommodate everyone who wanted to come to the fair. The hotels were standing room only. In the end, records showed a paid attendance for the five days of 125,000 people, well beating the attendance of the State Fair that had been held in Columbus just three weeks before. In fact, up until the last day of the State Fair, it looked like it was going to be a financial failure. Fortunately, about 26,000 people showed up the final day, which they bragged was the highest attendance ever reached in one day in the history of any state fair held in Ohio.

Of course Dayton was quite proud of itself and vowed to hold a fair every year. A large exhibition hall was built, as was a machinery hall and other buildings. The race track was enlarged and other improvements made, all at great expense. But, while the first fair was a great success as far as attendance was concerned, the receipts were not sufficient enough to pay for all of the improvements. The attendance of future fairs failed to meet the large expenses incurred in holding them. The last regularly held Southern Ohio Fair was in 1890.

September 30

Josephine Garrigus, had a great interest in airplanes. Her husband, Samuel, flew at night, advertising with neon signs attached to his airplane. Samuel was the only licensed one-arm pilot in the country. Josephine obtained her pilot's license on September 30, 1931, becoming the first woman from Dayton to do so.

Garrigus soon became friends with four other women with the same interest in flying: Iona Coppedge, Betty Hanauer, Sue Malone and Rosetta Zimmerman. In November, 1931, the group formed the Dayton Women Pilots' Club. They would meet monthly at the Miami Hotel. People came from far and wide to see and talk to the pilots.

Employed in the legal department at Wright Field, Coppedge obtained her license in February, 1932. Hanauer, whose husband ran the East Dayton airport, received her license in May, 1932. In her autobiography, Zimmerman states that she financed the club. She also says that she flew, but never mentions if she became licensed. The status of Malone's license is also unknown.

On February 11, 1936, Coppedge and Garrigus established a world's altitude record for light airplanes, flying 15,252 feet over East Dayton.

Members of the Dayton Women Pilot's Club. Left to right: Iona Coppedge, Josephine Garrigus, Rosetta Zimmerman, Betty Hanauer and Sue Malone.

October 1

On October 1, 1925, heavyweight boxing champion Jack Dempsey boxed two of his sparring partners in two two-round exhibition bouts at Memorial Hall, which was filled to capacity.

While Demspey was quite a draw all by himself, there were other compelling reasons why the crowd came to the hall. One was Dempsey's wife, Estelle Taylor, who was regarded as one of the most beautiful stars of silent films of the 1920's. The couple had met and married earlier that year.

Another draw was the rumor that the champ was in poor fighting shape. Instead of continuing to defend his title, Dempsey had spent the last two years earning money with boxing exhibitions, appearing in films, and endorsing products. It was also said that he partied more than he trained. His marriage to Taylor only led strength to the rumors.

Fight fans were also pleased to find out that Gene Tunney, another well-known heavyweight boxer, had been persuaded to attend the exhibition and be introduced at ringside.

In a twist of faith, when Dempsey finally decided to defend his title a year later, the man he fought was none other than Tunney. Tunney would win by a ten round unanimous decision. After losing to Tunney in a rematch in 1927, Dempsey would retire from boxing for good.

Gene Tunney and Jack Dempsey in the boxing ring at Memorial Hall in Dayton.

October 2

On October 2, 1874, the Fairgrounds was the scene of what was at the time the largest crowd that ever saw a horse race in the United States. It was estimated that between 80,000 and 100,000 people jammed the grounds on that day to watch Goldsmith Maid try to beat the record for a mile over a half-mile track.

Goldsmith Maid was a prominent Standardbred racemare in the 1870s that was called the "Queen of the Trotters". The race trial had been well advertised and people came in droves, with 60 carloads coming in on the street railway line. Street traffic was so heavy that thousands were unable to get to the fairgrounds until long after the race was over.

Goldsmith Maid was driven by Bud Doble in the trials. She was hitched to a high-wheeled sulky, a light two-wheeled horse-drawn vehicle for one person, used chiefly in harness racing. The time to beat was 2:18. In her first attempt, she finished the mile in 2:21. In her second try she came in at 2:18, tying the world record. The crowds went home quite satisfied.

Goldsmith Maid (1857-1885) had a harness racing career that spanned 13 years. Her last race was won at the age of 20 against a much younger horse named Rarus. She was inducted into the Harness Racing Hall of Fame in 1953.

October 3

The American Professional Football Association was organized in Canton, Ohio on September 17, 1920. Carl Storck, owner of the Dayton Triangles, was one of the founders. The league would be renamed the National Football League (NFL) in 1922.

On this day in 1920, history was made when the Dayton Triangles beat the Columbus Panhandles 14-0 in the first game between two teams of the American Football League. The Triangles' Lou Partlow scored the league's first touchdown and George "Hobby" Kinderdine kicked the first extra point. The game was held at Dayton's Triangle Park near Ridge Avenue and DeWeese Parkway. This is considered the very first APFA/NFL game.

In 1922, the other NFL teams were recruiting top college players, while Dayton continued to use mainly local players. This marked a decline in the team's performance, and the Triangles ceased being competitive in the NFL, winning just five of their 51 NFL contests from 1923–29.

On July 12, 1930, a Brooklyn-based syndicate headed by Bill Dwyer bought the Triangles. The franchise moved to Brooklyn and became the Brooklyn Dodgers. None of the Triangles players joined the Dodgers, although five of them went on to play for other teams.

A team photograph of the 1920 Dayton Triangles of the American Professional Football Association, later named the National Football League.

October 4

During World War I, the the United States Army Signal Corps asked Charles F. Kettering to design an unmanned "flying bomb" which could hit a target at a range of 40 miles. Kettering came up with a design, formally called the Kettering Aerial Torpedo, but later known as the Kettering Bug. The device was built by the Dayton-Wright Airplane Company. Orville Wright acted as an aeronautical consultant on the project, while Elmer Ambrose Sperry designed the control and guidance system.

On October 4, 1918, during a test flight, the Bug began to climb in ever widening circles, then went out of sight. Kettering and other engineers took off after it in their cars in fast pursuit. When they found the Bug a group of farmers surrounded the wreckage. Some of them had begun searching for the pilot. Wanting to keep the Bug's real purpose a secret, they told the farmers that the pilot had jumped from the airplane using a parachute and was only slightly injured. One of the farmers insisted he had seen the pilot fall from the plane and wanted to continue the search. Desperate, the engineers offered to take the man to see the pilot. Luckily, he declined.

Although several successful flights were made later, the device was never used in combat. Officials worried about the Bug's reliability when carrying explosives over Allied troops.

Prototype of the Kettering Bug.

October 5

On November 16, 1916, just seven years after joining the Dayton Police force, Patrolman Lucius J. Rice became the first black Dayton officer to be promoted to the rank of sergeant.

On September 30, 1939, Sgt. Rice was dispatched to the scene of a murder at 629 South Western Avenue. The victim was Scott Conner. Witnesses stated that a black man, Floyd McAlpin, had killed Conner during an argument over a woman. Rice was told that McAplin could be found at 515 College Street. Rice went to the address, where he was met by two other detective sergeants, Fred B. Smith and B. S. Benner. They found that the address belonged to an upstairs apartment, but that McAplin, whose real name was Eugene Harris, was living downstairs at 513.

When the three policemen entered the apartment, Benner stayed at the front entrance to block any attempts of escape, while the others began searching the rest of the apartment. When Sgt. Rice opened the door to the bathroom, Harris began to shoot. Rice and Smith returned fire. The gun battle ended with Sgt. Rice wounded in the abdomen and Sgt. Smith receiving a scalp wound. Harris was shot twice; one bullet entering his hip, the other into his shoulder.

Hearing the shots, Sgt. Benner ran toward the bathroom. When he saw Harris, Benner pulled his gun, but the cylinder fell open. Harris hit Benner over the head with the butt of his gun and escaped. But Harris' freedom was short-lived, for he was captured the next day.

Sgt. Lucius J. Rice died from his wounds on October 5, 1939. Harris was found guilty of murder and executed in the electric chair at the Ohio Penitentiary in Columbus on October 23, 1940. Harris is the first and only murderer of a Dayton police officer to be executed.

Sgt. Lucius J. Rice

October 6

The first time Elvis Presley performed in Dayton was on May 27, 1956, at 2 p.m. and 8 p.m., at the University of Dayton Fieldhouse. A review in the *Dayton Daily News* of the evening show stated that the 3,000 "mostly teenagers" screamed so much through the 30-minute performance that he doubted if anyone heard more than a couple of words from Elvis.

Elvis would come to Dayton three more times, performing at the University of Dayton Arena on April 7, 1972, October 6, 1974 and October 26, 1976.

To the delight of his fans, Elvis held concerts at 2:30 p.m. and 8:30 p.m. on October 6, 1974. The 13,500 fans attending the evening performance were rewarded with 24 songs, two more than he had sung earlier that day. Both began with set openers "C.C. Rider", "I Got a Woman / Amen", and "Love Me", and ended with "Can't Help Falling in Love".

"I have a lot of people that ask me if I play the guitar and the answer is no ... I mean, uh, yes I can!" Elvis said toward the end of the evening set, and then proved he could, playing an acoustic guitar for "That's All Right, Mama" and "Blue Christmas".

Fortunately for fans who were not there, both sessions were recorded with a direct connection to the soundboard. The matinee show was finally released 22 years later as part of a 4 CD box set called "A profile - The King on stage Vol. 2" in 1996. The evening show was released as "Breathing Out Fire" in 2000. A reviewer of the album wrote "This isn't Elvis Presley at his most intense, but the mutual warmth between singer and audience makes for a perfect time capsule of something now a quarter of a century gone: the 1974 Elvis Presley Show."

In 2009, the Gravel Road Music label released "A Day In Dayton", with both shows on two CDs. That same year, the Boxcar Label also released both shows on two CDs, but also included a 100 page glossy book with images and liner notes on the tour surrounding the two concerts.

Elvis Presley at U. D. Arena in 1974

October 7

In 1872, Buffalo Bill Cody began performing in a stage drama named *Scouts of the Plains*. He was joined by his friend, Texas Jack. In his autobiography, Buffalo Bill described the opening night of the play:

> "The Scouts of the Prairie was an Indian drama, of course, and there were between forty and fifty "supers" dressed as Indians. In the fight with them, Jack and I were at home. We blazed away at each other with blank cartridges, and when the scene ended in a hand-to-hand encounter, a general knock-down and drag-out, the way Jack and I killed Indians was "a caution". We would kill them all off in one act, but they would come up again ready for business in the next."

When the play reached Dayton on October 8, 1873, the troupe had been joined by the famous lawman and gambler Wild Bill Hickok. Held at the Music Hall (now the Victoria Theatre), the three men received applause throughout the show, with the *Dayton Daily Journal* stating that it was the most enthusiastic audience to ever assemble in the Hall.

Buffalo Bill must have loved Dayton, for he would bring his outdoor extravaganza, "Buffalo Bill's Wild West" show, to the city twenty times between 1875 and 1914.

"Buffalo Bill" in his later years

Left to Right:
James Butler "Wild Bill" Hickok
John Baker "Texas Jack" Omhaundro
William Frederick "Buffalo Bill" Cody

October 8

Edgar Cayce is well remembered as a psychic. While in a self-induced trance Cayce was said to have the ability to "read" the medical and physical conditions of people.

In 1923, he met Arthur Lammers, a successful printer from Dayton. Lammers was impressed with Cayce and invited him to Dayton to do a set of private readings. On October 8, 1923, the first in a series of readings on psychic phenomena was begun in room 115 of the Phillips Hotel. The room was to be the scene of extensive psychic work by Cayce over the next few months.

It was because of these readings that Cayce became convinced in reincarnation, after stating during his trance that he himself had once been a monk. Lammers persuaded Cayce that he should begin a psychic research society in Dayton. Cayce agreed and in 1923 opened the Cayce Psychic Institute in an office at the Phillips Hotel and began giving readings there.

Things did not go well in Dayton for Cayce. He wrote "Many were the days that we wondered when we left the house after breakfast to go to the office at the hotel whether there would be anything to eat when we returned in the evening." He eventually had to close the office in the hotel and set up a place at his residence at 322 Grafton Avenue, where he continued to do business until moving to Virginia Beach in September, 1925.

Edgar Cayce, circa 1910. Cayce would go on to gain national prominence in 1943 when an article titled "Miracle Man of Virginia Beach" appeared in Coronet magazine. Today, Edgar Cayce's not-for-profit organization, known as Association for Research and Enlightenment, has members in more than 70 countries.

October 9

The Dayton Typographical Union Local No. 57 was organized May 13, 1862. This appears to be the first union in the city. The organization was also involved in the first employee lockout. Early in 1886, John S. Doren, editor and manager of the *Daily Democrat*, discharged all of the union compositors employed on the paper. The Typographical printed a four-page sheet, *The Appeal*, which condemned Doren's actions and threatened political retaliation upon the Democratic party. On May 15, 1886, the Union accepted Doren's proposition to unionize employees of the newspaper.

On October 9, 1899, John Kirby, Jr., general manager of the Dayton Manufacturing Company, discharged 18 employees in the polishing and buffing department, saying that the work being done in the department was unsatisfactory. But the Metal Polishers, Buffers, Platers and Brass Worker's Union No. 5 countered that the only reason the men were fired was because they belonged to a union. This was the opening gun of the first serious battle of Dayton manufacturers with the forces of organized labor.

Dayton Manufacturing went to court, seeking protection from the Metal Polishers' Union. It charged that the men who were let go had formed a picket line, and were threatening to harm other employees of the company if they did not quit working there. The threats were taken more seriously when one of the workers, P. William Allinger, was attacked by a gang of 12 to 15 men and beaten within an inch of his life.

Some of the workers decided to leave, forcing Dayton Manufacturing to have a large portion of the polishing and buffing of the railway car trimmings they made to be done outside of the factory. Common Pleas Judge Kumler agreed to a temporary injunction forbidding the strikers to *"picket the plant, congregate or loiter about in the neighborhood, or in any manner interfere with the company or its employees"*.

On June 12, 1901, the injunction was made permanent. But by then the strike was over, the fired employees having all found work in other factories. Besides, the Metal Polisher's Union had bigger fish to fry - fighting the largest employer in Dayton - The National Cash Register Company. (*See May 3*)

October 10

Dayton's citizens were star-struck when Violet MacMillan came to Dayton to perform her vaudeville act at Keith's Theater. The actress got her start by winning the title of "Cinderella Girl" during a contest to discover a woman with feet small enough to wear a golden slipper that measured an 11½ children's size. This led to a leading part in the 1907-08 production of the musical, *The Time, The Place and The Girl*. But it was her roles in movies produced by L. Frank Baum that she is known for.

Baum's "Oz Film Manufacturing Company" was an independent film studio from 1914 to 1915. MacMillan played parts in the Oz movies that were produced, including Dorothy Gale in *His Majesty, the Scarecrow of Oz*.

Besides acting, MacMillan also added to her income by endorsing several businesses in each city wherever she appeared on stage. On October 10, 1917, an entire page of the *Dayton Daily News* was devoted to MacMillan's time in the Gem City. The actress touted the Overland Sedan, provided for her to use by Dayton Overland Sales; Steinway pianos, at Steinway & Sons; Sempre Giovine skin cleaner, available at Gallaher's Drug Store; and George W. Baker shoes, which could be found at Elder & Johnston.

Cinderella contests were held by local shoe stores. MacMillan would place one of her satin slippers in the store window. Anyone 18 or older that could put on the slipper and walk received a free theater ticket. It was the rare customer that was able to do so.

October 11

The Gem City Polo Club played hockey using roller skates instead of ice skates. They usually played on wooden floors - never ice. The sport was first known as "roller polo" due to the introduction of Polo in 1876. The sport was played for the first time in a roller skating rink in Dayton in 1882. On October 11, 1882 The National Polo League was organized. Chicago, Cincinnati, Cleveland, Columbus, Dayton, Louisville and Pittsburgh made up the seven founding cities of the new organization.

In the early days the Gem City Polo Club was the team to beat, becoming national champions during the 1882-1883 and the 1883-1884 seasons.

On March 1, 1903 The National Roller Polo League was organized in Dayton. Cincinnati, Columbus, Dayton, Hamilton, Indianapolis and Springfield made up the six founding cities of the new organization.

The sport still exists and is quite popular. Now known as rink hockey, the game is played in more than 50 countries worldwide.

The Gem City Polo Club won 53 out of 56 games in their 1883-1884 season.

October 12

On August 7, 1920, Franklin D. Roosevelt came to Dayton to meet with former Ohio Governor James M. Cox, the Democratic Party's presidential candidate, and accept the nomination for vice president. *(See August 7)*. On October 12, 1940, Roosevelt returned as President to inspect the progress at Wright Field and pay a visit to the Dayton Soldiers Home. Over 150,000 people filled the sidewalks as he drove by in his motorcade. Both Orville Wright and James M. Cox went along on the ride.

The trip to Dayton completed a two day check up on defense operations in Pennsylvania and Ohio. The president's son, Elliott Roosevelt, had reported to Wright Field earlier that month to begin a year of military service as captain in the specialist reserves. Elliott's appointment to a captaincy drew a bit of criticism at the time because he lacked military experience.

That evening Roosevelt gave an address on Hemisphere Defense. He stated that, while the U.S. did not want to go to war, the best way to avoid attack was to be prepared to meet it. So, in order to protect the western hemisphere, which included South America, the U.S. was going to begin to strengthen its military. Some countries viewed the speech as a step toward getting the United States into the war.

President Roosevelt and Orville Wright at Wright Field.

October 13

On October 13, 1950, the NCR Auditorium was the scene of a popular Cincinnati, Ohio television program, *Morning Matinee*. Hosted by Ruth Lyons, who was also known for her afternoon program, *The 50-50 Club,* the event allowed the audience to see first-hand how the popular WLW-TV star and her group staged their television show.

The show's special guests of honor that day were students of the Gorman Orthopedic Public School. Located on Grant Street, the school was named for Anna Barney Gorman, who had donated the land when the school was built in 1924. Students there were handicapped, most of whom suffered from polio or cerebral palsy. Gorman was also responsible for the Barney Community Center on Chapel Street, which provided residents free clinics, occupational therapy classes, a milk station and lunch program. This has since evolved into Dayton Children's Hospital.

During the *Morning Matinee* show Ruth Lyons presented Gorman School with a television set. Jeannette Wallace, principal of the Gorman School, praised the courtesy and helpfulness of the NCR guards in taking care of the children. Lyons also thanked NCR for allowing the show to be broadcast from "their beautiful auditorium."

Ruth Lyons (first woman on the left) and her gang at the NCR Auditorium.

October 14

In August, 1890, Rev. Carl Mueller, a minister at St. John's German Evangelical Lutheran Church, helped organize the Protestant Deaconess Society of Dayton, with the purpose of establishing a Deaconess Hospital. On October 18, 1891, a temporary hospital with thirty-seven beds was opened in Adam Pritz's house at 7 East Fourth Street. During the first year the hospital cared for eleven hundred patients, proving that there was a need to build a permanent hospital. That was when John H. Winters, president of Winters National Bank, and his wife, Sarah, came forward and donated some land along Main Street between Apple and Wyoming streets. About $150,000 was raised and on October 14, 1894 the new Deaconess Hospital was dedicated. The entrance to the hospital's main building was on the north side of Magnolia Street.

The hospital had a capacity of 150 beds and included a separate surgical suite. Private rooms could be had for $5 a week, while patients in the public wards were charged whatever they could afford.

Renamed Miami Valley Hospital in 1903, the facility provided Dayton with its first maternity ward and first emergency room. CareFlight, the region's first air ambulance, is but one example of the innovative ideas that contributes to the hospital's continued success.

Miami Valley Hospital's campus as it looked from Apple Street, circa 1912.

October 15

On April 12, 1862 one of the most daring exploits of the Civil War involved a young man by the name of James Reed Porter. The plan was for a group of Union soldiers to dress in regular clothing, board a train at Big Shanty, TN, then use it to destroy communication lines between Atlanta and Chattanooga, That would help Union forces take over the eastern part of Tennessee.

James J. Andrews, of the Secret Service, was given the assignment. After boarding, the men uncoupled the engine, along with three boxcars, from the rest of the train. Confederates caught up with the stolen train near Ringgold, Georgia. The frustrated Unionists stopped the engine and headed for the surrounding woods, but were soon captured. Andrews and several others were hanged as spies. The rest were given a stay of execution.

Although Porter and another soldier had overslept and missed the train they were later captured and thrown in jail for conspiracy. Porter, along with eight others, was able to escape the Fulton County Jail in Atlanta, Georgia on October 16, 1862.

For his part in the raid Porter was awarded the Congressional Medal of Honor, as were eighteen others, in part for the courage they all showed during the raid and for their capture by the enemy.

James Reed Porter, the last survivor of the men involved in what was to become known as "Andrews' Raid", passed away at his home in Dayton on October 15, 1923. He is buried at the Union Cemetery in McComb, Ohio.

Andrews and his men abandon the locomotive "The General". Eight of the men involved in the incident were hanged as spies in 1862.

October 16

In 1990, members of the 2003 Committee and Aviation Trail, Inc. approached the U.S. Department of the Interior about turning several historic sites in Dayton's Wright-Dunbar area into a national park. By then the city had already lost several buildings that were important in telling the story of Dayton's involvement in aviation, including the Wright home at 7 Hawthorn Street and the Wright Cycle Co. bicycle shop at 1127 West Third Street, where Orville and Wilbur Wright had constructed their gliders and the first airplane, the Wright Flyer. Both had been moved to Greenfield Village, in Dearborn, Michigan by Henry Ford in 1936. *(See July 3)* Orville Wright's laboratory at 15 North Broadway had also been razed in 1976 to make room for a gasoline station which was never built.

The proposed sites were the Wright Cycle Company at 22 South Williams Street, where Orville and Wilbur Wright sold bicycles and ran a printing operation from 1895 to 1897; Huffman Prairie Flying Field in Greene County, where the Wright brothers perfected the Wright Flyer III, the world's first practical airplane; the John W. Berry, Sr. Wright Brothers Aviation Center at Carillon Historical Park, which tells the story of the Wright brothers and showcases their original 1905 Wright Flyer III; and the Paul Laurence Dunbar State Memorial at 219 N. Paul Laurence Dunbar St., home of the first black American to achieve distinction in the literary field. *(See June 3 for more on the Dunbar home)*

Legislation was introduced in Congress on May 14, 1991 for the establishment of the Dayton Aviation Heritage National Historical Park. President George H. W. Bush signed the bill into law on October 16, 1992.

The Wright Cycle Co.

October 17

In 1959, Senator John F. Kennedy went on a "pulse-feeling" tour, traveling to a variety of states to see if he should become an active candidate for the presidency. On September 17, 1959, Kennedy arrived in Dayton to give a speech to the Dayton Bar Association at the Biltmore Hotel. Little did Kennedy know that, exactly 100 years prior to the day, Dayton had been visited by Abraham Lincoln. It was in front of the Old Court House on September 17, 1859, that Lincoln's bid for president was officially announced for the first time. Kennedy, however, was keeping his desire to be in the White House a secret, albeit one that most Democratic Party insiders already knew.

It wasn't until his return to Dayton on October 17, 1960 that Senator Kennedy would speak to a large crowd from the Old Court House about his political ambitions, having finally officially announced his presidential candidacy earlier that year. At the end of his speech, Senator Kennedy quoted Lincoln, saying:

"One hundred years ago in the campaign of 1860, Abraham Lincoln wrote to a friend: 'I know there is a God, and I know He hates injustice. I see the storm coming, and I know His hand is in it. But if He has a place and a part for me, I believe that I am ready.'

"Now, 100 years later, we know there is a God, and we know He hates injustice. We see the storm coming, and we know His hand is in it. But if He has a place and a part for us, I believe that we are ready. Thank you."

Hundreds came to see Senator Kennedy at the Old Court House when he revisited Dayton on October 17, 1960.

October 18

In 1867 the National Asylum for Disabled Volunteer Soldiers (more commonly called the Soldiers' Home) was opened in Dayton to take care of volunteer soldiers who had been injured during the Civil War. Several barracks were built, with each floor accommodating about forty men.

Unfortunately, the only clothing issued to the men were old wool uniforms from the war, which they had to wear year-round, even in the summer. And, for the first few decades, there was no air-conditioning to relieve them from sweating. As can be imagined, the barracks soon began taking on an unpleasant smell, especially as some of the residents were reluctant to take baths.

The managers at the Soldiers' Home did everything they could to make bathing a pleasant experience, to the point of constructing a brick building, with both hot and cold baths. But there were still holdouts to the idea. In fact, it was reported that "compulsion was sometimes necessary" in order to get the men to bathe. As it was, some had gone so far as to ask the doctor to be excused from bathing, but this was rarely granted.

On October 18, 1875, General Order Number 49 was posted, which commanded everyone in the barracks to take at least one bath a week. Tickets were issued to make sure that everyone complied with the order. Those who did not do so were hauled in front of the governor of the Home.

Bathing would do little toward keeping someone clean if they never changed their clothing. And so another rule was implemented stating that underwear and bed linens of each inmate had to be washed at least once a week.

October 19

During the Civil War, a Confederate cavalry, led by Brig. Gen. John Hunt Morgan, made their way into Kentucky, Indiana and Ohio. The raid took place from June 11 to July 26, 1863. As the cavalry made their way through the states, officials realized that they were unprepared for the war. Since the south had seemed so distant, no real effort had been made to prepare the states to defend against the enemy.

Martial law was declared in Cincinnati, Covington and Newport. Citizens were required to organize in accordance with the direction of the State and municipal authorities. In Dayton an organization was formed under the name of "Die Schuetzen Gesellschaft". There were twenty-four charter members.

To keep their shooting skills up, a Schützenfest was held at Oakwood Park on October 19, 1863. The Schützenfest ("marksmen's festival") was a target shooting competition, where contestants competed based on their shooting abilities.

Old-time, long-barreled, muzzle-loading squirrel rifles were used that first year, each man equipped with a powder horn, bullet pouch and cap box, and a soft hat with a feather. The targets were made of wood, 2½ feet in diameter and were named from the pictures painted on them – The Stag, The Hunter, Gambrinus and Winged Victory with Flambeau of Fame. In the center was a one-inch circle; five shots were fired from 100 yards and the one placing the most bullets in or nearest the center was declared the 'Schützenkönig' ("king of marksmen"). Their first King was William F. Sander.

The group decided to stay together and form a club after the war was over. In 1866 the organization was incorporated under the laws of Ohio and in 1870 the named was changed to Dayton Sharpshooters' Society.

Membership in the society grew to around 200 at its peak, but by its end very few were left. On October 17, 1917, the final tournament was held. Although the newspaper reported that the meet was "attended by practically all of the members and a number of visitors from Springfield, Troy, Xenia and other cities", only about two dozen shooters competed. As luck would have it, the event was won by none other than Gus H. Sander, the son of William F. Sander, who had won the first kingship.

October 20

Although parachutes were used during World War I by observers who were forced to jump from balloons, they were considered impractical for airplanes. General William Mitchell, Commander of the U.S. Air Force in France, pleaded for better parachutes for his pilots. In 1918, it was decided that a parachute facility should be established at McCook Field. The idea paid off when J. Floyd Smith developed a parachute enclosed in a pack that was opened by the operator after he jumped. This turned out to be quite lucky for Lt. Harold R. Harris, who was forced to make the first emergency parachute jump from an airplane on October 20, 1922.

Lt. Harris, Chief of the Flying Section at McCook Field, was conducting experimental tests on a Loening PW-2A when his control stick began to malfunction. The plane went into a dive at 2,500 feet. Lt. Harris bailed out, pulled the ripcord at 500 feet and landed unharmed in a grape arbor on the north side of town. The airplane Lt. Harris had been flying crashed a block away and was completely destroyed.

Harris' mishap inspired the "Caterpillar Club", whose membership is still open to anyone who has made an emergency parachute jump to save their life. Charles A. Lindbergh was the only person to qualify four times.

After Lt. Harris bailed out his airplane crashed at 403 Valley Street in Dayton.

October 21

In 1824, President Jean-Pierre Boyer made a plea for "descendants of the Africans" to move to his country, Haiti (also known as Hayti) where they would find equality, unlike the harsh and humiliating conditions that they were experiencing in the United States. He stated that "my heart and my arms have been open to greet, in this land of true liberty, those men upon whom a fatal destiny rests in a manner so cruel." President Boyer's hope was that Black migration would bolster the Haitian economy, something it desperately needed.

The Haitian government agreed to pay the emigrants travel expenses, give them free land, tools, schooling and full citizenship. President Boyer declared, "Those who come, being children of Africa, shall be Haytiens as soon as they put their feet upon the soil of Hayti." He also stressed that since Haiti was so close to the United States, emigrants would not be abandoning their enslaved brothers and sisters.

White advocates saw Haiti as a place to which undesirable free blacks could be deported and decided to help those who wanted to leave do so. And thousands did, including a third of the African Americans then living in Dayton.

On October 21, 1824, twenty-four of the seventy-three blacks residing in Dayton, amid "wild weeping, wailing, and shouting, and lamentations over the separation for life from friends and home", left for New York, where arrangements had been made with agents there to carry out the plan. Coffee from Haiti had been deposited with the agents, which they in turn sold to get the money to pay for the project. People arriving for the trip were supplied with food and clothing and safely conveyed on board a ship.

At first reports back were favorable, the emigrants praising the reception they had received in their new country. However, some of them found themselves confronting a number of problems. First, there were language barriers and religious differences. Settlers became frustrated with the process of land distribution, which was extremely slow in many cases. Worry spread that the Haiti government meant the new emigrants to be permanent laborers instead of independent landowners.

In 1825, Haiti's secretary general admitted that he believed nearly one-third of the original settlers had returned to the United States. Most of the twenty-four blacks who had left Dayton would eventually find their way back to the city.

October 22

If you wanted to pick out one of the strangest characters in Dayton's history, you wouldn't be far off the mark if you chose Dr. James S. Rose. Dr. William J. Conklin once described Dr. Rose as "unquestionably the most unique specimen who ever masqueraded under the pseudonym, 'Doc'".

"I can see him now leaning on his staff in the doorway of the old frame shanty on South Jefferson Street. Thin and wrinkled, and wizzen-faced, body bent to a quarter circle, eyes deep-set under shaggy brows, and a small and piercing like a serpent's beard, gray and long, covering the upper chest; a dressing-gown, red-figured and greasy, dangling from his misshapen shoulders, and an antique silk hat pushed far back over a bald and shining occiput - all in all, his appearance was uncanny enough to hurry school-children to their mother's knees and to give rise to the story of a haunted house."

Whenever a funeral procession would wind its way past his Jefferson Street office towards the cemetery, the eccentric physician would step into his yard and drop down a sign that read "Not My Patient". Another read "No poisoning or torturing, no burning and dissecting the living done here. Slaughter-pens farther up," referring to the offices of doctors on the same street.

Dr. Rose's first ad for his services appeared in the Dayton Daily Empire on October 22, 1860. One of his claims was the ability to cure Scrofula, or tuberculosis of the neck.

308

October 23

On the morning of October 23, 1906, Alonzo Souslin was painting a baseboard in one of NCR's new buildings, when a plank fell, striking him and breaking his neck. Souslin lay unconscious for eight days, then spent several months recovering from his injuries. A steel brace was made to try and keep pressure off of his neck.

Unable to work, Souslin came up with the idea to print postcards of himself and his family that he could sell to raise money. He also wrote a booklet, titled *My Own Story of a Broken Neck*, which told of how he was coping with the tragedy.

Before long Souslin's plight was printed in a number of magazines. The articles described the steel and leather contraption that held his neck in place. One article exclaimed that if Souslin so much as turned his neck even a sixteenth of an inch, death "would be instant".

Souslin eventually took to the road, traveling across the country, selling his postcards and booklet and giving lectures.

THEIR ONLY SUPPORT
Neck broken October 23, 1906, while decorating new office building, N. C. R., Dayton, O. Was stooped over in the act of removing rubbish, plank fell striking edgewise on back of neck.
A. Souslin, R. R. 15, Dayton, O.

Alonzo Souslin would continue to live another 16 years after the accident, dying at the age of 63 on March 22, 1923.

October 24

The Woman's Christian Temperance Union, founded in 1874, believed that the only way to save people from the temptation to drink was to outlaw the selling of liquor. One of the best known members was Carry Nation, who began her crusade in 1892. When one of her eloquent speeches was ignored by drinkers, she would resort to other means to get her message across. Armed with a hatchet, she would enter a saloon and smash bottles and furniture. This direct approach to the problem became known as a "Hatchetation".

In October 1904 Carry came to Dayton, selling her autobiography and souvenir wooden hatchets. Every day she gave a speech at a different church with hundreds of people attending. As the days went by and it came closer for her time to leave Dayton everyone became anxious, since they felt that Carry would not be able to hold back her tavern-smashing tendencies much longer.

One citizen decided not to wait.

On October 24, the newspapers reported of how Walter Ross, a true believer, had strapped a sunbonnet on his head, clothed himself in a black skirt and a Mother Hubbard and, procuring a wooden hatchet, had stopped in front of a Third street saloon and brandished the axe. A crowd gathered in expectation that a Carry Nation devastation was about to take place. Unfortunately for the crowd, it didn't happen. Two policemen happened by and stopped the man, taking him to police headquarters.

Disappointed Daytonians never did get to see a Hatchetation.

Carry Nation helped finance her trips by selling copies of her book and little wooden hatchets as souvenirs of her visit. The hatchets were so popular that, even at the cost of ten cents apiece, her entire supply of them were sold out.

October 25

On October 25, 1928, Babe Ruth and Lou Gehrig stopped in Dayton as part of a their barnstorming tour. Ruth's Bustin' Babes was made up of Dayton's amateur champions, the Thompson Yellow Jackets, while Gehrig's Larrupin' Lou's were the semipro champions, the McCall's. The game was held at the North Side Field northwest of Leo Street and Troy Pike. Both men were scheduled to both play first base and pitch.

While talking to *Dayton Daily News* Sports Editor Carl Finke, Ruth had one concern.

"Say Finke, can you find out what kind of baseballs they are going to use in today's game?" Ruth asked. "Over in Columbus, they had 50 cent balls that you couldn't hit hard. And then the fans were disappointed because Lou and myself didn't hit any home runs. The fans want to see us knock them out of the lot, and they are disappointed when we fail. If they use cheap balls today, I just won't play."

The balls must have had the right sort of stuffing, because "Iron Horse" Gehrig hit four consecutive home runs that day, including one over the center fence that was thought to be the longest ever hit at North Side Field.

But the "Emperor of Swat" did not let the 1,400 fans down that day, hitting a grand slam in the eighth inning.

Although Gehrig's McCall's team beat Ruth's Yellow Jackets 14-7, no one left the field disappointed.

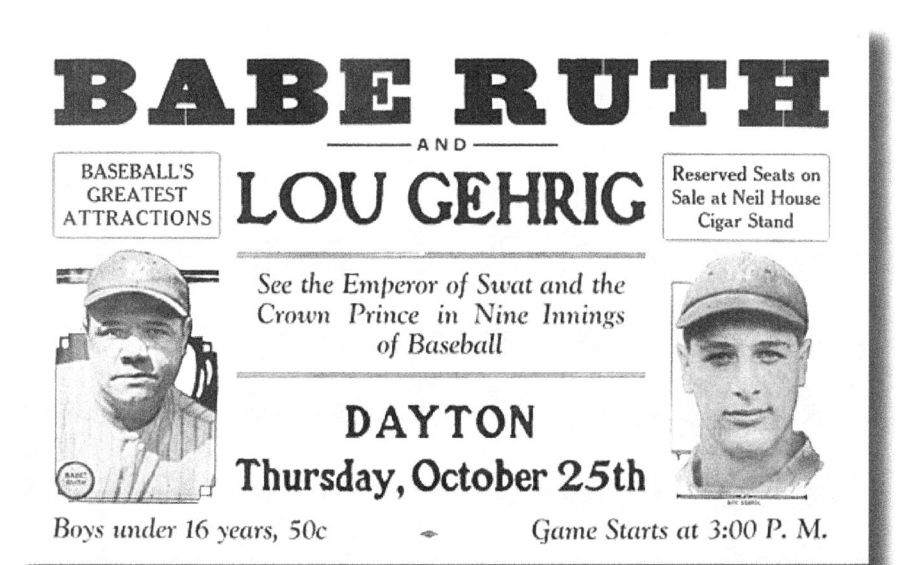

BABE RUTH
— AND —
LOU GEHRIG

BASEBALL'S GREATEST ATTRACTIONS

Reserved Seats on Sale at Neil House Cigar Stand

See the Emperor of Swat and the Crown Prince in Nine Innings of Baseball

DAYTON
Thursday, October 25th

Boys under 16 years, 50c — Game Starts at 3:00 P. M.

October 26

The Protestant Chapel was one of the first permanent structures to be erected at the Dayton Soldiers' Home and was dedicated on October 26, 1870. Built of stone quarried from the Home's grounds, the Gothic-style church was the first permanent government-constructed place of worship in the United States built for veterans and by veterans.

A spire was added to the chapel around 1872. Four years later a 1876 "Centennial Bell" was hung in the tower. Its inscription reads: "1776, Centennial Bell, 1876 made for the Church of the National Soldiers' Home Dayton, Ohio, from cannon captured from the enemy during the War of the Rebellion."

Morning and evening services were held in the church each Sunday. On occasion, guest speakers were asked to preach, including Bishop Milton Wright, father of Orville and Wilbur Wright, who held Sunday service in front of 350 veterans on January 10, 1897.

The pattern of the slate roof included fourteen stars framing a large cross. The tower included a large clock which could be seen from most of the campus.

October 27

On October 27, 1936, the citizens of Dayton started buzzing when they found out that Henry Ford was in town and visiting Orville Wright. It seems that Ford and his son, Edsel, had come to Dayton to see the Wright Cycle Co. building at 1127 West Third Street Henry had purchased earlier in the year. (*See July 3*) The idea was to move the bicycle shop to his museum in Dearborn, Michgan, named Greenfield Village, where Ford was busy relocating and restored historic structures

While in Dayton, Ford discovered that the old Wright home at 7 Hawthorn Street still existed as well. After Orville, Katharine and Bishop Milton Wright had moved to Oakwood in 1914, the home on Hawthorn was leased to Lottie Jones, the Wright's laundress. Jones would eventually buy the home, along with the furnishings the family had left behind, for $4,000. With Orville's help, Ford was able to purchase the home from Jones for $4,100.

In case you feel that Lottie Jones was somewhat cheated in the selling price of the house, know that she made up for it when it came to selling the furnishings and other items from the home. As Tom Crouch says in his book, *The Bishop's Boys*, Jones and her sons "milked the Ford establishment for all it was worth" by sending several shipments of "newly discovered" material to Detroit on consignment.

Today, both the Wright bicycle shop and Wright home are located at Greenfield Village.

The Wright family home at 7 Hawthorn Street as it looked in 1900.

October 28

After the stock market crash in 1929, the U.S. economy collapsed. People stopped buying anything that wasn't really needed. This led to factories shutting down, as many already had merchandise they couldn't sell. This, in turn, caused businesses to fail. By the end of 1930 it was estimated that 7 million people had lost their jobs. It was just the beginning of a depressed economy that would last over a decade.

A special dispatch to the *Cincinnati Enquirer*, dated October 28, 1939, reported a story of a desperate man who was willing to do anything to help his family. Unable to find work since he had been laid off from The Troy Sunshade Company 15 months before, Clyde M. Lowry placed an ad in a Dayton newspaper, offering to sell one of his eyes for $10,000.

"It might sound like a joke or a publicity stunt, but it is a serious matter to me," Lowry stated, adding that he had a wife and son to support.

Lowry appeared a few days later on the Cincinnati radio program, "I Need A Job", on WSAI, which tried to help jobless men find work.

Fortunately, Lowry did not have to sacrifice his eye to survive. Whether due to the publicity, or a turn in the economy, in just a short time he was hired as a factory foreman.

October 29

During the early 20th century William Ashley "Billy" Sunday was the nation's most famous evangelist, with his "old doctrine of damnation" sermons, as one journalist stated, and feverish, wild displays of running back and forth and even busting up chairs to make a point.

No regular church could hold the crowds that attended his sermons of salvation and so, before he came to Dayton on October 29, 1922, Sunday had a special temple built at what is now Riverview Park. Named the Billy Sunday Tabernacle, the huge wood building was 234 feet long by 136 feet wide and was capable of seating 6,472 true believers. A special platform was built 8 feet up off the floor and a thousand-watt light shined on it so that the crowd could get a good view of the preacher.

On December 18, when Rev. Sunday gave his final sermon, it was thought that about 750,000 souls had come to see the preacher while he was in Dayton. That final night alone, the collection plates were overflowing, bringing in over $25,000. Tired from seven weeks of preaching, Rev. Sunday and his wife boarded a train that evening and headed home.

During his stay in Dayton, Rev. Billy Sunday visited NCR and gave a "fire and brimstone" speech to employees there on November 10, 1922.

October 30

When the Civil War began, three groups of men were assigned to the 1st Regiment Ohio Volunteer Infantry for three months– the Lafayette Guard, the Dayton Light Guard and the Montgomery Guards. *(See April 17)*

After the term of service was over in August, a number of the men re-enlisted for 3 years in the reconstituted 1st OVI. The regiment was organized at Camp Corwin, which consisted of a house and land at Tates Point, just north of Huffman Hill. Colonel Edwin Parrott was in charge of the regiment during its time in Dayton. The officers lived in the house, while the men camped on the hillside. The regiment stayed at Camp Corwin until October 30, 1961, receiving muskets, uniforms, and other accoutrements.

Under Colonel Benjamin F. Smith, the 1st OVI was involved in 24 battles and skirmishes, including the Battle of Shiloh and the Battle of Chickamauga. The 1st Ohio Volunteer Infantry mustered out of the Union army from September 24 to October 14, 1864.

Above is a picture of the house at Camp Corwin. During its three years of service the 1st OVI lost 527 men in action and marched 2,500 miles.

October 31

During the Great Depression a number of banks across the United States collapsed. People feared that their bank would close since there were no guarantees on cash at the bank. That started a massive run on the banks to pull money out. Some banks were not able to fulfill the requests for withdrawal and closed their doors.

The Union Trust, Dayton's largest bank, failed and closed its doors on October 31, 1931. The next day Charles F. Kettering appeared on the floor of Winters National Bank and stated that everything was well and promised he would underwrite the bank with his own money if needed. He was believed, as he had already proven himself before, having once saved Winters Bank from collapse in 1924 by taking over its financing and helping guide it through troubled times. Kettering also paid a visit that day to other banks, brimming with self-assurance that things would turn out fine if everyone stuck together. It was agreed that the confidence which Kettering's presence gave to depositors at that critical time probably helped save several Dayton banks from closing.

Mutual Home and Savings, pictured on the left, also found itself in trouble. To build public confidence, the company erected a 20 story, $1.6 million building at 120 West Second Street in 1931. The building was an exceptional example, both inside and out, of art deco architecture.

On January 1, 1933, Mutual reduced their interest rate on mortgages from 7 percent down to 4.5 percent, the largest reduction made by any building association at the time. The extravagant gesture did not help. The company closed later that same year.

November 1

Dayton was, politically, a Democratic town at the time the Civil War began. The *Empire*, a decidedly Democratic newspaper, made it clear that it was against eliminating slavery. John F. Bollmeyer, editor of the *Empire*, encountered strong opposition to his views shortly after the war broke out; including receiving death threats. On November 1, 1862, Bollmeyer was shot to death by Henry N. Brown, an over-zealous supporter of President Abraham Lincoln's politics.

Afterward Brown gave himself up quietly to the police, who placed him in jail. That night hundreds of excited Democrats surrounded the jail, demanding the prisoner. Guards around the building were driven in with stones. As the police retreated they fired into the mob, who returned fire with pistols. Two cannons at the *Empire* office were seized and taken to the jail for use against it. The *Empire* protested later in its columns that the cannon had been taken by force and without the knowledge of the owners.

The fighting became so frantic that some loss of life seemed inevitable; but only three persons were wounded by the shooting, and several by stones. By 9:30 the tumult greatly subsided; and at 10:00 p.m., when a detachment of Federal troops arrived from Cincinnati, all was quiet.

Bollmeyer's friends wanted to erect a monument at Woodland Cemetery where he was buried, but his wife insisted on a marker instead. But when the trustees of Woodland heard what the inscription on the marker was going to be, they stated that she would not be permitted to place it in the cemetery.

However, whether it happened in the dead of night, as the trustees claimed, or the light of day, as the widow's friends insisted, the marker somehow ended up over the grave. It read: "He fell by the hand of an assassin, a martyr to the cause of liberty of speech and of the press."

Woodland trustees had the stone removed on the grounds that it was "offensive to a large portion of the lot owners."

The widow finally agreed to alter the inscription on the marker, which still stands today. It reads: "He fell by the hand of VIOLENCE Nov. 1, 1862. A Friend to the cause of Freedom of Speech and the Press."

November 2

Drive-in motion picture theaters had a reputation for being 'passion pits' almost from the very beginning. In 1957 a bill was introduced to the Ohio General Assembly by two Montgomery County delegates to ban unmarried persons under eighteen from attending movie theaters after midnight unless accompanied by parents or guardians. The measure was sponsored by State Representative Jesse Yoder and Charles W. Whalen, Jr. Yoder told the committee he had introduced the bill because "people are disturbed by the goings-on in drive-in theaters after midnight."

Harold B. LeCrone, assistant county prosecutor, told the house judiciary committee that "illegitimate births in the county are stemming primarily from one drive-in." He did not name the offending theater. "We know it must be happening," LeCrone continued. "The bars close and the dregs are using the places. They go off in a corner of the drive-in and park. It's a little cheaper than renting a motel."

Robert Wile, of the Theater Owners of Ohio, testified against the bill.

"You can't blame the illegitimate birthrate on the drive-ins because we are cheaper than motels. You should also keep eighteen year olds out of motels." He also stated that enforcing the law would be difficult since it would take theater operators "hours to check all the cars after midnight to see if there were any minors in them."

Part of the problem was due to the fact that during the early 1950's some of the local drive-ins began having all night movie marathons. The last movie of these 'dusk to dawn shows' sometimes didn't end until 4 a.m. or later.

Drive-in theater owners as far away as Troy, Miamisburg, Eaton and Springfield met at the Belmont Auto Drive-In to discuss the problem. They agreed to drop the dusk to dawn shows after November 2, 1957.

"When we saw they (dusk to dawn shows) were hurting the community, we decided to stop them," said Edward Parker, owner of the North Star Drive-In. "One of the theater operators had been holding out because he felt he was catering to a number of second shift factory workers, but we changed his mind."

The house judiciary committee shelved the bill after hearing that the number of films being shown would be reduced to three, which meant the box office closed at midnight. Owners also agreed to patrol the theater grounds for "unacceptable" activity, such as lovers and drinkers.

November 3

On July 14, 1851, Joseph Lebensburger purchased land on Rubicon Street on behalf of The Hebrew Society for use as a cemetery. The burial ground extended toward Stewart Street and back to Brown Street and covered about 300 feet by 150 feet. The cemetery opened in 1852.

The first burial, which took place on November 3, 1852, was seven-year-old Gelinde Friedlich. The last interment was made April 21, 1888. In 1889, John H. Patterson, president of NCR, bought the cemetery, as well as the Jewish Temple which stood at the corner of Fourth and Jefferson streets. With the transfer of the property, Patterson gave the congregation perpetual rights to the cemetery. The sale of the land was used to purchase eight acres on West Schantz Avenue, which became Riverview Cemetery. Disinterment began almost immediately. In 1967, Temple Israel moved the last of those buried on Rubicon Street to Riverview Cemetery.

A high stone wall was constructed in 1886 to block the view of monuments and tombstones. The Roundhouse at the fairgrounds can be seen on the upper left. Several of the homes on the right still exist. Today, most of the land is a parking lot.

November 4

James Ritty was the owner of a restaurant in Dayton called the Empire (which later became the Pony House). Ritty was frustrated by the fact that he was losing money due to his employees stealing from him. It was difficult to keep track of sales on the best of days, and impossible to know what the honest tally was at the end of the day.

While on a ship bound for Europe in 1878 Ritty found his answer. He was taking a tour of the vessel's facilities when he came across the cyclometer, a machine that automatically counted each turn made by the ship's propeller. Ritty immediately saw how that principle could be used to add up sales in his restaurant. When he returned to Dayton, he joined his younger brother, John, in the development of the cash register. They succeeded in doing so, receiving patent #221,360 for their idea on November 4, 1879.

Although several improvements were made to the cash register over time, the Ritty brothers became discouraged and sold their patent rights in 1881. The patent eventually found its way into the hands of brothers John H. and Frank J. Patterson, who would use it to start The National Cash Register Company (NCR). It was under their guidance that the cash register became one of the most important inventions in the world.

The early cash register model based on the Ritty patent looked more like a clock than a register. When a customer paid his bill, the cashier punched in the total amount. At the same time the machine would keep a running tally of total sales by adding successive entries.

November 5

On November 5, 1914, the "red light" district of Dayton, as it was delicately described in the newspapers, came under fire from City Manager Colonel Henry Matson Waite. With the help of several women from the police department, it was claimed that enough evidence had been gathered to ensure the eradication of vice districts in the city.

Waite had been hired as Dayton's first city manager on December 14, 1913. His main duty was to see that the laws and ordinances were enforced, including getting rid of prostitution and gambling. It had taken almost a year, but Waite finally had everything in place to carry out his plan without a hitch. Or so he thought…

Waite ordered the closing of 65 "houses of vice" and 15 "resorts" on Pearl Street, with a deadline of December 1. After that day, the full force of the police department would come to bear to make sure that the law was enforced.

However, Waite had forgotten one little detail. Estimates of the number of "fallen girls" working in the districts ranged from 60 to over 100. The Dayton Social Welfare League complained that the action by the city manager was a little precipitate. While they were pleased to hear that the houses were closing, the League wished that they had been included in the discussions, so that plans to try and find employment for that many woman might have been made. The worry was that, without jobs in place, many of the women might have to chose between remaining in their old line of work, or starving.

The Leagues's worries were well-founded. On December 3, 1914, it was reported that only two women had been offered jobs, both of them in hotels. Policewoman Catherine Ostrander said she had pleaded to housekeepers to place the girls to work in private homes, to no avail. Ostrander truly seemed puzzled as to how hard it was to get work for the girls, especially if the wives knew that their potential employee had worked on Pearl Street.

Although at first it seemed that the closings had worked, it was soon determined that the idea may not have been as good as it looked on paper. Before, the women were registered by the police and contained to certain areas, which meant better control of the situation. But the closing of the houses meant a wider area the police had to cover. By 1931, it was estimated that there were at least 300 women making a living walking the streets.

November 6

Phil Donahue began his career in 1957 as a production assistant at KYW radio and television in Cleveland, Ohio. He got a chance to become an announcer one day when the regular announcer failed to show up. He later became an anchor of the morning newscast at WHIO. Donahue also hosted Conversation Piece, a phone-in talk show from 1963 to 1967 on WHIO.

On November 6, 1967 The Phil Donahue Show debut on WLWD (now WDTN) in Dayton. In 1970, The Phil Donahue Show entered nationwide syndication. Donahue's syndicated show moved from Dayton to Chicago in 1974; then in 1984, he moved the show to New York City, where the show was shot at a studio at 30 Rockefeller Plaza, to be near his wife Marlo Thomas.

After a 29-year run, 26 years in syndication, and nearly 7,000 one-hour daily shows, the final original episode of Donahue aired on September 13, 1996, culminating what as of 2016 remains the longest continuous run of any syndicated talk show in U.S. television history.

Johnny Carson appeared on The Phil Donahue Show in Dayton on August 27, 1970.

324

November 7

At 10:45 a.m. on November 7, 1910, Philip Parmalee took off from Dayton in a Wright B Flyer. His destination: the Columbus Driving Park, a racetrack in Columbus, Ohio. Instead of a human, his passenger was 200 pounds of Rajah silk manufactured by Rogers and Thompson of New York City and valued at $600. The package was bound for the Moorehouse-Marten Department Store, which had paid the Wright Company $5,000 for the delivery. The distance of 60 miles was made in 56 minutes. This was much quicker than expected and so only about 1,000 people were there to meet the airplane when it landed.

The publicity stunt put Moorehouse-Marten on the map, with the news of the first cargo flight being covered in newspapers across the country. The silk was quickly cut up and sold to a fevered public. Swatches were attached to post cards that pictured a Wright biplane, while others were stamped with the legend, "This silk is a piece of the first merchandise ever carried in an airplane – Dayton to Columbus, November 7, 1910." The rest was made into men's ties and women's dresses. Sales of the silk came to over $6,000, more than recouping the investment in the flight.

This postcard of the Wright B Flyer in flight has a swatch of the silk attached to it in the upper right hand corner. Handwritten along the right side of the card is "Sample of first merchandise transported by Airplane. Dayton to Columbus Nov. 7th '10"

November 8

In the early 1900's the word THINK was a key slogan around the National Cash Register Company (NCR). John H. Patterson, President of the company, had THINK signs plastered liberally on the walls of the offices and factory buildings. It was also the title of a small pamphlet published in 1911, for salesmen to distribute to prospective customers. The small 2¾" x 4¼" - 16 page booklet was copyrighted October 12, 1911 and accepted and filed in the Library of Congress on November 8 of that same year.

Today, the slogan THINK is associated with IBM. While the company was not the first to use it, IBM's owner, Thomas J. Watson, may have been the person who originally came up with the idea.

Watson was first hired to work as a cash register salesman in NCR's office in Buffalo, New York in 1895. He eventually rose to the post of general sales manager of the company. Legend states that he tried to galvanize his team by saying "We don't get paid to work with our feet. We get paid to work with our heads," and wrote the word THINK on an easel. When Watson became President of the Computing-Tabulating-Recording Company(CTR), he began using his favorite slogan, THINK, which quickly became the corporate mantra. CTR would later become known as International Business Machines, or IBM.

Think!

Thomas A. Edison

THINK of what a great thing Thomas A. Edison did when he thought of the incandescent light.

The safe, economical and brilliant illumination which means so much to everybody was the result of Edison's THINKING.

The First Incandescent Light

326

November 9

In 1915, the Congressional Union, a suffrage organization, sponsored a cross-country trip from San Francisco to Washington DC, in which 500,000 signatures on a petition for a constitutional amendment giving women the right to vote would be personally handed to President Woodrow Wilson. Ingeborg Kinstedt and Maria Kindberg acted as chauffeur and mechanic, while Sara Bard Field gave speeches and collected more signatures along the way. Mabel Vernon would travel ahead, lining up welcoming parades and speaking engagements for Field.

Vernon must have been very good at her job, for when the ambassadors pulled into Dayton on November 9, 1915, they were warmly greeted with an automobile procession, which left Third and Ludlow at 11 a.m. and wound around the city, ending on Third and Main an hour later.

At the Old Court House, Marie Kumler welcomed the modern "Joan of Arcs". Judge Roland Baggott talked about how women wanted to vote, not just because they wanted to participate in an election, but also so that they could improve social conditions, provide better schools and help make the country a better place to live in. Sara Field drove home the point with an eloquent speech, while Mabel Vernon collected another hundred or so signatures on a petition that was already 4 miles long.

On December 6, 1915, the group reached Washington DC. President Wilson agreed to receive them and the huge spools the petition was rolled on, in the East Room of the White House. Though impressed, Wilson later stated that suffrage was an issue for each state to decide.

Sara Bard Field, Ingeborg Kinsteadt and Maria Kindberg in their Overland auto.

November 10

On this day in 1930, Frederick B. Patterson, president of NCR, opened the NCR City Club at Second and Ludlow streets as a relief kitchen. Known as "The Open Door", the relief station was open from four p.m. to seven p.m. Meals consisted of soup, hot mush, coffee or milk, and sandwiches. The dining room was brightened with curtains. The tables had a number of vases that held flowering begonias. Comfortable chairs and a radio playing music added to the experience.

After being fed, visitors were then offered candy and cigarettes, the latter being lit by the staff member handing them out. The company was proud to state that there was a large list of women from Dayton who were eager to help whenever needed.

About 750 people were served each day, no questions asked. Fred Patterson's kindness also extended to the dignity of those who used the service, insisting that the staff should never say or do anything that could embarrass anyone who ate there.

Jefferson Davis, self-proclaimed King of the Hoboes, was present the first day the kitchen opened. He praised Patterson for trying to help those in need.

"The feeding of these unfortunate people will be a wonderful protection for this community. It will prevent crime, insanity and suicide."

November 11

At the 11th hour on the 11th day of the 11th month of 1918, the Great War came to an end. At 5 a.m. on that day, Germany signed an armistice agreement with the Allies to go into effect at 11:00 a.m. Paris time.

Word of the signing reached Dayton shortly after 2 a.m. The news was announced by the ringing of a bell at the First Presbyterian Church, the same one that rang out the joyous news of various victories during the Civil War. Soon bells from other churches and whistles from dozens of factories joined in.

The last blast of the whistles had hardly died away when crowds of people began pouring into the streets, which grew by the minute. Almost every factory gave orders for closing down their plant. At 10 a.m., NCR's 5,000 employees joined in. When the 6,000 workers arrived at the Dayton Wright Airplane Company factory, they were told to punch in on the time clock and then told to fall in and march the four miles to downtown. From the moment they arrived, the streets were impassable.

Impromptu parades began, with companies carrying banners with messages like "Viva La France", and "Dayton Munitions, Money and Men Won the War". Confetti fell from windows like rain. It was estimated that over 150,000 people joined in on the celebration.

At the height of the demonstration, Howard M. Rinehart, chief pilot of the Dayton Wright company, flew over Third and Main, performing a number of stunts with his airplane.

As the revelers tired out, they all agreed that a real celebration should soon be held in the city. On March 17, a formal Victory event with a parade and speeches was given.

Although the Armistice was signed by 5:30 am., the fighting continued until 11 a.m. Sadly, at 6 a.m., Daytonian Sgt. Ralph B Clemens, of the 322nd Field Artillery, was struck by shell fragments while fighting in Ecurey, France. He died two hours later, just about the same time Dayton began celebrating the end of the war.

November 12

Due to the rise in the number of workers coming to Dayton to work in the factories during World War II, there was soon a shortage of housing. On November 12, 1942, the National Housing Agency opened the Dayton War Housing Center in order to centralize the demand for houses apartments and sleeping rooms from workers. To help solve the problem a number of mobile trailers were brought in to the city. There were also thirty-four trailer camps, including Forest Park, Ideal at Main and Shoup, and Riverside Trailer near Wright Field on Route 4, just past Harshman Road. Together, the camps held 1,026 trailers.

The reason trailers were used, instead of building permanent housing, was because a large number of war workers would move on after the war finished. To help ease the problems, several housing developments were either built or expanded during the war, including: Parkside Homes on Keowee Street, Edgewood Court on Edgewood Avenue, Summit Court on Summit and Riverview, DeSoto Bass Court on Germantown Street, Overlook on East Third and Smithville Road, and Greenmont on Waterviliet Avenue.

A number of mobile trailers, like this one at the site of the old McCook Field, were brought in for workers.

Parkside Homes

DeSoto Bass Court

November 13

On November 13, 1964 the Rolling Stones appeared for the first time in Dayton. They had toured the States once earlier in 1964 but were met with indifference, as by that time they had only managed two minor Top 30 hits. But by November the Rolling Stones' single *Time Is On My Side* was getting a lot of air time. The band had also made their first appearance on *The Ed Sullivan Show* the month before. Still, although advance publicity had claimed that the Stones were second only to the Beatles in popularity, fewer than 1,000 concert tickets for the 6,000 seats in Wampler's shiny new Hara Arena were sold. It didn't help that Brian Jones had just recently been admitted to Chicago's Passavant Hospital for pneumonia, with a fever of 105 degrees. This would cause Jones to miss four dates during the end of the band's U.S. tour. But what made it worse for those who did attend was the attitude of the rock band that night. The Rolling Stones stayed on stage for about 20 minutes and performed only eight songs.

Phil Gary, of Columbus, who had promoted the concert, figured he would lose $5000 on the show since the Stones were working on a flat guarantee, cash in hand before they went on. But it wasn't just Dayton concert-goers who seemed unimpressed by the band. The Stones had also bombed in both Ft. Wayne and Cleveland before coming here.

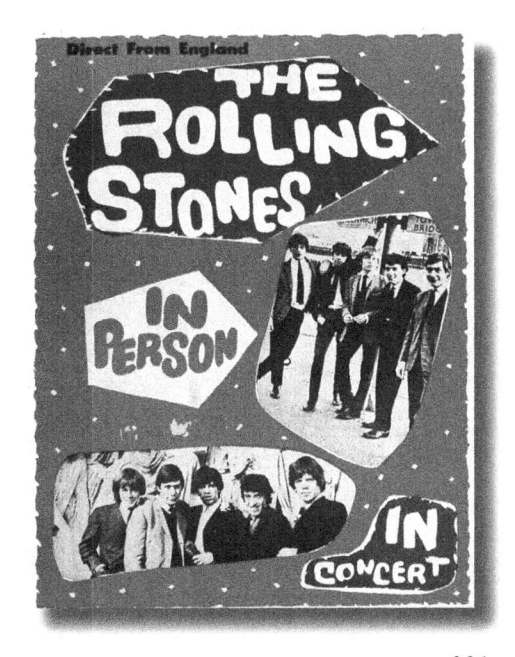

This poster was used during the Rolling Stones second U.S. tour, including their appearance in Dayton on November 13, 1964.

November 14

On November 14, 1882, Daytonians A. Ogden Huffman and Fred A. Brooks were granted Patent No. 267,348 for their grave vault. After the wrought iron vault was lowered into the grave, anchor irons or bolts were driven through sockets laterally into the earth, anchoring the vault so that it could not be raised back out of the grave. Once a coffin was placed in the vault, two self-locking lids would be closed. Once closed, the only way to get to the coffin would be to somehow smash through the wrought iron lids.

Why would such a vault be needed? The last line of the description of the invention says it all: *The above construction affords a vault which is easily made and is practically safe against grave-robbers.*

It's believed that between 1811 and 1881, just in Ohio alone, over five thousand bodies were stolen from their graves for the purpose of medical dissection. When the body of John Scott Harrison, the son of president William Henry Harrison and the father of future president Benjamin Harrison, was taken from its grave in 1878, a flurry of inventors filed patents on ways to make graves burglar proof. It is unknown if Huffman and Brooks ever manufactured their grave vault.

(No Model.)

A. O. HUFFMAN & F. A. BROOKS.

BURGLAR PROOF GRAVE VAULT.

No. 267,348.   Patented Nov. 14, 1882.

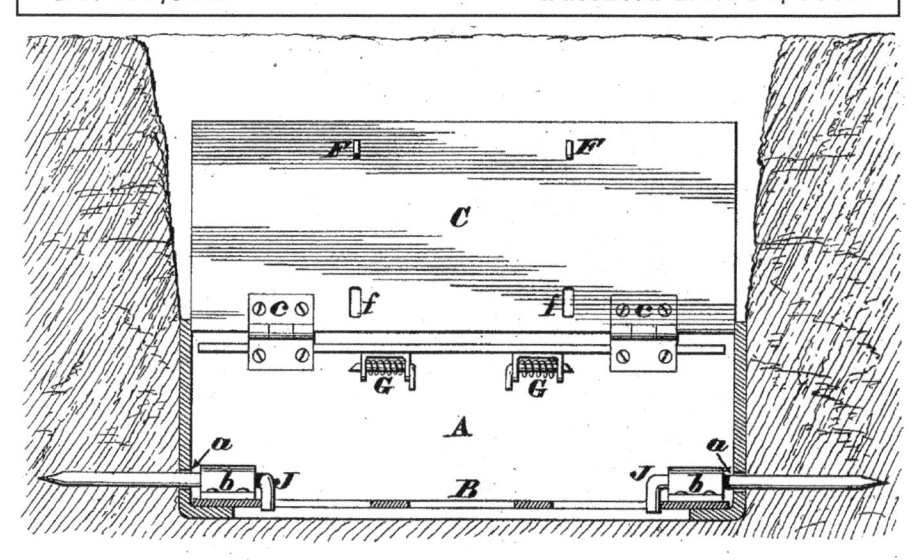

November 15

No one would have guessed from his track record in high school that Edwin Corley Moses would become one of the greatest athletes in the world. He ran some track at Fairview High, but didn't really stand out, being known more for his academics than his athletics. It wasn't until he tried out for track during his freshman year at Morehouse, an all-male, all-black Atlanta college, that Moses found his pace. He excelled at the high hurdles and would go on to win gold medals in the 1976 and 1984 Olympic Games in the 400 meter hurdles.

On November 15, 1984, at 10 am, a parade honoring Moses left Courthouse Square, travelled Main Street north to First Street and ended at Memorial Hall. Moses and his wife, Myrella, rode in a convertible, while over 1,000 Dayton public school children waved flags as they escorted the couple along the route. At the hall, Moses was given a standing ovation as he took the stage to give an Olympic Seminar. Afterwards, a luncheon sponsored by the Dayton Board of Education was held at the Ramada Inn downtown.

The following day a ceremony was held, changing the name of Miami Boulevard West and Sunrise Avenue to Edwin C. Moses Boulevard. Miami Boulevard West was chosen due to its connection with two major athletic facilities in Dayton, Welcome Stadium and the University of Dayton Arena. It was also the link between the two facilities and the River Corridor Bikeway, (now known as the Great Miami River Trail).

However, Moses' career was far from over. Between 1977 and 1987, Moses won 107 consecutive finals (122 consecutive races) and set the world record in the 400 meter hurdles event four times. Moses would finish third in the final 400 meters hurdles race of his career at the 1988 Summer Olympics in Seoul. During the 1990 World Cup at Winterberg, Germany, Moses and Brian Shimer competed in a bobsled race, winning the two-man bronze medal.

November 16

The Biltmore Hotel opened on the northeast corner of First and Main streets on November 16, 1929, less than a month after the stock market had crashed. A year later the hotel found itself in receivership, having to close all of its lower floors.

Fortunately, it was able to survive long enough to come back to life during World War II. Housing for factory workers was at a premium and many people became permanent residents. In 1944 the Hilton chain took over and began calling it the Biltmore-Hilton.

Biltmore's elegant interior included marble stairs, crystal chandeliers and the latest designer furniture. The Biltmore also boasted the biggest ballroom in Dayton. It was here that people gathered to watch Glenn Miller, Benny Goodman and Duke Ellington play. People still remember when local big-band leader Michael Hauer and his band played in the Kitty Hawk room, which was broadcast on the CBS Radio network.

In 1965, the Sharaton bought the lease from Hilton and renamed it the Dayton Sheraton, but its days as a hotel were slowly coming to an end. Now known as the Biltmore Towers, since 1980 the building has been a residential living complex for the elderly and handicapped.

Banquets were held in the Biltmore's large ballroom for a number of years. One of the more memorable events was the honoring of World War I ace Eddie Rickenbacker on his induction into the Aviation Hall of Fame.

November 17

During the first week of November, 1898 Bruno Kirves went over to his brother John's house to drink and play some cards. His wife Mary and his daughter Emma arrived soon after, and began nagging Bruno to come home with them. They wanted him to stop drinking, as he had been very abusive lately and alcohol made him even worse. A quarrel ensued and John's wife later decided to sue Mary for $10,000 for libel.

On November 16, 1898 Mary had been told by John that the case could be settled for $150. Bruno wanted her to pay the money, but Emma opposed the idea, since her parents would have to borrow the money from her to pay the debt. Mary's attorney advised her not to pay, saying that he would contact John and try and settle the case for less.

When Mary told Bruno of her meeting with the attorney, he became very upset and began threatening to kill her and Emma. He left the house and did not return home that evening.

The next morning Bruno returned home and killed his daughter with a shotgun he had stolen from a hunter drinking at a nearby saloon.

The case was given over to the jury for deliberation on February 22, 1898. He was found guilt of Murder in the First Degree. Bruno was sentenced to die by electrocution at the Ohio State Penitentiary on August 17, 1899.

At 12:21 am, the night of the execution, Warden Coffin signaled for the switch to be thrown. At first contact, bluish flames and blistering jets of steam appeared from under the black cap that covered Bruno's head. The body became rigid and the neck swelled to twice its natural size and turned white.

Bruno was examined but was found still alive. Another current was then sent through his body. Almost immediately the room began to fill with smoke and the odor of burning flesh and hair. One witness later described the smell as "sickening beyond description."

After examining Bruno a second time, the doctors had to admit that his heart was still beating. Again the current was turned on. Bruno's body gave a massive heave as it tried to escape its bonds, and the room became almost stifling under the stench of burning skin and muscle. After the current was turned off, the doctors finally pronounced that the prisoner was dead.

Bruno was later buried at Woodland Cemetery beside his daughter, Emma.

November 18

The Louisiana Purchase Exposition, held in St. Louis, Missouri, in 1904, commemorated the 100th anniversary of the purchase of the Louisiana Territory by the United States. One of the leading attractions at the fair was the Liberty Bell display in the Pennsylvania State Building. When the exhibit closed it was announced that the train transporting the bell to Philadelphia would stop in a number of towns along the way, including Dayton.

The excitement couldn't have been higher. Word spread that the train would arrive on November 18th at 3:10 and would stay for 15 minutes. Thousands showed up at the Union Depot to witness the unveiling of the Liberty Bell, the majority being children who had been let out of school early so that they could get to the depot in time. The Dayton Soldiers' Home band played patriotic songs as the crowd waited. Ten thousand copies of the song *America* were handed out and when the train carrying the Liberty Bell arrived the crowd greeted it by singing.

At 3:25 the bell was once again on its way towards home, with stops in other Ohio cities awaiting its arrival.

The Liberty Bell at the Union Depot in 1904. The bell had come to Dayton once before, on its way back home from the Chicago World's Fair, on November 1, 1893.

November 19

In the early days of motion pictures, Dayton theaters would show films that appealed to all ages. But after World War I, the various women's clubs, and mothers themselves, began voicing their concerns about children attending movies. The fear was that they might begin to imitate the actions they saw on the screen, like fighting, being too young to understand the difference between acting and reality.

On November 19, 1921, Dayton Loew's Theater held their first Saturday morning matinee. The program included films and vaudeville acts designed especially for children. At 10 a.m., the theater was packed with an eager crowd of youngsters, who had paid 10 cents to get in. Besides cartoons, there were two movies. "Now or Never" was a comedy starring Harold Lloyd, in which a young man, unaccustomed to children, must accompany a young girl on a train trip. "Nobody's Kid" starred Mae Marsh as a neglected and mistreated girl in an orphanage, who is happily rescued in the end.

The "Children's Saturday Show", which the program was first called, would soon have a new name. On those magical Saturday mornings the theater would temporarily transform into the "Children's Playhouse".

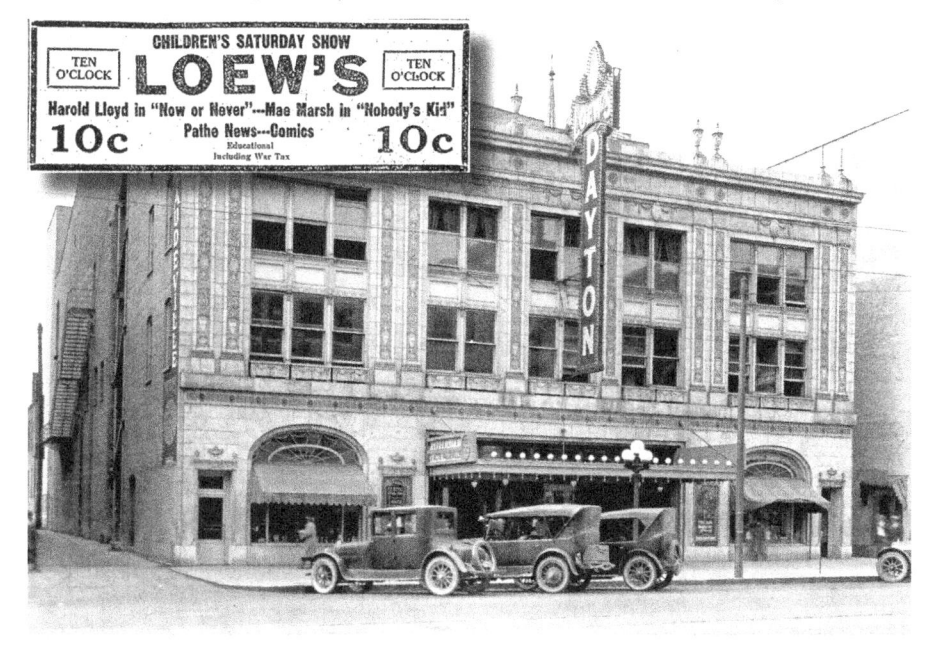

Dayton Loew's Theater was located on 125 North Main Street. The ad is for the first Children's Saturday Show, held on November 19, 1921.

November 20

W. C. Fry owned a gravel pit located just beyond the Davis Sewing Machine Works on Linden Avenue and along the Panhandle Railroad tracks. While working in the pit on November 20, 1904, Fry noticed what looked to be a human bone projecting from the gravel. On closer inspection he found that it was the entire skeleton of a man, imbedded under six feet of soil and resting on a gravel bed. From all appearances the body looked to have been washed there by a current of water, as its peculiar location on the gravel did not indicate that it had been buried in a grave.

Measurements of the skeleton indicated that the man had been between eight and nine feet tall. The length of the leg between the knee and the ankle was six inches longer than an average sized man. The thickness of the skull was about three-eighths of an inch and looked to be two to three times larger than a normal skull. Unfortunately, when Fry touched the skull, it crumbled to pieces. The teeth were in the skull and were in perfect condition. They seemed to be somewhat worn, which led Fry to believe that the skeleton had belonged to an old man.

After hearing of the discovery, Professor Sigmund Metzier, principal of the Sixth District School, and August Foerste, a professor of physics at Steele High School, went out to look at the bones. Unfortunately, Fry was out rabbit hunting when they came and they did not get to look at it. A group of men visited the pit a few days later and dug for several hours around the spot where the skeleton had been found, but they failed to find any other bones.

This wasn't the first time that a giant skeleton had been found in the area. On January 21, 1899, it was reported that a skeleton, calculated to be that of a man 8 feet 1 1/2 inches in height, had been found in a gravel pit a half mile of Miamisburg, in a locality which contained a number of relics of the mound builders. The bones were fossilized. The drawing above was included in the 1899 article and was said to depict the well-proportioned skeleton.

November 21

John and Rachel Aiken owned two prime lots in Dayton, close to the river. They paid their taxes on time and never had any disputes with their neighbors, or each other for that matter, at least nothing that involved the local justice of the peace. They were a typical pioneering husband and wife, building a home on land that was primarily still in the heart of the wilderness.

But the event that took place November 20, 1806 was far from normal for the small community. On that day John, "not having the fear of God before his eyes but being moved and seduced by the instigation of the devil", beat his wife about the head and stomach to the point where she was mortally injured. Rachel languished until the next day, dying from her injuries on November 21.

On November 25, 1806 a special Court of Common Pleas session was held on the second floor of Hugh McCollum's Tavern, which had replaced Newcom's as the legal center of Dayton. The Associate Judges were Benjamin Archer, Isaac Spinning and John Ewing.

Due to guilt, or maybe fear, John had a complete breakdown that day, to the point that he was unable to speak. When it came time to leave for court, John collapsed entirely and had to be carried from the jail to the Courthouse.

Sheriff George Newcom brought Aiken before the judges. Since the crime had occurred only a few days before, neither side was prepared for a trail to begin. The judges ordered that several people be subpoenaed to appear before them as soon as possible. Bond was set in the sum of $1000. Various friends and family of Aiken swore in court that they would be responsible for payment of the money. John Aiken was reminded that he had to appear at the next term of the Court of Common Pleas held in Dayton, at which time he would have to answer any charges against him and abide by the final judgment of the court.

The cause of what happened next remains a mystery. Only a short time after appearing before the judges, John was dead. Heart attack? Suicide? Court records state that Aiken had gone on to his "long home", or heaven, before he was even able to leave the courthouse that day.

Although no trial was held, this is considered the city's first murder.

November 22

When Wilbur Wright was in New York in 1909, Clinton R. Peterkin came to see him. He asked Wilbur if there might be a chance that the brothers would be interested in opening an airplane factory if funding could be found. Wilbur was probably amused by the twenty-four year old man standing before him, but he gave Peterkin a true answer: they might well be interested, but only if men of some importance were willing to invest in such a company. Peterkin took Wilbur at his word and talked to J. P. Morgan. Morgan told him that not only would he take stock in the company, he would also order some for his friend Judge Elbert H. Gary, head of the United States Steel Corporation.

Word trickled down of Morgan's interest and soon other men in high positions wanted in on the deal. The list of investors included Theodore P. Shonts (President of the Interborough Rapid Transit Company), Morton F. Plant (Chairman of the Board of Directors of the Southern Express Company, and Vice President of the Chicago, Indianapolis & Louisville Railroad), E. J. Berwind (President of Berwind-White Coal Mining, who had made a fortune selling coal to steamship lines), and Cornelius Vanderbilt (who built his wealth in railroads and shipping). These men who were involved with transportation, were also quite interested in the potential of the transportation of men and goods by aircrafts.

The one thing that held back some of the stockholders was the fact that J. P. Morgan and Elbert H. Gary were involved. It was thought that perhaps Morgan, with his larger than life personality, might be too controlling. In the end, Morgan agreed to withdraw the offer to buy stock he had made for Gary and himself.

The Wrights stated that they wanted their friends Robert J. Collier, publisher of Collier's Weekly, and brothers Russell A. and Frederick M. Alger, stockholders in the Packard Automobile Company, to be involved. The other investors readily agreed.

On November 22, 1909, The Wright Company incorporated. In exchange for all rights to their patents in the United States, Orville and Wilbur received stock and cash, plus a guarantee of ten percent royalty on all airplanes sold by the company. Another very important provision was that The Wright Company would also pay for any expenses incurred from prosecuting anyone who infringed on the Wright patents. The first building in the United States constructed specifically for an airplane factory was completed for the Wright Company in Dayton in 1910.

November 23

On November 23, 1910, Philip Herbert was sent to clean out a vat that contained lard oil in the basement of the Brooks Sons' plumbing establishment at 42 North Jefferson Street. Herbert, who was 17, was an apprentice plumber for the company.

Suddenly, Herbert began screaming. Several of his fellow workers rushed into the cellar. There they saw Herbert standing in the middle of the 40 inch high vat, calling hysterically for help, while trying to beat out flames that were leaping up from the oil in the container. In seconds his clothes were on fire.

Three men, John L. Gridley, Henry S. Blank and David McGallard rushed to his rescue. Blank attempted to lift Philip and then called Gridley to help. As they tried to drag Herbert from the vat, burning oil was thrown all over them. They raised Herbert about a foot when Gridley slipped and fell. His clothes caught fire. In a panic, Gridley ran out into the street, causing his clothes to burn even faster. Blank, with his trousers burning, ran to the top of the stairs, where another man helped to extinguish the flames. Blank sustained burns on his hands and ankles.

Finally, the boy was pulled unconscious from the fire. When Dr. H. H. Herman arrived he found Herbert burned from head to foot. Although the boy was rushed to the hospital, he did not survive. Gridley died on December 3, 1910, at Miami Valley Hospital as a result of severe burns he had received during the rescue attempt.

Word of the attempted rescue of Herbert reached the Carnegie Hero Fund Commission. Started by Andrew Carnegie in 1904, its purpose was to recognize "civilization's heroes" and to provide financial assistance for those disabled and the dependents of those killed helping others.

On April 26, 1912, Blank received a bronze medal and $1,000 from the commission. John's widow, Emma L. Gridley, was also awarded a bronze medal, plus a life pension of $30 per month.

As of 2016, there have been 18 heroes from Dayton who have received an award from the Carnegie Hero Fund Commission. Unfortunately, four of them lost their lives in their attempt to save others. If you know of someone who may qualify for this award, please visit the Carnegie Hero Fund Commission website at www.carnegiehero.org.

November 24

On November 23, 1950, Daytonians gathered with their friends and families to celebrate Thanksgiving. Then, as now, many were anticipating doing a little early Christmas shopping the next day. Instead, any guests who had not quite left for home yet were going to be staying a little longer, for no one was going anywhere for the next few days.

On November 24, nearly a foot of snow fell over a two-day period in Dayton. Combined with high winds and cold temperatures near zero, the storm turned into the city's worst blizzard on record up to that time. With drifts rising 5 feet or more in some areas, all schools and most industries were closed for several days, as was public transportation. Dayton Mayor Louis W. Lohrey declared a state of emergency, but with no guardsman in town, the best he could do was to order residents to stay off the streets until they could be cleared. The cost of removing the snow was estimated to be over $100,000.

Dayton wasn't the only city in Ohio affected by the storm. In fact, it was one of the luckier ones. The eastern sections measured depths of 20 to 30 inches, while Steubenville reported an unheard of 44 inches.

It was estimated that at least 55 people had died in Ohio due to the blizzard, including three from Dayton.

Not everyone heeded Mayor Lohrey's advice to stay off the roads. Scenes like this showing cars stuck on Main Street greatly hampered clearing the streets of snow.

November 25

On Easter Sunday, 1900, William H. Starry, was standing at a window of his home on 830 South Main Street sharpening a knife. Distracted by some boys, he glanced out the window. When he looked back at the stone, he was shocked to see what looked to be the outline of a face. He immediately showed the stone to several neighbors, some of whom agreed that the stone seemed to have a portrait of Christ on it. In order to protect it, Starry sealed the stone in a box with a glass lid and gave it to the Dayton Public Library and Museum for their collection.

There it sat for over four years until someone noticed that the face was seemingly becoming more distinct each day, the lips parting and becoming pink, and teeth beginning to show. Before long, the whetstone mystery was the talk of the town. When a picture of the stone was placed in the *Dayton Daily News*, people began flocking to the library to see it, but Starry had already taken the whetstone back in order to sell it.

In order to drum up even more interest, Starry held the first public exhibit of the stone at the Raper M. E. Church at Fifth and Jackson on November 25, 1904. Admission was free and hundreds came to see it. The fame of the stone grew to the point that its story and image were published in the April 1905 edition of *Popular Mechanics* magazine.

When asked the selling price of the whetstone, Starry replied that he would not think of taking less that $1,000 for it. There were no takers.

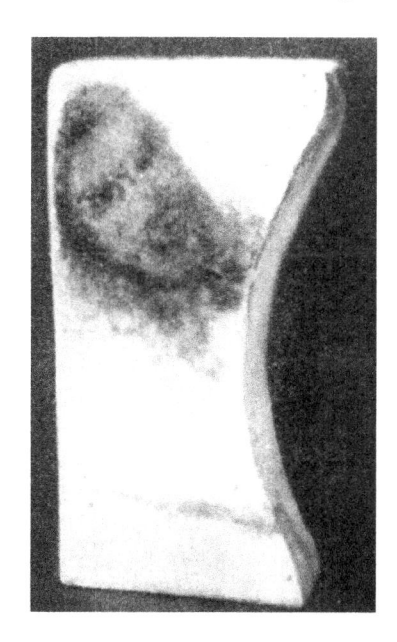

When William H. Starry died on December 30, 1906, the whetstone became part of his estate. The stone still bore the mysterious image and it was wondered what his widow would do with it. The final fate of the stone is unknown, although a newspaper account in 1910 mentions that it was thought that one of the children of the family had accidentally dropped it into a tub of boiling suds one day, which made the picture disappear.

November 26

Dayton ranked first in the nation in terms of patents granted per capita as early as 1870 and continued to retain that ranking for decades. What is rarely discussed are the early women inventors from the Gem City.

The first to receive a patent was Hannah D. Conrad, for improvement in setting and threading needles in sewing machines. Her invention received Patent #34,407 on February 18, 1862.

Other women soon followed. Hannah Conway patented an improved hospital bed in 1868 and Connie S. Murphy would patent a flexible urinal in 1883.

One of the more prolific inventors was Edith E. L. Boyer. She was co-inventor with her husband, Israel Donald Boyer, of a wrapping machine in 1896, and a caramel candy-making machine and two mechanical toys - a spinning top and a locomotive toy - in 1897. Six months after her husband's death, Edith was granted a patent for a triple-action jack.

By 1902, Edith had begun a business manufacturing price tags, so it seems only natural that her next invention would be a machine capable of easily affixing labels to round cans and bottles. Edith's labeling machine would be granted patent #871,776 on November 26, 1907.

But Edith wasn't done yet. In 1920 and 1924, she would again be co-inventor, this time with her son, Frederick G. L. Boyer, involving indicating devices for scales.

November 27

When the Keith's theater opened on November 27, 1922, it was thought to be the most beautiful theater in the state, if not in the Midwest. And no wonder. No expense was spared to build the five-story structure.

While in the beginning Keith's was a major vaudeville palace, by 1929 live acts were phased out as the popularity of motion pictures grew. The following year the theater became RKO Keith's.

During World War II the theater held special showings to help in the war effort. In 1943, a scrap collection by Dayton Girl Scouts topped the two-ton marker after several dozen girls paid their way into a Christmas movie by bringing five pounds of paper each.

Television was too popular to ignore, so in the early 1950's equipment was installed at the theater for television productions. Closed-circuit television shows included boxing matches and UD basketball games.

Unfortunately, by the 1960's, Keith's was very large and economically unfeasible to operate with the growing number of theaters being built in shopping centers. The theater was demolished in November 1967.

The theater was demolished to make way for the Grant-Deneau Building (now called 40 West 4th Center). Ironically the final movie was entitled Once Before I Die.

November 28

Although built to take care of Union soldiers who had been disabled through loss of limb, wounds, disease and other injuries, the Dayton Soldiers' Home (now known as the VA Medical Center) was also quite beautiful. In 1876 Col. Edwin F. Brown, Governor of the Dayton Soldiers' Home, made the following report:

> "The Homes have become so attractive and interesting that they draw many thousands of visitors annually. By actual count of the gate-keepers, the visitors to the Dayton Home last year numbered over 100,000. They come singly and in parties, as societies and churches, in excursion trains, hundreds at a time, and mostly to spend an entire day with the veterans."

One of the major attractions at the Soldiers' Home was a Deer Park. Several acres were enclosed by fencing, where as many as one hundred-fifteen deer were kept over the years, many of them sent from Lookout Mountain. An old soldier who had once been the deer keeper for the King of Prussia was chosen to take care of them.

It was said the deer were so tame that, instead of running away, they would allow themselves to be petted. Others might disagree about just how tame the deer were. Colonel William J. White, namesake of Colonel White High School and Governor of the Home at the time, was walking in the Deer Park when he was attacked by a buck. Colonel White struggled for his life against the buck for two hours and was badly injured. The Colonel never fully recovered and died on November 28, 1920.

November 29

When it came to merchandising, Rike's couldn't be beat. During the Christmas season of 1922, the company started a campaign called "A Million in December", with the goal of selling a million dollars worth of merchandise during that month. A daily newspaper, *Pep*, was given to Rike's employees. It was filled with suggestions for sales, inspirational stories and notes on which departments were reaching their quota for sales. A thermometer both inside and outside the store showed how close the company was to their goal. To nearly everyone's surprise, the goal was reached, with a little over $6,000 to spare.

The next year, Rike's started their advertising early. On Thanksgiving Day, November 29, 1923, Rike's held its first Toy Parade. People lined the streets to watch the numerous decorated floats, clowns and various characters from nursery rhymes go down Main Street. The final float would usher in Santa Claus, who would then ascend a ladder which led to a chimney located on top of Rike's. The event took nearly a year to plan and involved well over 1,000 Rike's employees to pull it off.

Jack Spratt and friends during Rike's Thanksgiving Parade in 1935. The tradition lasted until 1942, when the trucks and men were commandeered for the Army.

November 30

The first association organized to preserved the history of Dayton dates back to The Pioneer Association of Dayton. For some time, before anyone thought of organizing a historical society, *the Dayton Daily Journal* had frequently been publishing reminiscences of some of the oldest settlers in the city. The series of articles proved quite popular.

On November 25, 1867, the *Dayton Daily Journal* asked for "the old folks" to meet at City Hall on November 30 to organize a society. The invitation was open to "all persons born in this county before 1820 or having immigrated to Dayton prior to that date."

In spite of some nasty winter weather, thirty-seven of the city's oldest residents decided to attend the meeting. A record was made of everyone present who, by reason of having been born prior to 1820, were eligible to membership. The group agreed that "the object of the Association shall be for the collection and preservation of the traditions, incidents, experiences and records of the first settlements and early settlers of Montgomery County." Membership was $1.00 for enrollment and $.50 annually thereafter.

Annual meetings were held at Newcom Tavern on May 1, the date being chosen because Montgomery County had been organized on that day in 1803. While somewhat active at first, the membership was necessarily made up of older people and around 1888 the society was disbanded.

It would take until after the centennial anniversary of Dayton in 1896, before another historical organization would form. The numerous events held in Dayton that year, especially the saving of Newcom Tavern from near destruction, once again spurred the interest in preserving the city's past. On April 1, 1897, the Dayton Historical Society was organized, it's purpose being to "collect and preserve everything relating to the history and antiquities of Ohio and especially of the County of Montgomery and the City of Dayton and the dissemination of knowledge."

In the 1960s, Dayton Historical Society became The Montgomery County Historical Society and relocated from Newcom Tavern to the Old Court House. In 2005, Carillon Historical Park merged with The Montgomery County Historical Society to create Dayton History, whose headquarters are located at Carillon Historical Park.

December 1

America entered World War II after the Japanese attack on Pearl Harbor on December 7, 1941. When the Japanese invaded the Dutch East Indies, the U.S. supply of rubber was cut off. This affected the availability of tires.

The government reasoned that rationing gasoline, would help conserve rubber by reducing the number of miles Americans drove. Deadline for the first registration for the "A" ration coupon books was December 1, 1942. By the end of the deadline 95,000 residents of Montgomery County had signed up, leaving 18,000 cars not registered to receive gasoline. The unregistered cars were thought to be either owned by men in the armed forces, cars sold to dealers and not purchased yet, or people who misunderstood the fact that they wouldn't receive gasoline without the coupons.

President Franklin D. Roosevelt called on citizens to contribute scrap rubber, tires, rubber raincoats, garden hoses, and even bathing caps to help out in the war effort. In only two weeks Montgomery County citizens had donated 3,740,281 pounds of rubber to the cause.

To help conserve tires, Daytonians were asked to share rides and to avoid rough roads. Proper auto maintenance was more important than ever. Brake adjustment, wheel alignment, tire inflation, tire rotation, and repair of holes all prolonged the life of the tires.

December 2

The first wireless voice transmission from an airplane pilot to the ground was demonstrated at Langley Field in the fall of 1917. The Army was so impressed that it ordered the equipment for all of its existing airplanes. Still, there were a number of problems to overcome, including finding a smaller power source capable of running the equipment in the airplane, overcoming interference caused by the airplane's ignition system and creating a way for the pilot to hear better over the noise of the engine.

On December 2, 1917 an official demonstration was held at Wright Field involving two airplanes in the air as well as a wireless telephone on the ground. The two-seated airplanes each held a pilot and an observer. The ground outfit included a speaker so that all of the officials from the Aircraft Production Board and the officers from the Army and Navy could hear both the orders issued to the airplanes and the communications from the airplanes.

The demonstration went even better than expected. Not only could the pilot and observer hear every order given from the ground, the observer within each airplane could talk to the other, and the pilot and observer in an individual airplane could talk to each other. This was a tremendous advantage, solving the problem of pilots and observers not being able to communicate due to engine and propeller noises.

The equipment proved to work at a distance of 10 miles, even though the airplanes were outside of visual range. The airplanes were also able to talk to each other over the same distance.

The demonstration showed the success of the new system and made such an impression that large orders were immediately placed by both the Army and Navy. The equipment was also obtained by the Allied Forces and used during World War I.

After the war, a series of experiments using the same type of equipment were held at McCook Field. On April 9, 1920, a recording of a Sousa march was played on a phonograph and broadcast to receivers in Dayton, as well as Columbus, St. Marys, Lima, Cincinnati and Tipp City. The experiment proved to be a success.

December 3

Amy Florence Acton was born in Australia in 1867 and came to the United States when she was 5 years old. Her desire to help the poor, especially women, led her to go to school to become a lawyer. In 1894, while still taking classes at the Law School of Boston University, Acton passed the Massachusetts bar.

In 1895, she was offered a position to work as assistant council for NCR in Dayton. This was unprecedented, for no corporation before that time had ever hired a woman as a lawyer. Acton agreed and on December 3, 1895 she went to Columbus for examination for admission to the Ohio Bar. NCR must have known what they were doing in hiring Acton, for she scored higher than any of the fifty-two men who had also taken the examination that day.

During her three years in Dayton, Acton helped form, and was elected the first president of, the Woman's Century Club of NCR. Organized in part to help educate its members in literary, musical and current events, the women also called on the sick and helped families in need.

In May 1898, Acton returned to Boston to open her own law office. She became known for giving free legal assistance to poor women and working with the Massachusetts Board of Charities. Amy Florence Acton passed away in 1918 at the age of 51.

December 4

On October 13, 1917, the Signal Corps Office released Memorandum No. 22, stating that the Engine Design Section and the Plane Design Section from Langley Field were being merged into a single organization to be know as the Airplane Engineering Department. Its headquarters were to be located in a temporary experimental station in Dayton, Ohio.

Sitting on 254 acres, the site of the station was bounded on the north and west by the Great Miami River, on the south by Herman Avenue and on the east by Keowee Street. The field was named for the McCook family who had once farmed on part of the land where it was located. The family was known as the "Fighting McCooks", for the 17 men who fought for the Union during the Civil War. Daniel and John McCook, and thirteen of their sons saw service. George McCook, and his son, George Jr., were volunteer surgeons. Six McCooks reached general officer rank. Four were killed in action or died from their wounds.

Work had already begun at the site even before the memorandum had been announced. By the first week in December 1917, enough buildings at McCook Field had been completed to allow key personnel to move from downtown Dayton to the new installation. McCook Field officially opened on December 4, 1917, becoming the first military aviation research and development center in the United States.

The motto "This Field Is Small - Use It All" was a reminder to pilots that the runway was only 1,000 feet long. This resulted in a short approach and takeoff distances due to surrounding trees, the river and other buildings. As aircraft grew in size and power, using the runway was no longer feasible and the activities at McCook Field were forced to move to Wright Field in 1927.

December 5

Dayton's first school opened on September 1, 1799 with a small class of pupils in a log blockhouse built at Water Street (now Monument Avenue) and Main Street. The blockhouse had originally been built to in case of an attack by Indians, but was fortunately never used for that purpose.

A visitor to the blockhouse would have seen students seated on low block stools and hewed slab benches, reciting lessons in spelling, reading and arithmetic to Dayton's first schoolmaster, Benjamin Van Cleve; or bent over a long, narrow table, covered with a smooth layer of sand, where they would trace letters of the alphabet from hand-made charts in front of them. Early students learned the A B C's without slates, pencils or paper.

Among the early schools was the Dayton Academy, a private school for boys. Starting in 1808, the classes were held in a two-story brick structure on the west side of St. Clair Street between Second and Third.

The first public, or "free," school was opened on December 5, 1831, on Jefferson Street, near First Street, with Sylvanius Hall as instructor. Although public money was used, there were not sufficient donations to pay expenses, so each pupil was assessed a dollar a year.

From then on schools were given increasing public encouragement. In 1850, Central High School became Dayton's first high school. Central's first high school graduation class in 1854 consisted of two students.

Steele High School would replace Central High in 1889.

In 1850, Central High School opened in this building at the corner of Fourth and Wilkinson Streets. The school had originally been built for the Dayton Academy, which had moved to the new location in 1833.

December 6

During WWI, behind high board fences, with armed sentries at the gates, the Maxwell Motor Company and Platt Iron Works were busy making Renault FT war tanks. No one but the two thousand workmen in the shops knew about the tanks. Due to the speed needed for production, not all of the parts could be made by the two companies, and so as many as 500 local sub-contractors furnished various parts to finish the tanks, most of them never knowing how the parts were being used. There were some difficulties, including translating building plans written in French, but by using French tanks as models, approximately 450 tanks were built before the war ended.

Although construction in Dayton began in December, 1917, it wasn't until November 17, 1918, when the tanks rolled down the streets of the city during an Armistice celebration, that the secret became widely known.

On December 6, 1918, *Dayton Daily News* reported that about 400 members and guests of the Noontide Club had been treated to a tank demonstration. Slide shows and speeches concerning the manufacture of the tanks were given at the Masonic Temple, followed by rides in the tanks at the testing field located at the Maxwell Motor Company.

The Renault FT tank held two men and was armed with either a machine gun or 37 mm field type gun. For years storage buildings at the Platt Iron Works were filled, ceiling high, with parts of tanks that had been completed but never used.

December 7

Until early 1804 Cincinnati was the nearest post office. Benjamin Van Cleve was the first postmaster in Dayton, the post office being in his home on the southeast corner of First and St. Clair streets. Until 1806 everyone north of Dayton, as far as Fort Wayne, had to come here for their mail. The mail route was up the Little Miami River, through Lebanon and Xenia to Urbana, and down through Piqua, Dayton, and Hamilton to Cincinnati. On December 7, 1808, a contract was signed with George F. Tennery, of Troy, Ohio for him to be responsible for the mail being delivered between Dayton and Urbana.

> "AGREEMENT, made and concluded this seventh day of December 1808, between William George, William McClure, and Joseph Peirce, committee, in behalf of the undertakers for carrying the mail from Dayton to Urbana, of the first part:
>
> "WITNESSETH, That the said George, on his part, binds himself, his heirs, etc., to carry the mail from Dayton to Urbana once a week and back to Dayton for the term that has been contracted for between Daniel C. Cooper and the postmaster general, to commence on Friday, the ninth instant (to-wit): leave Dayton every Friday morning at six o'clock; leave Urbana Saturday morning and arrive at Dayton Saturday evening, the undertakers reserving the right of altering the time of the starting and returning with the mail, allowing the said George two days to perform the trip, the post-rider to be employed by the said George to be approved by the undertakers. They also reserve to themselves the right of sending way letters and papers on said route, and the said George binds himself to pay for every failure in the requisitions of this agreement on his part the sum equal to that required by the postmaster general in like failures. The said committee on their part agree to furnish the said George with a suitable horse, furnish the person carrying the mail and the horse with sufficient victuals, lodging, and feed, and one dollar for each and every trip, to be paid every three months. In witness whereof the parties have hereunto set their hands the day and year above mentioned."

In 1825, the first experiment was made to establish a line of stagecoaches through Dayton. Timothy Squier contracted to use the line to run the mail between Cincinnati, Dayton, and Columbus once a week. Before long enough passengers were also using the service for travelling that the mail was being delivered to Dayton nearly every day.

December 8

A long standing disagreement between the Wright brothers and the Smithsonian Institute began due to the museum's misleading display of the aeronautical achievements of its former Secretary, Samuel P. Langley. Langley had successfully flew unmanned powered model aircrafts, but the two tests of his manned "Aerodrome No. 5" airplane were complete failures. Nevertheless, the Smithsonian later displayed Langley's airplane with a label stating that it was the "first man-carrying aeroplane in the history of the world capable of sustained free flight."

Orville responded by loaning the 1903 Kitty Hawk Flyer to the London Science Museum in 1928. It wasn't until 1942 that the Smithsonian finally published an article recanting its views on the Langley matter.

On December 8, 1943, Orville wrote a letter to inform the director of the London museum that he would be asking for the return of the Flyer once WWII was over and the craft could be safely transported. After the war was over, Orville agreed to leave the Flyer at the Science Museum until they could make a copy of it for permanent display.

Orville died suddenly of a heart attack on January 30, 1948, while the Wright Flyer was still in England. His intention on what he had wanted done with the Flyer once it had been returned was made clear in an unsigned will Orville had been working on just before his death. It stated:

"I give and bequeath to the U.S. National Museum of Washington, D.C., for exhibition in the National Capital only, the Wright aeroplane (now in the Science Museum, London, England) which flew at Kitty Hawk, North Carolina, on the 17th of December, 1903."

The executors of his estate fulfilled his wishes and brought the treasured artifact home. It was installed at the Smithsonian on December 17, 1948, 45 years to the day after its history-making flights.

December 9

On December 7, 1941, the day of the attack on Pearl Harbor, Dayton Chief of Police Rudolph F. Wurstner stated that there were very few Japanese in Dayton, but that the bus and train lines had been notified not to sell tickets to any Japanese who wanted to leave Dayton.

On December 9, 1941 twenty men and thirteen women, subjects of Germany and Italy and technically classed as enemy aliens, were denied American citizenship papers by Federal Judge Mel G. Underwood. The naturalization was the first in Dayton since the war had begun, and Judge Underwood made a decision to withhold the papers at least another four months. This did not stop him from administering the oath of citizenship to 80 others who were not of those nationalities.

The U.S. Treasury Department also closed the Oriental Trading Company store at 126 N. Main Street. The owners, Shaji and Mary Okino, were American citizens of Japanese descent. Treasury agents said that plans were being considered to sell the store, with the funds to be placed in a government agency trust. Four days later, however, the shop was allowed to reopen.

On February 19, 1942, President Franklin D. Roosevelt signs Executive Order 9066, which included the removal of resident enemy aliens from the West Coast. About 5,000 German-Americans and Italian-Americans were rounded up for questioning, with most being released within a year. Unfortunately, the same could not be said for the 127,000 Japanese-Americans living in the United States at the time. All Japanese, both American and foreign-born, were removed from their homes along the coast and in defense areas and taken to relocation centers, where they were carefully examined by the FBI to determine their loyalty to the U.S.

Eventually, Japanese-Americans who satisfied the authorities of their loyalty were permitted to leave the camps, on the condition that they had jobs. Many were relocated to Dayton in the early fall of 1943. Most of them were employed at the Red-Bar Battery Company, McCall and the Federal Housing Authority. Many also accepted farm work, where their knowledge of gardening on small acreage was said to have "proved a boon to agricultural communities" in the Dayton area.

Fred Stroop, president of the Stroop Agricultural company, hired a number of Japanese-Americans to assist on farms managed by the company.

"They have proven highly efficient and very acceptable- really, God sent!" claimed Stroop.

December 10

During WWII dogs were recruited for the war effort by the "Dogs for Defense" (DFD). The first dog donated for service from the Dayton area was named Wright Rudder. "Ruddy", as he was called by the family, was a two-year-old pointer owned by Mrs. F. O. Carrol, whose husband was a brigadier general stationed at Wright Field. Mrs. P. W. Kline's dog, 2 year-old Mr. Chips, an elegant Collie, was also selected to work for the Army. "If you can give your son, you can give your dog, too," stated Mrs. Kline. Her son, Richard, was a seaman at Norfolk, Virginia, and, of course, he wanted his dog to go to the Navy, but stated that he was "mighty proud" that Mr. Chips would serve in the Army.

Eleven-year-old Emerson Robinson had a good reason for enlisting his German Shepherd Dog, Rex. "I'm going to send him to the army and then when I'm old enough I'll go, too," he explained. Emerson's mother agreed with the decision. The rest of the Robinson family was involved in the war effort, so it was only fitting that Rex should be as well. Besides a son in the navy, two other daughters worked at a local military base, and she worked for the signal corps. The first dogs donated from Dayton left for the Cincinnati induction center on December 10, 1942.

Mrs. William H. McHugh was placed in charge of recruiting dogs for army work in the Dayton area. She said that seeing the parting of the dogs and their owners was the worst part of her job. Some of the owners couldn't bear to watch their dogs leave, and would stay away from home until she had taken their pet away.

People who owned dogs who did not qualify for service were offered another way to enlist their pets. The *Journal Herald* began conducting a campaign for the War Dog Fund. Pet owners could make contributions that paid for an honorary rank for their "recruits". Ranks ranged from private to four-star general or admiral of the fleet, depending on the size of the owner's contribution. The pet received a certificate denoting his rank and a tag for his collar showing membership. Contributions were used to help with the expenses of kenneling and feeding of dogs before they reported for final examination.

After the war the dogs were discharged from the K-9 Section and returned to their families.

December 11

In 1899 the decision was made to decorate Steele High School. A plaster-of-Paris lion was purchased from the Pan American Expo when it closed. The plaster lion looked fierce on his pedestal when he was dedicated in 1902. Unfortunately, by 1904, the cold, rain and snow had turned the once brave lion into a heap of broken pieces.

It was decided that another, sturdier, lion needed to be obtained. Anna Vaughn Hyatt was commissioned to create a bronze statue. She left for Naples in 1907, where she had a studio that was a cave cut into the soft, rocky cliff. She worked all that winter modeling the large lion. Hyatt would later recall her time at the foundry where the lion was cast.

"The place was lit only by oil torches. An image of the Virgin was conspicuous and during the crucial pourings of the bronze, the excited workmen knelt to pray for the success of the pouring."

On December 11, 1908 a large crowd gathered at Steele High School to see the new sculpture. Unfortunately, there was a problem with pulling the canvas covering off. A high school student was persuaded to climb up the pedestal and unveil "Leo" the lion.

Steele High School closed in 1940. The venerable lion was moved in 1955 to stand guard outside the Dayton Art Institute.

The statue was based on Sultan the Lion that Anna Vaughn Hyatt saw at the Bronx Zoo.

December 12

On Sunday, December 12, 1915, the West Dayton Civic League began filming local churches as part of a project to document the West Side. The four days of filming also included public schools, manufacturers such as the Wright Company, the Charles Sucher Packing Company, and the Gem City Ice Cream Company, as well as two-thirds of the retail merchants. A view was filmed from the rear of a railway car as it traversed from the western end of the Third Street bridge, through the business sections of Third and Fifth streets. Hungarian dancers performed in full costume for the cameras at McCabe Park.

On December 15, it was announced that, although the film was not yet complete, it would be shown at the Midget Theater on Friday, December 17. This proved to be a mistake. Cloudy weather caused poor lighting for filming, and the moisture made it difficult for the film to dry. More than four hundred feet of film that showed cards describing the action in the movie was destroyed. The haste in getting the film out did not allow for reshooting and the first showing did not contain the cards.

In spite of this, "Real Life on the West Side", as the film was named, proved to be a hit. Hearty applause was given as each school and church was shown and the audience loved seeing the interior of the factories.

Unfortunately, no known copies of the film exist today.

Looking east down West Third Street from Williams Street in 1914.

December 13

John and Michael Schiml started the J. & M. Schiml Brewery in 1852, on the corner of Wayne and Hickory. The first lager beer of Montgomery County was believed to have been made there on December 13 that same year. A cousin of the Schiml's who was a brewer brought the stock yeast necessary for making it from Boston, Massachusetts. The first year the brewery made 1,200 barrels of lager beer.

On September 5, 1858 John died and Michael took over the brewery, renaming it first the Oregon Brewery and later the Wayne Street Brewery.

In July 1881, a fire destroyed a stable and its contents, including four horses, the roof of the ice house, and over 3,000 bushels of malt. Michael took the disaster in stride, enlarging the brewery to 38' x 140', and three stories high, plus building an ice house in connection capable of storing 1,500 tons of ice. Both buildings were made of brick, with cellars underneath. At the time of the fire the brewery was producing 4,400 barrels of lager annually, but the new building had the capacity to double that amount. In 1882 sales were up to $35,000.

Andrew Schiml and Frank J. Bucher became partners in the Wayne Street Brewery and changed its name to the Pioneer Brewing Company in 1889. On August 20, 1900 Louis L. Wehner bought the business, but closed it a year later, using the equipment for another brewery he owned.

December 14

On December 14, 1944, Charles Goodwin Bickham, Dayton's first person to be awarded the Congressional Medal of Honor, passed away at the age of 77. His heroism is rarely remembered today.

Bickham began his career in the military by serving as a Colonel on the staff of Gov. William McKinley in 1891. During the Spanish-American War he was a Private in Company G, 3rd Regiment, Ohio National Guard and was later commissioned Captain in the 9th U.S. Volunteer Infantry. He was then appointed Captain in the 28th U.S. Volunteer Infantry during the Philippine Insurrection until the unit was mustered out of service in May, 1901. Bickham became a First Lieutenant in the 27th U.S. Infantry Regiment the following month, returning to the Philippines, where he commanded Company F in operations in Mindanao.

It was here, on the battlefield of Bayan, near Lake Lanao, that Lieut. Bickham earned his medal. On May 2, 1902, an orderly was sent to get more ammunition, but was quickly wounded by Filipino soldiers. Seeing that the soldier was dangerously exposed, Bickham ran into the line of fire and placed the wounded man on his back. Bickham's actions drew heavier fire in his direction, but he was able to stagger to safety.

For his actions of "saving life on the battlefield at the risk of his own," Lieut. Bickham was awarded the Congressional Medal of Honor. Although it was issued on April 28, 1904, he would not receive the medal for several weeks. It was presented to Bickham in June, 1904, by Brig. Gen. Fred Dent Grant, son of President Ulysses S. Grant. The ceremony took place at Fort Sheridan, Illinois, where the lieutenant was stationed at the time.

Charles G. Bickham, circa 1901

December 15

In 1916, magician and escape artist Harry Houdini spent a week in Dayton performing at the Keith's theater on 141 South Ludlow in the old Colonial Theater building. On December 11, his first day in the city, Houdini was strapped into a regulation straitjacket and suspended by his ankles from the side of the *Dayton Daily News* building. Over 6,000 people watched as Houdini made his escape in only three minutes. But his most popular performance took place on December 15.

Two days before, Houdini had received a letter from employees of the Olt Brewing Company challenging him to escape from a cask containing 60 gallons of Olt's beer. Houdini accepted. After lowering himself into the beer-filled barrel, the lid was fastened down by a group of Olt employees.

Although Houdini released himself in less than three minutes, it took longer than that to recover from the effects of the fumes he had inhaled while struggling in the cask. A non-drinker, Houdini found it necessary to take a brisk walk in the cold air before he was able to continue his show.

On December 12, 1916 the Dayton Daily News printed this drawing of Houdini and some of the acts he would perform at Keith's Theater.

December 16

On this day in 1811, the first of many earthquake shocks were felt in Dayton. The most intense shock was felt between two and three o'clock that morning. It was so severe that almost everyone in the city was awakened. Many of them ran outside their homes, terrified at the unusual phenomenon. Aftershocks were felt the rest of that day and into the next. But it was only the beginning.

On the morning of January 23, 1812, another shock of earthquake was felt. It was agreed that it was more intense than any of the ones from the month before. It was also reported to have been just as bad in Cincinnati and other adjacent towns. Several considerable shocks followed, the most severe occurring on the morning of the 27th. It shook houses considerably, and articles suspended in stores were kept in motion for over a minute.

On 3:45 a.m. on the morning of February 13, the towns people were once again awaken from their slumber. Two shocks were felt in quick succession. A rumbling noise was distinctly heard just before the first shock occurred. At first the noise appeared to be subsiding, but then began increasing in loudness, and continued through the second shock. It was agreed that this was much worse, both in its severity and the length of its duration, of any of the shocks that had been felt in Dayton, and the terror it caused left an impression upon everyone who experienced it. Stories written on the incident decades later stated that people who were children when the earthquake occurred still spoke of it in old age with a shudder of horror.

But evidentially not everyone felt that way. In the book, *Early Dayton*, Robert and Mary Steele tell the story of how a "flighty little woman, who, partly for the purpose of asserting her own courage, of which, in fact, she had not a particle, and partly from a spirit of mischief and desire to shock her awestruck friends, threw herself laughingly on the ground, exclaiming: 'How delightfully the world rocks! I like the motion.' The poor, frightened lady probably thought it better philosophy to laugh than to cry; but the village gossips considered such conduct very unbecoming, and proof positive that she was an atheist."

December 17

On January 22, 1948, "Project Sign", an official U.S. government study of unidentified flying objects (UFOs), was begun. Sign was part of Air Technical Intelligence Center (ATIC) at Wright-Patterson Air Force Base. Although most of the project's personnel seem to agree that extraterrestrials were involved, Project Sign's final report in 1949 stated that while some UFOs appeared to represent actual aircraft there was not enough data to determine their origin. Sign was dissolved and replaced with Project Grudge.

It seems that Project Grudge tried to find ways in which the vast bulk of UFO reports could be explained away as normal phenomena. The final report stated that "All evidence and analyses indicate that reports of unidentified flying objects are the result of:
- Misinterpretation of various conventional objects.
- A mild form of mass-hysteria and war nerves.
- Individuals who fabricate such reports to perpetrate a hoax or to seek publicity.
- Psychopathological persons.

Project Blue Book, which started in 1952, was headquartered at Wright-Patterson Air Force Base. Although a total of 12,618 UFO sightings were reported from 1947 to 1969, the conclusions of Project Blue book were: (1) no UFO reported, investigated, and evaluated by the Air Force has ever given any indication of threat to our national security; (2) there has been no evidence submitted to or discovered by the Air Force that sightings categorized as "unidentified" represent technological developments or principles beyond the range of present-day scientific knowledge; and (3) there has been no evidence indicating that sightings categorized as "unidentified" are extraterrestrial vehicles. The project ended on December 17, 1969.

A U.S. Air Force Fact Sheet was distributed by Wright-Patterson AFB in January 1985. It stated, in part: "Since Project Blue Book was closed, nothing has happened to indicate that the Air Force ought to resume investigating UFOS. Because of the considerable cost to the Air Force in the past, and the tight funding of Air Force needs today, there is no likelihood the Air Force will become involved with UFO investigation again."

December 18

George de Bothezat was a Russian refugee who had fled to the United States in the wake of the Russian Revolution. Having written and lectured extensively on rotorcraft theory, de Bothezat received a contract from the United States Army in 1921 for the construction of an experimental helicopter.

Establishing a workshop at McCook Field, de Bothezat completed a helicopter in December 1922. Known as the "Flying Octopus", the aircraft had four massive six-bladed rotors attached to girders, which were braced with piano wire. On December 18, 1922, the aircraft made its first flight, hovering to a height of six feet. On other tests the helicopter held up to three "passengers", if you consider holding onto the frame for dear life a way to travel.

Although hailed by Thomas Edison as "the first successful helicopter" the aircraft never flew for more than 2 minutes 45 seconds nor reached any higher than 30 feet. Also, the machine needed a favorable wind to fly forward. In 1924, the Army cancelled the contract and ordered the helicopter to be scrapped. However, the aircraft's control column has survived, and is on display in the Smithsonian Institution's Steven F. Udvar-Hazy Center.

The Army abandoned the helicopter partly because de Bothezat was difficult to work with. When it ended, the government had spent $200,000 on the project.

December 19

For years tradition dictated that each December a large evergreen would be cut down and taken to a park in Dayton and decorated by the city for Christmas. But in 1914 it was suggested that a permanent growing tree be planted instead. When Frank M. Tait, president of Dayton Power & Light, learned of the suggestion, he offered to have his company buy an evergreen and have it planted in Cooper Park, near the entrance to the Children's section of the downtown library.

Naturally the offer was accepted and on December 19, a 30-foot high Norwood Spruce was transplanted. A conduit was built so that the tree could be decorated with electric lights. Dayton Power & Light also agreed to furnish free electricity and maintain the tree's lights in the years to come.

That Christmas Eve, thousands gathered to celebrate the season, singing Christmas carols and hymns, led by a large choir and band. Over 2,000 boxes of candy were handed out to children. Gifts of money, clothing and food were also brought to the tree and turned over to organized charities in Dayton, to be distributed to the needy.

This is a view of the St. Clair Street side of the Dayton Public Library building, showing the community Christmas tree on the left hand side.

December 20

On May 21, 1921 the United States Patent and Trademark Office, received a letter from Weston Green, president of The Green & Green Company in Dayton, asking that they be allowed to trademark the logo "Cheez-It". He stated that the company had begun using the logo on their Cheez-It Cheese Crackers on March 31, 1921. The company, which had started business in 1896, was well known for its Edgemont crackers and its nutty-flavored Dayton cracker, which was stamped with the name "Dayton". The logo was approved on December 20, 1921.

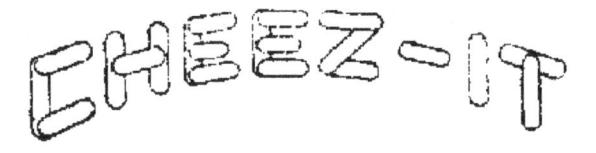

After the Wall Street Crash of 1929, The Green & Green Company was acquired by The Sunshine Biscuit Company. The Keebler Company acquired Sunshine in 1996, and Keebler was in turn acquired by Kellogg in 2001.

In 2016, there are over 26 varieties and flavors of Cheez-It being offered.

The original Cheez-It packaging was a combination of light and dark green (what else would you use when your business name is Green & Green?) The oval in the middle allowed customers to see the cheese crackers inside the box.

December 21

Hayner Distilling Co. began in 1866 in Troy, Ohio, as "Lewis Hayner, Distiller, Pure Copper Distilled Rye and Bourbon Whiskies." In 1885, Lewis' nephew, William M. Hayner, opened the Hayner Distilling Co. in Springfield, Ohio and began selling the whiskies by mail-order. By 1898, their main office and shipping depot was in Dayton. William's brother-in-law, Walter S. Kidder, became manager of the location.

By the 1890s, many parts of the country began outlawing the sale of beverages that contained alcohol. Whiskey, however, could still be shipped to "dry" cities, and Hayner became the source of alcohol to desperate customers that could not get it at their local stores or bars.

In 1891, William Hayner married Mary Jane Harter Coleman. Mary's father, Samuel K. Harter, owned Dr. Harter Medicine Company. The St. Louis based company was well-known for its many cure-all medicines, most of which contained quite a bit of alcohol. In 1895, Harter longed to come back to his boyhood stomping grounds in Troy, and so he formed a partnership with William Hayer and Walter Kidder. The Dr. Harter Medicine Company moved to Dayton, which was big enough to handle the 20 million pieces of printing material the company distributed each year to potential customers. Hayner Distilling doubled its production of alcohol that same year, due to it being used in Harter's medicines. When Samuel Harter died in June, 1898, Hayner and Kidder decided to sell the business and turn their full attention to the Hayner Distilling Co.

When William Hayner passed away in 1912, Kidder became president of the company. The Webb-Kenyon law went into effect the following year, closing the loophole that allowed dry states to import alcohol for personal use. Hayner Distilling eventually began distributing cigars by mail, but that didn't make up for the sales that were being lost as more and more states went dry.

On August 1, 1917, the Senate passed a resolution to present a constitutional amendment prohibiting the sale or consumption of alcohol. Seeing the writing on the wall, Hayner Distilling announced that it was closing its doors in Dayton on December 21, 1917. Instead, the building would be the home of the Thompson Printing Company, run by none other than Kidder, with the help of his partner, Herbert Thompson, who had been in charge of the printing and mailing department for Hayner Distilling for the past eleven years.

December 22

Levitt Luzern Custer had always been interested in how things worked. Born in Dayton, he graduated from the Massachusetts Institute of Technology in 1913. Custer's first invention was the Custer Bubble Statoscope, which registered the rise and fall of aircraft. By 1916, the Statoscope had proven so popular that Luzern had a four-story brick building constructed on Franklin Street and the Custer Specialty Company was born.

Then came World War I. By the time it ended, over 4,000 amputations had been performed on U.S. soldiers, many of whom came to the Dayton Soldiers' Home (now called the V.A. Medical Center) for rehabilitation. This prompted the invention of the Custer Invalid Chair, a three-wheel motor vehicle that ran on batteries. Designed to be used by invalids as a sort of self-propelled wheelchair, it would travel 10 to 15 miles before it needed recharging. Custer was granted design patent #D53,891 for his electric motorized wheelchair on October 7, 1919.

Unfortunately, while Custer's invention allowed the veterans to travel into town, since the Soldiers' Home was on a hill, many times the chair would run out of power on its way back. This led Custer to invent a gasoline version of his invalid car. Custer's gasoline-powered wheelchair was granted patent #2,306,042 on December 22, 1942.

The gasoline-powered version of Levitt Luzern Custer's Invalid Car

December 23

President William McKinley was well-loved in Dayton. After he was assassinated in 1901, citizens of the city tried to find a way to honor him, including the possibility of placing a statue in Cooper Park. (*See April 7*)But Daytonian Lewis G. Reynolds, wanted to do something more, something that would keep McKinley's memory fresh in the minds of the entire nation.

On December 23, 1902, Reynolds began promoting an organization know as the "Carnation League of America". The name came from the fact that the carnation was McKinley's favorite flower, which could be found on his lapel most of the time. Reynolds' idea was to have everyone wear a carnation every year on the anniversary of McKinley's death, on September 14. This was soon changed to the president's birthday, January 29, so that it would be a celebration of his life, not his untimely death.

The idea quickly took hold, with thousands of people asking how to become members. Newspapers across the country published a form that could be sent in. In Dayton, School Superintendant Edwin J. Brown authorized the wearing of the carnations on that day. Both the county and city employees also joined in. It was later estimated that millions of people across the county wore carnations on January 29, 1903.

On February 3, 1904, the scarlet carnation was adopted as the state flower of Ohio, "as a token of love and reverence for the memory of William McKinley." Today, the Ohio Statehouse still honors McKinley's birthday with it's annual Red Carnation Day.

Enrollment form for The Carnation League of America, 1903

December 24

On December 24, 1903, the Dayton Board of Public Service decided to give some of their prisoners an early Christmas present by having them transferred to the workhouse in Xenia, Ohio. It seems that the Dayton police were cracking down on vagrants and petty offenders in an effort to clean up the city. However, their efforts were so robust that the workhouse was overcrowded and the workshop facilities were insufficient to keep the prisoners busy.

Such was not the case in Xenia. The city there had a fine pile of stone that could be busted up by the convicts with sledgehammers, which would then be used in public construction projects, like repairing roads. The hard labor was considered part of the punishment and a deterrent that would encourage the prisoners to behave in the future. Those who refused to work were placed in the dungeon, where they were given only bread and water until they agreed to be good. The law at the time allowed prisoners to be fed only bread and water for up to 30 days.

Another decision that went into effect that same day was to begin using workhouse prisoners at the Dayton garbage dump. The city had no garbage crematory set up at the time and had to pay for men to dig trenches, dump trash into them, and then cover the holes back up. Dayton decided to save this expense by having the prisoners sent to the dump to do the work.

In order to make sure that no one wandered off from the job, the Dayton Board of Public Service bought 100 balls and chains, which were then placed on any prisoners that worked at the garbage dump. The balls were of heavy iron, attached to a length of chain. The other end of the chain was fastened to a leg bracelet, which went around the ankle of the prison worker. Although the balls and chains were expensive, the money was made up by the free labor at the dump.

December 25

Located at 1125 West Fifth Street, the Palace Theater opened on Christmas Day in 1927 to an overflowing crowd of theater-goers. Patrons were greeted by music from a $25,000 Wurlitzer organ. The ceiling and dome of the main auditorium was decorated with clouds and shooting stars that glowed in the electric lighting. The theater had a seating capacity of 1300 in the main section and 500 in the balcony, making the show house one of the largest in the Midwest at the time. In back of the forty foot stage were individual dressing rooms for the actors that would appear under the theater's spotlights. An attached ballroom held 1000 people.

Built by the Dayton West Side Amusement Corporation, the Palace was planned as an amusement center for the black population of Dayton, who were barred from downtown theaters. Although movies were shown, vaudeville was the theater's bread and butter. Bessie Smith was a headliner, as were Butterbeans and Susie, S. H. Dudley and his mule, and Sweet Mama Stringbean, to name just a few.

In 1941, the theater was purchased by the Palace Amusement Co. The building was completely remodeled, with 1,100 seats, new carpet and air conditioning. Up to this point, most of the movies had been action or western films. The new owners began adding more romance and adventure films, as well as the usual serial chapter and bonus cartoons.

By 1968, the theater was in bad shape and in need of improvements. Patrons complained that the food was stale and Kool-Aid was being served instead of soft drinks. The theater closed later that year.

December 26

On December 17, 1832, a canal boat arrived from Cincinnati carrying twenty-five German emigrants on board, with one dead and several others ill with cholera. Fortunately, due to other cities in Ohio having already been hit by the disease, a Board of Health had been appointed in Dayton earlier that fall. The passengers were quarantined together in a small room. Despite precautions, two of the older passengers died on December 26. Seven other deaths soon followed, including two local nurses who had taken care of the patients.

Although the disease abated during the winter months, it came back with a vengeance the following year. From June into September, 1833 there would be thirty-three more deaths. While not a doctor himself, Daniel Stutsman, a sickle-maker, devoted his entire time and energy to nursing the sick during this period. Stutsman would become the last person stricken with cholera, on September 5, 1833. When he died the following day his last words were, "This is the happiest day of my life, for I shall see my Savior."

After the crisis had abated, the board of health was abolished. In its place the city council passed an ordinance in December, 1835, instructing "physicians, keepers of public houses, and commanders of canal boats" to report cases of smallpox, cholera, or any other unusual diseases to the mayor. A place to establish an emergency hospital if any contagious disease appeared was agreed on and all persons with the disease were to be sent there if willing to go. It was also agreed that for anyone who objected going to the hospital, a notice or sign naming the disease was to be put up in a conspicuous place on the outside of the house where they were, on penalty of a fine. Persons suffering from such diseases were also to be fined if they left the house before they were well.

This plan proved well enough for a smallpox epidemic that hit the city in 1836, but was no match for the second epidemic of cholera during the spring and summer of 1849 in which over 200 people would die. *(See May 18)*

December 27

During World War I, The United States Treasury issued Liberty Bonds, War Savings Certificate stamps and Thrift stamps as a means of financing the war effort. Liberty Bonds were sold to businesses at high dollar amounts, but a person could buy one for as low as $50.

To encourage support of the war effort among people who could not afford a Bond, the Treasury Department also decided to issue Thrift Stamps and War Savings Stamps. Thrift stamps cost 25 cents and bore no interest. However, once sixteen were collected and pasted into a stamp booklet, they could be exchanged for a War Savings Certificate stamp. The War Savings Certificate stamps bore interest compounded quarterly at four percent and were tax free. War Savings stamps could be registered at any post office, insuring the owner against loss. These could then be sold back to the government through any post office with ten days written notice.

On December 27, 1917, the Dayton Post Office received 120,000 War Savings Certificate stamps and 600,000 Thrift stamps. Montgomery County's quota was set at $2 million dollars and the first shipment made up $644,000 of that amount.

The campaign began on January 2, 1918 and closed at the end of the year. The War Savings Certificate stamps were set to mature on January 1, 1923, with a value of $5.

The stamps were a success. A number of clubs were formed in Dayton, which allowed members to pool their resources together to buy multiple stamps. This proved especially popular among classes of school children.

War Saving stamps were affixed to a folder which carried the name of the purchaser, and could only be redeemed by that individual.

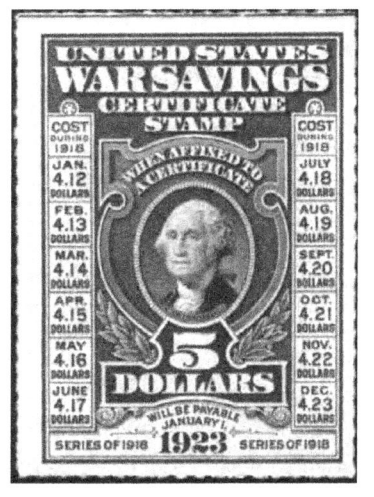

375

December 28

Three brothers, David, Edwin and Wesley Ingle, were grocers in Dayton in the early 1900s. They were familiar with the usage of tokens as a way to extend credit to customers. Instead of businesses keeping credit ledgers listing each item and its price for credit purchases, a certain amount of credit was extended to a customer, which was given to them in tokens in the amount of credit extended. The tokens could be spent the same as cash with the issuing merchant.

Unfortunately, tokens could easily be counterfeited, which could bankrupt a business. All that was needed was a token from a business. It could then be sent to a token manufacturer, with an order that a few hundred of them be made as close as possible to the original. The token manufacturers rarely checked to see if the person ordering the tokens actually owned the business it came from.

The Ingle brothers developed unique tokens which they initially test marketed in Dayton in 1909. The idea was to patent a design to be placed on one side of the coin, along with a patent date, so that the token couldn't be copied by other token manufacturers without breaking patent laws. The design they patented was the words Ingle System over a triangle logo. There were two base designs for the tokens, one with a patent date of June 1909 and the later one with a patent date of April 7, 1914. The other side would include the name of the business using the tokens and the amount the coin would be worth in credit. The tokens caught on and Ingles began distributing them nationwide. The business grew so large that the brothers decided to incorporate as The Ingle System Company on December 28, 1911.

Example of the front and back of a token made by The Ingle System Company. The Ingle System Company was succeeded by the Insurance Credit System in 1919.

376

December 29

Pole sitting, radio listening, dance marathons... People came up with a number of unusual ways to entertain themselves, and others, during the Great Depression.

Dance endurance marathons, where couples danced almost non-stop for hundreds of hours, were quite popular during the Depression. As usual, Dayton was no exception.

On December 29, 1929 the "Marathon and Endurance Carnival", as it was quite aptly called, began at the Eagles' Auditorium. Along with the dancers, a rocking chair and bicycle endurance contest was held as well. Couples danced, walked, shuffled and sprinted around the clock. A 25 cent admission fee entitled viewers to a box seat to watch as long as they pleased.

Contestants were required to remain on the dance floor for 45 minutes each hour, the other fifteen minutes was allotted for rest on cots. A live band played at night, whereas a record player usually sufficed during the day.

In order to bring in paying customers, other entertainment was also offered. One night included a mock wedding performed by a shuffling bride and groom. Mardi-Gras Nite saw contestants in full costume.

The longer the marathon wore on, the more endurance events the contestants found themselves subject to. Sprint races, no rest periods and fast walking soon whittled down the number of participants.

After enduring an incredible 1,878 hours, or about 2 and a half months on the dance floor, Dick Driscoll was the last person left standing, his partner having dropped out earlier in the contest.

In December, 1930, the Dayton City Council passed an ordinance that prohibited dance marathons within the city limits. Opponents to dance endurance events included movie theater owners, who lost money when their patrons attended a marathon instead of a motion picture. The police found that the marathons attracted an undesirable element, and churches did not like the close holding of the dancers in public.

Why would contestants endure weeks of dancing, knowing that only one person or couple would win? Participation meant a roof over their head, free meals and a possibility of money and fame.

December 30

In 1884, Mark Twain was about to publish his latest book, *Adventures of Huckleberry Finn*. Twain knew that a lecture tour was a good way to advertise and promote a new book, and so he had his agent contact George Washington Cable, author of *The Grandissimes* and other fiction about New Orleans, to accompany him as a performer. The tour, billed as "The Twins of Genius," travelled to about 80 cities between November 5, 1884 and February 28, 1885.

Twain' originally planned was to presell 40,000 books by December 15, publish that day, and hope to pick up more sales in bookstores in time to "catch the holiday trade." Unfortunately, from accident, or due to a prankster, one of the book's illustrations was considered obscene enough that it had to be replaced, which delayed publication until 1885. Still, as they say, the show must go on.

Twain and Cable rode the train all day and on December 30, 1884, gave a reading in the Grand Opera House. Twain had decided to make the last section of his forthcoming novel, in which Tom and Huck set out to free Jim, the major feature of the evening's performance. According to a *Dayton Daily Journal* reporter, that was the right choice to make.

"Laughter comes easy to an audience of Twain's, and having once started to laugh people are kept in a titter for the remainder of the evening. His fun is of the "dry" variety, not appreciated by the lover of the broad jokes and antics of the circus or minstrel show. In appearance he resembles the Nast caricatures of Whitelaw Reid, tall, gaunt, with long neck, heavy moustache and lots of hair. He wears a dress suit, but it is awfully wrinkled, and Mark looks as uneasy in it as a young man from the country. While speaking he holds up his right arm with his left hand, fingering his chin with his right hand in a nonchalant manner. He drawls his words, keeps a sober face, with rather an anxious, earnest look, and tumbles along into his story in a hesitating sort of way, very well imitating the characters supposed to be in conversation, and fetching a laugh about four times a minute. The best thing was his selection from his unpublished book--Huckleberry Finn, a companion to Tom Sawyer.

"The audience was very large, and apparently highly pleased."

December 31

In 1911, Thomas Midgley, Jr. came to Dayton and began working in NCR's invention department. In 1916, he joined forces with Charles F. Kettering, who had formed Dayton Engineering Laboratories Company (Delco). Delco was eventually sold to General Motors and became the foundation for the General Motors Research Corporation of which Kettering became vice-president in 1920.

General Motors had been making electrical refrigerators under the name Frigidaire in Detroit, Michigan for several years. In 1921, their production of the refrigerator was moved to Dayton. In 1926, Frigidaire became a GM subsidiary.

At the time, materials used for refrigeration; methyl chloride, ammonia and sulfur dioxide, were flammable and highly toxic. Even a minute leak in a refrigerator's system would give an unpleasant smell and breakdowns would release a poisonous gas.

In 1928 Kettering asked Midgley to search for a refrigerant that would be safer to use. Three days later he got his wish, when Midgley discovered chlorofluorocarbons, or CFC's, which was later given the name Freon©.

On December 31, 1928, Charles F. Kettering applied for a patent on a refrigerating apparatus that would use the gas, assigning it to Frigidaire. It would take until November 1, 1932 before Patent #1,886,339 would be issued.

In 1930 Midgley demonstrated before the American Chemical Society the safety of his creation by inhaling a lungful of the gas and breathing it onto a candle, which was extinguished, proving the gas was not harmful and was nonflammable.

Most uses of CFCs are now banned or severely restricted, as they have been shown to be responsible for ozone depletion. Today there are types of Freon that contain partly chlorinated and fluorinated hydrocarbons (HFCs) instead. These have replaced many uses of the older version, but they, too, are under strict control, as they are thought to be "super-greenhouse effect" gases. They are no longer used in aerosols, but are still used for refrigeration, due mainly because no suitable general use alternatives have been found that are not flammable or toxic - the same problems the original Freon was devised to avoid.

APPENDIX

A SKETCH IN THE SETTLEMENT AND PROGRESS OF DAYTON.
READ BEFORE THE DAYTON LYCEUM
AT ITS ANNIVERSARY MEETING ON AUG. 27, 1833.

In the latter part of the year 1791, the army of Gen. St. Clair, on its advance into the Indian country built Fort Hamilton, where the town of Hamilton now is, and another fort about six miles northerly of the present town of Easton. Gen. Wayne afterward built others which formed a chain of posts extending from Cincinnati to the mouth of the Auglaize. At length his victory over the Indians, on the 20th of August, 1794, brought on a general treaty with all the hostile tribes, which was concluded on the 3rd day of August, 1795, by which peace was established, boundaries were defined, and the country was thrown open for settlement.

Seventeen days after the treaty was concluded, Arthur St. Clair, James Wilkinson, Jonathan Dayton and Israel Ludlow made a contract with John Cleves Symmes, who assigned them his claim to two ranges of land extending from the Great Miami to the Little Miami, upon their binding themselves to make three settlements within their purchase – one at this point, one upon the Little Miami and one on Mad river. On the 21st of September, 1795, they dispatched two parties of surveyors from Cincinnati – one under Mr. Daniel Cooper, to survey and partially to clear out a road from that place to the mouth of Mad river, and the other under Capt. John Dunlap, to run the boundaries of their purchase. Dunlap's party was accompanied by a man named Bedell, who was moving to a point about six miles west of Lebanon where he was about to make a settlement, which was the first one established in advance of the old stations. Previous to that time, the frontier in that direction was a station on Mill creek, only 11 miles from Cincinnati. At that point the surveying parties separated, and that of Dunlap arrived at this place on the 27th of September, and on the banks of Mad river, about 30 miles from its mouth, found a party of six Wyandot Indians encamped.

From having been so long accustomed to consider each other as enemies, both parties were at first a little alarmed and manifested some shyness, but soon became friendly and confident, and made exchanges of provisions, knives, belts and other articles. Shortly afterwards, Mr. Cooper's party arrived, in company with some men from Kentucky who had come to view the country with an idea of becoming settlers. But on the next day, they went a mile or two up the river and finding the land covered with vines and rank weeds, so that it was difficult to get through them, they became discouraged and returned to Kentucky. Mr. Cooper's party started back to Cincinnati, and the other proceeded to finish their survey, which employed them about a week longer, during which their c amp was visited by some Indians, who robbed them of their provisions, and threatened the pack-horseman and hunter who had charge of it but did not attempt to do them any personal injury. The party reached Cincinnati on the 5th of October.

About the first of November Mr. Ludlow, one of the proprietors, came up and finished laying out the town. Having finished his work on the 4th, he gave it the name of Dayton. In order to promote the speedy settlement of the place the proprietors had offered certain donations and privileges to such as would engage to become settlers, and 46 persons had accepted the proposals and entered into engagements to that effect. They were each to have an in-lot and an out-lot in the town and the privilege of purchasing 160 acres of land at the rate of one French crown per acre. On the day after the town was laid out a number of them attended, and a lottery was held in which they drew lots for themselves and their friends. Out of the 46, however, only 15 fulfilled their engagement.

On the first day of April, 1796, four of them arrived here in a periauger after a passage of 10 days down the Ohio and up the Miami rivers. Two or three others had arrived during the winter and the remainder soon followed, together with four more who had entered into the engagement with the proprietors, subsequently making 19 persons who entitled themselves to donation lots by becoming settlers. Those 19 persons were William Gahagan, Samuel Thompson, Benjamin Van Cleve, William Van Cleve, Solomon Goss, Thomas Davis, John Davis, James McClure, John McClure, Daniel Ferrell, William Hamer, Solomon Hamer, Abraham Glassmire, John Dorough, William Chenoweth, James Morris, William Newcom and George Newcom. The only one of the number now a citizen of Dayton is George Newcom, and only two of the others are supposed to be yet living.

About the time that the first residents of this place removed here a few families located themselves where Miamisburg has since been laid out, the place then being called Hole's Station; a few settled upon Clear creek, about where Franklin now is; and some on the Big Prairie, a little below Middletown. Shortly after, during the same spring Jonathan Mercer settled on Mad river, eight or nine miles above this place, and some other persons established themselves higher up the river at its fork, some on the Miami at the mouth of Honey creek, and some at Piqua. The people at Mercer's Station at one time became so much alarmed at the conduct of the Indians, by some of whom they were threatened and abused, that they abandoned the place, but in a short time returned again. The other settlements were not molested in any manner, except by having horses stolen.

The ground which is now laid off into out-lots on the west side of the town was an open prairie when the people first removed to this place and they raised a considerable crop off corn upon it the first season of their residence here. Until that was gathered they were obliged, of course, to bring all their provisions of that kind from Cincinnati, where a barrel of flour cost them $9 and a bushel of corn meal $1, while the transportation to this place was an additional expense of $2.50 per hundred weight.

These disadvantages and the other difficulties incident to the settlement were gradually over come and the people began to acquire the necessities of life from their own fields. The town was advancing a little in population and improvement and the land in the neighborhood began to be taken up for farms. A difficulty, however, soon arose with respect to the titles, both to the lots in the town and the land around it, which checked the progress of the settlement for some time.

The settlers had all made their purchases and expected to receive their titles from St. Clair, Wilkinson, Ludlow and Dayton, the assignees of Judge Symmes; but Symmes found himself unable to fulfill his contract and make pay for the whole of the purchase; and the government at length gave him a patent for the amount of land he was able to pay for, and took back the residue in which were included the two ranges of townships which he had assigned and relinquished to St. Clair, Wilkinson, Ludlow and Dayton. When this became known the people were very much alarmed on account of the apparent danger that they would lose their lands and with them all the labor they had expended in their improvement, and all the advantages they had expected in becoming settlers.

They had ventured into the wilderness considerable in advance of the frontier – they had encountered difficulties without number, labored under many disadvantages, expended their limited means, worked hard and suffered privations to provide homes for their families, and, after all, found it doubtful whether they should be able to preserve them. The situation of things, while it disheartened those who had already located themselves here, and caused some of them to abandon the country and remove to other parts where the same difficulties did not exist, discouraged and prevented other persons from coming who otherwise would have done so. The title under Symmes had failed and the government had not yet made provisions for the sale of the land at the public land offices. The country, therefore, promised nothing but loss and disappointment to those who were already here, and offered no inducement to others to come.

Affairs remained in this state some time. At length, on the petition of inhabitants, congress on the 2nd day of March, 1799, passed an act, usually known by the name of the pre-emption law, by which all persons who had made any contract in writing with John Cleves Symmes previous to the 1st of April, 1797, for the purchase of lands between the Miami rivers, not comprehended in his patent, were to be entitled to a preference in purchasing the same lands of the United States, at the price of $2 an acre, to be paid in three annual installments. This law, however, did not give sufficient relief, and only three or four persons accepted its conditions and entered their lands.

During the summer of 1799 the people of the Miami county became alarmed at the disposition manifested by the Indians, who, it was supposed, had been operated upon by the British traders among them, and had become dissatisfied with the cession that had been made of their lands and the boundaries established. The alarm was so great as to cause the people in all the different settlements to build block houses for protection. One was build in Dayton, on the river bank, at the head of Main st. The Indians, however, remained quiet and did not engage in hostilities, and the feeling of security was again restored.

On the 3rd of March, 1801, congress passed another pre-emtion law, extending the privileges granted by the first act to all persons who had made contracts in writing with Judge Symmes, or his associates, or had made payments of money, for the purchase of lands, and giving longer time to substantiate claims and make payments. In addition to the price of $2 an acre it provided that the claimant should pay surveyor's fees and some other incidental expenses. The price which Judge Symmes was to pay for his land was two-thirds of a dollar per acre, and his assignees, St. Clair, Wilkinson, Ludlow and Dayton, would have had their purchases at the same rate.

Accordingly, the settlers who had bought lands of them had generally bargained for them at a small advance on that price and probably had not, in any case, agreed to give as much as $2 per acre. The pre-emption law, therefore, although it afforded them a considerable relief, of which they were glad to avail themselves, did not place them in as good a situation as they would have been if they could have got their lands according to the terms of their contracts with St. Clair and his associates, and those who had entitled themselves to donations, by becoming settlers under their agreement with the proprietors, lost their gratuities and were only permitted to enter their town lots at the price of $2 an acre in preference to any other persons.

St. Clair and his associates, if they had chosen to do so, might have availed themselves of the law and entered the whole tract which Judge Symmes had relinquished to them; but in that case they would have had to pay the government $2 an acre, instead of 66c, which they would have cost them under the contract with Judge Symmes. This rise in the price, and perhaps the circumstance that they had sold out a considerable quantity of land at less than $2 an acre, and would have to complete the titles to the purchase at a positive loss to themselves instead of realizing a profit if they purchased the land of the United States, determined them to abandon their speculation and decline availing themselves of the benefit of the law.

They accordingly notified the commissioners, who had been appointed by the government to examine and decide upon claims to the rights of the preemption, of their relinquishment of their right, and assisted the settlers who had purchased of them in obtaining the allowance of their claims. Accordingly, all those who chose to do so procured patents, not only for their lands but also for their inlots in Dayton – for which they paid at the rate of $2 an acre – making the lots, with the additional fees, cost about $1 each.

At the same time that the pre-emption law took effect, the land offices were opened for the general ale of the government land, and the country commenced filling with inhabitants. The year 1801, therefore, may be considered as the real beginning of this improvement and consequent prosperity. During that year a list was taken of the free males who were 21 years of age in Dayton township, which then formed a part of Hamilton co., and included the whole Miami co. north of a line running a short distance below Miamisburg. There were 28 west of the Great Miami, 20 east of the Little Miami, and 382 between, making 430 in all.

The opening of the United States land offices gave an impulse to emigration into the eastern portion of the territory, that soon increased the population to the number requisite to entitle it admission into the Union; and on the 30th of April, 1802, congress passed an act authorizing it to form a constitution and to enter into a state government. The convention met for the formation of a constitution on the first of November following, and the first state legislature assembled on the first of March, 1803.

Among its earliest acts was one for the division of the counties of Hamilton and Ross. Hamilton co. which then comprised the whole Miami county was reduced to its present limits; Butler and Warren were organized with their present boundaries; and Montgomery was established with a view to its ultimate reduction to its present size, but for that time was made to include all the country north of Butler and Warren, to the northern boundary of the state; out of which has since been formed the counties of Preble, Darke, Miami, Shelby and seven others. Dayton was made the county seat and courts were directed by the act to be held at the house then owned by George Newcom and now by John Thomson at the head of Main st. It is now the oldest building in the town and when it was erected was the best, the others being all cabins.

Previous to the establishment of the county seat in Dayton, many of the first inhabitants had removed to farms in the country and at that time there were only five families residing in the place. They all lived near the river bank and that neighborhood remained the principal part of the town for many years. From then it gradually spread in different directions and the business removed further away from the river, until it became stationed about the four corners at the intersection of Main and First sts. In 1805 the first brick building was erected. It was the one on Main st. now occupied by the Franklin Coffee House. In 1806 the courthouse was built and within a year or two after that three other brick buildings.

In 1810 the population had increased to 383. The war commenced two years afterward and Dayton then became a thoroughfare for the troops on their way to the northwestern frontier and a place of collection and deposit for provisions. The improvement and population of the town advanced rapidly. At the close of the war the business had increased and spread further south; so that it extended down to the corner of Main and old Market st. Improvements continued to progress rapidly after the war, particularly in 1816, and by the year 1820 the population had increased to 1139, which was very near three times what it was in 1810.

Soon afterward the general breaking up of the banks in the western country took place; the flood of paper money with which the country was inundated sunk away; the prices of every description of property fell and a great depression ensued in all kinds of business. All improvements ceased in Dayton and the place remained at a standstill, neither gaining nor losing much in the amount of its population until the commencement of the canal gave it new life.

The division of the Miami canal extending from Middletown to Dayton was put under contract in May, 1827, and during that year building recommenced with considerable activity, and old neglected houses were repaired and crowded with inmates until dwellings could with difficulty be secured as fast as the increase of population required them. In May, 1828, a census was taken and inhabitants were found to amount to 1697, showing an increase from 1820 of 558, nearly all of which had taken place within the preceding year. In June, 1830, when the inhabitants were enumerated by a United States deputy marshal, the population had increased to 2954, the gain in a little over two years having been 1237. Eighteen months afterward, at the close of the year 1831, the census was again taken and the inhabitants amounted to 3258.

The improvement of the town in the meantime set pace with the increase of its population. At the end of the year 1828 the whole number of buildings amounted to 370, of which 125 were of brick, six of stone, 239 of wood. In 1829, 46 brick buildings were erected and 54 of wood, making a total of 100. In 1830 the new houses built were 35 of brick and 46 frame, total 81. In 1831 the number was still greater, brick dwellings amounting to 50 and those of wood to 62, in all 112. In 1832, 51 brick buildings and 44 of wood were added.

The canal was opened for navigation to this place early in January, 1829. The population in the preceding May was less than 1700, and it is now probably 4000. The number of houses was then 370 and 388 have been erected since that time, greatly superior to those built before both in average size and quality.

In connection with this sketch of the commencement of the settlement and the progress of the improvements of the town, some other circumstances may be noted which will probably not be uninteresting.

In the spring of 1805 Dayton was inundated by an extraordinary rise of the river. In all ordinary freshets the water used to pass through the prairies at the east side of the town, where the basin now is, but the flood of 1805 covered a great portion of the town itself. There were only two spots of dry land in the whole place. The water came out of the river at the head of Jefferson st. and ran down through the commons at the east end of old Market st. which a horse could not cross without swimming, leaving an island between it and the mill. A canoe could be floated at the intersection of First st. with St. Clair, and the first dry land west of that point was about where the house of Mr. Brabham now stands.

The western extremity of that island was near the crossing of Main and First sts., from whence it bore down in a southern direction, toward where the saw mill now stands leaving a dry strip from the point on the south side of Main cross between Jefferson st. and the prairies to the river bank at the head of Main st. Almost the whole of the land was under water, with the exception of those two islands, from the river to the hill which circles around east and south of the town from Mad river to the Miami. The water was probably eight feet deep in Main st., at the courthouse, where the ground has since been raised several feet.

In consequence of the flood, a considerable portion of the inhabitants became strongly disposed to abandon the present site of the town; and the proposition was made and urged very strenuously that lots should be laid out along the plain upon the second rise southeast of the town through which the Waynesville road passes and that the inhabitants should take lots there in exchange for those which they owned upon the present plot, and thus remove the town to a higher and more secure situation. The project, however, was defeated through unyielding opposition of some of the citizens, and it is no doubt for the advantage and prosperity of the place that it was.

Some time afterward a levee was raised across the low ground at the grist mill to prevent the passage of water through the prairie in freshets; but not being built of sufficient strength and elevation, the floods rode over it and washed it away several times, until at length it was made high and strong enough to resist the greatest rises of water that have occurred since 1805, although one like the one of that year would still pass over it. The last time it was washed down was in August, 1814, and this time the water was deep enough to swim a horse where the warehouses stand at the head of the basin, and a ferry was kept there for several days. The water at that time also passed through a considerable current, from the head of Jefferson to the east end of Old Market st., and through the hollows in the western part of the town; and the plain through which the feeder passes east of the mill race was nearly all under water.

Before the erection of the numerous mill dams upon the Miami, it was navigable during the principal part of the year for keel boats by which considerable business was done upon it, above Dayton as well as below. A few years before the war a couple of the citizens of this place built two small keel boats, in Main st., opposite the court house, from whence they were hauled to the river and launched. Having ascended the river to Loramie, one of them was taken out of the water and hauled over to St. Marys river, a distance of about 12 miles and thus a connected line was established – one boat plying upon the Miami and the other upon the Maumee with which the parties carried on a considerable trade from some time, making tolerably regular trips. Some business continued to be done on the Miami, with keel boats as late as the year 1820, when navigation became so much impeded by mill dams.

At the same time that the price of wagon transportation between Dayton and Cincinnati had dropped down to such a low rate that they could no longer be run with a profit, and ceased to be used. From that time until the construction of the canal the only species of navigation witnessed by Dayton, was the descent of the flatboats bound for New Orleans, a considerable number of which were usually freighted and taken down every spring. Boats of that kind ran from Dayton as early as 1809, if not previously.

On the 25th of January, 1829, the first boat from Cincinnati arrived in our basin. She was called the "Gov. Brown," and there was something appropriate in that name, being borne by the first boat that traversed the Miami canal, from Cincinnati to Dayton. Gov. Brown as long back as 1819, was engaged in urging the connection of the two places by means of a canal and was one of the most energetic and efficient of the public men in our state in devising and carrying into execution the grand scheme of internal improvements, which has so much exalted the character of Ohio.

A postoffice was established in Dayton in 1803. For some years, the only mail received in the place was one which left Cincinnati once a week, and went up the Little Miami through Lebanon and Xenia, and then down through Dayton and Hamilton, to Cincinnati again. Thus a letter from Cincinnati to this place went the whole route, by Lebanon, Urbana and Piqua, before it reached its destination; and one from Dayton to Piqua, or from Franklin to Dayton had to go down to Cincinnati in the first place, and take the whole circuit of the post route, and would then be received at the place to which it was directed, a week after it was mailed.

The first improvement upon this state of things was a weekly mail from Zanesville, by way of Franklinton and Urbana, to this place, and that was succeeded by one through Chillicothe which continued to be the principal channel of communication with the east until a few years ago when a more direct line was established through Columbus. In the spring of 1825, the first experiment was made in the establishment of a line of stages through Dayton. It was undertaken by Mr. Timothy Squier, who formed a connection with the mail contractors between this place and Cincinnati and Columbus, and commenced by running a stage once a week, occupying two days in coming from Cincinnati to Dayton.

The undertaking was considered hazardous by many who thought the country too new to support it; but instead of its failing for want of support, the increase of travel soon demanded further facilities, and the stages commenced running twice and three times a week, and with increased speed; and at length a daily mail was established. Lines of stages have also been put in operation in other directions, affording means for traveling which leave little more to be desired, except a general improvement of the roads to put the country on an equal footing in this respect, with that east of the mountains.

The first newspaper printed in Dayton was called the Dayton Repertory. It was issued by William McClure and George Smith on the 18th of September, 1808. The first five numbers were printed upon common writing paper and the publication was then suspended for nearly four months for want of paper. After that it was issued regularly on a sheet of the ordinary size then used for newspapers in the western country, and a paper has been published in Dayton ever since.

When the county was organized, Benjamin Archer, Isaac Spinning and John Ewing were appointed associate judges of the court of common pleas, and Francis Dunlavy of Warren co. was president of the circuit. The first court was held in Dayton in July, 1803. Mr. Newcom, in whose house it was held, kept the only tavern in the place, and a part of his house was occupied by the only store. He had been elected sheriff of the county and his house, therefore, was courthouse, jail, tavern, store and dwelling. At the first term of the court one civil action was commenced, and a grand jury found three indictments for assault and battery.

When the first settlers came to Dayton the ground which the town occupied was covered by a growth of scrub oak, hawthorn, plums and other small trees, but had very little heavy timber on it. Its appearance was very similar to that of the margins of our barren prairies. While the inhabitants all lived upon the river bank, it was no uncommon thing for strangers, on coming into the place, after threading their way through the brush until they had passed through the whole town plat from one extremity to the other, and arrived at the first of the few cabins that constituted the settlement, to inquire how far it was to Dayton.

They were of course informed that they had just passed through it and had arrived in the suburbs. The fact seemed rather ridiculous and it was very natural for them to think that the projectors of the town had calculated much too largely in laying it out upon so extensive a scale. The inhabitants themselves, indeed, partook of the same opinion. The lots on the east side of Main st. opposite the courthouse were considered so far out of the way that it was not thought probably that the town would extend much beyond that, and they were accordingly appropriated for a graveyard, and remained so until the year 1805, when the present burying ground was selected, which has been used by the town and adjoining county ever since.

The business and improvements of the place, instead of being limited to the vicinity of the river as was then expected, have spread very generally over the whole ground originally laid out in the building lots, and additions have been made to them on every side. Those who have been citizens for only a few years have witnessed principal improvements that have taken place, and doubtless have taken much interest and pleasure in seeing it advance in prosperity; but they who have seen it and the surrounding country change from its wilderness state to what it is now, must possess their feelings of interest and gratification in a high degree.

End

INDEX

10 Wilmington Place, 261
10th Ohio OVI, 119
11th Ohio OVI, 119
134th Field Artillery, Battery D, 177
1st Regiment OVI, 117, 316
2003 Committee, 302
27th U.S. Infantry Regiment, 362
28th U.S. Volunteer Infantry, 362
322nd Field Artilery, 329
372nd Infantry Regiment, 82
372nd Infantry Regiment, Company G, 82
3-D motion pictures, 153
3rd Regiment, Ohio National Guard, 362
40 West 4th Center, 345
50-50 Club, The (television show), 83, 299
661st Air Force Band, 221
6th Regiment of the U.S. Engineers, 102
9th U.S. Volunteer Infantry, 362
Abernathy, John, 140
Abernathy, Louis, 140
Abernathy, Temple, 140
Acton, Amy Florence, 351
Adams, MA, 107
Adelphic Society of The Dayton Academy, 73
Advance Department, NCR, 133
Adventures of Huckleberry Finn (book), 378
Aerodrome No. 5 (airplane), 356
Africa, 307
African American veterans, 82
After Taxes I Still Have You (song), 105
Aida (opera), 253
Aiken, John, 339
Aiken, Rachel, 339
Air Force, 365
air raid sirens, test, 157
Aircraft Production Board, 350
Airless Tire, 183
Airplane Engineering Department, 352
Akron, OH, 243
Alderman, Edwin E., 49
Alder's Home Store, 35
Alexander Film Company, 108
Alexander Industires, Inc., 108
Alexander, Ray, 30
Alger, Frederick M., 340
Alger, Russel A., 340
All-American Soap Box Derby, 243
Allinger, P. William, 295

Alpha (canal boat), 259
Altherr, Jacob, 118
altitude record set, 65
Alton, IL, 136
America (song), 336
American Chemical Society, 379
American Elm (tree), 147
American Expeditionary Force, 102
American Football League, 289
American Legion, 102
American Mutoscope and Biograph Co., 58
American National Association of Masters of Dancing, 202
American Professional Football Assn, 289
American River, 47
American Vaudeville Company, 277
American Veterans Heritage Center, 110
Amiens Defense Line, 102
Amiens, France, 102
Amry, 350
Amtrak, 213
Ancient and Accepted Order of Scottish Rite of Dayton, 212
Anderson, Carl, 249
Andrews' Raid, 301
Andrews, Frank Mills, 72
Andrews, James J., 301
annex of 1868, 174
annexation of 1930, 89
Antietam (battle), 119
Anti-Noise Society, 57
Antioch Shrine Temple, 20
Anti-Saloon League, 187
Anti-Slavery Society, 32
Antler Hotel, 29
Aplco, 280
Apollo Theater, 130
Appeal, The (four-page sheet), 295
Apple Electric Company, 280
Apple, Vincent G., 280
Arcade Market, 72
Archer, Benjamin (Judge), 339, 388
Archibald, J. D. (Capt.), 31
Arir Techincal Intelligence Center (ATIC), 365
Army, 80, 108, 358, 366
Army-Navy "E" Award, 80
Arnold, Hap (Gen.), 246
Arrears of Pension Act of 1879, 51

389

Assn. for the Remebrance of the Sabbath, 37
Assn. for Research and Enlightenment, 294
astronaut maneuvering device, 234
Atlanta Campaign (battle), 119
Atlanta, GA, 301, 333
Atlantic City, 277
Atlas Hotel, 140
Audobon, John, 97
Auglaize River, 380
Australia, 351
autographic register, 141
Avery Dennison Corporation, 176
Aviation Hall of Fame, 19
Aviation Trail, Inc., 302
B & O Passenger Train #59. 257
B-17 (airplane), 201
Baby's Milk Fund, 123
Bachman, John, 97
Bag of Nails (song), 122
Baggott, Oliver P., 119
Baggott, Roland (Judge), 327
Baker, John L., 241
ball and chain, for prisoners, 372
Baltimore, MD, 168
Bank Flyer (automobile), 30
Bank One Corporation, 109
Banvard, John, 168
Barauska, Elias Joseph, 135
Barling Bomber (airplane), 246
Barling, Walter H., 246
Barnett, Joseph (Senator), 174
Barney and Smith Car Works, 228-229, 237
Barney Community Center, 299
Barney, Eugene, 72
Barnum & Bailey (circus), 217-218
Barrett, Edward, 167
Barrymore, Lionel, 58
barter system, 215
bathing, forced at Dayton Soldiers' Home, 304
Battle of Chickamauga, 316
Battle of Gettysburg (cyclorama), 238
Battle of Shiloh, 316
Battle of Slim Buttes, 53
Baum, L. Frank, 205-296
Bayan, Philippines, 362
Beach Boys, 149
Beatles, 149, 331
Beckel Hotel, 66, 94, 132, 154
Bedell, 380
beer hall, Dayton Solider's Home, 9
Beerman Realty Co., 35
Beerman Stores, Inc., 35

Beerman, Arthur, 35
Beers, John (Judge), 116
Belgium, 103, 159
Bell, Alexander Graham, 66
Bell, John S. (Chief of Secret Service), 210
Belmont Auto Theater, 153
Belmont, 89
Beneath the 12-Mile Reef (motion picture), 153
Benjamin Kuhns & Co., 113
Benner, B. S. (Detective), 291
Benzoin Elixer (patent medicine), 128
Berlin, Germany, 49
Berwind, E. J., 340
Berwind-White Coal Mining, 340
Beter Films Committee of Atlanta, 108
BHA, 166
Bickham, Charles Goodwin, 362
Bickham, William D. (major), 242
Big Prairie, 381
Big Shanty, TN, 301
billboards, law regulating, 95
Billy Sunday Tabernacle, 315
Biltmore Hotel, 303, 334
Biltmore Towers, 334
Biltmore-Hilton, 334
Bimm Dayton Ice and Cold Water Supply, 199
Bimm's Park, 156
Bishop's Boys, The (book), 313
Bissett, Joe, 146
Black Hill Rangers, 53
Black Locust (tree), 147
black veterans, 82
Black, David, 196
blizzard of 1950, 342
Blnk, Henry S., 341
Bloch, C. C. (Admiral), 80
blockhouse, 353
Blue and Grey, The (song), 124
Blue Christmas (song), 292
blue laws, 37
Board of Health, 148
body snatching, 332
Bois des Tallious (woods) 102
Bois-de-Bonseil, France, 177
Bolling Field, Washington, D.C., 158
Bollmeyer, John F., 319
Bombe, 77
Bombeck, Erma, 121
Bomberger, William, 134
Bond, Hugh L. (Judge), 268
Bonebrake Theological Seminary, 76

390

Book Giving Week, 172
Boone, Charles (Cadet), 127
Boonshoft Museum of Discovery, 271
Boston Dry Goods Store, 35
Boston University, 351
Boston, MA, 351, 361
Bott, Fenton I., 202
Bott's Studio, 202
Boxcar lable, 292
Boyer, Edith E. L., 344
Boyer, Frederick G. L., 344
Boyer, Israel Donald, 344
Boyer, Jean-Pierre (President of Haiti), 307
Boyer, O. P., 218
Brabham (Mr.), 385
Braun, Bob, 83
Breathing Out Fire (music album), 292
Bridal Chariot (balloon), 248
Bridge Street bridge, 34
Brill T-40 (electric trolley bus), 123
Brimhall, William, 240
British Fifth Army, 102
Broadbent, Betty (tattooed lady), 217
Broadway, 89
Broadwell, Simeon, 15
Brock, Isaac (Gen.), 163
broken neck, lived with a, 309
Bronx Zoo, 359
Brook Sons', 341
Brooklyn Atlantics (baseball team), 156
Brooklyn Dodgers (football team), 289
Brooks, Fred A., 332
Brown (Gov.), 387
Brown School, 264
Brown, Don, 255
Brown, Edwin F. (Col.), 279, 346
Brown, Edwin J., 371
Brown, Eleanor Gertrude, 150
Brown, Henry N., 319
Brown, Mike, 125
Brown, Robert (Justice), 116
Bruges, Belgium, 247
Brush Motor Car, 140
Bucher, Frank J., 361
Buck Rogers, 234
Buckeye Blossoms (book), 242
Bucking Bronco (motion picture), 277
Buffalo Bill's Wild West Show, 277, 293
Buffalo, NY, 326
Buffum, Edward Gould, 47
Build for Tomorrow (book), 258
Bull Moose Party, 145

bullfight, 253
Bulter County, 23
Burba, Francis, 180
Burba, George F., 180
Burba, Howard L., 191
Burbank, CA, 126
Bureau of Air Commerce, 129
Burkham, E. G., 99
Burkhardt Building, 130
Burkhardt, William, 279
Burkhart, Edward E. (Mayor), 95
Burnett, Sophia Greene, 254
Bush, George H. W. (President), 302
Bustin' Babes (baseball team), 311
Butler County, OH, 191, 384
Butlerville, IN, 191
Butterbeans and Susie (vaudeville actors), 373
By Your Leave (stage play), 79
C.C. Rider (song), 292
C-69 Constellation (airplane), 126
Cable, George Washington, 378
Caldonia (motion picture), 249
Californian, The (newspaper), 47
California, 47, 235
Callahan Building, 12
Callahan, Dan, 240
Calvary Cemetery, 206, 233
Cambridge University, 216
Camp Chase, 24
Camp De Souge, 177
Camp Sheridan, 177
canal, 31, 259, 272, 374
Can't Help Falling in Love (song), 292
Canton, OH, 289
Cap Corwin, 316
cardiac massage and resuscitation device, 42
Cardinal, The (motion picture), 79
CareFlight, 300
Carillon Historical Park, 41, 175, 244, 302, 348
Carley, F. G., 191
Carmen's Deli, 109
Carnation League of America, 371
Carnegie Hero Fund Commission, 341
Carnegie, Andrew, 63, 341
Carnell, Julia Shaw, 13
Carprarola, Italy, 13
Carrol, F. O. (Mrs.), 358
Carson City, 198
Carson, Johnny, 324
Carter, Jimmy (President), 169
Case, Ann, 96
Case, Phil, 96

cash register, invented, 322
Caterpillar Club, 306
Cates, Diane, 207
Cates, Joseph (Mrs.), 207
Cayce Psychic Institute, 294
Cayce, Edgar, 294
CBS Radio, 334
CBS, 135
Cedar Grove Cemetery, Flushing, NY, 216
Cedar Rapids, Iowa, 190
Celoron Park, NY, 262
Centennial Bell, 312
Central High School, 12, 73, 178, 353
Central Market House, 67
Century of Service, A (book), 172
CFCs, 379
Chachet G!, 144
Champios, Bernice, 170
Channel 22, 255
Chapman, Ray, 270
Charity Circus, 204
Charles McCaul Company, 94
Charles Sucher Packing Company, 360
Chase Bank, 109
Chattanooga, TN, 301
Cheez-It Cheese Crackers, 368
Chenoweth, William, 381
Chevrolet, 243
Chicago Electrical Vehicle Company, The, 237
Chicago World's Fair, 336
Chicago, IL, 28, 166, 237, 297, 324, 331
Chicago, Indianapolis & Louisville Railroad, 340
Chicago's World Fair, 61
Chickamauga (battle), 119
Chifos, Theodore C., 130
Chiko (chimpanzee), 218
children's meetings, NCR, 219
Children's Parade and Pet Show, 181
Children's Playhouse, 337
Children's Saturday Show, 337
Chillicothe, OH 212, 387
cholera epidemic of 1833, 148
cholera epidemic of 1849, 148
cholera, 374
Christ, 343
Christmas, 373
Church of Jesus Christ of Latter-Day Saints, 220
Cincinnati Associated Artists, 168
Cincinnati Daily Chronicle (newspaper), 242
Cincinnati Enquirer (newspaper), 51, 124, 314

Cincinnati Red Stockings (baseball team), 156
Cincinnati, Hamilton & Dayton Railroad, 52, 213
Cincinnati, OH, 47, 83, 118, 148, 168, 265, 285, 297, 299, 305, 314, 350, 355, 364, 374, 380, 386-387,
Cinderella Girl, 296
CinemaScope, 153
Cinerama (motion picture process), 253
Cinerama Holiday (motion picture), 253
circus parade, 31
Citizens National Bank, Piqua, OH, 30
Citron Balsam (patent medicine), 128
City Brewery, 279
City Hall, 42
city manager-commision government, 236
City Railway company, 186, 232
City Workhouse, 240
Civil War, 11, 24, 53, 62, 70, 82, 110, 114, 117, 119, 124, 168, 203, 223, 235, 238, 301, 304, 305, 316, 319, 329, 352
Clark, David (Sheriff), 116
Clark, Edward, 57
Clark, Harry, 277
Clark, Henry, 136
Classic Theater, 249, 262
Clemens, Ralph B. (Sgt.), 329
Clements, William T., 102
Cleveland Indians, 270
Cleveland, OH 28, 104, 136, 270, 285, 297, 324, 331
Click Camera and Video, 144
Click, Clarence B. (Private), 177
closed-circuit television shows, 345
Coca-Cola, 154
Cody, Buffalo Bill, 53
Cody, William Frederick "Buffalo Bill", 53, 241, 293
Coffee House, 118
Coffin (Warden), 335
Coleman, Henry, 212
Coleman, Mary Jane Harter, 369
Collier, Robert J., 340
Collier's Weekly (magazine), 340
Colonel (dog), 90
Colonel White High School, 346
Colonel White's regiment, 127
Colonial Theater, 89, 249, 278, 363
Columbia University, 150
Columbian Exposition, 271
Columbus (elephant), 122
Columbus band, 204

Columbus Driving Park, 325
Columbus Panhandlers (football team), 289
Columbus, OH, 25, 83, 97, 104, 117, 150, 158, 166, 245, 261, 276, 285, 291, 297, 311, 325, 331, 350-351, 355, 387
Commercial Club, 107
Common Council of the Town of Dayton, 15
Community Chest, 194
Community Golf Course, 159
Community Hall, NCR, 103
Community War Chest, 164
Compound Syrup of Poke Root, 128
Computing-Tabulating-Recording Company, 326
Congressional Medal of Honor, 362
Congressional Union, 327
Conklin, Oliver F., 7
Conklin, William J. (Dr.), 308
Conner, Scott, 291
Conrad, Hannah D., 344
Consul (monkey), 189
Consul Crosses the Atlantic (motion picture), 189
Consul the Educated Monkey (toy), 189
Convention Center, 277
Conversation Piece (talk show), 324
Converse, Elijah, 16
Conway, Edward, 85
Conway, Hannah, 344
Cook, Frederick A., 74
Cooper Medicine Company, 139
Cooper Park, 14, 55, 73, 107, 163, 179, 271, 367, 371,
Cooper, Daniel C., 50, 55, 84, 254, 265, 281, 380
Cooper, David Zeigler, 55
Cooper, Harry, 254
Coppedge, Iona, 286
Corbett, James J., 198, 228
Corcoran, Noreen, 149
Coronet (magazine), 294
Corpus Christi Church, 269
Corridors of Light (book), 150
Council of Social Agencies, 89
Count Basie, 249
County jail, 125
Courier (automobile), 226
Courier Car Company, 226
Courier Clermont (automobile), 226
Court of Common Pleas, 339
Courthouse (1884), 81
courthouse of 1806, 384

courthouse of 1815, 14, 32
Courthouse Square, 81, 121, 169
Covington, KY, 305
Cow, The (song), 209
Cox, James M. (Jr), 173, 180
Cox, James M., 98, 129, 173, 175, 186, 231, 298
Crable, Mace, 23
Craighead, Samuel (Prosecuting Atty.), 116
Crane, Joseph H. (Judge), 96
Crane, Noah, 274
Crawford, Jack (Capt.), 53
Crickets (singing group), 149
Croatia, 151
Croix de Guerre with Palm, 82
Crook, George (Gen.), 53
Crook, Oliver (Dr.), 128
Crosley Broadcasting Corporation, 83
Cross, (Prof.), 204
Crothers, Benjamin "Scatman", 154
Crouch, Tom, 196, 313
Crouse, John, 119
Crowne Plaza Dayton, 19
Crume, P. M. (Dr.), 191
CSS Virginia (ironclad ship), 62
Cuba, 127
Cumberland, MD, 25
Curby Crusaders, 59
Curby the Cardinal, 59
curfew, for children, 164
Curley (dog), 119
Curry, E. W. B. (Rev.), 188
Curry, John (Col.), 184
Custer Bubble Statoscope, 370
Custer Invalid Chair, 370
Custer Specialty Company, 370
Custer, Levitt Luzern, 114, 191, 370
Custer, Randall, 243
Cypress Gardens, 253
D.& X. (railway company), 186
Dahomey Park, 115
Daily Democrat (newspaper), 295
Dalton, William (policeman), 233
Dalton, William, 71
dance marathons, 377
Dance Pavillion, Island Park, 182
Darke County, 384
Darlington, Jeanie, 96
Darlington, Sandy, 96
Darrtown, OH, 191
Daughters of Jerusalem, 82
Daughters of the American Revolution, 108

Dauphin, PA, 185
Davids Cemetery, 170
Davis Girls' Bicycle Club, 108
Davis Sewing Machine Company, 7, 44, 232, 284, 338
Davis Tri-Car Chemical (fire apparatus), 44
Davis, Bing, 121
Davis, Jefferson, 328
Davis, John, 101, 381
Davis, Thomas, 381
Day in Dayton, A (music album), 292
DAYCO, 183
Dayton & Springfield Turnpike Co., 25
Dayton & Union Railroad, 52
Dayton & Western Turnpike Company, 25, 52
Dayton Academy, 353
Dayton Airport, Inc., 129
Dayton and Montgomery County Federation of Churches, 164
Dayton Arcade Company, 72
Dayton Arcade, 72
Dayton Art Institute, 13, 359
Dayton Association of Cooperative Production Units, 194
Dayton Aviation Heritage National Historical Park, 302
Dayton Bar Association, 303
Dayton Board of Education, 73, 333
Dayton Board of Health, 374
Dayton Board of Public Service, 372
Dayton Breweries Company, 187
Dayton Buggy Works, 111
Dayton Canoe Club, 102, 170, 182
Dayton Chamber of Commerce, 275
Dayton Children's Hospital, 299
Dayton City Commission, 236
Dayton City Council, 84, 377
Dayton City Planning Board, 227
Dayton Clearing House Association, 30
Dayton Coca-Cola Bottling Company, 18
Dayton Convention and Exhibition Center, 19
Dayton Council for Defense, 157
Dayton Country Club, 92
Dayton Cup, 275
Dayton Daily Empire (newspaper), 85, 293, 308, 348, 378
Dayton Daily News (newspaper), 29, 53, 59, 71, 74, 86, 90, 98, 107-108, 134, 173, 175, 180, 200, 202, 228, 231, 237, 243, 255, 292, 296, 311, 343, 348, 354,
Dayton Daily News Building, 363
Dayton Development Coalition, 109
Dayton Division of Police, 175
Dayton East Drive-in, 149
Dayton Electrical Manufacturing Company, 280
Dayton Engineering Laboratories Co., (DELCO), 40, 161, 379
Dayton Evening News (newspaper), 173, 231
Dayton Fan and Motor Co., 7
Dayton Federation of Women's Clubs, 150
Dayton Female Association, 113
Dayton Fire Department, 18, 179, 200
Dayton Flyer (name of cigar), 192
Dayton Flyer Cigar, 192
Dayton Foundation, The, 109
Dayton Fun House and Riding Device Co., 160
Dayton Gas Light and Coke Company, 43
Dayton Glee Club, 11
Dayton Glove Company, 18
Dayton Guards, 259
Dayton Herald (newspaper), 178
Dayton Hickory Club, 14
Dayton Historical Society, 348
Dayton History, 348
Dayton Home Guard, 159
Dayton Hospital for the Insane, 261
Dayton incorporated, 50
Dayton Indians, 83
Dayton Industrial Exposition, 275
Dayton Journal (newspaper), 39, 43, 70, 191, 223, 242, 251, 275, 277,
Dayton Library Association, 73
Dayton Light Guard, 117, 316
Dayton Loew's Theater, 337
Dayton Lyceum Association, 251
Dayton Lyceum, 73
Dayton Malleable Iron Company, 112
Dayton Manufacturing Company, 295
Dayton Marcos (baseball team), 115
Dayton Masonic Center, 212
Dayton Mental Health Center, 261
Dayton Metal Products Company, 283
Dayton Metro Library, 55
Dayton Motor Car Company, 226, 237
Dayton Municipal Airport, 129
Dayton Municipal Building, 70
Dayton Museum of Fine Arts, 13
Dayton Mutual Exchange, 215
Dayton National Cemetery, 24, 48, 135, 203, 268
Dayton Opera House, 178
Dayton Orphan Asylum, 113
Dayton Overland Sales, 296

Dayton Philharmonic Concert Band, 196
Dayton Police Department, 227, 233, 241, 291
Dayton Power and Light, 169, 197, 367
Dayton Public Library, 63, 172, 271, 343, 367
Dayton Public Schools, 150
Dayton Purchase, 254
Dayton Racquet Club, The, 109
Dayton Realty Company, 229
Dayton Repertory, The (newspaper), 274, 287
Dayton Rubber Manufacturing Company, 183
Dayton Sharpshooters' Society, 305
Dayton Sheraton, 334
Dayton Silk Company, 75
Dayton Social Welfare League, 323
Dayton Soldiers' Home Band, 248, 336
Dayton Soldiers' Home cemetery, 24
Dayton Soldiers' Home Panorama Company, 238
Dayton Soldiers' Home, 9, 24, 48, 51, 53, 62, 82, 119, 124, 132, 145, 155, 191, 203, 210, 235, 248, 268, 279, 298, 304, 312, 346, 370
Dayton Speedway, 83, 120
Dayton Spice Mills Company, 282
Dayton State Hospital, 261
Dayton Street Railway Company, 123, 186
Dayton Tattler, The (newspaper), 69, 178
Dayton Thorobred Cord (tire), 183
Dayton Township, 384
Dayton Transportation Center, 19
Dayton Triangles (football team), 289
Dayton Turngemeinde, 204
Dayton Typographical Union, 295
Dayton VA Medical Center, 24, 48, 110, 114, 135, 203
Dayton Veterans (baseball team), 270
Dayton View Bridge, 8, 34, 155
Dayton War Housing Center, 330
Dayton West Side Amusement Corporation, 373
Dayton Women Pilot's Club, 286
Dayton Women's Christian Association, 22
Dayton, Jonathan, 251, 254, 380, 382-383
Daytona Beach, FL, 185
Dayton-California Association, 47
Dayton-Montgomery County Salvage Committee, 264
Daytons (baseball team), 156
Dayton-Wright Airplane Company, 143, 161, 283, 290, 329
Dayton-Wright South Field, 143
de Bothezat, George, 366
de Havilland DH-4 (airplane), 143, 158, 283

Deaconess Hospital, 300
Dearborn, MI, 195, 302, 313
Death Song, A (song), 188
Deeds' barn, 88
Deeds Carillon, 247
Deeds Park, 114
Deeds, Charles, 88
Deeds, Edith Walton, 247
Deeds, Edward A. (Col.), 45, 88, 161, 236, 244, 247
Deer Park, 203
Deer Park, 346
Deerwester, Raymond Louis, 105
Delco Light System, 283
Deluge (fire company), 138
DeLuise, Dom, 255
Dempsey, Jack, 287
Denello (Detective), 210
Department of Public Welfare, 89
depression of 1874, 21
depression of 1893, 204
Desch, Joseph, 77
DeSoto Bass Court, 330
Detroit News (newspaper), 195
Detroit, MI, 166, 379
Devoe, Fred, 275
Dewitt, (policewoman), 202
Dickerson, Charles, 125
Die Schutzenfest Gesellschaft, 305
Diehl Band Shell, 182
Diehl, Leslie L., 182
Dillinger, John, 30
Disbrow, Henry, 274
Division of Self-Help Cooperatives, 194
Dixie Drive-In, 149
Dobbins, John, 118
Doble, Bud, 288
Dogs For Defense (DFD), 358
dogs, quarantined, 57
Domestic Engineering Company, 283
Donahue, Phil, 324
Doren, Electra C., 13
Doren, John S., 295
Dorothy Lane Market, 37
Dorough, John, 101, 381
Downtown Dayton Days, 144
Downtown Merchants Retail Association, 144
Dr. E. Conway's Linimentum, 85
Dr. Harter Medicine Company, 369
Dresser, Paul, 124
Driggs, Nelson, 210
Driscoll, Devoss W., 108

395

Driscoll, Dick, 377
Drive-In East, 131
Drive-In Theater, The, 131
Drive-In theaters, 320
Drive-In West, 131
Drury, Augustus Waldo (Rev.), 76
Dudley, Colonel (dog), 61
Dudley, S. H., 373
Dunbar, Matilda, 165, 188
Dunbar, Paul Laurence, 12, 48, 69, 115, 121, 165, 178, 188
Dunbar, Paul Laurence, home of, 302
Dunlap, John (Capt), 380
Dunlavy, Francis, 388
Dunlevy home, 70
DuPont, 183
Dutch East Indies, 349
Dutch Elm disease, 147
Dutch Java Blend, 282
Dwyer, Bill, 289
Eagles' Auditorium, 377
Early Dayton (book), 364
Earp, Wyatt, 198
earthquake of 1811, 364
East Carnegie Branch, 63
East Dayton airport, 286
East Liverpool, OH, 124
East Lynne (stage play), 79
East Park, 89
Easter, 343
Easton, OH, 380
Eastwood Park, 54
Eaton, OH, 320
Ebenezer, OH, 170
Ecker, Mary Bell, 70
Ecurey, France, 329
Ed Sullivan Show, The (television show), 331
Edgewood Court, 330
Edison Institute, 195
Edison, Thomas, 277, 366
Educational Novelty Company, 189
Edward, 101
Edwards, Cecil E. (Judge), 37
Edwin C. Moses Blvd. named, 333
El-Bee Shoe Outlet, 35
Elder & Johnston, 35, 176, 296
Elder, Robert (Mrs.), 67
Elder, Thomas, 35
Elder-Beerman, 35, 144
electric automobiles, 237
electric tricycle, 7
Ellignton, Duke, 249, 334

Ells, Benjamin Franklin, 209
Elmwood Park, 54
Emm, Lou, 255
Emmanuel Church, 239
Empire (newspaper), 273, 319, 322
Empire Saloon, 228
Engineers Club of Dayton, 41
England, 356
English and French School for Young Ladies, 228
Enigma, 77
Enon, OH, 25
envelopes, embossed, 104
envelopes, printed stamped, 104
Erie Dispatch-Herald (newspaper), 49
ethyl gasoline, 40, 283
Etna (paper mill), 104
Evening Item, The (newspaper), 69, 222
Eversull, Solomon, 259
Ewing, John (Judge), 339, 388
Executive order 9066, 357
Eyck, Sidney Ten, 154
eyes frozen during flight, 65
Fair, George Washington (Private), 114, 223
Fairborn, OH, 25
Fairfield, OH, 25
Fairview Elementary, 264
Fairview High School, 333
Fairview Park, 270
Fansher Bros., 142
Far Hills, 214
Far West, MO, 220
Faries, Elizabeth, 172
Farnum, William, 34
Fashion Cents, 144
FBI, 357
Federal Aviation Administration (FAA), 263
Federal Building, 94
Federal Communications Commission, 83
Federal Emergency Relief Administration, 194
Federal Housing Authority, 357
Federal Surplus Commodities Corp., 167
Ferrell, Daniel, 101, 381
ferries, 34
Fidelity Building Association, 60
Fidelity Building, 60
Field, Sara Bard, 327
Fifth Street Railroad bridge, 52
Fifth Street Railway Company, 232
Fifth-Third Center, 86
Fighting McCooks, 352
Finke, Carl, 311

Fire Engine House No. 14, 200
fire pumper, 200
fire, Morrison's Shop, 138
fireless steam locomotive, 244
fires, 18
Firestone Tire and Rubber Company, 183
first air ambulance, 300
first air raid drill, 207
first all talking motion picture shown, 278
first AM Stereo radio station, 154
first American tire of synthetic rubber, 183
first amusement park for blacks, 115
first annex west of the Great Miami River, 174
First Baptist Chruch, 36
first battle of Spanish-American War, 127
first bird strike on an aircraft, 263
first black to be born in Dayton, 254
first bridge built, 34
first broadcast license for television, 83
first canal boat, 259
first carbon-free typing paper, 197
first cargo flight, 325
first circus in Dayton, 122
first civil act in Dayton, 116
first dog catcher, 57
first drive-in theater, 131
first drive-in with 3-D movies, 153
first drive-in with CinemaScope, 153
first drive-in with heaters, 153
first drive-in with stereo sound, 153
first electric powered street cars, 232
first emergency parachute landing, 306
first ferry across the Great Miami River, 76
first fire engine, 84
first fire of consequence, 84
first food stamp program in Ohio, 167
first fraternal organization, 212
first history of Dayton printed, 251
first in nation for patents per capita, 344
first jury sequestered in United States, 269
first lager beer, 361
first lion in Dayton, 122
first log cabin in Lexington, KY, 214
first low-pressure tire, 183
first murder in Dayton, 96, 339
first murderer of Dayton police officer executed, 291
first newspaper printed, 387
first newspapers printed in a balloon, 191
first Ohio state memorial to honor African American, 165
first paid firemen, 138

first parking meters installed, 227
first passenger depot, 33
first patent for tree granted in U.S., 147
first patent granted to Daytonian, 16
first patrol wagon, 241
first policeman killed in line of duty, 23
First Presbyterian Church, 174, 329
first public library, 39
first public playground, 134
first radar speeding arrest, 175
first regatta, 182
first school, 353
first scratch and sniff product, 197
first settlers of Dayton, 84
first sorter for phosphorescent stamps, 225
first spacewalk, 234
first speeding ticket, world, 175
First Street Bridge, 8
first successful helicopter, 366
first telephone book in Dayton, 66
first theater owned and operated by blacks, 249
first theater to sell popcorn, 130
first trackless trolleys, 123
first union in Dayton, 295
first volunteer fire department, 84
first wedding, 252
first woman to obtain pilot license, 286
Fishback, Frank S., 282
Fitsimmons, Robert, 198
Fitzgerald, Ella, 249
Flagg, James Montgomery, 103
Flips and Flops, toy, 26
flood of 1805, 50, 251, 385
flood of 1814, 251, 386
flood of 1832, 34
flood of 1852, 34
flood of 1886, 142
flood of 1897, 142
flood of 1898, ,142
flood of 1913, 63, 93, 112, 148, 182, 236, 244,
Flushing, NY, 216
flying bomb, 290
Flying Octupus (helicopter), 366
Flyover (monument), 196
Foerste, August (Prof.), 338
Folkerth, John (Judge), 39
Food and Drugs Act of June 30, 1906, 282
food stamps, 167
Ford, Edsel, 313
Ford, Gerald (President), 169
Ford, Henry, 195, 302, 313
Forest Park ad Zoological Garden, 160

Forest Park, 330
Forrer (canal boat), 31
Fort Detroit, 163
Fort Hamilton, 380
Fort Laramie, 53
Fort Sheridan, IL, 362
Fort Sumter, 117
Fort Thompson, KY, 102
Fort Wayne, IN, 355
France, 82, 103, 159
Francis, John, 23
Franciscan Medical Center, 239
Frank, Alfred Swift, 67
Franklin Coffee House, 384
Franklin, OH 104, 381, 387
Franklinton, OH, 387
French Maids (burlesque act), 95
Freon, 379
Friedman, Joseph, 192
Friendlich, Gelinde, 321
Frier, Robert (Mrs.), 181
Frigidaire, 80, 379
Fry, W. C., 338
Frye, Jack, 126
Ft. Wayne, IN, 331
Fulton County Jail, Atlanta, GA, 301
Funkhouser, G. A. (Rev.), 188
Fussbudget, Ferdie, 166
G. S. Outfitters, 144
G.A.R., 11
Gage, OK, 185
Gahagan, William, 101, 381
Galinger, Father, 269
Gallaher's Drug Store, 296
Gallery Jewelry, 144
Gano, John Stites, 101
garbage dump, 372
Garfield, James A. (President), 62
Garfield, The (man-of-war ship), 62
Garrigus, Josephine, 286
Garrigus, Samuel, 286
Garst, Michael (Dr.), 148
Gary, Elbert H. (Judge), 340
Gary, Phil, 331
gasoline rationing, 349
Gaudy, Albert, 240
Gayety Theater, 95
Gear, W. C. (inspector), 245
Gebhart's Opera House, 277
Gehrig, Lou, 311
Geiger, Albertus (Dr.), 118, 128
Gem City Ice Cream, 360

Gem City paper-mill, 242
Gem City Polo Club, 297
Gem City, 242
Gemini 4 (space capsule), 234
General Conference of the United Brethren Church, 190
General Marion (canal boat), 31
General Motors Research Corporation, 379
General Motors, 129, 283, 379
General Pike (canal boat), 31
General, The (locomotive), 301
Genos, Italy, 151
George Grove's hat store, 84
George W. Baker (shoes), 296
George, William, 355
German Naval Enigma, 77
Germania Building Association, 60
Germantown, OH, 118
Germany, 329
giant skeleton found, 338
Gibbons Hotel, 86
Gibbons, Michael, 72
Gibbs, E. D., 58
Gilbert, Johnny, 83
Giles, Goodrich, 249
Gilmore, William (Gen.), 184
Girl Scouts, 345
Girls on the Beach, The (motion picture), 149
Gish, Dorothy, 58, 79
Gish, Lillian, 58, 79
Glassmire, Abraham, 381
Glenville track, Cleveland, OH, 28
Go Home, 144
Goddess of Liberty, 223
Godfrey, Arthur, 154
Goetz, Anthony, 17
Goforth, William, 101
Gold Star Mothers Memorial, 221
Goldsmith Maid (racehorse), 285, 288
Goodman, Benny, 334
Gore, Leslie, 149
Gorman Orthopedic Public School, 299
Gorman, Anna Barney, 299
Goss, Solomon, 101, 381
Governor Brown (canal boat), 31, 387
Grace M.E. Church, 82
Grand Army, parade, 223
Grand Moving Panorama of the Bible (panorama), 168
Grand Opera House, 198, 378
Grand Rapids Stags (baseball team), 270
Grandissimes, The (book), 378

Grant, Fred Dent (Brig. Gen.), 362
Grant, Ulysses S. (President), 362
Grant-Deneau Building, 345
Grassmire, Abraham, 101
Grauser, Charles (police officer), 23
grave vault, 332
Gravel Road Music, 292
graveyard, 388
Great Depression, 54, 89, 104, 123, 129, 160, 167, 172, 183, 194, 215, 243, 257, 314, 317, 377,
Great Miami River Trail, 333
Great Miami River, 52, 93, 137, 174, 182, 208, 223, 251, 352, 380, 384
Great River Road (postage stamp), 225
Great Sioux War, 53
Greater Dayton Association, 155
Gree, Weston, 368
Green & Green Company, 108, 368
Green Hornet, 166
Green, Barrett K. 197
Greencastle Cemetery, 10
Greene County, OH, 302
Greene, Charles R., 266
Greenfield Village, Dearborn, MI, 41, 195, 302, 313
Greenmont, 330
Gridley, Emma L., 341
Gridley, John L, 341
Griffith, D. W., 79
Grimes Tavern, 34
Grinnell College, Iowa, 83
Gross, Charles E. (police officer), 71
Grove, George, 84
Grub Steak Restaurant, The, 146
Gunckel, Lewis B., 273
Gurley, Phineas D. (Rev.), 174
Guy, Homer, 130
Guyon, James, 210
Gwindle, (Prof.), 204
gypsies, 267
H. E. Talbott & Company, 208
H. R. Blagg Company, 212
Hagerstown, MD, 158
Haiti, 307
Hall, Sylvanius, 353
Hamer, Mary, 101
Hamer, Solomon, 381
Hamer, William, 101, 381
Hamilton Co, OH, 384
Hamilton Journal (newspaper), 275
Hamilton, OH, 191, 297, 355, 387

Hampton, Robert, 240
Hanauer, Betty, 286
Hans Wagner (horse), 200
Hara Arena, 331
Hard Tack (motion picture), 108
Hardin, Ken, 166
Harding, Warren G. (President), 231
Harlem Racetrack, Chicago, IL, 28
Harley-Davidson Motor Company, 284
Harness Racing Hall of Fame, 288
Harris, Eugene, 291
Harris, Glover, 240
Harris, Harold R. (Lt.), 306
Harrison, Benjamin (President), 332
Harrison Township, 267
Harrison, John Scott, 332
Harry K. Thaw's Fight for Freedom (motion picture), 269
Harter, Samuel K., 369
Hartford, CT, 35
Hartrum, Della, 136
Hartsville University, IN, 190
Hatfield, W. S., 23
Hauer, Michael, 334
Hauser, John, 241
Havana Harbor, Cuba, 127
Havana, Cuba, 192
Hawaii, 349, 357
Hawkins, Betty, 108
Hawthorn Hill, 78, 184
Hawthorne, Thomas (Private), 177
Hayes, Rutherford B. (President), 268
Hayner Distilling Company, 369
Hayner, Lewis, 369
Hayner, William M., 369
Hayti, 307
Hayworth, Rita, 153
Headquarters Building (VA Center), 110
Heald, Charles D. (Atty), 212
Hearts of the World (motion picture), 79
Hebrew Society, The, 321
Heck, Mathias (Prosecutor), 193
Heinman, Samuel, 228
helicopter, 366
Hemisphere Defense, 298
Henderson, 235
Henry Ford Museum, 41
Herbert, Philip, 341
Heritage Sculpture, The (sculpture), 121
Herman Avenue Bridge, 170
Herman, H. H. (Dr.), 341
Hess, Mary, 148, 239

HFCs, 379
Hickok, James Butler "Wild Bill", 293
High Diver (roller coaster), 160
Hillgruber, F. J. , 181
Hills and Dales Lookout Tower, 54
Hills and Dales Park, 171
Hillsboro, OH, 166
His Majesty, the Scarecrow of Oz (motion picture), 296
History of the city of Dayton and Montgomery County, Ohio, 76
Hix, John, 61
Hoadley, George H. (Gov.), 223
Hobo Philosopher, The (pamphlet), 216
hoboes, 22
hogs, 281
Holes Creek, 259
Hole's Station, 381
Holly (cat), 185
Hollywood, CA, 149
Holy Trinity Church, 269
Holyke Daily Transcript (newspaper), 139
Hoosier (hot air balloon), 191
Hopkins, James (Patrolman), 175
Horseless Age, The (magazine), 111
hosiery, recycling for war effort, 56
Hotel Atlas, 90
Houdini, Harry, 363
How the West Was Won (motion picture), 253
Howard (paper mill), 104
Howard, John (Major), 148
Howdy, Honey, Howdy (book), 165
Howell, Frederick W. (Judge), 37
Hoyt, Charlie, 277
Huffman Hill, 316
Huffman MetroPark, 220
Huffman Prairie Flying Field, 302
Huffman Prairie, 263
Huffman, A. Ogden, 332
Huffman, W., 220
Huffman, William, 122
Hughes, Howard, 126
Hughes, Pat (police officer), 23
Hull, William (Gen.), 163
Hunter, William (Jr), 35
Huston Hall, 118
Hyatt, Anna Vaughn, 359
Hyre, Etta, 170
I Got a Woman/Amen (song), 292
I Need a Job (radio program), 314
IBM, 326
ice skating, 8

Ideal, 330
Idylwild, 170
Illinois, 25
Illustrated American, The (magazine), 210
Imperial Shrine Council, 20
In Dahomey (stage play), 115, 165
Independence Hall, Philadelphia, PA, 168
Indiana, 25, 305
Indianapolis, IN, 25, 297
Indians, 382-383
Ingle System Company, The, 376
Ingle System, 376
Ingle, David, 376
Ingle, Edwin, 376
Ingle, Wesley, 376
Inspector General, The (stage play), 79
Insurance Credit System, 376
Interborough Rapid Transit Company, 340
International Business Machines (IBM), 326
International Envelope, 104
International Wizard of Oz Club, The (205)
Into the Light (book), 150
Irwin, May, 277
Isaacson, Max, 42
Island Park Dam, 8, 258
Island Park, 54, 170, 182, 202
It's a Mad, Mad, Mad, Mad World (motion picture), 253
J. & M. Schiml Brewery, 361
Jackson, Andrew (President), 14
Jackson, George, 23
Jacobs, Charles, 279
Jacobs, Nicholas, 279
Jacobson, Jack, 166
jaffe & Gross Jewelry, 144
Japan, 56
Jay's Seafood Restaurant, 228
Jefferson Street Baptist Church, 168
Jefferson Street Market House, 73
Jefferson, Thomas (President), 25, 265
Jeffries, James J., 228
Jennings, Michael J., 29
Jennison, William, 272
Jeremiah (male stripper), 255
Jerry Lewis MDA Labor Day Telethon, 255
Jersey Baking Soda, 282
Jersey Coffee, 282
Jersey Spices, 282
Jet over Capitol (postage stamp), 225
Jewett, Henry S. (Dr.), 23
Jewett, Hibbard (Dr.), 32
Joanna (chimpanzee), 218

John W. Berry, Sr. Wright Brothers Aviation Center, 302
Johnston, J. Russell, 35
Jones, Brian, 331
Jones, Garfield (Sgt.), 82
Jones, Lottie, 313
Jordan, Louis, 249
Jordan, Marsh & Co., Boston, MA, 35
Journal (newspaper), 138, 273
Journal-Herald (newspaper), 54, 153, 278, 358
Judah, Dorothy Patterson, 171
Jung, Paul, 217
Jung, Walter, 217
Junior News, The (newspaper), 180
Juvenile Manufacturing Company, 88
Juvenile Songster, The (book), 209
Kammer, K. M., 275
Kany, A. S., 153
Keebler Company, 368
Keely Gold Cure Club, 9
Keith Theater, 249
Keith's Theater, 90, 249, 296, 345, 363
Kellogg Company, 368
Kellogg's Sugar Smacks (cereal), 217
Kemper, Sarah Lawson, 252
Kennedy, John F. (President), 303
Kenny Roberts Show, 166
Kentucky, 305
Kepler, Carl, 180
Kepler, Ralph, 180
Kepler, Ross, 180
Kett, Christina, 17
Kett, Christine, 17
Kett, Frederick, 17
Kettering Aerial Torpedo, 290
Kettering Bug, 290
Kettering Tower, 109
Kettering, Charles F. 40, 45, 92, 109, 215, 280, 283, 290, 317, 379,
Kettering, Eugene, 109
Kettering, Virginia, 109, 121
Keyes, W. A., 130
Kidder, Walter S., 369
Kiefaber Café, 140
Kimmerle, Frank, 279
Kindberg, Maria, 327
Kinderdine, George, 289
King of Prussia, 346
King of the Hoboes, 328
King, William, 76, 174
Kinsey, Eva, 203
Kinsey, Hannah, 203

Kinsey, Henry, 203
Kinstedt, Ingeborg, 327
Kirby, John (Jr.), 295
Kirk, Steve, 255
Kirkbride, Thomas (Dr.), 261
Kirtland, OH, 220
Kirves, Bruno, 335
Kirves, Emma, 335
Kirves, John, 335
Kirves, Mary, 335
Kiser & Co., 175
Kiser, Earl H., 28
Kitty Hawk Flyer, 356
Kitty Hawk Room, 334
Kitty Hawk, NC, 196, 356
Kline, P. W. (Mrs.), 358
Kline, Richard, 358
Knickerbocker Trust Building, 173
Knights of Pythias, 82, 103
Knights of St. John, 204
Knights of Tabor, 82
Knights of United Brotherly Friendship, 82
Knox, Herbert B., 94
Kohan, George C., 61
Kohnle, Frederick, 176
Kool-Aid, 373
Korean Veterans Memorial, Washington, D.C., 230
Korean War Veterans Memorial (postage stamp), 230
Korean War, 221, 230
Kossuth Colony, 229
Kramer, John (traffic officer), 71
Krebs, Frank M. (Mayor), 157, 164
Kroger's, 59
Krohn, Stanley M., Jr., 154
Kuhns Building, 98
Kuhns, Benjamin F., 113
Kumler, Marie, 327
Kumpler, Alvin W. (Judge), 206, 295
Kuralt, Charles, 135
Kwesell, Bob, 255
KYW, 324
L-049 Constellation (airplane), 126
Labor Day, 255
Labrobe, Charles Joseph, 97
Lacey, William, 98
Ladies Home Journal (magazine), 202
Lafayette Guard, 117, 316
Lake, Ann, 169
Lakeside Park, 89, 145, 202
Lakewood Cemetery, Cleveland, OH, 270

Lamar Advertising, 59
Lammers, Arthur, 294
Landis, James M., 207
langley Field, 350, 352
Langley, Samuel P., 356
largest pork tenderloin user in Ohio, 146
Larrupin' Lou's (baseball team), 311
Laspe, Harold, 170
last solo flight, Orville Wright, 143
law against hogs running loose, 281
Law School of Boston University, 351
law, billboards, 95
law for selling fruit/vegetables in Ohio, 245
laws, blue, 37
laws, unusual, 15
Lawson, Gene, 120
Lazarus, 87
Le Havre, France, 177
League of Nations, 99
Lebanon, OH, 274, 355, 380, 387
Lebanon, PA, 190
Lebensburger, Joseph, 321
LeCrone, Harold B., 320
Leo the Lion, 359
Leopard People, 217
Levin, Al, 149
Levin, Lou, 149
Levin, Sam, 149
Levis, W. P., 242
Lewis Hayner, Distiller, 369
Lewis, Diocletian (Dr.), 64
Lexington, KY, 91, 214
Liberty Bell, 336
Liberty Bonds, 375
Liberty Society of Dayton, 73
Library Building, 271
library museum, 271
Library of Congress, 326
Life With Father (stage play), 79
Liggett Drug Company, 86
Lights of New York (motion picture), 278
Lily Brew (beer), 187
Lima, OH, 350
Lincoln Memorial University of Tennessee, 108
Lincoln, Abraham (President), 86, 117, 124, 174, 273, 303, 319
Lincoln, Mary Todd, 273
Lindbergh, Charles, 184, 306
Lindemuth, George, 118
Little Miami River, 251, 355, 380, 384, 387
Little Playhouse Theater, 130

Little, Tess, 121
Lloyd, Harold, 337
Lloyd, William, 235
Lloyd, Willie, 235
Lockheed Corporation, 126
Loening PW-2A (airplane), 306
Lohrey, Louis W. (Mayor), 342
London Science Museum, 356
Lone Ranger, 166
Long Branch, NJ, 78
longest concrete bridge in the world, 208
Lookout Mountain, 346
Loramie, OH, 386
Lorenz and Williams, 94
Louisiana Purchase, 336
Louisville, KY, 168
Love Me (song), 292
Lowry, Clyde M., 314
Lucky the Ladybug, 59
Ludlow, 382-383
Ludlow, Israel, 251, 265, 380 - 383
Lukeman, Augustus, 107
Lutheran Church, 212
Lynam, Lee (police officer), 23
Lyons, Ruth, 299
Lyons, Ruth, 83
Lyric Theater, 277
M.I.T., 77
MacMillan, Violet, 296
Mad River and Lake Erie Railroad, 33
Mad River Park, 54
Mad River, 34, 50, 93, 101, 220, 267, 275, 380, 381, 386
Maddox, Preston, 240
Madison Square Garden, 269
Madison, James (President), 163
Magical Mimics of Oz, The (book), 205
Main Line Broadcasting, 154
Main Street Bridge, 8, 155, 208, 223
Majestic Theater, 269
Malin, C. Fred, 27
Malleable Iron Works, 229
Malone, Sue, 286
Maltin, Leonard
Mam'zelle Champagne (play), 269
Man on the Street (radio program), 154
Mansffield, OH, 285
Manufacturers' Aircraft Association, 152
Marathon and Endurance Carnival, 377
Marbache, 177
Marine Corps (postage stamp), 225
market house, Central, 67

market house, Jefferson Street Market, 73
market house, Wayne Avenue, 67
Market Wine, 144
Marsh, Mae, 337
Marshall, James, 47
Martial law, 305
Martin, Robert (Judge), 264
Masonic Temple Association, 212
Masonic Temple, 354
Massachusetts Board of Charities, 351
Massachusetts Institute of Technology, 370
Massachusetts, 3512
Matanzas Harbor, 127
Matrimony, or The Prisoners (stage play), 122
Matteawan State Hospital for the Criminally Insane, 269
Matthews, Henry, 30
Maumee River, 386
Maxwell (paper mill), 104
Maxwell Motor, 237, 354
May Irwin Kiss, The (motion picture), 277
Mayfair Theater, 277
Mayne, Calvin D., 37
McAfee, Dolly, 96
McAfee, John, 96
McAfee's Confession (ballad), 96
McAplin, Floyd, 291
McCabe park, 194, 360
McCall, 357
McCalls (baseball team), 311
McCleallan, George (Col.), 191
McCleary, Nat, 32
McClure (widow), 101
McClure, John, 391
McClure, William, 274, 355, 387
McCollum's Tavern, 339
McCook family, 352
McCook Field, 65, 129, 158, 246, 306, 330, 350, 352, 366
McCook, Daniel, 352
McCook, George (Jr.), 352
McCook, George (Sr.), 352
McCook, John, 352
McDonald, Malcom D., 37
McGallard, David, 341
McGee, James H. (Mayor), 19
McGowan and Lake, 267
McHugh, William H. (Mrs.), 358
McKinley home, Canton OH, 277
McKinley Park, 155
McKinley, William (President), 55, 107, 127, 362, 371

McLardie, John D., 136
McLaren, Jack, 125
McMaken & Hilton, 259
McPherson, Aimee Semple, 136
Mead Engine Company, 112
Mead, Cyrus, 112
Mecca Theater, 249-250
Mechanic's Institute, 73
Medal of Honor, 301
Medlar, D. L., 273
Meigs Camp, 163
Meigs, Jonathan (Governor Return), 163
Memorial Hall, 11, 53, 99, 136, 145, 287, 333
memorial, Dunbar House, 165, 302
memorial, Korean War, 221
memorial, North Dayton Patriots Memorial, 221
memorial, Ohio Korean War Veterans Memorial, 230
Memphis Belle (name of airplane), 201
Mendelson Liquidation Outlet, 144
Mercer, Jonathan, 101, 381
Merchantile Corporation, 104
Metal Polishers, Buffers, Platers and Brass Workers Union No. 5, 295
Methodist Church, 33
Metropolitan Band, 204
Metropolitan Club of New York, 158
Metzier, Sigmund (Prof.), 338
Meuse-Argonne, France, 177
Mexican War, 117
Miami Beach, FL, 28
Miami Canal, 259, 385, 387
Miami Chapel Road, 10
Miami City, 174
Miami City, 52
Miami County, OH, 382, 384
Miami Hotel, 87, 286
Miami Paper Company, 59
Miami River, 8, 50, 132, 179, 199, 275, 381, 386
Miami Valley Council, Boy Scouts of America, 61
Miami Valley Hospital, 36, 300, 341
Miami Valley Research Park, 153
Miami Valley Screen Review, The, (motion picture), 108
Miami Wood Specialty Company, 26
Miamisburg, OH, 14, 125, 233, 259, 320, 338, 381, 384
microencapsulation, 197
Middle Lake, Dayton Soldiers' Home, 62

403

Middle West Supply Company, 104
Middletown, OH, 47, 381, 385
Midget Theater, 262, 360
Midgley, Thomas (Jr), 40, 379
Midwestern Hayride (television show), 83
Mikulec, Joseph Frank, 151
Milk White Flag, The (motion picture), 277
Miller Florist, 144
Miller, Emma L., 23
Miller, Glenn, 334
Miller, Ivonette Wright, 36, 184
Miller, John L. (Mayor), 241
Miller, Lester (Major-General), 201
mills, Daniel Cooper's, 84
Mindanao, 362
Miracle man of Virginia Beach (article, 294
Miss Sadie Thompson (motion picture), 153
Miss Susie Slagle's (stage play), 79
Missouri Legend (stage paly), 79
Mitchell, Gee, 149
Mitchell, William (Gen.), 246, 306
Monarch Marking System Company, 176
Monschke, Virginia, 211
Monschke, Wallace, 211
Monseiur Tonson (recital), 122
Montgomery County Children's Home, 113
Montgomery County Commissioners, 113, 174
Montgomery County Fairgrounds, 179, 181, 206, 218, 2331, 276, 288, 321
Montgomery County Historical Society, 348
Montgomery County juvenile court, 164
Montgomery County Medical Society, 128
Montgomery County Solid Waste District, 59
Montgomery County, OH, 348, 384
Montgomery Guard, 117, 316
Montgomery, AL, 177
Monument Avenue Bridge, 34
monument, Dayton Soldiers' Monument, 24
monument, Flyover, 196
monument, German gun, 177
monument, Gold Star Mothers, 221
monument, Leo the Lion, 359
monument, McKinley, William (President), 55, 107
monument, Soldiers' Monument, downtown, 155
monument, Soldiers' Monument, Soldiers' Home, 223, 268
monument, Spanish American War, 11
monument, stone tablet, World War I, 177
monument, Victory Oak Knoll, 159
monument, World War I, 11

monument, Wright Flyer III, 137
Moore, Marion, 115
Moore, Moses C., 115
Mooreshouse-Marten Department Store, 325
Moraine Ash (tree), 147
Moraine Honeylocust (tree), 147
Moraine Locust (tree), 147
Moraine Park School, 45
Moraine Sweet Gum Tree, 147
Morehouse College, 333
Morgan, Arthur E., 45
Morgan, J. P., 340
Morgan, John Hunt (Brig. Gen.), 305
Mormon Migration, 220
Mormons, 220
Morning Matinee (television show), 299
Morris, James, 101, 381
Morris, Thomas (Senator), 32
Morrison's Shop, 138
Morrow, Jeremiah (Ohio Gov.), 31
Moses, Edwin Corley, 333
Moses, Myrella, 333
Moskowitz, Jacob, 229
Motion Picture Operators Union, 106
motor, rotary, 112
Mount Auburn, 89
Mr. Chips (dog), 358
Msuse-Argonne advance, 82
Muddy Water White (cat), 185
Mueller, Carl (Rev.), 300
Mulharon, Henry, 9
mummy, Indian, 122
Muncie, IN, 243
Munday, William, 148
Munger, Warren, 15
Municipal Building, 106
murder, 9, 17
Murlin Heights, OH 170
Murphy, Connie S., 344
Murphy, Harold (Patrolman), 175
Murray, Jacob, 116
Murray, John, 116
Murray, Samuel, 116
Muscular Dystrophy Association, 255
Museum of Natural History, New York, NY, 218
Music Hall, 241, 293
Mutual Home and Savings, 317
My Gal Sal (song), 124
My Own Story of a Broken Neck (booklet), 309
Myers, Frank, 235

Myers, Harry J., 175
Myers, Harry, 175
NAACP, Dayton branch, 249
Narrison, William H. (Gen.), 174
Nation, Carry, 310
National Air and Space Museum, 196
National Asylum for Disabled Volunteer Soldiers, 304
National Cash Register - see NCR
National Defense Research Committee, 77
National Football League (NFL), 289
National House, 31
National Housing Agency, 330
National Polo League, 297
National Recovery Administration (NRA), 215
National Register of Historic Places, 229
National Road, 25
national VA History Center, 110
National War Labor Board, 186
National Youth Administration (NYA), 54
Native Americans, 101
Navy Academy, 127
Navy Board for Production Awards, 80
Navy, 80, 108, 235, 350, 358
NCR Auditorium, 219, 299
NCR City Club, 328
NCR Factory News (newsletter), 80
NCR Hall of Industrial Education, 219
NCR power house, 219
NCR Schoolhouse, 219
NCR, 12, 36, 58, 77, 80, 91, 99, 103, 108, 133, 155, 171, 181, 189, 197, 201, 214, 219, 244, 295, 299, 309, 315, 321-322, 326, 328, 329, 351
Negro National League, 115
Neil, (Dr.), 237
Neil, Juanita Achey, 237
Neon Movies, 253
Nesbit, Evelyn, 269
Nethersole, Olga (95)
New Jersey, 254
New London, OH, 51
New Neon Movies, 253
New Orleans, LA, 378, 387
New York City, NY, 58, 79
New York Herald (newspaper), 53
New York Times, The (newspaper), 9, 12
New York, NY, 103, 140, 173, 269, 307, 324, 325, 340
Newcom Tavern, 339, 348
Newcom, George, 101, 339, 381, 384, 388
Newcom, Mary, 101

Newcom, William, 101, 381
Newhall, John, 16
Newman, David S. (Dr.), 148
Newman, Walter (police officer), 71
Newport News, VA, 62
Newport, KY, 305
Nexstar Mdia Group, 83
NFL, 289
Niagara Falls, 277
Niehus, Gustave A., 130
Niles, OH, 235
Nina Dodd's White Star Kennels, 78
Nixon, Richard (President), 169
Nobody's Kid (motion picture), 337
Noontide Club, 354
Norfolk, VA, 358
North Dayton Patriots Memorial, 221
North Pole, 74
North Side Field, 311
North Star Drive-In, 320
Nosey the Clown, 166
Now or Never (motion picture), 337
Oak and Ivy (book), 12
Oakwood Park, 305
Oakwood Street Railway company, 186
Oakwood, OH, 37, 184, 313
Ochs, Herbert, 131
Odd Fellows, 82
Office of Civilian Defense, 157, 207
Ogden, UT, 235
Ohio Agricultural Commission, 245
Ohio Assn. of Union Ex-Prisoners of War, 62
Ohio Board of Agriculture, 276, 285
Ohio Court of Appeals, 245
Ohio Electric company, 186
Ohio General Assembly, 320
Ohio Historical Society, 220
Ohio House of Representatives, 37
Ohio Korean War Veterans Memorial, 230
Ohio Legislature, 165
Ohio Lunatic Asylum, Columbus, OH, 261
Ohio Nation Guard, Third Regiment, 155, 204
Ohio Penitentiary, Columbus, OH, 23, 125, 291, 335
Ohio State Fair, 276, 285
Ohio State School for the Blind, 150
Ohio State University Extension Master Gardener, 110
Ohio Supreme Court, 245
Ohio Watchman, The (newspaper), 34
Ohio, 25, 305
Ohio, admitted to Union, 25

Okino, Mary, 357
Okino, Shaji, 357
Oklahoma Territory, 140
Oklahoma, 140
Old Court House, 81, 116-117, 121, 161, 169, 273, 303, 348
Old Guard G.A.R hall, 11
Old Reliable Coffee, 282
Oldt, William (Sheriff), 125
Olt Brewing Company, 363
Olympics, 1984, 333
Omhaundro, John Baker "Texas Jack", 293
On the Banks of the Wabash (song), 124
Once Before I Die (motion picture), 345
One Dayton Centre, 86
Open Doot, The, 328
Oregon Brewery, 361
Oregon District, 169
Orientla Trading Company, 357
Orphans of the Storm (motion picture), 79
orphans, 113
Ostrander, Catherine (policewoman), 323
Our Dumb Animals (magazine), 242
Overland (automobile), 296, 327
Overlook, 89, 330
Owens, William, 204
Oz Film Manufacturing Company, 296
ozone depletion, 379
Packard Automobile Company, 340
Palace Amusement Company, 373
Palace Theater, 262, 373
Pan American Expo, 359
Pannes, 177
parachute developed, 306
Parish House of Christ Church, 106
Park Theater, 277
Parker, Edward, 320
parking meters, 227
Parkmoor, 211
Parkside Homes, 330
Parmalee, Philip, 325
Parrott, Edwin (Col.), 316
Partlow, Lou, 289
Passavant Hospital, Chicago, IL, 331
patent medicines, 85, 209
Patient Library (VA Center), 110
Patterson Elm, 91
Patterson Field, 106
Patterson, Frank J., 133, 322
Patterson, Frederick B., 151, 160, 328
Patterson, Harry, 90
Patterson, John H., 91, 99, 103, 121, 133, 151, 155, 171, 214, 236, 244, 321-322, 326
Patterson, Robert (Col.), 91, 133, 214
Paul Dixon Show, (television show), 83, 105
Paul Laurence Dunbar State Memorial, 302
Paul Pry (resort), 32
Paule, Barbara, 185
Paule, Bill, 185
Payne, Roger, 216
Pearl Harbor, 49, 106, 349, 357
Peary, Robert E, 74
Pegram, Albert, 71
Peirce, Joseph, 355
Pennsylvania Academy of the Fine Arts, 168
Pennsylvania State Building, 336
Pennsylvania Volunteers (regiment), 53
Pennsylvania, 143
penny books, 209
Peoples Railway company, 186
Pep (newspaper), 347
Perrine, James, 43
Perry, Oliver H. (Commodore), 265
Peterkin, Clinton R., 340
Peters and Burns, 73
Pfieffer, Wendell, 130
Phil Donahue Show, The (talk show), 83, 324
Philadelphia, PA, 168, 248, 261, 336
Philharmonic Society, 188
Philippine Insurrection, 362
Phillips Building, 73
Phillips House, 86, 273, 294
Phillips, George L., 66
Phillips, H. G., 84
Phillips, J. D., 43
Philomathean Society, 12
phosphorescent stamps, 225
Pickett's Charge, 238
Pickford, Mary, 58
Pickford, Mary, 79
Piersol, James, 195
Pinkney, Charles (Jr.), 270
Pioneer Association of Dayton, The, 348
Pioneer Brewing Company, 361
Piqua, OH, 30, 249, 355, 381, 387
Pittsburgh Chamber of Commerce, 143
Pittsburgh, PA, 269
Plant, Morton F., 340
Platt Iron Works, 354
Polk, James K. (President), 47
Pony House, 228, 322
Popular Mechanics (magazine), 343
Porter, James Reed, 301
Porter, M. E. (Mrs.), 242

Portugal, 218
Post Office, 94, 225, 375, 387
post office, various locations, 355
Potterf, Benjamin F., 262
Potterf, Sadie, 262
Potterf, Sherman W., 262
Praying Woman's Crusade, 64
Preble County, OH, 384
P'reonne, France, 102
Presley, Elvis, 292
Press-Gazette (newspaper), 166
Pretzinger, Albert, 173
Price Brothers, 170
Price Stores, 144
price ticket machine, 176
Price, Harry, 258
Principi, Anthony J. (VA Sec.), 110
prison escape, 240
Pritz, Adam, 300
production units, 194
Progressive Party, 145
Project Blue Book, 365
Project Crudge, 365
Project Sign, 365
Protestant Chapel (VA Center), 110, 312
Protestant Deaconess Society of Dayton, 300
Prugh, Joyce and Rike, 87
Public School Library, 73
Puckett, John D. (Cpl.), 177
Pueblo, CO, 45
Purple Heart (postage stamp), 230
Purple Heart, 230
Putnam Library, Dayton Soldiers' Home, 51
Pyramid Film Company, 108
racetrack accident, 120
Rags, 135
Ramada Inn, 333
Ramby, Frank D. (Fire Chief), 95
Rapallo, Iraly, 79
Raper M. E. Church, 343
Rapid Arthmetical Selector, 77
Rarus (racehorse), 288
Rauh, Hazel, 187
REACH, 121
Reader's Digest (magazine), 164
Real Life on the West Side (motion picture), 360
Recko, Paula, 121
Red Carnation Day, 371
Red Cross, 171, 159
red light district, 323
Red-Bar Battery Company, 357

Redwood City, CA, 158
Refiners Oil Station, 40
Regan, Ronald (President), 169
Regimental Band, 117
Reibold Building, 35
Reichenbacher, Edward "Eddie", 158
Reid, Gordon, 120
Reid's Inn, 122
Religious Telescope (magazine), 190
relocation of Japanese during WWII, 357
Remodeling Her Husband (motion picture), 79
Renault FT (war tanks), 354
Renfax Musical Talking Motion Pictures, 262
Rennie, James, 79
Republic (automobile), 275
Republican National Convention, 145
retailers stay open longer, 21
Revigny, France, 177
Revolutionary soldiers, 14
Revolutionary War, 91
Rex (dog), 358
Reynolds & Reynolds, 175, 199
Reynolds, Edward, 175
Reynolds, Lewis G., 371
Rice, John C., 277
Rice, Lucius (Patrolman), 291
Richards, William C., 138
Richmond, IN, 25, 52
Richter, George, 27
Rickenbacker, Edward "Eddie", 158, 334
Rieman, Anna L., 134
Rike, Frederick H., 236
Rike-Kumler Company, 87, 92, 347
Rike's Toy Parade, 347
Rinehart, Howard, 161, 329
Ringgold, GA, 301
Ringling Bros and Barnum & Bailey, 217
Ringling Bros. World's Greatest Shows, 217
rink hockey, 297
Ripley's Believe It Or Not (comic strip), 61
Ritty, James "Jake", 228, 322
Ritty, John, 228, 322
Ritzert, Oliver J., 27
River Corridor Bikeway, 333
Riverdale Methodist Church, 92
Riverdale, 89
RiverScape Park, 137
Riverside Park, 221
Riverside Trailer Park, 330
Riverview Cemetery, 321
Riverview Park, 114, 315
RKO Keith's, 345

Robert Blvd., 8
Robert's Fill, 8
Robertson, William Henry, 189
Robinson, Emerson, 358
Rochester of the West, 242
Rochester, NY, 167
Rockaways' Playland, 253
Rockhold, Joe, 166
Rogers and Thompson, New York, NY, 325
Rogers Theater, 276
roller polo, 297
Rolling Stones, 331
Rome, 13
Romola (motion picture), 79
Roosevelt, Elliott, 298
Roosevelt, Franklin D. (President), 194, 207, 231, 298, 349, 357
Roosevelt, Theodore (President), 98, 140, 145
Rose, James S. (Dr.), 308
Ross County, OH, 384
Ross, Walter, 310
Rotary Club, 155
rotorcraft, 366
Roundhouse, 321
Royal Ribs, 146
rubber collecting during WWII, 349
Russ, Nellie, 248
Russ, William Earl, 134
Rutenber engines, 112
Ruth, Babe, 311
S & V Office and Furniture, 144
S. N. Brown company, 7
Sacred Heart Church, 135, 233
Saint Bartholomew's Episcopal Church, 79
Salem Drive-In, 149
Salvation Army War Cry (magazine), 235
San Francisco, CA, 327
Sander, Gus H., 305
Sander, William F., 305
Sandusky, OH, 285
Sandy, Gary, 196
Sao-ke-Sze (Chinese Minister), 108
Sapho (stage play), 95
Savings Bonds (postage stamps), 225
Sawyer, Charles, 154
Scarborough, W. S. (President), 188
Scatman, 154
Schantz, Adam (III), 215
Schantz, Adam, 279
Scheidt, Ed, 125
Schenck, Peirce D., 112
Schenck, Robert C., 273

Schenghof, Father, 269
Schiml, Andrew, 361
Schiml, John, 361
Schiml, Michael, 361
Schirmer, Theodore, 141
Schleicher, Lowell, 197
Schroeder, Rudolph W. (Major), 65
Schultz, Charles A. (City Sealer), 245
Schuster Performing Arts Center, 87
Schutzenfest, 305
Schutzenkonig (king of marksmen), 305
Scipio (dog), 78
Scolding Life Reclaimed (recital), 122
Scott, Myron E., 243
Scouts of the Prairie (stage play), 293
scratch and sniff, 197
sculpture, The Heritage Sculpture, 121
Search for Paradise (motion picture), 253
Seasholes, Charles Lyon (Dr.), 36
Second Bull Run (battle), 119
Secret Service, 210, 301
Seeburg Orchestra (piano), 250
Seeger, Mike, 96
Select Council of the Town of Dayton, 50
Sempre Giovine (skin cleaner), 296
Seneca (work engine), 33
Settlement and Progress of Dayton (speech), 251
Seven Wonders of the World (motion picture), 253
Shadow Rogers, 217
Shaffer, Ruby Ellen, 120
Shaggy Man of Oz, The (book), 205
Shawen Acres, 113
Shelby County, OH, 384
Shellabarger, John (Mrs.), 119
Sherbrooke, Quebec, 269
Sherman, John Q., 141
Sherman's March to the Sea (battle), 119
Sherwood Drive-in, 149
Shilito-Rikes, 87
Shimer, Brian, 333
shimmy music, 202
shipping bill register, 141
Shonts, Theodore P, 340
Shoup, Hettie, 96
Shriners, 20
Siebenthaler Company, The, 147
Siege of Atlanta (battle), 119
Siege of Chattanooga (battle), 119
Sifferman Fish Market, 71
Signal Corps Office, 352

Simba (lion), 160
Simm's Station, 275
Simms, Charles, 20
Simply Fashions, 144
Sinclair, David A., 70
Sines, Ed, 69
Sioux (Native American tribe), 53
Sir Gallhad (horse), 217
Six Months in the Gold Mines (book), 47
Sixth District School, 338
slaghterhouses, 279
Slutz, Frank Durward, 45
smallpox, 374
Smilg, Benjamin, 42
Smith, Benjamin F. (Col.), 316
Smith, Bessie, 373
Smith, Fred B. (Detective), 291
Smith, George, 274, 387
Smith, J. Floyd, 306
Smith, Owen, 138
Smith, Silas H. (Dr), 148
Smithsonian Institute, 196, 356, 366
Snow, Jack, 154, 205
Social Library Society of Dayton, 39
Soldiers' Monument, Soldiers' Home, 24
Soldiers' Monument, downtown, 114, 155, 231
Soldiers' Service Club Review, 106
Soldiers' Service Club, 106
Solly, Cornelius, 203
Sons of Union Veterans, 114
Sons of Veterans, 11
soup kitchens, 22
Sousa march (song), 350
Souslin, Alonzo, 309
South America, 298
South Park Business Men's Association, 181
South Park Savings (bank), 30
South Park, 181
South Sea Adventure (motion picture), 253
Southern Express Company, 340
Southern Ohio Fair, 285
Southern Ohio Lunatic Asylum, 261
Southern Ohio Stock Yards Company, 279
SPAD S.XIII C.1. (airplane), 158
Spain, 127
Spanish American War, monument, 11
Spanish-American War, 127, 362
Speedwell Motor Car Company, 112
Sperry, Elmer Ambrose, 290
S-PH-L-S (patent medicine), 128
Spinning, Isaac (Judge), 339, 388
Spirit of Lincoln, The (motion picture), 108

Spirit of St. Louis (airplane), 184
Springfield, OH 212
Springfield, OH, 25, 33, 140, 152, 211-212, 220, 285, 297, 305, 320, 369
Squier, Timothy, 355, 387
squirrel hunt, 97
St. Clair, Arthur (Gen.), 380, 382-383, 251, 254, 265
St. Elizabeth Hospital, 29, 233, 239
St. Francis Sisters of the Poor, 239
St. Henry's cemetery, 206
St. Henry's Chapel, 206
St. John's German Evangelical Lutheran Church, 300
St. John's Lodge No. 13, 212
St. Louis, MO, 184, 336, 369
St. Mary's College, 260
St. Mary's Institute, 260
St. Marys River, 386
St. Mary's School for Boys, 260
St. Marys, OH, 350
stagecoaches, 355, 387
Stahl, Ferdinand, 248
Standard Register Company, The, 141
Stanley, Ed, 125
Stanley, Levi, 267
Stanley, Matilda, 267
Star Spangled Banner, The (song), 159, 179
Starry, William H., 343
State Bureau of Aeronautics, 129
State Theater, 70
Steele Building, 73
Steele Dam, 8, 170, 258
Steele High School, 53, 111, 338, 353, 359
Steele, Mary, 364
Steele, Robert, 364
Steely Building, 271
Steinway & Sons, 296
Steinway (piano), 296
Steubenville, OH, 342
Steven F. Udvar-Hazy Center, 366
Stewart (dog), 29
Stickle, Jacob, 279
stike, molders and metal polishers, 133
Stillwater River, 8, 93, 182
Stites, Benjamin (Major), 101
Stoddard Manufacturing Company, 237
Stoddard, John W. 137
Stoddard-Dayton, 226, 237
Stolz, Arthur, 114
stone with portrait of Christ, 343
Storck, Carl, 289

Strange As It Seems (comic strip), 61
Stranger, The, 9
street car strike, 186
Stroop Agricultural Company, 357
Stroop, Fred, 357
Stutsman, Daniel, 374
Sugar (cat), 185
Sullivan, Charles F., 8
Sullivan, John L, 228
Sultan the Lion, 359
Summit Court, 330
Sunday Morning Show, 135
Sunday, William Ashley "Billy" (Rev.), 315
Sunshine Biscuit Company, The, 368
Supreme Court, 206
Sutter, John, 47
Sweet Mama Stringbean, 373
Switzer, J. M. (Mayor), 159
Symmes, John Cleves, 101, 251, 254, 380, 382-383
Taft, Howard (President), 74
Taft, William Howard (President), 74, 99, 145, 173
Tait, Frank M., 367
Tamplin, Mary, 252
Tanlac (patent medicine), 139
Tarantino, Quentin, 253
Tates Point, 316
Taylor Corp. 141
Taylor, Charles, 41, 195, 280
Taylor, Estelle, 287
Temple Israel, 321
Tennery, George F., 355
Tennessee, 108, 301
Tetzlaft, Joseph (Rev.), 260
Texas Jack, 293
Thanksgiving, 342, 347
Thatcher, Robert (Special Policeman), 120
That's All Right, Mama (song), 292
Thaw, Harry K., 269
The Bowery News (newspaper), 216
The Dayton Foundation, 109
The Dayton Song (song), 105
The Landing, 70
The Letter That Never Came (song), 124
The Poet Scout (book), 53
The Poisoned Wife (ballad), 96
The Rambler in North America (book), 97
The Truth About the Pole (lecture), 74
The Village Lawyer (stage play), 122
The Widow Jones (stage play), 277
Theater Owners of Ohio, 320

Think! (brochure), 326
Third Street Bridge, 155
Third Street Presbyterian Church, 132
This is Cinerama (motion picture), 253
Thomas, Marlo, 324
Thompson Printing Company, 369
Thompson Yellow Jackets (baseball team), 311
Thompson, Billy (Co.), 198
Thompson, Catherine, 101
Thompson, Herbert, 369
Thompson, Matthew, 266
Thompson, Samuel, 101, 381
Thomson, John, 384
Thorpe, Phyllis, 207
Thorpe, Richard (Mrs.), 207
Thresher (electric automobile) 111
Thresher, E. M., 213
Thrift Stamps, 375
Throm, John A., 148
Tiber River, 101
ticket machine, 176
Tiffany, 187
Time Is On My Side (song), 331
Time, the Place and the Girl, (stage play), 296
time-release medicine, 197
tin can collecting during World War II, 264
Tin Town (neighborhood), 194
Tipp City, OH, 350
tokens, 376
Tokyo, Japan, 49
Toledo, OH, 166, 285
toll bridge across the Miami River, 76
Tom Mix Show, 166
Tomlinson, John, 223
Tony Stein Post 619, American Legion, 221
Toulmin, Henry, 152
toy, Flips and Flops, 26
toy, invented by Orville Wright, 26
tramps, 22
Trans World Airline, 126
Transylvania University, 214
traveling museum, 122
Traxlers, 176
Triangle Club, 103
Triangle Park, 177, 202, 289
trolley, electric, 123
Trouble on the Street Corner (article), 164
Troy Sunshine Company, 314
Troy, OH, 305, 320, 355, 369
Tuffy Muffler Shop, 144
Tunney, Gene, 287
Turner Opera House, 122

Turner, Robert, 243
Twain, Mark, 98, 378
Twentieh Century Fox, 153
Twins of Genius, The (stage act), 378
Ty Cobb (horse), 200
U.S. Air Force, 306
U.S. Army Air Service, 283
U.S. Army Signal Corps, 46
U.S. Bankruptcy Court, 94
U.S. Colored Troops (USCT), 48
U.S. D-9 (airplane), 158
U.S. Department of Agriculture, 282, 302
U.S. National Museum of Washington, D.C., 356
U.S. Patent and Trademark Office, 16, 192, 368
U.S. Treasury Department, 357, 375
U.S.S. Battleship Maine, 127
U-boats, 77
UFOs, 365
UltraPanavision (moton picture process), 253
Uncle Orrie, 166
Underwood, Mel G. (Judge), 357
Union Biblical Seminary, 76, 190
Union Cemetery, McComb, OH, 301
Union Station, 22, 58, 145, 213, 336
Union Stock Yards Company, 279
Union Trust (bank), 30, 317
United Brethren Building, 73
United Brethren Church, 64, 190
United Brethren Printing Establishment, 69
United Nations, 99
United Presbyterian Church, 94
United Registration Bureau for the Tobacco Industries, 192
United State Steel Corporation, 340
United States Army Air Forces, 201
United States Army Signal Corps, 290
United States Bank, Philadephia, PA, 248
United States Envelope Company, 104
United States Hotel, 210
United States Motor Company, 226, 237
Universal Film Company, 143
University of Dayton Arena, 292, 333
University of Dayton Fieldhouse, 292
University of Dayton, 89, 260, 292
Urbana, OH, 104, 355, 387
USS Cumberland (sailing frigate), 62
USS New York, 127
VA Medical Center, 232, 238, 268, 346, 370
Valeria Beauty Center and Day Spa, 144
Valley City, 242
Van Cleve Park, 114, 179

Van Cleve, Benjamin, 39, 101, 251-252, 353, 355, 381
Van Cleve, John W., 252
Van Cleve, John, 251
Van Cleve, Mary, 101
Van Cleve, William, 101, 381
Van Schaik, Peter N., 234
Vandalia, OH, 129
Vaszin, Aurel, 160
Verizon, 109
Vernon, Mable, 327
Veterans Clubhouse (VA Center), 110
Vicksburg, MS, 267
Victoria Theatre, 58, 71, 74, 198, 241, 291
Victorio's War, 53
Victory (sirens), 157
Victory Oak Knoll (monument), 159
Victory Theater, 71
Vienna Boys' Choir, 253
Vietnam War, 230
Vigilance (fire company), 138
Villa d'Este, 13
Villa Farnese, 13
Village People, 196
Virginia Beach, 294
Vitascope Company, 277
Wahoo (game), ,193
Waite, Henry M. (Col.), 323
Waite, Henry, 258
WAJU, 166
Wake Up America (lecture), 103
Walker, George, 115
Walker, Johnny, 255
Wall Street, 368
Wallace, Jeanette, 299
Wallace, Marjorie, 136
Wampler family, 331
War Chest, 161
War Dog Fund, 358
War of 1812, 163, 203, 239, 251, 384
War Production Board, 264
War Production Planning Committee, 201
War Savings Certificate Stamps, 375
War Savings Stamps, 375
Ward, Clarence E. 223
Warfusse-Abancourt, France, 102
Warner Brothers, 278
Warren County, KY, 122
Warren County, OH, 384, 388
Washington Square Arch, New York, NY, 269
Washington Street Bridge, 155
Washington, Booker T., 98

411

Washington, D.C., 99, 126, 158, 180, 230, 246, 327
Watch Dayton's Broadcast Station, 154
Watermelon Contest (motion picture), 277
Watson, Thomas J., 226
Wayne Avenue Market House, 27, 67
Wayne Street Brewry, 361
Wayne Theater, 27
Wayne Township, Montgomery County, 128
Wayne, Anthony, 265, 380
WDBS, 154
WDTN, 83, 324
Webbert, Charles, 195
Webb-Kenyon law, 369
Wehner, Louis L., 361
Welch's Hippodrone, 276
Welcome Stadium, 333
Wellmeier Plat, 89
Wendler, B. H., 191
Wesley Chapel, 70
West Carnegie Branch, 63
West Carrollton, OH, 59, 125
West Dayton Civic League, 360
West Side News (newspaper), 69, 178, 222
West Side, 142, 174, 279, 360
West Virginia, 104
West, Martin, 149
Western Ohio Hospital for the Insane, 261
Western Union Telegraph Office, 66
Westwood, 89
WFO (radio station), 92
Whalen, Charles W. (Jr.), 320
Wharton, Thomas K., 272
wheelchair, electric, 114, 370
wheelchair, gasoline powered, 114, 370
Wheeler, Benjamin, 130
Wheeling, WV, 25
Wheelock, Carl, 170
Whidden, Charles, 88
Whidden, Evan, 88
WHIO-TV, 83, 166, 324
White (Col.), 127
White City (park), 182
White City Amusement Park Company, 182
White Line Railroad Company, 232
White, Edward (II), 234
White, Stanford, 269
White, William J. (Col.), 346
Whitten, Mary, 252
Who's Who in Oz (book), 205
Why Should We Be Lonely? (album), 96
Wilberforce College, 188

Wilbur Wright High School, 150
Wild Bill Hickok, 293
Wilde, Oscar, 132
Wile, Robert, 320
Wilkinson, James, 251, 254, 265, 380, 382-383
Williams' Great Painting of the American Rebellion (panorama), 168
Williams, Bert, 115
Williams, John Insco, 168
Willowview Cemetery, 170
Wilson, Woodrow (President), 145, 327
Wine of Tar (patent medicine), 128
WING, 154, 205
Winterberg, Germany, 333
Winters Bank Building, 109
Winters Bank Tower, 109
Winters National Bank, 21, 27, 109, 300, 317
Winters, David (Father), 248
Winters, John H., 300
Winters, Sarah, 300
Winters, Valentine, 13
Winton (automobile), 175
Wisconsin, 231
Wise, Thomas, 118
Withoft, Frecerick, 94
Withoft, Mabel, 98
Witte, Belle, 48
Witte, Theodore C., 48
Wizard of Oz, The (book), 205
WKRP in Cincinnati (television show), 196
WLWD, 83, 324
WLWT, 83
WLW-TV, 299
Wolf Creek, 93, 142
Wolf, Hannah, 203
Wolf, Jacob, 203
Woman's Century Club of NCR, 351
Woman's Christian Association, 98
Woman's Christian Temperance Union, 64, 310
Women's Clubs (postage stamps), 225
Wonderful World of the Brothers Grimm, The (motion picture), 253
Woodhull, Morris, 111
Woodland Cemetery, 28, 36, 102, 148, 188, 251, 267, 319, 335
Woodruff, James, 240
Wood's Station, 191
Work Projects Administration (WPA), 54
Works Progress Administration (WPA), 129
world altitude record for light airplanes, 286
World Cup, 1990, 333

World War I, 82, 99, 102-103, 108, 151, 158, 161, 177, 180, 186, 221, 230, 283, 290, 306, 329, 337, 350, 354, 375
World War I, monument, 11
World War II, 56, 77, 80, 126, 157, 183, 201, 221, 264, 330, 334, 349, 356, 358
World War II, retailers stay open, 21
WPA, 182
Wright airplane engine, 41
Wright airplane factory, 140
Wright B Flyer (airplane), 325
Wright Bicycle Shop, 195
Wright brothers airplane, 192
Wright Brothers celebration, 179
Wright brother's first flight, mosaic mural of, 19
Wright brothers home, 41
Wright Brothers Maple (tree), 147
Wright brothers, 41, 46, 86, 222, 275, 340, 356
Wright C Flyer, 143
Wright Celebration, 192
Wright Company, The, 340, 360
Wright Cycle Company, 1127 West Third, 41, 195, 302, 313
Wright Cycle Company, 22 South Williams Street, 302
Wright Field, 36, 106, 126, 164, 171, 184, 211, 246, 286, 298, 330, 350, 352, 358
Wright Flyer (airplane), 195
Wright Flyer III (airplane), 41, 137, 263, 302
Wright home, 7 Hawthorn Street, 195, 302, 313
Wright laboratory, 302
Wright Rudder (dog, 358
Wright, Ida, 190
Wright, John, 41
Wright, Katharine, 78, 190, 313
Wright, Lorin, 26, 190
Wright, Marion, 137
Wright, Milton (Bishop), 41, 69, 312
Wright, Orville, 26, 36, 41, 45, 69, 78, 190, 121, 126, 137, 143, 152, 178-179, 184, 192, 195-196, 263, 275, 280, 290, 298, 302, 312, 313, 340, 356,
Wright, Otis, 190
Wright, patent on airplane, 152
Wright, Reuchlin, 190
Wright, Susan, 190
Wright, Wilbur, 26, 69, 121, 137, 140, 152, 178-179, 190, 192, 195, 263, 280, 302, 312, 340
Wright, Wilkinson, 137

Wright-Dunbar area, 302
Wright-Patterson Air Force Base, 234, 365
WSMK, 154
WSPD, 166
Wullkotte, Bernard A., 255
Wurlitzer (music organ), 373
Wurstner, Rudolph F. (Chief of Police), 357
WXAX, 154
WXYZ, 166
Wyandot Indians, 380
Wyse, David, 243
Xenia, OH, 33, 305, 355, 372, 387
XNBL-1 (airplane), 246
Yanks Are Coming, The (motion picture), 143
Yeager, Wmeline, 209
Yoder, Jesse, 320
Young Love (stage play), 79
Young McAfee on the Gallows (ballad), 96
Young Men's Christian Association (YMCA), 7, 70, 164
Young Women's League home, 98
Young Women's League, 98
Zanesville, OH, 285, 387
Zimmerman, Rosetta, 286
Zooilogical Gardens, Lisbon, Portugal, 218
zoological museum, 272
Zwiesler, John, 239

Photo Credits

AAF Materiel Command: 126

Dayton Daily News: 298

From the collections of Dayton History: 5, 54, 109, 123, 249, 287, 373

Dayton Metro Library: 8, 20 (top), 31-33, 35, 55, 60, 63 (both), 66-68, 72, 86, 91, 93, 98, 107 (left), 113, 116-117, 127-128, 134, 150, 155, 159, 165, 172-173, 223, 179, 195, 198 (bottom), 203, 212, 214, 228, 239-241, 257-258, 261, 271-272, 281, 288, 297, 300, 316-317, 325, 334, 337 (bottom), 345-346, 352-353, 359 (top), 361-362, 367, 370

Dayton Police History Foundation: 30

From the DPL Collection at Dayton History: 342

Elvis Australia: 292

Gerald Ford Presidential Library: 169

Stephen Grismer: 175

Jeff Iula: 243

John F. Kennedy Presidential Library: 303

From the Albert Kern Collection at Dayton History: 62

Library of Congress: 28, 44, 46, 74, 78-79, 107, 132, 136, 140, 145, 161, 184, 213, 263, 273, 293 (right), 313, 327

From the Mayfield/Christian Collection at Dayton History: 191, 200, 336

Montgomery County Solid Waste Management District: 59

NASA: 234

National Park Service: 163, 178

National Tribune, February 23, 1888 (Washington, D.C.): 119

From the NCR Archive at Dayton History: 12, 36, 45, 95 (bottom), 99, 147, 151, 171, 181, 186, 197, 201, 206, 217, 219, 226, 244, 250, 299, 315, 321-322, 326, 328, 330, 351, 360

NSA: 77

Courtesy of the Ohio History Connection, Ohio Guide Photograph Collection: 13, 129, 227, 347

Jenny Paxton: 130

Skip Peterson: 120

Franklin D. Roosevelt Presidential Library: 56, 231

Harry Seifert: 41, 312

U.S. Air Force: 158, 290, 306

U.S. Army Air Service: 366

U.S. National Archives and Records Administration (NARA): 80, 82

VA Medical Center: 24, 48, 51, 110, 304

Wikipedia Commons: 53, 95 (top), 188 (picture taken by Drabikrr), 198 (top), 294, 324

Photographs not listed are property of the author

Made in the USA
Coppell, TX
07 February 2021

49590423R10227